CPG Series of Comparative Constitutional Law, Politics and Governance

Edited by the
German-Southeast Asian Center of Excellence for Public Policy and Good Governance

Vol. 4

Henning Glaser (ed.)

# Talking to the Enemy

## Deradicalization and Disengagement of Terrorists

Nomos

**The Deutsche Nationalbibliothek** lists this publication in the Deutsche Nationalbibliografie; detailed bibliographic data are available on the Internet at http://dnb.d-nb.de

ISBN 978-3-8487-0433-0 (Print)
978-3-8452-4739-7 (ePDF)

**British Library Cataloguing-in-Publication Data**
A catalogue record for this book is available from the British Library.
ISBN 978-3-8487-0433-0 (Print)
978-3-8452-4739-7 (ePDF)

**Library of Congress Cataloging-in-Publication Data**
Glaser, Henning
Talking to the Enemy
Deradicalization and Disengagement of Terrorists
Henning Glaser (ed.)
374 p.
Includes bibliographic references and index.

ISBN 978-3-8487-0433-0 (Print)
978-3-8452-4739-7 (ePDF)

1. Edition 2017

## Preface

This book was made possible by the contributions and support of a number of individuals and institutions to whom we would like to express our gratitude.

First and foremost, sincere thank is owed to the authors for their time and efforts devoted towards this book. Out of their busy schedule they greatly helped realize this publication.

We would like to also thank at least some of our long standing partners and friends who have supported our Center's activities in the field of security on many occasions in the recent years, namely Supt. Mohd Zaini bin Mohd Akhir, Maj. Gen. Srisaran Dhiradhamrong, Lt.-Col. Doan Quang Thuong, Prof. Hall Gardner, Brig. Gen. Dr. Reinhard Golose, Wilfried Herrmann, Maj. Gen. Ashok Hukku, Gen. Lt. Suthin Khiewratana, Prof. Klaus Larres, Col. Bernhard Müller, Angkhana Neelaipaijit, Prof. Amara Pongsapich, Sr. Col. Amnat Pooksrisuk, Pol. Col. Songsak Raksaksakul, Col. Sayed Sajid Raza, Gen. Pahol Sanganetra, Karl-Peter Schönfisch, Gen. Vaipote Srinual, Col. Eko Sudarto, the Ministry of Defense of Thailand, the Royal Thai Army, the Royal Thai Police, the Hanns Seidel Foundation, the Taiwan ASEAN Research Center, the Department of Special Investigation, the National Human Rights Commission, the Muslim Attorney Council and many unnamed security officers, human right defenders and Muslim friends who all shared their experiences and opinions. Their ideas, insights and advice have been a constant source of support for the work of CPG.

Of different nature but equally important is the contribution of the Federal Foreign Office, the German Foreign Ministry, and the German Academic Exchange Service (DAAD). We would like to thank both institutions for their financial and administrative support provided to us.

Thanks go furthermore to Prof. Dr. Ingwer Ebsen, Prof. Dr. Dr. h.c. Dirk Ehlers, Prof. Dr. Robert Esser and Prof. Dr. Udom Rathamarit, representing the four CPG-forming Universities of the Frankfurt am Main, Münster and Passau as well as Thammsat University. Their constant endorsement of and contribution to the work of CPG is an indispensable condition for the success of CPG's activities.

For technical and editorial support we would like to acknowledge the contributions of Adam Reekie, Dr. Lasse Schuldt, Dr. Duc Quang Ly, Dr. Sabine Carl, Oliver Fleig, Wang Xiaochuan, Markus Friedrich and Badreddine Berkhli.

*Henning Glaser*

## Table of Contents

*Part I: Articles*

# *Part I: Articles*

# Talking to the 'Enemy': Counterterrorism and Communication – An Introduction

*Henning Glaser*

## *A. Introduction*

Since the 9/11 attacks in 2001, counter-terrorism has undergone a profound transformation concerning its outlook and overall impact. Since then it has become a dominating and encompassing policy paradigm in domestic and international constitutional politics, a decisive driver and subject of major international and domestic legislation. As such it has strongly advanced what might be called the rise of the 'security constitution'. It is not exaggerated to say that this new counter-terrorism (CT) has shifted into the pivot of national and global security agendas to a historically unprecedented degree, whereas security governance became strongly valorized and quickly entangled with a broad range of central policy fields which were originally not linked to national security. As a consequence of this process CT moved more into the focus of a large number of academic disciplines and public discourses. This book is meant to make a modest contribution to the current debate focusing on some aspects of the 'communicative' dimension of CT and its practical implications since 9/11.

As a reference to the fact that the epistemic, political and strategic frame of the contemporary CT discourse is the 'Global War on Terror' (GWOT), including its iconic imagery of the terrorist as a *hostis generis humani*, an enemy of mankind, deeply sated with legal and policy claims, our interests in the general theme of 'talking to the terrorists' might also be addressed as 'talking to the enemy'. By this, we want to underline one of the heuristic anchors of the current debate: the dominating and yet contested assumption that there is a war waged against terrorism as an enemy of mankind. By this reference to the dominating imagery, idiom and conception of CT, an initial problem of all communication-related CT measures is already indicated, namely the fact that some of these measures like counter- and de-radicalization efforts are somehow framed by the overarching paradigm of the GWOT. Evidently, in a war-like scenario the various means of how to communicate with terrorists and those who might support them or turn into terrorist themselves one day will have a particularly defined design and underlying rationale.[1] It has yet to be remembered that the GWOT is not the only available approach to conceive CT but by far the dominant one. Thus, the issue of 'talking to the enemy' has to be analyzed in more depth, also with respect to the broad field of CT measures.

'Talking' in this sense might initially be understood as all forms of deliberate communication with terrorists, with those who support them and even all those to whom the terrorists might appeal to. The corresponding counter-terrorism measures, policies and strategies encompass 'soft' and 'hard', direct and indirect approaches, language-based and symbolic forms of communication. That includes for example all measures of retaliation and counter-terrorism that are meant to send a message of deterrence to the enemy and its support base, but also judicial discourses, the engagement in counter-radicalization and winning the 'hearts-and-minds' campaigns, as well as peace-talks and processes of de-radicalization, disengagement and rehabilitation.

Some of these approaches have been subject of research, counseling and training activities of the German-Southeast Asian Center of Excellence for Public Policy and Good Governance (CPG) in whose publication *Series of Comparative Constitutional Law, Politics and Governance* this book is published. It brings together a number of articles (first part) and a longer study (second part) rounded off by some additional material (third part). While most contributors to the book's first and third part are longstanding partners of CPG's engagement in security studies, the subsequent essay reflects the results of CPG's own research efforts and practical activities in the field of security law, policy and governance.

Getting back to the overarching theme of this book, 'talking to the enemy', the outburst of political violence and destruction in the Middle East with all its accompanying consequences, especially in Iraq, Libya, and Syria, is pointing at some interesting issues that should be taken into consideration to conceive the outlook of contemporary CT, especially with respect to its communicative dimension.

---

1 Black, "Terrorism as Social Control," 2004, p. 15, states, that where "greater violence" seems to offer a promising strategy while "a negotiation of peace is conceivable as well", the actual course of CT "depends on the social geometry of the conflict" which is attributed here to the basic attitude towards CT, the then dominating CT paradigm.

First of all, the success of violent Islamist groups in the Levant, Iraq and beyond might well be understood as a reflection of an obvious failure of CT and counter-insurgency (COIN) in the framework of the post-9/11 GWOT. A failure, which is understood here as at least partly representing a failure of 'talking to the enemy'. This becomes especially obvious if the term is more narrowly understood in the sense of counter-radicalization, disengagement, de-radicalization, and rehabilitation. Evidently, the region has not been pacified and de-radicalized. Rather, it has plunged into chaos and destruction.

Second, it is this – in this respect largely failed – GWOT that might be acknowledged as a kind of CT/COIN campaign different from previous ones where it comes to the GWOT's inner nature and overarching impact as an encompassing and dominating paradigm that became the pivot for central processes of normative ordering and public policy on the domestic, regional and international level in the post-9/11 world. Never before has CT stood so much at the center of constitutional politics and never before did it offer a comparable level to unfold hegemonic politics of global scale. Never before has CT had such a broad, deeply entrenched and transformative impact (see the second part of this volume).

Pertaining to the first assumption, it has to be stated that the initial overwhelming military success of the U.S.-led coalition in *Operation Iraqi Freedom* increasingly devolved into the creation of a huge 'radicalization engine' of global reach. Triggered by the GWOT paradigm and largely resulting also from failed occupation policies, the various emerging violent Islamist groups soon encroached on large parts of the region while the Taliban re-conquered territory after territory in Afghanistan. At the same time, the broader geopolitical constellation contributed to a steady worsening of the situation in the Middle East further driving the GWOT into the midst of attempts of the involved external powers to gain relative control over the region. Yet, not only the balances of power shifted with an increasingly fierce resistance against the plans that had been made for the future especially of Iraq, but also the strategic focus in the frame of the further reproduced GWOT. For the U.S., only some years after the total military defeat of the Baath regime, regional hegemony, on the basis of classical nation building approach, seemed either not viable anymore, or, given the inherently close ties between the new Shiite government in Iraq and their Iranian cousins in faith, not attractive with an Iranian, Iraqi, Syrian and, ultimately, Russian axis looming. The changing situation seems to have left not many options. By having carried the GWOT on legally more than questionable grounds to Iraq in 2003, the U.S. had confirmed their firm decision to dominate the region at high costs. However, even after "the surge" of 2007 – the large U.S. troop increase in Iraq – had eventually ebbed away with the 'official' U.S. withdrawal[2] without having achieved its purpose, the initial and maintained strategic decision to dominate the region seems to have remained conceivable by only one option. That option was to preserve the gained strategic position in the destabilized region by maintaining a *relative* control in form of a flexible and dynamic hegemony in the midst of growing chaos.[3]

This strategy is much relying on the ability to engage in shifting state and sub-state alliances without holding a massive troop presence on the ground and the maintenance of military bases to uphold the necessary air-control, as well as the ability to quickly deploy special operation forces and to supply the local allies. Still, the GWOT is the central avenue to pursue this strategy, paradoxically reproducing its own raison d'être.

In particular the consequential refugee crisis that is carrying the failure of the GWOT into some of those countries that had been supportive of waging it, once more raises the question of what could be learnt in terms of conducting CT. With the probability that the consequence of the refugee

2 The withdrawal did not affect the remaining significant number of military personal at the U.S. biggest embassy in the world, the continuing presence of private military contractors and especially the presence of Special Operation Forces which spearhead the U.S. GWOT, be it officially deployed, covert or semi-covert in the context of 'trainings' of Iraqi counterparts. Where Special Operation Forces of the Joint Security Operation Command are officially deployed to Afghanistan, they have been put under CIA control since 2014 so that Washington can claim that U.S. troops were no longer present (see Kibbe, "Covert Action and the Pentagon," 2014, p. 230).

3 Interesting is the formulation in the National Security Strategy of the United States of America 2015: "We have drawn from the experience of the last decade and put in place substantial changes to our efforts to combat terrorism, while preserving and strengthening important tools that have been developed since 9/11. Specifically, we shifted away from a model of fighting costly, large-scale ground wars in Iraq and Afghanistan in which the United States – particularly our military – bore an enormous burden. Instead, we are now pursuing a more sustainable approach that prioritizes targeted counterterrorism operations, collective action with responsible partners, and increased efforts to prevent the growth of violent extremism and radicalization that drives increased threats. Our leadership will remain essential [...]. [...] we will train and equip local partners and provide operational support to gain ground against terrorist groups." NSS 2015, p. 9, accessible at: http://nssarchive.us/wp-content/uploads/2015/02/2015.pdf.

crisis will remain acute for a long time and an increasing risk of terrorist incidents in Europe, the general environment seems, however, not favorable towards a rethink of the dominating approach of 'talking to terrorists' in a way that could claim to be built on lessons learnt. On the contrary, both, the centripetal and the centrifugal powers created by the pull of the emerging IS in the center of the Middle Eastern power vacuum, the influx of 'foreign fighters' on the one side and the surge of refugees created by the chaos and destruction on the other side, will strengthen only those dynamics that are inclined to perpetuate the initial CT failure.

In other words, any contemporary reflection of CT gains from starting with the insight that there has been no successful thrust of counter-radicalization, disengagement, de-radicalization and rehabilitation respectively in the Western conduct of the GWOT but only massive radicalization and instigation of insurgent/terrorist fury. The central question is: Will this change? Will a new approach of 'talking to the enemy' become the hallmark of an adjusted CT paradigm that will successfully engage political and religious extremism and its radicalization? – The answer is already indicated: Most probably not, at least not as a dominating project on the current and future CT-agendas (see also *Banlaoi* and *Gunaratna*). The practical impact of this assumption is reinforced by the further assumption that CT has, after all, to be understood as being more than just a loose bunch of policies, strategies and tactics. Especially with the sustaining implementation of the GWOT paradigm at heart of domestic and international politics it is rather a comprehensive and dominating regime and *dispositif* in the *Foucauldian* sense. Any single initiative and measure is thus to a certain degree influenced by the super-ordinated whole, the underlying superstructure. While it is possible that certain policies of counter-radicalization, disengagement, de-radicalization and rehabilitation might be suggested with a notion that deviates from the GWOT paradigm in the wake of spiraling violence to come not only in the Middle East but also in Europe they would most probably not set the tone. A dominating account on CT based on a notion of 'talking to the enemy' that would break with the established 'war-paradigm' is very unlikely to emerge after the GWOT achieved such a pivotal role as indicated above. Rather than decreasing in influence, the civil and proxy wars in the Middle East, with their expansion of violent extremist groups and increasing streams of refugees will only entrench the GWOT as the dominating CT paradigm, notwithstanding that these developments are at least partly direct expressions of its failure in the past.

While there might indeed be more public talk on 'talking with terrorists', radicals and extremists in Europe, the frame of the corresponding discourses and project developments will be eventually defined by the continuation of the rigid GWOT paradigm as the underlying rationale and driver of the geopolitically relevant 'politics of counter-terrorism' (see *Glaser*).

For Europe and even more for the U.S., all in all, it might thus be assumed that the discussion on CT will not dominantly focus on what could be called 'a lesson learnt' from the Iraq debacle. On the other hand however, the continuing if not increasing importance of CT might well create some interest also in dialogue-oriented forms of 'talking to the enemy' that are not necessarily in line with the GWOT paradigm at the margins of the mainstream discourses.

They will, however, remain relatively marginalized alternative approaches that might as such be tolerated even if not carefully supported by the hegemonic structure for the purpose to contain them. In this respect, such alternative CT approaches might even serve the dominating trend as a form of mimicry, a mimicry of affirmation of constitutional core values in a CT project that is easily inclined to challenge these values by further advancing the 'security constitution'.[4]

Somehow different is the picture in parts of Southeast Asia and the Middle East. Especially in predominantly Muslim countries, governments are inclined to employ counter-radicalization, disengagement, de-radicalization and rehabilitation to a greater degree and as a more important part of their CT strategies than it is normally the case within the GWOT framework. Such projects of 'talking to the terrorist' are often – not always – not primary supposed to emerge into real dialogue here either, but rather represent unilateral attempts to maintain or regain state control or at least influence over the definition of Islamic orthodoxy. In this sense, they offer a tempting potential of social disciplining and an opportunity to observe and control those parts of the population that is displaying a more extremist leaning.

---

4 See in this sense the U.N. High Level Panel Report 2004 which referred to the critique that "the current 'war on terrorism' has in some instances corroded the very values that terrorists target: human rights and the rule of law […]." Report of the High-level Panel on Threats, Challenges and Change, *A more secure world: Our shared responsibility*, United Nations 2004, http://www.un.org/en/peacebuilding/pdf/historical/hlp_more_secure_world.pdf, p. 48.

This form of 'talking' can on the other side produce much closer relationships between state representatives and the stakeholders of an Islam of potentially violent radical provenance than it is imaginable in Europe. Moreover, the legal-political marginal conditions for state-faith encounters and entanglements are also essentially different in these predominant Islamic countries compared to those in the 'West'. Partly, these legal-political marginal conditions somehow *require* such closer contacts between the state and a fundamentalist political Islam due to a shared Islamic identity. The latter might even be part of the constitutional basic structure or encompass serious challenges of this basic structure that can only be avoided to be fueled by staying in dialogue to the contenders of a more moderate interpretation of political Islam. On the other side, the state's communication with terrorists, their supporters and sympathizers is also less framed by procedural or substantial restraints in terms of constitutional and plain law than it is in Western constitutional states. That enables the state to force targets and potential addressees of counter/de-radicalization, disengagement and rehabilitation programs much easier into compliance with dialogical settings than it is the case in the 'West'. Paradoxically, however, it is the established and frequently employed body of the old colonial emergency legislation (mostly of British provenance), which proved to be one of the major tools of such an enforced compliance with communication-based CT measures in Southeast Asia (see also *Banlaoi*).

## B. *(De-)radicalization, Disengagement and Rehabilitation: Processes, Programs and Marginal Conditions*

To take account of these regional differences in CT, the first part of this volume collects presentations providing both, Eastern and Western perspectives on the communicative dimensions of CT, namely by *Arabinda Archaya, Rommel Banlaoi*, *Rohan Gunaratna* and *Thomas Koruth Samuel* as well as *Michael Fischer* and *Eva-Maria Reh*, *Oliver Gerson* and *Eelco Kessels* and *Orla Hennessy.* The common thread running through most of the papers is the communicative dimension of CT in form of (de-)radicalization, disengagement and rehabilitation with one paper (*Kessels/Hennesessy*) addressing one of the marginal conditions of successful communication based CT campaigns, the crime-terror nexus.

The first view on the issue provided by *Acharya* offers an encompassing and critical analysis of the broad spectrum of the various CT measurers and approaches against jihadi terrorism starting with some typical features of the American-led GWOT which are contrasted with strategies to engage the (potential) enemy in various forms of 'talking' and preventive CT policies. His account on the GWOT starts with the assumption that this 'war' has failed given the fact alone that years of massive military campaigning did not eradicate international terrorist attacks at all. On the contrary, terrorist incidents have surged significantly while, according to *Archaya*, 'kill and capture' operations and like-minded measures like enhanced interrogations have only produced a whole new breed of terrorists all over the world. For him the GWOT is primarily characterized by the forceful application of the most repressive among the available CT means exemplified by the predominantly militarily driven rationale of preemption. Its application is inclined in *Archaya's* account to amount to a flat denial of core principles of the established legal frameworks of national constitutional law and international law. The underlying spirit of this paradigmatic CT approach is captured well by *Archaya* quoting an Israeli intelligence head saying, "that there is no fair war against terrorists. Never has been. Never will be."[5] The legal transgressions that have become a regular and deliberately calculated practice in the wake of the GWOT, he points out, are expressed by a new willingness not only of the U.S. but also numerous other countries like Australia or India to also launch preemptive strikes against their designated terrorist enemies without consent of the affected host governments. Altogether, the consequences, *Archaya* resumes, are devastating. They might not only create a serious source of interstate tensions, but, for sure, one of deep radicalization of broad parts of the affected populations and those feeling solidarity with them. In essence, for *Archaya*, the U.S. modified doctrine of preemptive self-defense is exemplifying the GWOT paradigm as eventually leading to a vicious circle of increasing brutality whose "results [in terms of humanitarian grief] are identical" for both sides, those of the terrorists and those of the state trying to defeat them (*Archaya*).

Opposing those who advocate an abandoning of the principle of proportionality in the asymmetric warfare with 'evil' terrorists, *Archaya* underlines that the observance of such central principles of constitutional and international law is especially relevant in the context of conflicts like those

5 Archaya quoting Avi Dichter, Head of Shin Bet (2000-2005), with a remark from 2003.

related to or affected by the GWOT. His critical assessment leaves the impression that, notwithstanding the fact that a certain degree of violent responses might be inevitable, aggressive intimidation and the excessive use of force as the hallmarks of the actually *dominant* CT approach can finally lead to strategic failure only.

Starting from this result, *Archaya* explores those means of CT that represent a language-based concept of communication with the 'enemy' and his/her potential or actual support and supply base in the population. This includes "communication management" and the informed surveillance of vulnerable groups, sensible counter-radicalization campaigns, a strengthening of moderate Islamic discourses, well-crafted and executed de-radicalization, disengagement and rehabilitation programs and a bunch of policies that are addressing the root causes of radicalization, including educational reform (see in the same direction *Banlaoi*). An interesting remark in this context pertains to counter-radicalization campaigns. When *Archaya* describes them as aiming at discrediting the respective dangerous worldview in form of "traditional psychological warfare (PSYOP)", he points to the classical understanding that has been developed in the context of colonial counter-revolutionary warfare which is contrasted by less manipulative and more principled forms of dialogical counter-radicalization. What becomes visible here is the fact that it is not only the selection of single CT measures but very much also the underlying rationale of their employment that makes the decisive difference of the various CT approaches. Very similarly, de-radicalization or disengagement programs can be designed with a purely instrumental notion that is easily compatible with very harsh measures while they can also represent approaches based on the acknowledgment of rights and of the essential subject-quality of the hostile counterpart when engaging.

*Banlaoi*, discussing the same arsenal of communication-related CT measures with a more regional and comparative focus on Southeast Asia, adds for the Philippines an interesting point to the long and differentiated discussion of prison radicalization.[6] Instead of focusing on regular prison sentences *Banlaoi* highlights especially *investigative detention* practices in the Philippines as an engine of radicalization of detainees. The major

6 See Page, *Prisons, Peace, and Terrorism: Penal Policy in the Reduction of Political Violence in Northern Ireland, Italy and the Spanish Basque Country, 1968-97*, 1998; Silke, *Prisons, Terrorism and Extremism: Critical Issues in Ma-nagement, Radicalization and Reform*, 2014.

problem he highlights here are the largely flawed judicial procedures that are leaving detainees often without effective remedies in great uncertainty for prolonged periods of time. In this respect, *Banlaoi* points to two important marginal conditions of (de-)radicalization in general: Firstly, the situational vulnerability of detained persons especially in the context of police arrest and investigative detention where experiences of injustices often tend to leave the deepest marks on detainees due to their overall situation which is more precarious than during regular prison terms. Secondly, the basic importance to maintain the rule of law at least at a minimum level to not alienate and enrage vulnerable individuals who might seek to strike back to perceived injustice otherwise.

*Fischer* and *Reh* then approach the challenge of disengagement, de-radicalization, rehabilitation with the aim to provide an understanding of how radicalization works as a precondition for the design and implementation of CT programs in terms of disengagement, de-radicalization, rehabilitation and counter-radicalization. In this respect, *Fischer* and *Reh* give a differentiated account on the characteristics and processes of radicalization, extremism and violent engagement and the corresponding avenues to drop out. What *they* are unfolding conceptually is then reflected by *Samuel's* presentation of his year-long practical engagement with radicalized youths. *Samuel's* fascinating account on his methodology and the challenges he has to overcome in his work is complemented by *Gunaratna*, *Banlaoi* and *Gerson* who each review a broader number of de-radicalization, disengagement and rehabilitation programs. Like *Samuel*, *Banlaoi* and *Gunaratna* bring along with them rich practical experiences and insights from the field. Their accounts, which are based both on external perspectives and own involvements reflect different grades of actual achievements. This poses the crucial question in how far the various de- and counter-radicalization, disengagement and rehabilitation programs are eventually successful and which factors are inclined to render success or failure to which degree. Interesting in this context is the explicit skepticism *Banlaoi* holds towards the Philippine CT approach pointing to the general fact that successful CT means more than just putting well sounding policies and programs in place. Among the multiple factors that might be contemplated in terms of success and failure are those pertaining to the very design of CT measures (see *Samuel*), the relevant marginal conditions that are influencing the implementation of well-designed programs and very much also the basic underlying spirit that is defined by the ultimate question of what conception of CT is leading the engagement with the enemy (see *Glaser*).

Among the many marginal conditions influencing the communication between the state on the one hand and the terrorists, their actual and potential supporters and sympathizers on the other hand, are two which are specifically addressed or frequently touched upon throughout several of the presented papers respectively. The first pertains to the involvement of societal actors that can contribute to CT communication strategies (see *Banlaoi*, *Gunaratna*, *Samuel*), the second is the crime-terror nexus (*Kessels* and *Hennessy*).

The involvement of privates in dialogue-based CT – namely the involvement of NGOs and individuals that might provide leadership, counsel and orientation in the context of de-radicalization, disengagement and rehabilitation – is as crucial as ambiguous for the success of such measures. While *Samuel* himself is an example of an authentic and consistent involvement in dialogue based CT measures that are successfully addressing the youth, *Gerson* gives the warning example of a failed – almost not responded to – disengagement program for radical Islamists (HATIF) which was run by one of the German intelligence agencies. To openly entrust an intelligence agency with the task to facilitate dropouts from groups which the very same agency is targeting as adversaries is one thing, another one is the ability of such agencies to display a credible commitment that would bridge the natural gap between the state and those considered to be its potential or actual enemies. Two problems come together here: One is the principled credibility of the state as an actor engaging in dialogue with radicalized adversaries, the other the ability of the state to get 'close' enough to the 'other' to engage in meaningful contact, to be able to understand and address the other's worldview. The lack of both conditions was the problem of the said German program whose bureaucratic setup seems to strongly contrast the passion and empathy that is resounded by *Samuel's* description of his daily work with the Muslim youth. The juxtaposition of these very different programs generally points to the potential of non-state actors in CT programs attempting to de- or counter-radicalize target groups that are principally alienated from them.

However, as useful as it might be, the employment of private actors in such contexts can also entail serious problems. Generally, the tension addressed by these reflections might be described in terms of distance and closeness: Evidently, CSOs and individuals who successfully engage with target populations for the sake of counter- and de-radicalization do so because they can *reach* their audience. For them, the ability to reach out as a consequence of their closeness to the target population is not only a potential but a necessity as these private actors have less incentives and disincentives at their disposal than state agencies to establish a communicative setting. In other words, closeness to the target population is the very raison d'être to employ civil society actors in CT. Accordingly, many successful programs addressing right-wing or Islamist extremists are based on the participation of former activists, often even people with a violent past, who have successfully dropped out from their former extremist environment (see *Samuel* with several examples and *Gerson* referring to the German *EXIT* program).[7] On the other hand, not all 'charismatic religious practitioners' (*Gunaratna*) who are employed by the state to counter- or de-radicalize their brothers and sisters in faith are actually close enough to the extremist scene. An example is the Singaporean setting (see *Gunaratna* and *Banlaoi*), which points to a fundamental problem of many, especially Islamic countries engaging in CT-related communication with radical Islamists. This is the paradox of a state attempting to control a religion which is universalistic at heart and thus claiming to transcend the borders and definitional supremacy of the state. In this sense, it has been considered highly problematic for the Singaporean case that the private religious counselors employed by the state's counter and de-radicalization programs are members of or regarded as being closely linked to the Majlis Ugama Islam Singapura, the primary religious body in Singapore, which is ensuring a strict state control over the religious activities of the people in the city state.[8] Therefore, while single counselors might be personally convincing and credible, their institutional background seems to be largely rejected 'on the ground' by the targeted representatives of a marginalized Muslim population.[9] The problematic closeness between the state and the

---

7 This fact points to the constructive horizon of de-radicalization and disengagement in general: As empirical findings show, "today's gunmen can be tomorrow's community activist or peace worker". Ferguson, "Disengaging from terrorism," 2011, p. 117.

8 See for the state's approach towards religion in Singapore Thio, "Constitutionalism and Religious Diversity in Singapore: A *via media* between principle and pragmatism?," 2015, pp. 197-236.

9 See Wikileaks, "SINGAPORE'S COUNTER-RADICALIZATION PROGRAM CLAIMS ZERO RECIDIVISM, BUT SKEPTICS REMAIN," Date: 2009 October 7, 03:43 (Wednesday), Canonical ID: 09SINGAPORE982_a, Original Classification: SECRET, Current Classification: SECRET.

religious counselors of the Singaporean "winning hearts and mind, promoting harmony"-program compromises the latter as agents of a state that is principally distrusted by the endangered parts of Singapore's minority Malay Muslim youth.

On the other side, the ideological credibility and 'closeness' between some of those who are involved in religious counseling and those they are supposed to keep away from violence might occasionally also lead to a dangerous collusion and eventual reinforcement of the potentials of radicalism. This is the case when religious counselors disguise their true intention or radicalize themselves. In certain cases, Muslim clerics who were initially supported by the state as advocates of a non-violent Islam turned out to gradually become much more extreme than initially believed. In some cases, they had been hiding their true intention from the beginning, in others, their creed underwent substantial transformation, often under the impression of the GWOT. An example for the latter is the first American citizen who was exterminated by a drone based missile strike as a designated target on presidential order, Anwar al-Awlaki. After having started preaching a peaceful Islam he became such an important recruiter for violent jihad on the Internet that it landed him on the U.S. president's kill or capture list.

However, to turn it once again, it is nevertheless possible and successfully practiced to employ persons of fundamentalist, yet non-violent Islamic provenance to counter- and de-radicalize brothers and sisters in faith, endangered to shift into the dangerous waters of violent jihad. This observation emphasizes a crucial borderline, the line between non-violent and violent fundamentalists (see *Fischer* and *Reh*). Like almost any other line in the context of CT, this line too, is occasionally blurring and often neutralized on the analytical and conceptual level. Yet, to principally uphold it seems to be one of the essential conditions of successful CT, especially in Islamic contexts as it not only prevents detrimental encroachments on constitutional core values on the side of the state that is conducting CT, but also processes of further alienation and radicalization of the populations at risk in form of a self-fulfilling prophecy. In fact, there is a growing tendency in the public perception to equate very different forms of radicalism, especially to put non-violent and violent forms of radicalism on one level. For *Gerson* for instance 'Islamism', 'Salafism' and 'Wahhabism' are not only expressions of "religious fanaticism" but, under the common label of "fundamentalism", all basically characterized by the "necessity" to wage jihad. Despite detailed efforts to reconstruct the phenomenology of jihadi extremism, the decisive borderline between violent and non-violent forms of fundamentalist Islamism remains largely irrelevant in this account. The equation of fundamentalist Islam and violent jihad surfaces here again in the assumption that "European citizens convert to radical Islam with the intention to travel to civil war regions such as Syria or North Africa, in order to take part in the "Jihad" *(Gerson*). It might, however, be argued that barely any significant number of converts did actually choose Islam just for the purpose to wage jihad. It rather seems that many newly converted Muslims are endangered to be especially quickly radicalized for certain reasons until some of them might eventually join the jihad, – often to take side of their grieving Muslim brothers and sisters (see *Samuel*). To contra-factually equate fundamentalism in general and violent extremism in particular might be seen as a negative marginal condition for radicalization itself, as one of the pushes that alienate Muslim populations on a broad scale.[10] Even where such a notion is not pushing formerly peaceful fundamentalists over the red line to violent engagement, the alienation it causes also diminishes the willingness of many others to co-operate with the state in CT. The pattern is the same domestically as well as internationally. The U.S. sponsored UN Counter-Terrorism Task Force's Working Group on Radicalization for instance has soon been "disestablished" – while its tasks were overtaken by the UN Interregional Crime and Justice Research Institute (UNICRI) in Turin – much due to the perception of such a principled bias against fundamentalist Islam by some of the Muslim members. Among the governments which were represented in the group – for instance Egypt, Yemen, Saudi Arabia, Morocco, Pakistan, Norway, Italy, Spain, France, UK, Algeria, and the U.S. – some Muslim government representatives developed severe problems with what they saw as the "construction of de-radicalization" as a notion to target Islam itself.[11] From another perspective, the levelling point of view that too easily equates any fundamentalist creed with the intention to engage in violence is instructive as an example to point out the contradictions of the GWOT and its perception of the Muslim adversary. After

10 See Gardner, *Averting Global War: Regional Challenges, Overextension and Options for American Strategy*, 2007, pp. 16 f.

11 See Wikilwaks, "COUNTER TERRORISM – UN DISBANDS WORKING GROUP ON 'RADICALIZATION'," Date: 2008 November 20, 22:48 (Thursday), Canonical ID: 08USUNNEWYORK1098_a, Original Classification: UNCLASSIFIED, Current Classification: UNCLASSIFIED.

all, Saudi-Arabia as a major partner of the U.S.-led war on terror in the Middle East is *the* (fundamentalist) Wahhabi Kingdom and nevertheless known for having an extended and somehow successful de-radicalization program that earned the country the very optimistically claimed reputation to be "the master of de-radicalization".[12] Yet, from the very same country rooted in a fundamentalist state Islam and running this de-radicalization program flows support for violent extremist groups in the Syrian civil war like Jaish al-Islam and Ahrar al-Sham that are phenomenologically only marginally different from the IS pertaining to both their ideology[13] and the violent means they employ against civilians. This, however, is hardly justifying the equation of Islamic fundamentalism with violence. The instrumentalization of violent extremist groups by external players to achieve their aims by proxies does not justify to extrapolate a general rule that 'Islamism', 'Salafism' and 'Wahhabism' are finally well characterized by the defining intention to wage violent jihad. In fact, numerous countries and individuals adhere to a fundamentalist Islam without being violent or supporting violence at all. Paradoxically, those actors who are willing to employ proven violent extremists for the sake of their own cause are often the same who support a view that blurs various lines: the line between fundamentalists and violent extremists, between suspects and sentenced culprits, between terrorists, supporters and sympathizers, between criminal investigation, intelligence operations and warfare. At the same time, this kind of CT actors cannot do much with the dialogue related forms of CT that acknowledge the inalienable rights of the terrorist adversary, accept his/her political and moral stance with principled empathy – not sympathy – and try to engage vulnerable groups by generally respecting their 'otherness' as a basis for dialogue (see *Samuel*). Against the background of several empirical studies on successful de-radicalization and disengagement processes, it seems indeed to be inevitable to take a differentiated approach towards fundamentalism and extremism. Successful dropouts seem, however, to be the result of such complex processes of gradual dissociation that the ability to apprehend and address even the subtle distinctions on the side of the adversary seems to be essential for success.[14]

---

12 El-Said and Barrett, "Saudi Arabia – The Master of De-Radicalization," 2013, pp. 194-226.

13 Ideology-wise Jaish al-Islam distinguishes itself from IS basically by the fact that the former does not claim the caliphate.

14 See Bjorgo and Horgan, "Introduction," 2009, p. 6.

The last paper in the book's first part is the only one not directly addressing the question of 'talking to the enemy'. In their contribution *Eelco Kessels* and *Orla Hennessy* deal not with the communicative dimension of CT itself, but with one of its marginal conditions, the link between terrorism and organized crime. To take this nexus into account seems indeed to be very useful and occasionally even indispensable to design and apply a comprehensive communication based CT approach. It is as old as terrorism itself and, as often, history offers some interesting lessons.

In 1907 for instance, a band of violent political extremist raided and robbed an armored gold transport of the Tiflis branch of the Russian Empire's state bank causing a blood bath that left more than 40 people dead.[15] This "great Tiflis bank robbery" was the work of an assault troop of Russia's Bolsheviks and supposed to finance the Bolshevik under-ground network. Aside, the robbery was the stage for Stalin's (then aka Koba) first broadly recognized appearance in revolutionary circles.[16] Remarkable is an episode after the robbery[17]: Agents of Russia's feared secret security service, the Ochrana[18], questioned Stalin who used to play a triple game as their disloyal informant. When the agents pressured him on why he had not informed them appropriately, Stalin and one of the agents engaged in a prolonged argument until the outraged agent finally lost control and struck Stalin in his face. The other agents were not sure if they could believe Stalin or not and finally intervened, recorded both Stalin's and their colleague's testimony and send it to their supervisor who himself remained unsure and further forwarded the testimonies to St. Petersburg. Soon, the agent who had struck Stalin was suspended while Stalin himself was ordered to leave Tiflis for Baku.[19] The episode is interesting for it is representing not only an early and quite significant criminal activity of a violent political extremist group, but also because of the surprisingly restrained security approach of Russia's Ochrana behaving almost true to the rules. More importantly, it also highlights another dimension of the crime-terror

15 In Latin America the Sendero Luminiso, Tupac Amaru or AVC were robbing banks as well as the Irish PIRA, or the PLO with the latter working together with the Corsican mafia and the Lebanese Phalange, normally one of the PLO's enemies, when staging one of the greatest robberies in the history of terrorism in Beirut.

16 See Brackman "Chapter 7: The Great Tiflis Bank Robbery," 2000, pp. 58-65.

17 See for the episode Brackman, "Chapter 7: The Great Tiflis Bank Robbery," p. 59.

18 Vassilyev, *The Ochrana: The Russian Secret Police*, 1930.

19 Brackmann, "Chapter 7: The Great Tiflis Bank Robbery," p. 59.

nexus that is not covered by *Kessels* and *Hennessy*, i.e. the link between violent extremist organizations/irregular fighters, organized crime and the state.[20] To apprehend this complex and covert dimension in the relations between terrorism and CT, a differentiated assessment of the mutual relations between terror and crime offers the ideal gateway.

*Kessels* and *Hennessy* give a fairly detailed account of the phenomenology of the crime-terror nexus, its different forms, motifs, incentives and disincentives included. The question is in how far CT, especially its communicative dimension, benefits from this perspective. In fact, the awareness of the frequent and various relations between crime and terrorism might prove to be highly relevant not only as a general precondition to get to know the 'enemy', but also due to the opportunities it might offer to communicate target-oriented with the terrorists. To further explore the potential of the 'crime-terror-nexus' the latter has to be acknowledged as almost forming a constant marginal condition of terrorist movements that results from at least two factors.

Fundamentally, the relation between crime and terrorism is influenced not only by the illicit character that both phenomena are sharing, but also by the fact that violent extremist groups and irregular fighters are inherently dependent on maintaining a certain inflow of the necessary resources when the state starts to successfully cut off their overt and legal supply lines. Especially where terrorist/insurgents are fighting against more or less well functioning states and a professional security apparatus, the more successful a terrorist/insurgent campaign develops, the more it will be accompanied by increasing state pressure leading to their increasing social and material isolation. In the latter situation, it is difficult and risky to obtain financial and other resources openly and legally. Yet, such a detrimental situation for the terrorists can be easily outbalanced if they succeed to exert control over significant non-illicit societal segments by activities and practices that typically include criminal ones, especially by the control of or participation in illicit economies. The options for the terrorists/insurgents are basically the establishment of own criminal structures, of links to (organized) crime operating independently from the terrorists, or both. From this point of view, the affinity to engage in organized crime tends to be greater than to engage in normal crime for a variety of reasons. One is

20 An example among many are the entanglements between Italy's security services, the NATO backed Gladio structure, right wing terrorism, the mafia and the secret society Propaganda Due.

that organized crime offers a much larger potential in terms of supply and control, notwithstanding the fact that other organized criminal groups might emerge as dangerous competitors in the illicit markets, which is reinforcing the incentive to partner up. Moreover, while single occasional criminal transactions like bank robberies by terrorists on the run create and significantly increase the state's chances to track and capture the terrorists, already well established criminal structures provide a potential 'safe haven' in times of increasing 'enforcement stress'. Thus, more occasional criminal activities have to be distinguished from continuous, regular criminal engagement. For the latter, it has to be differentiated if terrorist/insurgent movements operate fully independent in regular crime or cooperate with independent (organized) criminal entities raising the question of the respective balances of power and the factors influencing them. Generally, organized criminal engagements of terrorists/insurgents, on own accounts or in cooperation with 'independent' criminals, for which *Kessels* and *Hennessy* give a range of examples, bear the potential not only to extract a constant stream of supply and resources but often also to entrench the respective movement into social and politically supportive society segments. By its criminal structures, the violent extremist group can often connect and develop close ties with other societal groups in a comparatively intense way.[21] This criminal engagement might even enable the occupation of a controlled territory and the development of ordering structures parallel to those of the state that generate additional support for the terrorists from the affected sub-society segments (*Kessels* and *Hennessy*). Besides the offer of a more efficient and predictable normative order than those of the state, the political-criminal rule of the terrorists/insurgents often also

21 Such popular support is an essential stabilizing factor for any partisan movement and has been famously underlined by Mao lead to the colonial COIN practices of counter-revolutionary warfare to re-concentrate whole populations in Cuba, South Africa, the Philippines, Malaya, Kenya or Algeria in areas beyond the terrorists' reach. Support of the population is, however, partly dependent of the nature of the criminal involvement by the terrorists/insurgents. When non-state armed groups gain for instance access to resources largely independent from the support of the population, they will be inclined to become more repressive, more indiscriminately violent and to stronger blend into brutal organized crime if the revenues gained by criminal activities are higher than necessary to maintain the basic military operations. Then, security forces might attempt to split the terrorists/insurgents from their popular support base if they can provide the necessary security for collaborators. See Weinstein, *Inside Rebellion: The Politics of Insurgent Violence*, 2006.

enables the direct or indirect economic participation of the normal population in criminal activity, which intensifies the terrorists' 'community bonds'. The classical example is the planting and marketing of illicit drugs. Cooperation of the terrorists with independent organized crime on the other side might stabilize terrorist/insurgent movements if it provides powerful external support for the terrorists/insurgents that can complement their own limited scope of illicit expertise and contacts or provide them with supply, cover or shelter in times of increasing state pressure.[22]

Assessing the various forms of engagement in the large spectrum of the crime-terrorism nexus, it is important to consider that crime is value-neutral and profit-oriented while terrorism is primarily ideologically determined. Notwithstanding this basic distinction, the entanglement of groups and activities on the two sides of the basic separation of crime and terrorism can also lead to a blurring of the lines dividing them according to their respective leading rationales. Criminal groups might develop increasingly ideological interests in this sense while violent extremist groups often develop dominating criminal profit oriented interests. Decisive for the emerging dynamics is the question which rationale is dominant in a given scenario. Such knowledge generally exposes a lot of a violent extremist group´s strength and weaknesses which can be addressed by various CT means. It can help for instance to identify conflicts within or between target groups on which the state can capitalize by catalyzing their destabilizing potential for example if the criminal engagement of terrorists/insurgents can be communicated as compromising the groups ideology. If group members or supporters feel such a 'contamination' of the initial moral commitment and ideological claim of their group, this might lead to an increasing lack of credibility and leadership legitimacy. The resulting fissures and cracks might result in swindling support, policy driven infights or splits. Additionally, not only such moral/ideological but also genuine criminal interests can contaminate the base of internal cohesion when they lead to a disconnection from the integrating ideological mission and evolve into clashes resulting from conflict over the stakes of criminal engagement. This is the other possible effect of an increasing criminal in-

22 However, the history of CT especially in the Cold War environment proves that organized time as an external factor is not only stabilizing but also destabilizing terrorist movements. As much as organized crime often fosters clandestine contacts to terrorist organizations as much does it do the same with intelligence agencies which frequently have turned criminal organizations against the terrorists.

volvement of violent political groups, its potential to destabilize the group due to shifting priorities and an emerging internal competition that weaken the organizational integrity and cohesion. Under these conditions the state might facilitate or catalyze such internally destructive dynamics by increasing the pressure on the group, creating distrust by disinformation campaigns, open up spaces for infiltration and approach potential defectors. To explore the status and dynamics of criminal engagement of political extremist groups might thus serve as an important basis for a broad range of CT measures and prove particularly valuable for disengagement and counter-radicalization campaigns, de-radicalization and rehabilitation efforts as well as criminal investigations and intelligence gathering.

Even if the economic factor is only one aspect of the crime-terror nexus, it is a central one which has been focused on from other angles as well. Another perspective on the illicit economic involvement of violent political groups has been developed for instance to explain the internal drivers and decisive dynamics of asymmetric conflicts from a more general perspective. Following what could be called the 'economic turn' in analyzing violent extremist groups that can be located in the late 1990s, the assumption has been stated that the moving force behind these conflicts would be "greed not grievance".[23] The consequences of this basic assumption for CT and COIN are profound: Based on such an assumed political economy of violent conflict without politics, the conflict and its actors will be approached totally differently on the communicative axis than if being based on an imagery of politically and even morally moved actors. Generally, such a predominantly economically defined perspective would make the state inclined to take a kind of response to terrorist/insurgent groups which is not addressing inherently ideologically defined political actors but rent-seeking criminals.[24] In this approach the conflict is not analyzed by including a criminal element on the side of the target in the considerations but focused on or even reduced to such an element. Such a dominating paradigm of a political economy of criminal violence might seem to be appropriate for some conflicts. It does, however, run counter to the findings of a number of scholars and professionals describing a broad range of other conflicts. Notwithstanding strong pulls of criminal interests that

23 Sanín, "Telling the Difference: Guerillas and Paramilitaries in the Colombian War," 2008, p. 3.

24 Sanín, "Telling the Difference: Guerillas and Paramilitaries in the Colombian War," p. 4.

'contaminate' the causes of the involved actors, these conflicts are also shaped by an ideological if not moral rationale, forming one of the central threads of the normative and motivational fabric of the respective terrorists/insurgent movements (see *Samuel*, *Fischer* and *Reh*).[25] Even if 'greed' might indeed be an important motif for some, it is rejected here as sufficient subject for an overarching analytical tool in perceiving the dynamics of violent extremist groups in general. Rather, it is quite a range of motifs and interests of equal or higher importance that moves terrorist and insurgents. Beyond the mentioned moral and political causes mental dispositions should for example also be considered, be they expressed as narcissistic, erotic, psychopathological or other dispositions.[26]

Nevertheless, economic incentives obviously do play an important role in the recruitment and maintenance of violent extremist groups even if they do so not always dominantly and pervasively. Vice versa successful CT campaigns regularly include various forms of material support to the addressees of counter- and de-radicalization efforts. Here, however, it is not 'greed' which is responded to by such CT measures but 'need'. This applies for example to support granted to CT targets for the sake of enabling their disengagement or their and their families' ability to reintegrate into normal life (*Gerson*, *Gunaratna*, *Samuel*).

From the perspective on the crime-terror nexus as addressed by *Kessels* and *Hennessy* the focus shall finally be slightly shifted to another, often overlapping and at least equally important aspect of this marginal condition of CT: the covert involvement of the state in the crime-terror nexus. This covert and secretive dimension of CT represents yet another variant of the abovementioned difficulty with 'distance and closeness' in CT. The operative need to establish a certain proximity to control and combat violent extremist movements always involves also the potential of a counterproductive collusion with the target.

Only some aspects of this complex relation will be pointed out. Firstly, it has to be acknowledged that successful CT is not exhaustively described as a series of single interventions bringing 'bad' people to justice or stopping plots to unfold (see also *Samuel*). Rather, the state will often have to be in a more continuous informal contact with the potential source of

25 For the causes of terrorist engagement in this sense see for instance Browne and Silke, "The impact of the media on terrorism and counter-terrorism," 2011, pp. 89 ff., 97 ff.

26 See Zulaika, *Terrorism: The Self-Fulfilling Prophecy*, 2009, pp. 63-107.

threat in one or the other way prior to, in between and subsequent to single disruptive interventions if investigative and intelligence operations shall be successful in the long term. If an operative need to establish a certain informal contact to targets can be claimed for some sort of criminal investigation and prevention, it is even more obvious for intelligence operators. The more the target of CT measures is subject of intelligence coverage, the greater is thus the likelihood that such an imperative of an informal involvement and entanglement with the terrorist/insurgent is felt in the sense that "cops want to arrest the bad guys while spies want to recruit them".[27] On this shaky and shadowy ground the crime-terror-nexus displays another facet. Not only are violent political extremist instrumentalized by intelligence services against adversary states, the struggle against such groups – CT and COIN – often also involves other non-state actors, be they adversary violent extremists or organized criminals. Especially the latter can be used to infiltrate, observe and manipulate violent extremist targets due to the crime-terror-nexus. This might often be preferable for the state rather than running own operations for a number of reasons. Most important beside the given 'closeness', the whole dimension of entanglement with crime and violent political extremists is a grey, if not black zone, nothing in which the state wants to be involved without flexible exit options and sufficient deniability.

The potential obstacles of this CT dimension are evident. Not only does it run counter to constitutional core values with the rule of law leading the way, but it also blurs the lines that are separating the 'good' and the 'bad' cause, those of the state and those of its extremist adversary. This might contaminate the state's legitimacy in CT, instigate more radical responses and poses the question to which end the terrorists are eventually combated. Strategic, tactical and operational decision-making in CT is, however, more constraint than it might sometimes appear as *Glaser* exemplifies in a longer essay, which makes up the second part of this volume. He deals with the question in how far future CT might be adjusted to the changing CT environment in the Middle Eastern theaters of the GWOT and its repercussions on the situation in Europe.

Understanding the GWOT as more than just a CT approach but as a governance paradigm of great weight and reach that serves not only the purpose to combat terrorism but also the project to preserve the post-Cold

---

27 Clark, *Intelligence and National Security*, 2007, p. 88.

War hegemonic position of the U.S., *Glaser* distinguishes two ideal-typical approaches towards CT. They are defined by the way in which they perceive and configure the position of constitutional core values, the preferable mode to communicate with the adversary and the dominant imagery of this adversary. Whereas the GWOT, which represents one of these ideal-types, has dramatically failed to eradicate terrorism, it is by far too important and entrenched as a governance paradigm not to be further reproduced in the times to come. Due to this single fact, the effective margin of maneuver of any adjustments of the CT approaches in terms of communicating with the adversary is already tightly defined. It might indeed be expected that a growing radicalization of Muslims in Europe and Europeans towards Muslim in the wake of the intensifying disaster in the Middle East might lead to a more vivid discussion of communicative CT approaches that would typically express the alternative CT paradigm competing with those represented by the GWOT. Yet, according to Glaser, these approaches will either remain marginal or subjugated to the GWOT rationale neutralizing their effectiveness.

The volume is rounded off by an appendix in which an interview with Gen. Maj. Ashok Hukku, former chief intelligence advisor to the Indian government, deals with the Islamic State and its impact on geopolitics, once more reflecting the fact how the current CT agendas are entangled with complex realities – and a report by Dr. A.S. A. Safras informing about the Sri Lankan rehabilitation program for combatants of the Liberation Tigers of Tamil Eelam.

## *Bibliography*

Bjorgo, Tore, and John Horgan,"Introduction," in *Leaving Terrorism Behind: Individual and Collective Disengagement*, ed. Tore Bjorgo and John Horgan, London/New York: Routledge, 2009, pp. 1-14.

Black, Donald, "Terrorism as Social Control," in *Terrorism and Counter-Terrorism: Criminological Perspectives*, ed. Mathieu Deflem, Amsterdam et al: Elsevier JAI, 2004, pp. 9-18.

Brackman, Roman, "Chapter 7: The Great Tiflis Bank Robbery," in idem, *The Secret File of Joseph Stalin: a Hidden Life,* Portland, Oregon: Psychology Press, 2000, pp. 58-65.

Browne, Deborah, and Andrew Silke, "The Impact of the Media on Terrorism and Counter-Terrorism," in *The Psychology of Counter-Terrorism*, ed. Andrew Silke, New York/London: Routledge, 2011, pp. 89-110.

Clark, J. Ransom, *Intelligence and National Security: A Reference Handbook*, Westport, Connecticut/London: Praeger Security International, 2007.

El-Said, Hamed, and Richard Barrett, "Saudi Arabia: The Master of De-Radicalization," in *Deradicalizing Violent Extremists: Counter-Radicalization and Deradicalization Programmes and Their Impact in Muslim Majority States*, ed. Hamed El-Said and Jane Harrigan, London/New York: Routledge, 2013, pp. 194-226.

Ferguson, Neil, "Disengaging from Terrorism," in *The Psychology of Counter-Terrorism*, ed. Andrew Silke, New York/London: Routledge, 2011, pp. 111-122.

Gardner, Hall, *Averting Global War: Regional Challenges, Overextension and Options for American Strategy*, New York/Basingstoke: Palgrave Macmillan, 2007.

Gutiérrez Sanín, Francisco, "Telling the Difference: Guerillas and Paramilitaries in the Colombian War," in *Politics and Society* 36, 1 (2008): 3-34.

Kibbe, Jennifer D., "Covert Action and the Pentagon," in *Essentials of Strategic Intelligence*, ed. Loch K. Johnson, Connecticut/London: Praeger Security International, 2014, pp. 217-236.

Page, Michael Tangen, *Prisons, Peace, and Terrorism: Penal Policy in the Reduction of Political Violence in Northern Ireland, Italy and the Spanish Basque Country, 1968-97,* New York/Basingstoke: Palgrave Macmillan, 1998.

Silke, Andrew, *Prisons, Terrorism and Extremism: Critical Issues in Management, Radicalization and Reform*, London/New York: Routledge, 2014.

The White House, "National Security Strategy of the United States of America 2015," at http://nssarchive.us/wp-content/uploads/2015/02/2015.pdf.

Thio, Li-Ann, "Constitutionalism and Religious Diversity in Singapore: A *via media* between principle and pragmatism?," in *Norms, Interests, and Values – Conflict and Consent in the Constitutional Basic Order*, ed. Henning Glaser, Baden-Baden: Nomos, 2015, pp. 197-236.

United Nations, *A More Secure World: Our Shared Responsibility*, Report of the Secretary-General's High-level Panel on Threats, Challenges and Change, 2004, at http://www.un.org/en/peacebuilding/pdf/historical/hlp_more_secure_world.pdf.

Vassilyev, Aleksei Tikhonovich, *The Ochrana: The Russian Secret Police,* ed. and with an introduction by Fülöp-Miller, René, London: George G. Harrap and Co. Ltd., 1930.

Weinstein, Jeremy, *Inside Rebellion: The Politics of Insurgent Violence*, Cambridge: Cambridge University Press, 2006.

Wikileaks, "SINGAPORE'S COUNTER-RADICALIZATION PROGRAM CLAIMS ZERO RECIDIVISM, BUT SKEPTICS REMAIN," Date: 2009 October 7, 03:43 (Wednesday).

Zulaika, Joseba, *Terrorism: The Self-Fulfilling Prophecy*, Chicago/London: The University of Chicago Press, 2009.

# The Right War, the Just War? Assessing the Fight against Terrorism since 9/11

*Arabinda Acharya*

> The mind of the enemy and the will of his leaders is a target of far more importance than the bodies of his troops.
> Samuel B. Griffith II, On Guerrilla Warfare, 1961

## A. *Introduction*

It is now more than 12 years since the terrorist attacks on 11th September 2001 (hereinafter called the 9/11 attacks) in the US and the "global war on terror," the metaphor that was used to describe our response to the attacks. Throughout these years, the question whether we are "winning or losing" the fight against terrorism has been debated among the policy makers, military strategists and academia. However, given the fact that there are no clear battle fronts in this kind of fight, it is difficult to assess if the killing of Osama bin Laden and other key figures of Al Qaeda and its affiliated or associate groups, the end of military engagement in Iraq in 2010 and the up-coming pull back from Afghanistan could be considered as significant milestones towards victory. This becomes more complicated when we assess if the world has become a safer place than what it was before 9/11.

According to a report of the Institute for Economics and Peace, in the ten years after 9/11, international terrorist attacks have gone up by 460 percent with a 195 percent increase in fatalities and 224 percent increase in injuries.[1] Considering the number, the spread and the lethality of the attacks and the metamorphosis of the terrorist groups, it is quite difficult to say if even the basic objectives of the fight against terrorism have even been accomplished. These objectives, as laid out by the US which leads the fight against terrorism, involved not a single military strike or was

1 Institute for Economics and Peace, "The 2012 Global Terrorism Index: Capturing the Impact of Terrorism for the Last Decade," (December 2012), http://www.visionofhumanity.org/sites/default/files/2012_Global_Terrorism_Index_Report.pdf.

simply not "a matter of capturing people and holding them accountable, but removing the sanctuaries, removing the support systems, ending states who sponsor terrorism."[2] The initial gains achieved through killing and capturing many top ranking terrorist leaders and the destruction of bases and training facilities have been reversed by the emergence of a new breed of terrorists all over the world and new safe havens and sanctuaries in Pakistan, Iraq, Yemen, Somalia, Nigeria to name a few. Even the state sponsorship of terrorism has resurfaced albeit in a different form and manifestation. Thus, as Bernard Finel posits, we are no closer to victory. "Successes are matched by reversals. As one country gets better, another gets worse."[3]

This reinforces the fact that the objectives of the "global war on terror" were based on an inappropriate characterization of the adversary and the nature of the fight involved in the first place, besides being too ambitious and ambiguous and internally inconsistent.[4] Moreover, focus on thwarting the terrorists through predominantly military means and consequent extensions of government powers with less legislative or judicial oversight and limited access to due process has resulted in compromising civil and human liberties.[5] This is not discounting the money spent on prosecuting the fight in multiple theaters and diversion of resources from other public goods.

### *B. Knowing the Enemy*

In warfare – conventional or otherwise, it is extremely important to know the enemy. As Sun Tzu articulated centuries ago:

> If you know the enemy and know yourself, you need not fear the result of a hundred battles. If you know yourself but not the enemy, for every victory

---

2 United States Department of Defense, "DoD News Briefing: Deputy Secretary Wolfowitz," *News Transcript*, (13 September 2001), http://www.defenselink.mil/news/Sep2001/t09132001_t0913dsd.html.

3 *Finel,* "The War on Terrorism: Are We Winning?" *UCF Today* (20 January 2011), http://today.ucf.edu/the-war-on-terrorism-are-we-winning/.

4 See Crenshaw, "The War on Terrorism: Is the U.S. Winning?," 2006, p. 1.

5 See Haque "Government Responses to Terrorism: Critical Views of their Impacts on People and Public Administration," 2002, pp. 170–180; Herman," The USA Patriot Act and the U.S. Department of Justice: Losing Our Balances," 2001, pp. 5-6.

> gained you will also suffer a defeat. If you know neither the enemy nor yourself, you will succumb in every battle.[6]

In conventional warfare, it is rather easy to identify who we are fighting against. But today, the wars have changed; the nature of the conflict, the actors involved, and the tactics and strategies they use have become markedly different. The National Commission on Terrorist Attacks Upon the United States (9/11 Commission), which enquired into the 9/11 attacks, noted that the adversary in the conflict today is characterized by "loose, far-flung, nebulous conspiracies with no territories or citizens or assets that could be readily threatened, overwhelmed, or destroyed."[7] Moreover, these entities do not have clearly articulated objectives which could be subjected to non-military solutions such as negotiations. Overall, the lack of a clear picture of the adversary has contributed to the construction of broad symbolic enemies and goals which has complicated the overall counterterrorism efforts both at the national and international level.

Thus, even after more than 12 years of 9/11, there is no unanimity as to whether the threat is from organized groups such as Al Qaeda and its associates, or from an "ideology" that underlies global jihad, or from new breed of so called homegrown jihadists. The characterization of the global jihad itself differs – from being a mass movement, loose confederation of allies or a franchised model with autonomous operational units at the local level.[8] No one is sure if the fight is against a single entity like Al Qaeda or from a variety of groups including for example, the Islamic State of Iraq and Syria (ISIS) now. This is largely an outcome of the attempt to aggregate dispersed local conflicts and groups and issues and motivations into a unified threat, without differentiating these on the basis of their respective geographical, social and political contexts.[9] As a result, as Ashley Tellis tells us, there has been an overall failure to perceive the threat in clear terms.[10]

---

6 See Wee, *Sun Zi: Art of War*, 2003.

7 National Commission on Terrorist Attacks Upon the United States, *The 9/11 Commission Report: Final Report of the National Commission on Terrorist Attacks Upon the United States*, 2004, p. 348.

8 See Bergen, *Holy War, Inc: Inside the Secret World of Osama bin Laden*, 2001.

9 See Kilcullen, "Countering Global Insurgency," 2005, pp. 597-610.

10 See Tellis, "Assessing America's War on Terror: Confronting Insurgency, Cementing Primacy," 2004, p. 7.

Admittedly, the difficulty in understanding lies with the type of threat those groups like Al Qaeda and its associates such as Jemaah Islamiyah (JI) or the Al Qaeda in Arabian Peninsula (AQAP) and Al Qaeda in the Islamic Maghreb (AQIM) pose to security. In Bin Laden's construction of the adversary, America was identified as the main enemy, but it nevertheless also encompassed the "alliance of Jews, Christians and their agents," and included Muslim regimes seen to be corrupt or apostate.[11] This became the template for the jihadists in many parts of the world. Justifying the October 2002 bombings in Bali in Indonesia, Imam Samudra, one of the masterminds of the attacks contended that Islam is currently being attacked on a global scale and hence Muslim responses to this hostility should be in kind, and, not to be restricted only to areas with active conflicts.[12] An article in the Al Qaeda military journal Al-Battar also reinforced this:

> In the beginning of their war against Islam [the West's] had announced that one of their main goals was to destroy the Al Qaeda organization in Afghanistan; and now, look what happened? Thanks to God, instead of being limited to Afghanistan, Al Qaeda broke out into the entire Islamic world and was able to establish an international expansion, in several countries, sending its brigades into every Islamic country, destroying the Blasphemers' fortresses, and purifying the Muslims' countries.[13]

Second, the nature of the threat changed dynamically after 9/11 and after the US invasion of Afghanistan and Iraq. Due to the killing and capture of key terrorist leaders and the destruction of their bases and training camps the terrorist universe has become disaggregated and diffused. This also led to the emergence of micro actors – the homegrown jihadists. The decline of the "established" terrorist organizations and the phenomenon of "leaderless jihad" moved the threat from commander-cadre organizations to diffused networks or cells which are self-sufficient and mostly autonomous

---

11 "Declaration of Jihad Against the Americans Occupying the Land of the Two Holy Mosques," in *Compilation of Usama Bin Ladin Statements 1994 – January 2004*, FBIS Report (January 2004), http://www.fas.org/irp/world/para/ubl-fbis.pdf.

12 See Hassan, *Unlicensed to Kill: Countering Imam Samudra's Justification for the Bali Bombings*, 2006, p. 84.

13 Cited in Kilcullen, "Countering Global Insurgency," p. 598.

in their operations, thereby making detection and pre-emption by law enforcement agencies quite difficult.[14]

This explains why the nature of the threat is being articulated in terms of competing narratives such as being another Cold War or a clash of civilizations, among others. Though such discourses are subject to contestation, it suffices to say that post-9/11 terrorism has transformed from a subnational instrument of political change to one which almost invariably and inescapably transcends national boundaries in terms of tactics and targets."[15] As Paul Pillar observes, "terrorism's reach is now worldwide" and "terrorists have extended their reach by building globe-circling infrastructures."[16]

## *C. The Right War?*

An unfortunate outcome of these developments has been the failure to grasp the nature of the fight involved. As Carl von Clausewitz urged, the most important strategic consideration that a statesman and the commander have to make is to establish the "kind of war on which they are embarking, neither mistaking it for, not trying to turn it into, something that is alien to its true nature."[17] But as the course of the post-9/11 fight against terrorism demonstrates, this has not been the case.

First, the characterization of the fight as a "global war on terror" was inherently wrong and contradictory. Though the perception that this was an act of war was based on the extraordinary destructiveness of the 9/11 attacks, the use of the phrase "war on terror" instead of what is in essence a fight against "terrorism," was an aberration which also signified a state of intense or extreme fear.[18] There were also some unwelcome consequences to responding to the terrorist threat with war like strategies and resources. As Sir Michael Howard argued:

---

14 See Acharya and Marwah, "Nizam la Tanzim (System not Organization): Do Organizations Matter in Terrorism Today? A Study of November 2008 Mumbai Attacks," 2011, pp. 1-16.

15 Kegley, "The Characteristics, Causes, and Controls of the New Global Terrorism," 2003, p. 8.

16 Pillar, "Terrorism Goes Global," 2001, pp. 34-37.

17 Clausewitz, *On War*, 1976, p. 88.

18 See Wedgwood, "Al Qaeda, Terrorism, and Military Commissions," 2002, p. 328; Aly and Green, "Fear, Anxiety and the State of Terror," 2010, pp. 268-281.

> To declare war on terrorists or, even more illiterately, on terrorism is at once to accord terrorists a status and dignity that they seek and that they do not deserve. It confers on them a kind of legitimacy … But to use, or rather to misuse, the term "war" is not simply a matter of legality or pedantic semantics. It has deeper and more dangerous consequences. To declare that one is at war is immediately to create a war psychosis that may be totally counterproductive for the objective being sought. It arouses an immediate expectation, and demand, for spectacular military action against some easily identifiable adversary, preferably a hostile state – action leading to decisive results.[19]

In fact, the war on terror narrative took ideological dimensions; the "loaded and elastic frame" implicit in the metaphor was used to justify fast-track policies and became a camouflage for discourses such as pre-emptive strikes, regime change, democratic transformation and the like.[20] In many countries, the war on terror framework was used to tighten control over their own people, to restrict individual rights in the name of common defense against insecurity.[21]

Second, there was a tendency to conflate not only the threat, but also the enemy. Understandably, the September 2001 attacks prompted the construction of the enemy as seen in the eyes of the immediate victim – the United States of America. Washington put all groups – those operating "primarily within a single country," those that "operate regionally... transcend[ing] at least one international boundary," and those with "global reach," together. This was based on the argument that these groups share intelligence, personnel, expertise, resources, and safe havens and subscribe to the same ideological agenda.[22] Accordingly, all of these groups became the target of the war on terror, regardless of their location, objectives and whether they pose a threat to America's interests or not.[23] Also in the target were rogue states, especially, Iraq, Iran and North Korea and any individuals or entities which could provide weapons of mass destruc-

---

19 Howard, "What's in a Name? How to Fight Terrorism," 2002, pp. 8-13.

20 See Lewis and Reese, "What is the War on Terror? Framing Through the Eyes of Journalists," 2009, pp 85-102; Reese, "Militarized Journalism: Framing Dissent in the Gulf Wars," 2004, p. 247; Reese, "The Framing Project: A Bridging Model for Media Research Revisited," 2007, pp. 148-54.

21 See Hoffmann, "Clash of Civilizations," 2002, p. 104.

22 The White House, "National Strategy for Combating Terrorism: February 2003," (February 2003), pp. 8-10, http://www.iwar.org.uk/homesec/resources/counter-terror/counter_terrorism_strategy.pdf.

23 See Record, "Bounding the Global War on Terrorism," 2003, p.12, http://www.globalsecurity.org/military/library/report/2003/record_bounding.pdf.

tion (WMD) to terrorist organizations or the technology to acquire the capability; and states that willingly or unwillingly provide safe haven and assistance to the terrorist groups.[24]

This resulted in discourses such as those on "international terrorism" or "global jihad" and responses predicated on the assumption that the nature and the impact of terrorism is the same or similar for all the countries in the world and hence could be dealt with "one size fits all" policies. But both historically and as post-9/11 developments demonstrated, different countries' experiences with terrorism are quite dissimilar not to mention the root causes of the conflicts that spawns terrorism in each country. Groups involved in these conflicts also differ in terms of motivations, targets and tactics.[25]

### D. *The Just War?*

This also brings up the question whether the war on terror adheres to the long-established norms of warfare. In other words, there are concerns as to whether military action in a state of asymmetric warfare is justifiable in terms of the "just war" theory and the laws on war respectively. The debate about the just war and the use of military force could be traced to Paul Ramsey's The Just War: Force and Political Responsibility, and Michael Walzer's Just and Unjust Wars: A Moral Argument with Historical Illustrations.[26] This was pioneered by the Greek and Roman political thinking which was captured by Augustine in his treatise The City of God against the Pagans.[27] The just war theory, in its classic form, was based on the justified use of force, set squarely within a normative consensus on the purpose of political order.[28] The concept was refreshed during the Cold War years in the 1960s and 1970s.[29]

---

24 See "National Strategy for Combating Terrorism: February 2003," pp. 8-10.

25 See Acharya and Acharya, "The Myth of the Second Front: Localizing the 'War on Terror' in Southeast Asia," 2007, p. 80.

26 See Ramsey, *The Just War: Force and Political Responsibility*, 1983; Walzer *Just and Unjust Wars: A Moral Argument with Historical Illustrations*, 1977.

27 See Lovin, *Reinhold Niebuhr and Christian Realism*, 1995.

28 See Weigel, "The Development of Just War Thinking in the Post-Cold War World: an American Perspective," 2007, p. 19.

29 See Johnson, "Just War Thinking in Recent American Religious Debate over Military Force," 2007, pp. 76-98.

The "just war" theory is explained and interpreted in many ways, but there were inherent concerns about proportionality and costs. The issue of proportionality is complex but relevant especially in the context of asymmetric warfare. This gets more complicated when one of the parties to the conflict is concerned about democratic norms and values. The paradox here is that while the adversary (terrorists) could seek to compensate for the power asymmetry by resorting to unconventional tactics – suicide bombings for example –, the state gets condemnation if any of its counterterrorism measures impede rights and liberties of its citizens.

There is also a belief that once the concept of proportionality is abandoned there are no limits to brutality entrapping all parties of the conflict in vicious cycles fed by revenge rather than logic. The results are identical – grieving families, confusion, and a profound desire for revenge and the perpetuation of violence.

### *E. Preemption*

Linked to the use of military force is the doctrine of preemption. The legal and moral permissibility of preemptive military strikes has been one of the most controversial subjects in the war *on terror. Preemption as a strategy was outlined by President Bush in his June 2002* Commencement Address at the United States Military Academy in West Point. *Bush said that*

> *[d]*eterrence -the promise of massive retaliation against nations-means nothing against shadowy terrorist networks with no nation or citizens to defend. Containment is not possible when unbalanced dictators with weapons of mass destruction can deliver those weapons on missiles or secretly provide them to terrorist allies.[30]

*Thus,* America would take preemptive action even before threats fully materialize. This became the cornerstone of successive National Security Strategies beginning 2002.[31]

A 1988 memo of the US Department of Defense defines "preemption" (preventive attack) as an "attack initiated on the basis of incontrovertible evidence that an enemy attack is imminent." Whereas "preventive war" is initiated in the belief that military conflict, while not imminent, is in-

30 The White House, "The National Security Strategy 2002," (September 2002), http://georgewbush-whitehouse.archives.gov/nsc/nss/2002/.

31 See The White House, "The National Security Strategy 2002,".

evitable and any delay to respond would involve greater risk.[32] Though the definitions make it clear that there are in fact two different levels of anticipatory self-defense, the way the words "preemption" and "prevention" have been used, especially in the US, imply a certain subjectivity that allows for interpretation in each case in which it is applied.[33]

However, America was not the only country embarking on mechanisms such as preemption. Countries like Australia and India have also discussed preemptive strikes as a strategy to combat terrorism with or without the tolerance of the concerned host governments especially where the groups hostile to these countries (Jemaah Islamiyah and Laskhar-e-Toiba respecttively) operate in other countries (Indonesia and Pakistan respectively). Preemption has long been an essential component of Israel's war strategy, whether it was against states hostile to Israel, or against non-state actors like Hamas, Hezbollah, and other Palestinian groups. As Avi Dichter, Head of Shin Bet, said in 2003, it is "not an eye for an eye. It's having him for lunch before he has you for dinner. [...] If we miss this opportunity, more Israelis will die.[...]There is no fair fight against terrorists. Never has been. Never will be."[34]

However, preventive wars are controversial since like deterrence, they rely on what *Brian Angelo Lee* terms "retrospectively disproportionate violence."[35] Preemption, critics argue involves the use of military force to thwart an attack that has not yet occurred and perhaps never will occur. Such a policy therefore is both incompatible with international law and norms and a reckless abandonment of the long-established rules of engagement.[36] Moreover, as Harvey Rishikof pointed out, "although some

---

32 Department of Defense, "Dictionary of Military and Associated Terms," (12 April 2001; as Amended Through 19th August 2009), pp. 428 and 432, http://www.fas.org/irp/doddir/dod/jp1_02.pdf.

33 Aggelen, "The Consequences of Unlawful Preemption and the Legal Duty to Protect," 2009, pp. 23-24.

34 Cited in Rishikof, "Morality, Ethics and Law in the Global War on Terrorism (the Long War)," 2007, pp. 112-113.

35 Lee, "Preventive *War*, Deterrent Retaliation, and Retrospective Disproportionality," 2009, p. 253.

36 See Crawford, "The Slippery Slope to Preventive War," 2003, p.17; Rocheleau, "Preventive War and Lawful Constraints on the Use of Force: An Argument Against International Vigilantism," 2007, pp. 18, 202.

forms of terrorism may be containable by deterrence, all terrorism is not."[37]

*F. Reciprocity*

A concomitant aspect of the just war argument is the principle of reciprocity. The question here is whether Al Qaeda's provocations delivered by the 9/11 attacks could justify the violation of positive and customary rules that prohibit reprisals against civilians, without any recognition of basic harbeas corpus rights, sustained detention, coercive interrogation and targeted killings.[38] This is also linked to the question whether just war principles can be applied to adversaries like Al Qaeda or for that matter the jihadist movement. Mark Osiel argues that the US-Al Qaeda confrontations could reasonably be regarded as a transnational armed conflict in which case, Al Qaeda's disregard for just war principles – indiscriminate killing of non-combatants including women and children – would justify similar actions by the US or the international community.[39]

There are a number of implications following from the above. First, it challenged the central assumption of early U.S.-led counterterrorism policies that the destruction of Al Qaeda would end the war on terror. Second, although military force was necessary in the initial years of the fight, in the long term, strategies to curb Al Qaeda and global jihadism through decapitation have not been successful. As a result, the world is left to fight an almost perpetually elusive target, with a constantly moving center and focal point, which is becoming progressively harder to counter.[40]

Third, by conflating the issues and perceived enemies, the war on terror rhetoric widened the fissures between the West and Islam. Historically, U.S. policies in the Middle East have fuelled suspicions that Washington has an anti-Muslim agenda.[41] Many Muslims see the U.S.-led war on ter-

---

37 Rishikof, "Morality, Ethics and Law in the Global War on Terrorism," p. 110.

38 See Osiel, *The End of Reciprocity: Terror, Torture and the Law of War*, 2009, pp. 2, 56.

39 See Osiel, *The End of Reciprocity*, pp. 2-3.

40 See Cohin, "How Al Qaeda Ends: The Decline and Demise of Terrorist Groups," 2006, p. 7.

41 See Surin, "Strategic Challenges Facing Islam in Southeast Asia," Lecture delivered at the *Institute of Defence and Strategic Studies and the Centre for Contemporary Islamic Studies*, (Singapore: 5 November 2001).

ror as actually a war on Islam and a ruse to help maintain the status quo in countries with pro-U.S. regimes. Others see it as part of a religiously based war between the Muslim world and a Judeo-Christian West.[42] For example, Muslims view Washington's Iraq invasion as reflective of "an increasingly violent culture," and its policies in Iraq and Iran "as a prelude to the fourth World War."[43] In sum, the rhetoric of the "war on terror" took a one dimensional view of what essentially was a multidimensional problem.[44]

What about the costs? "Absolute military power" generates a very particular kind of arrogance and corruptibility. This is manifest in the willingness to suspend basic human rights. This "apart from being counter-productive, has taken attention and resources away from other, more promising, approaches to dealing with terrorism."[45] There is also a concern that the war on terror has pushed democratic projects – human rights and human security – to the backyard and substituted development goals in favor of militarization. There are now questions about if there must be a trade-off between waging an effective fight against terrorism and the protection of fundamental liberties.[46]

The trade-off issue is also important in respect of states' ability to provide other public goods such as human security. The 9/11 attacks exposed the limitations in the core arguments of the proponents of the human security discourse that the state is not a good or sufficient provider of human security. The scale of responses required to cope with security concerns involving post-September 2001 era terrorism was beyond the competency of any other agency except the state. At the same time, primacy of hard security measures both in policy making and in allocation of resources risks denting state's capacity in fighting poverty and unemployment, crime and domestic violence and deal with natural disasters and other consequences of climate change and the like. Despite non-agreement among

---

42 See Pillar, "Counter-terrorism after Al Qaeda," 2004, p. 108.

43 "Mahathir: U.S. Policy in Iraq, Iran Preclude to 4th World War," *China Daily*, 8 June 2006, http://english.people.com.cn/200606/08/eng20060608_272051.html. Mahathir described the Cold War as the Third World War.

44 See Byford, *"The Wrong War,"* 2002, p. 34.

45 Keen, *Endless War?: Hidden Functions of the "War on Terror", 20*06, p. 2.

46 Weinberg et al., "The Cost of Terrorism: The Relationship Between International Terrorism and Democratic Governance," 2008, pp. 257-270; and Robison, "Terror's True Nightmare? Reevaluating the Consequences of Terrorism on Democratic Governance," 2010, pp. 62-86.

scholars, these issues have significant impact on terrorism and counterterrorism.

The situation is one typically faced by democratic countries when split between conflicting ideas and courses of action. The difficulty is when deciding between providing protection and security to citizens, i.e. limiting the freedom of individual terrorists, terrorist groups, and support networks to operate freely in a non-regulated environment and maintaining, in full or part, the tenets of democracy, especially the provision of individual liberty and human rights that form the core values of democratic societies. The efforts to combat terrorism are further complicated by the trend of globalization, which requires open trade, commerce and borders, and deregulation.

### G. Limits of Coercive Power

Arguably, in counterterrorism, the use of force would always be the first line of defense to reduce the immediate threat. As Joseph McMillan and Christopher Cavoli argue, waiting passively for attacks to happen would undermine "government's legitimacy in proportion to the terrorists' capacity to inflict harm." Therefore there is a need to seize the initiative and if necessary preempt the attacks.[47] Inevitably, it is the security and the military apparatus that the concerned government would use in the immediate instance. It is still necessary to eradicate specific terrorist assets or capabilities that pose a clear and present danger and cannot be dealt with by other means.[48] This explains why the fight against the jihadist threat has developed primarily within a law enforcement paradigm at least in the early stages of the campaign.[49]

However, the use of the military means has limits and often leads to undesirable consequences. Its unrestrained or indiscriminate use could create new resentments, new grievances and even the next generation of terrorists. As former U.S. diplomat John Brady Kiesling cautioned, "The more aggressively we use our power to intimidate our foes, the more foes we create and the more we validate terrorism as the only effective weapon of

47 See McMillan and Cavoli, "Countering Global Terrorism," 2008, pp. 26-27.

48 See McMillan and Cavoli, "Countering Global Terrorism," p. 32.

49 See Cortright and Lopez, "Strategic Counter-Terrorism," 2007, p. 1.

the powerless against the powerful."[50] In fact, repression provides evidence of the effectiveness of the terrorists campaign and therefore a reason to persist.[51] Moreover, governments, especially liberal democratic ones, operate under a number of legal and ethical, cultural and system level constraints that inhibit a full-spectrum response.[52] Terrorists, as Paul Wilkinson points out, typically hope for indiscriminate crackdowns and repressive, heavy-handed responses. Their hope is to "alienate the public from the government."[53] An indiscriminate or repressive state response could therefore undermine people's support for counterterrorism measures. [54]

Thus, there is now a growing recognition of the limits of coercive power and understanding that violence is an appallingly blunt instrument for the solution of difficult political, economic or social problems. Traditional strategies of deterrence are unlikely to work; instead there is a need to adopt a strategy of containment and address the underlying causes of discontent.[55]

It is not that there was no appreciation for the non-military strategies in the past while responding to the terrorist threat. Nations have recognized its importance and come out with a laundry list of strategies including intelligence enhanced law enforcement, strategic communication, public diplomacy or propaganda response to counter or refute hostile ideology, economic sanctions or inducements, political and socioeconomic reforms, empowering moderate Muslims, negotiated settlement and advancement of "effective democracies." These also include targeting financing of terrorism international cooperation and multilateral efforts and new structures and institutions to put forth a combined front against the threat as a whole. Needless to say that some of these measures are necessary and proven to be highly effective while few others such as the efforts to ad-

---

50 Kiesling, "Diplomatic Breakdown," *The Boston Globe Magazine*, (27April 2003).

51 See Guelke, *The Age of Terrorism and the International Political System*, 1995, p. 180.

52 See Campbell and Weitz, *Non-Military Strategies For Countering Islamist Terrorism: Lessons Learned From Past Counterinsurgencies*, 2006, p. 6.

53 Wilkinson, "Maintaining the Democratic Process and Public Support," 1986, pp. 177-178.

54 See Holmes, *Terrorism and Democratic Stability*, 2001, p. 197.

55 See Simon, "The New Terrorism: Securing the Nation against a Messianic Foe," Brookings Review, 21, (Winter 2003), http://www.brookings.edu/articles/2003/winter_terrorism_simon.aspx.

vance effective democracies have become controversial and even as in some cases, counterproductive.

A number of non-kinetic measures also form part of prescriptions in analytic and academic scholarship. Though these measures are as varied as the number of analysts and scholars who write on the subject, certain commonalities could be compiled. First is an almost total recognition that use of military force, though necessary, is not enough to counter the terrorist threat. As McMillan and Cavoli caution, both "excessive" and "inadequate" use of force could lead to strategic failure. Therefore, the key is in using "minimum effective force."[56] Second is the need to address the broader political, social and economic aspects of the fight to undercut the importance of the issues and grievances that the jihadists exploit to mobilize the members of the community. Third is the imperative of engaging with the broader Muslim community, majority of which is moderate, with a view to insulate potential recruits from jihadist propaganda and recruitment. As Mackenzie Eaglen observes, "many Muslims reject terrorism, even in countries where the official rhetoric comes across as warlike," and that "many Islamic scholars argue that terrorism – the intentional murder of innocents to achieve political goals – is completely illegitimate."[57] It is these viewpoints that need to be encouraged and given as wide a platform as possible to be heard and resonate in the hearts and minds of those who have fallen prey to the jihadist propaganda.

### H. Countering Radical Ideology

The root of the conflict is a radical ideology that, like Marxism-Leninism in the past, serves as an intellectual, political, and emotional foundation of a worldwide revolutionary movement.[58] Hence, the radical ideology must be countered and discredited. This is all the more important as it is critical to defeat the enemy "without radicalizing or alienating the population to the point that the security forces become recruiting agents" for the jihadists.[59] In the battlefront of ideas, as Brian Jenkins reminds us, we must

56 McMillan and Cavoli, "Countering Global Terrorism," p. 30.

57 Cited in Zellen, "Whither Victory in the War on Terror?" 2007, http://www.nps.edu/Academics/centers/ccc/publications/OnlineJournal/2007/Mar/zellenMar07.pdf.

58 See Lord, "Psychological-Political Instruments," 2004, pp. 220-221.

59 See Kilcullen, "Countering Global Insurgency," p. 29.

defeat the jihadists' missionary enterprise.[60] Jihadists typically operate with a "religious or ideological agenda which so totally rejects the existing political and social order that there is no basis for negotiation with democratic government on political, social and economic demands." [61] As Mahathir Mohamad, the former prime minister of Malaysia commented, it is not Islam which obstructs its progress, but its "wrong and rigid interpretations."[62] The trick therefore, according to Paul Wilkinson, "is to harmonize strategy on both the security and political fronts: this is the only basis for a winning strategy."[63]

There are a number of interrelated elements in the counter-ideology strategy – de-radicalization or disengagement, religious rehabilitation, education reforms and the like. All the elements of counter-ideology strategy are variants of traditional psychological warfare (PSYOP) which is "the planned use of communications to influence human attitudes and behavior. PSYOP consist of political, military and ideological actions conducted to induce in target groups' behavior, emotions, and attitudes that support the attainment of national objectives."[64] These strategies are primarily directed at the mind of the adversary rather than his body.[65] These are the essential elements that "precede, accompany and follow" military measures as part of a comprehensive counterterrorism strategy.[66]

### *I. De-radicalization/Disengagement*

De-radicalization implies a cognitive shift, a fundamental change in understanding of the jihadist version of the religion. Disengagement – a term often used interchangeably with de-radicalization – "refers to a behavioural change, such as leaving a group or changing one's role within it.

---

60 See Jenkins, *Unconquerable Nation*, p. 15.

61 Wilkinson, *Terrorism versus Democracy: The Liberal State Response*, 2001, p. 230.

62 Mahathir Mohamad, "Breaking the Muslim Mindset," *The Sunday Times*, (Singapore: 28 July 2002).

63 Wilkinson, "Maintaining the Democratic Process and Public Support," p. 177.

64 Paddock, Jr., "Military Psychological Operations," 1989, p. 45.

65 Bernstein, "Political Strategies in Coercive Diplomacy and Limited War," 1989, p. 145.

66 Paddock, Jr., "Military Psychological Operations," p. 45; Also see Post, "The Key Role of Psychological Operations in Countering Terrorism," 2007, p. 381.

It does not necessitate a change in values or ideals, but requires relinquishing the objective of achieving change through violence."[67] A disengaged terrorist may not be "de-radicalized" or repentant at all. Often physical disengagement may not result in any concomitant change or reduction in ideological support.[68] Nevertheless, both aim at one objective – undermining the jihadist narrative, which is related to its practical as ideational aspects.

Given the alienated and uncompromising worldview of the radical ideologues in the jihadist movement, it might not be easy to wean the mainstream Muslims away from their influence through the fear of force or political concessions, amnesties or other personal incentives. The same is true in respect of attempts to divide the community into progressive or fundamentalist belief systems.[69] A better chance of success is to counter the narrative by openly contesting extremist views and offering alternatives and fostering deeper ideological debates.[70] This involves engaging in dialogue, especially the most vulnerable segments in the community, to demonstrate how they are being misled and manipulated by perverted and corrupt interpretation of the religious texts and to convince them that there could be better alternatives to acts of violence. Another component of this strategy is social, political, cultural, and economic reforms that touch all individuals and institutions involved in the socialization process.[71]

Identifying the most vulnerable is a challenge because; there is no single profile of a jihadi or a single pathway to radicalization.[72] Social, economic, psychological and ideological factors play critical roles though it is difficult to determine whether these variables could be individually or col-

---

67 Fink and Hearne, "Terrorism: Deradicalization and Disengagement from Violent Extremism," 2008, p. 3.

68 See Horgan, "Individual disengagement: a psychological analysis," 2009, p. 27.

69 See Jenkins, *Unconquerable Nation: Knowing Our Enemy, Strengthening Ourselves*, 2006, p. 121.

70 See Carpenter and Levitt, "We must challenge the ideology driving terrorism," *The Australian*, (16 November 2010), http://www.theaustralian.com.au/news/opinion/we-must-challenge-the-ideology-driving-terrorism/story-e6frg6zo-122595404797.

71 See "Saudi Paper Publishes Study of Saudi Counterterrorism Strategy," *Riyadh Al-Jazirah,* (31 December 2005), http://www.al-jazirah.com.

72 See HM Government, "Delivering the Prevent Strategy: An updated guide for local partners," (August 2009), p. 9, http://www.dcsf.gov.uk/violentextremism/preventstrategy/downloads/2009%20Updated%20guide%20to%20local%20partners.pdf.

lectively implicated. This is where the literature on radicalization is most fragmented which has led to sweeping generalizations; focus on situations in which people may become radicalized without examining the underlying dynamics, or simply explanations that are inadequate. As Yusuf bin-Ahmad al-Uthaymayan, a Saudi exponent of the need for a comprehensive counter-terrorism studies put it, "We have to know accurately the intellectual atmosphere, cultural sources, social grounds, institutions, and activities that nurture terrorism within the society, reproduce it, regenerate it, spread it, propagate it, and make it glamorous and 'attractive' to the hearts and minds of the youths and sympathizers."[73] It is a difficult but not an impossible task.

Another challenge is that a simple strategy of coming up with good counterargument to jihadists' worldview might not be sufficient since, for the adherents, the primary attraction, is to radicalism per se. The narrative simply serves as a vehicle to express and justify this psychological and emotional predisposition.[74] Similarly, since counter-ideology programs include a significant theological component, many countries especially non-Muslim ones, find it difficult to counter particular arguments purportedly based on Islam.[75]

Despite the difficulties, a number of countries have de-radicalization/disengagement programs in place. Though the ultimate objectives of these programs are the same – to wean away the ones already indoctrinated and/or to insulate potential adherents or recruits – the specifics differ reflecting the specific circumstances under which radicalization takes place in the particular country concerned. In other words, there is no single formula to disengagement or de-radicalization and it would be a mistake to attempt to implement a particular strategy which might have been successful or largely effective in a given context, universally. This is because the reasons for becoming a terrorist, staying a terrorist, and then disengaging from terrorism have often been different and context-specific.[76] Thus, the

73 "Saudi Paper Publishes Study of Saudi Counterterrorism Strategy." The English version of the quote is cited in Bard O' Neil, "Responding to Psychological, Social, Economic and Political Roots of Terrorism," 2007, p. 316.

74 See Hoffer, *The True Believer: Thoughts on the Nature of Mass Movements,* 1951; Also see Robbins, "Battlefront in the War of Ideas," 2007.

75 See Rabasa et al., *Deradicalizing Islamist Extremists*, 2010, p. 122.

76 See Horgan, "Psychological Factors Related to Disengaging from Terrorism: Some Preliminary Assumptions and Assertions," 2005, p. 67.

process of radicalization could be specific to particular cultures and societies, which makes generalizations difficult and self-defeating.

### J. Rehabilitation

One important component of any de-radicalization program is rehabilitation, more specifically religious rehabilitation. In fact, in almost all cases, counter-ideology programs have started with religious rehabilitation of detained militants. Moreover in many cases prisons have become one of the major sources of radicalization and recruitment. As Harvey Kushner, an American criminologist found, the Western prisons are one of the main recruitment grounds for Al Qaeda.[77] Similarly, a 2010 study by the International Centre for the Study of Radicalization and Political Violence (ICSR) concluded that prisons are "places of vulnerability," which provide near-perfect conditions in which radical, religiously framed ideologies can flourish.[78]

At the same time prisons could also be the incubators of peaceful change and transformation. In many countries, rehabilitation programs have already made significant contribution in reversing the process of radicalization and undermining the jihadists' campaigns.[79] Rehabilitation is also a panacea especially in respect of those countries which had to detain terrorist suspects effectively indefinitely without trial (Singapore and Malaysia under the Internal Security Act and the U.S. in Guantanamo as war criminals). In the case of Singapore, through structured and comprehensive rehabilitation programs, the government was able to release a substantive number of such detainees without any case of recidivism. Malaysia has also released most of the JI detainees after they went through rehabilitation programs. The similar trends are now emerging in many oth-

---

77 See Kushner, *Holy War on the Home Front*, 2004.

78 See "Prisons and Terrorism: Radicalisation and De-radicalisation in 15 Countries,": Report published by the International Centre for the Study of Radicalisation and Political Violence (ICSR) in partnership with the National Consortium for the Study of Terrorism and Responses to Terrorism (START), (2010), p. 2, http://www.icsr.info/publications/papers/1277699166PrisonsandTerrorismRadicalisationandDeradicalisationin15Countries.pdf.

79 See "Prisons and Terrorism," p. 8.

er countries.[80] These programs, with variations, are designed to combat the ideological motivations of suspected terrorists and their supporters in the community. The central focus of these rehabilitation programs is to reorient religious beliefs of the detainees and in many cases their family members away from extreme interpretations that encourage or justify violence through re-education.

However, it is difficult to measure the overall success of such programs. Rehabilitation has always been an integral part of the criminal justice system. But the impact of terrorist/extremist rehabilitation programs is not easily determinable. First, the initiatives are rather new and upcoming and need to have sufficient lead-time to demonstrate the impact. Second, the number of persons going through religious counseling is small and even if there is a very high rate of success with regard to such individuals, the extent to which this would reduce radicalization and extremism in the broader community is difficult to ascertain. As Brig. Gen. Tito Karnavian, deputy head of Indonesia's National Anti-Terrorism Agency (BNPT), admitted, "Our de-radicalization program isn't working as fast as they [extremist ideologues] can radicalize new members."[81] As with Yemen there are reports of high recidivism though recidivism rates may not be the best parameters to measure the success.[82] Moreover, disengagement and deradicalization programs are not implemented in isolation. Hence, the effectiveness of such programs cannot be judged without considering the respective political and social milieu.[83] In any case, rehabilitation is more important than prosecution or indefinite detention especially if it can be used to discourage indoctrination and recruitment to the jihadist movement.[84]

---

80 For a discussion on rehabilitation and deradicalization of detained militant in various countries, see Gunaratna, *Terrorist Rehabilitation and Counter-Radi-calization: New Approaches to Counter-terrorism*, 2011.

81 Arnaz, "Police Say Antiterror Program is Faulty," *The Jakarta Globe* (27 June 2011), http://www.thejakartaglobe.com/home/police-say-antiterror-program-is-faulty/449266.

82 See Porges and Stern, "Getting Deradicalization Right," *Foreign Affairs*, (May/June 2010), http://www.foreignaffairs.com/articles/66227/marisa-l-porges-jessica-stern/getting-deradicalization-right.

83 See "Prisons and Terrorism," p. 49.

84 See Jenkins, *Unconquerable Nation*, p. 129.

## K. Education Reform

A related counter-ideology strategy is to promote secular education. The common thread running across various conflicts involving Muslims is the role of Islamic religious educational institutions. As former U.S. Defense Secretary Rumsfeld commented in October 2003, "Are we capturing, killing or deterring and dissuading more terrorists every day than the madrassas and the radical clerics are recruiting, training and deploying against us?"[85] Some of these institutions have become the main disseminator of the jihad cult and the breeding grounds for the jihadist movement. This was due to increasing radicalization of education with perverted readings of the Quran and attempts to cloak political issues in extremist terminology.[86]

The religious schools have also become one of the instruments to strengthen ties among the dispersed jihadists and ensuring that their ideology is passed down to a new generation.[87] This form of religious education has thrived in most of the under-developed regions, where the concerned governments are not capable of or willing to provide minimum levels of education to all its citizens. Given the fact that much of the Islamic educational system is being misused by the radicals, it is necessary to ensure that states provide universal education based on a curriculum that promotes tolerance and respect for other cultures and religions.

But the nature and the extent of involvement of the Islamic schools in violent conflict are poorly studied. As such there is a need to understand the roots, nature and the extent of this involvement. Available research suggests that only a small percentage of Islamic religious schools have

---

85 DOD memo, Rumsfeld to Myers, Wolfowitz, Pace, and Feith, "Global War on Terrorism," (16 October 2003), http://www.usatoday.com/news/washington/executive/rumsfeld-memo.htm.

86 See Desker, "The Jemaah Islamiyah Phenomenon in Singapore," *Contemporary Southeast Asia*, 2003, p 495.

87 See "Jemaah Islamiyah in South East Asia: Damaged but Still Dangerous," *International Crisis Group*, Asia Report, 63, (6 August 2003), p. 26, http://www.crisisgroup.org/~/media/Files/asia/south-east-asia/indonesia/063%20Jemaah%20Islamiyah%20in%20South%20East%20Asia%20Damaged%20but%20Still%20Dangerous.pdf; Also see "Pakistan: Karachi's Madrasas and Violent Extremism," *International Crisis Group*, Asia Report, 130, (29 March 2007), http://www.crisisgroup.org/en/regions/asia/south-asia/pakistan/130-pakistan-karachis-madrasas-and-violent-extremism.aspx.

been infiltrated by terrorist and extremist groups. However, many of the teachers in these schools are increasingly found to be associated with extremism and terrorism. Therefore, it is necessary to prepare and disseminate guidelines for self-regulation and procedures for management of religious educational institutions drawing from global best practices. The idea is to counter the radical ideology which is based on a misinterpretation of the holy text and promote moderation, tolerance and dialogue.[88] The Asatiza Recognition Scheme in Singapore is an example of how to ensure that the teachers in Islamic schools develop an outlook that is progressive and resilient in its religious and social life.[89]Another example of best practice in this regard is the Madrasah Comprehensive Development & Promotion Program (MDCDPP), in Davao city in the Philippines which is based on community initiative to insulate the schools and the teachers from radical ideology.[90]

### *L. Communication Management*

Since the media, especially the tools of new media such as the Internet, has become one of the most important means to disseminate the ideology, it is also important to devise appropriate strategies of intervention. A quick-fix solution is to take down the jihadist websites but in practice this would be of no consequence and could even be counterproductive. The jihadists would come back with new websites in no time. On the contrary, the Internet could be of a greater value as an intelligence source than "if they were to disappear."[91] Taking down a website could disrupt monitoring or investigation by the law enforcements agencies. Therefore, as Aaron Weisburd commented: "The object isn't to silence them – the object is to keep them moving, keep them talking, force them to make mistakes,

---

88 See O' Neill and Alberts, "Responding to Psychological, Social, Economic and Political Roots of Terrorism," 2007, p. 316.

89 See "Asatizah Executive Development Programme (AEDP)," http://www.Muis.gov.sg/cms/services/Islamic.aspx?id=4718.

90 Author's interview with A'Lem Jamal S. Munib Executive Program Director of MDCDPP, Ustadz Mohammad Pasigan, Grand Mufti and Ustadz Omar Piang, Secretary of Madrasah Association, (Davao City: 22 August 2006).

91 Aftergood, cited in Lasker, "Watchdogs Sniff Out Terror Sites," *Wired News*, (25 February 2005), http://www.wired.com/news/privacy/0,1848,66708,00.html (12 Dec. 2005).

so we can gather as much information about them as we can, each step of the way."[92]

The second option following from the above is monitoring. Monitoring jihadi websites helps understanding extremists' philosophical and religious views, their views on grievances and root causes and other topical issues; innovation and changes in tradecraft including support activities and methods of attack; and linkages among various groups spread across the globe. Monitoring websites could be passive or active. Active monitoring involves covertly engaging the members of the forums in jihadi websites to elicit information for purposes of thwarting a potential terrorism-related activity.[93] This monitoring requires penetration into forums and chat rooms which are always password protected. But with adequate training, patience and understanding of the nuances of the way jihadists communicate; it is not a difficult task and in fact is already being done in many countries.[94]

The third option is "contamination", which is deliberately diluting the contents especially those on tradecraft – i.e., bomb making – with wrong or misleading details. According to a report, the British intelligence substituted instructions on bomb-making in the English-Language e-magazine – Inspire – published by the Al Qaeda in Arabian Peninsula and replaced them with cupcake recipes.[95] Over a period of time, this could undermine the confidence of the online community on the overall materials posted on the Internet by the jihadists. To target the ideological content, moderate Muslim individuals and groups could be given opportunity and technical and material assistance to create their own websites. However, while considering the intervention strategy, the legal and moral aspects and issues

---

92 Weisburd, cited in Lasker, "Watchdogs Sniff Out Terror Sites".

93 See Theohary and Rollins, "Terrorist Use of the Internet: Information Operations in Cyberspace," *Congressional Research Service*, R41674, (8 March 2011), p. 8, http://www.fas.org/sgp/crs/terror/R41674.pdf.

94 See Hinnen, "The Cyber-Front in the War on Terrorism: Curbing Terrorist Use of the Internet," 2004, pp. 1-42.

95 See "Cyberattack Wipes Jihadist Forum off the Web," *The Associated Press*, (1 July 2011), http://www.todayonline.com/World/EDC110701-0000308/Cyberattack-wipes-jihadist-forum-off-the-Web.

such as the protection of human rights and the legality of investigative instruments should not be lost sight off.[96]

## *M. A Platform for the Moderate Voice*

The challenge to radical views that supports acts of terrorism is likely to succeed only when it comes from deep within the Islamic tradition. Therefore it is vital that, "Muslims must conduct it."[97] Those challenging the radical's worldview must themselves be as deeply steeped in Islamic doctrines and be able to argue on the basis of the texts so frequently cited by the radicals. It is in fact for the Muslim community to rescue key concepts of the ideological discourse from the rigid pedagogical structures that have kept it in static mode and enthused it with inherent conservatism. As the 9/11 Commission Report succinctly observed, Muslims themselves would have to reflect upon such basic issues as the concept of jihad, the position of women, and the place of non-Muslim minorities. "The West can promote moderation, but cannot ensure its ascendancy. Only Muslims can do this."[98]

Moreover, the initiative of public diplomacy or a "propaganda" response to refute hostile ideological messages depends to a large degree on how the contents are prepared and delivered and which agency does so. As Raphael Perl points out, the U.S. sponsored more informal channels like Radio Free Europe and Radio Marti were generally accepted as believable and trusted medium of communication, while the Strategic Information Initiative (SII) – a direct U.S. DoD initiative, was not. Moreover, the SII was viewed as a tool for disinformation as opposed to traditional public diplomacy.[99] An ineffective counter-ideology campaign can be counter-

96 See "Countering Terrorist Use of the Internet – Legal Aspects," *The United Nations, Counter-Terrorism Implementation Task Force*, Draft (28 November 2010), http://www.un.org/terrorism/pdfs/2010_ctitf_legal_short_version_draft.pdf.

97 Kinnane, "Winning Over the Muslim Mind," 2004, p. 98.

98 National Commission on Terrorist Attacks upon the United States, *The 9/11 Commission Report,* p. 376.

99 Perl, "International Terrorism," p. 28; see also, "Propaganda – Cold war," *Encyclopedia of the New American Nation*, http://www.americanforeignrelations.com/O-W/Propaganda-Cold-war.html.

productive and may lead to distrust of and even animosity against the agency or the individual conducting the campaign.[100]

It is therefore necessary to create an international network of moderates and to provide platforms to amplify their message.[101] This is similar to the Social Democrats that represented one of the strongest bulwarks against the communist ideology.[102] At present, moderates are unwilling to confront the radicals. This could be due to lack of courage or a pervasive sense of helplessness, which according to Shibley Telhami is a function of the historical legacy of self-consciousness and a sense of inability to wage collective battles.[103] They could also be wary about the consequences of challenging the radicals or due to the values and the belief systems and the visions of the future social order that both moderates and the radicals share together.

Co-opting moderate leaders and influential clerics who could then affect larger public opinion is especially important given that a more direct [government] effort would likely have less impact [or even negative].[104] This might appear a difficult task to accomplish, but not an impossible one and not without precedent either. One example is the work of Mohammed Haniff Hassan – *Unlicensed to Kill: Countering Imam Samudra's Justification for the Bali Bombing*. In this volume, which was translated in Bahasa Indonesia and Melayu and widely circulated, Hassan provided a point-by-point rebuttal to Imam Samudra's justification of October 2002 Bali bombings using the same Quoranic verses to undermine the actions which Imam Samudra used to justify the killings.[105] There are in fact a growing number of respected and influential individuals in this category and we need to ensure that their theological and religious standing comes to the notice of those affected by the jihadists' deviant rhetoric.

In fact, proactive attempts to engage the Muslim community are already gaining momentum. In many countries of the world, including in the U.S., Muslims are working with the governments to delegitimize the appeal and

---

100 See Cragin and Gerwehr, *Dissuading Terror: Strategic Influence and the Struggle against Terrorism*, 2005.

101 See Rebasa et al., *Building Moderate Muslim Networks*, 2007.

102 See Campbell and Weitz, *Non-Military Strategies for Countering Islamist Terrorism*, p. 15.

103 See *Telhami,* "Understanding the Challenge," 2002, pp. 9-10.

104 Campbell and Weitz, *Non-Military Strategies for Countering Islamist Terrorism*, p. 15.

105 See Hassan, *Unlicensed to Kill.*

influence of the jihadists. Hussein Ibish, executive director of the Hala Salaam Maksoud Foundation for Arab-American Leadership, points out that, "most of the major successes the government claims within the United States have actually involved cooperation with the local Muslim communities" particularly for example, the neutralization of the "Lackawanna Six," the group of six Yemeni Americans who were reported by a local store owner who called the authorities on a suspicious request to copy a jihadi videotape.[106]

The same is the case with many other countries. In Singapore, for example, the Muslim community works closely with the government, not only to help identify potential recruits, but also by offering religious counseling to detainees and their families, (Religious Rehabilitation Group – RRG and Singapore After-care Association – SACA); determining the curriculum in religious schools and vetting and training teachers (Asatizah Recognition Scheme – ARS, and Asatizah Executive Training Programme – AEDP) for these schools. In Davao city in the Philippines, the local Muslims came forward to help the government respond to the terrorist threat immediately after the 2003 bombings in the city Airport and Sasa Wharf perpetrated by the Abu Sayyaf Group.[107]

As most analysts agree, the success of the strategy against jihadism will ultimately be based on the ability to counter the ideology and effective media propaganda and community engagement, thereby breaking the cycle of recruitment and resurgence that has helped the movement to survive. This would involve a mindset change in targeting and identifying the adversary and would require broader consensus and cooperation to go about destroying the enemy. The more than 12 years long fight has been characterized by wrong identification of the enemy and the inability of the governments to use soft power to reach out the Muslim masses.

The April 2006 report of the UN Secretary-General's High-Level Panel on Threats, Challenges and Change acknowledged that "a global strategy of fighting terrorism" needs to address root causes and strengthen responsible states and the rule of law and fundamental human rights." Counter-terrorism is a political-military action that requires simultaneous use of

---

106 See Kaplan, "American Muslims and the Threat of Homegrown Terrorism," *Council for Foreign Relations*, (May 2007), http://www.cfr.org/publication/11509/american_muslims_and_the_threat_of_homegrown_terrorism.html.

107 Author's interview with *A'Lem Jamal S. Munib*.

military, together with state-political socio-economic measures.[108] More specifically, as Francis Fukuyama emphasized, the struggle against global jihadism is more of a political battle, a "contest for the hearts and minds of ordinary Muslims around the world."[109]

From an operational perspective, a combination of hard and soft power is paramount to the success of any strategy against terrorism. This requires nuance, patience, and a comprehensive understanding of the threat and the operating environment, as well as how a government's actions can impact either of them.[110] Though a late starter, such initiatives are getting increasingly entrenched in strategies to fight the terrorism with good measures of success.

## *Bibliography*

Acharya, Arabinda, and Sonal Marwah, "Nizam la Tanzim (System not Organization): Do Organizations Matter in Terrorism Today? A Study of November 2008 Mumbai Attacks," *Studies in Conflict and Terrorism* 1 (2011): 1-16.

Acharya, Amitav, and Arabinda Acharya, "The Myth of the Second Front: Localizing the 'War on Terror' in Southeast Asia," *Washington Quarterly* 4 (2007): 75-90.

Aggelen, Johannes van, "The Consequences of Unlawful Preemption and the Legal Duty to Protect," *Case Western Reserve Journal of International Law* 1/2 (2009): 21-89.

Aly, Anne, and Leila Green, "Fear, Anxiety and the State of Terror," *Studies in Conflict and Terrorism* 3 (2010): 268-281.

Arnaz, Farouk "Police Say Antiterror Program is Faulty," The Jakarta Globe, (27 June 2011), at http://www.thejakartaglobe.com/home/police-say-antiterror-program-is-faulty/449266.

"Asatizah Executive Development Programme (AEDP)," at http://www.Muis.gov.sg/cms/services/Islamic.aspx?id=4718.

Author's interview with A'Lem Jamal S. Munib Executive Program Director of MD-CDPP, Ustadz Mohammad Pasigan, Grand Mufti and Ustadz Omar Piang, Secretary of Madrasah Association, (Davao City: 22 August 2006).

108 See Ganor, *The Counter-Terrorism Puzzle: A Guide for Decision Makers*, 2007, p. 38.

109 Fukuyama, "After Neo-Conservatism," *New York Times Magazine*, (19 February 2006), http://www.nytimes.com/2006/02/19/magazine/neo.html?pagewanted=print.

110 See Forest, "Strategic and Tactical Considerations: An Introduction," 2007, p. 5.

Bergen, Peter, *Holy War, Inc: Inside the Secret World of Osama bin Laden*, London: Weidenfeld & Nicolson, 2001.

Bernstein, Alvin H., "Political Strategies in Coercive Diplomacy and Limited War," in *Political Warfare and Psychological Operations*, ed. Carnes Lord and Frank R. Barnett, Washington, DC: National Defense University Press, 1989, pp. 111-138.

Byford, Grenville, "The Wrong War," *Foreign Affairs* 4 (2002): 34-43.

Campbell, Kurt M., and Richard Weitz, "Non-Military Strategies For Countering Islamist Terrorism: Lessons Learned From Past Counterinsurgencies," The Princeton Project Papers, September 2006, pp. 1-36.

Clausewitz, Carl von, *On War*, ed. and transl. Michael Howard and Peter Paret, Princeton, New Jersey: Princeton University Press, 1976.

Cohin, Audrey Kurth, "How Al Qaeda Ends: The Decline and Demise of Terrorist Groups," *International Security* 1 (2006): 7-48.

Cortright, David, and George A. Lopez, "Strategic Counter-Terrorism," in *Uniting Against Terror: Cooperative Nonmilitary Responses to the Global Terrorist Threat*, ed. David Cortright and George A. Lopez, Cambridge, Massachusetts: The MIT Press, 2007, pp. 1-22.

Carpenter, J. Scott and Levitt, Matthew "We must challenge the ideology driving terrorism," *The Australian*, (16 November 2010), at http://www.theaustralian.com.au/news/opinion/we-must-challenge-the-ideology-driving-terrorism/story-e6frg6zo-1225954047 97.

Crawford, Neta C., "The Slippery Slope to Preventive War," *Ethics and International Affairs* 30 (2003): 30-36.

Cragin, Kim, and Scott Gerwehr, *Dissuading Terror: Strategic Influence and the Struggle against Terrorism*, Santa Monica: Rand Corp., 2005.

Crenshaw, Martha, "The War on Terrorism: Is the U.S. Winning?," *Analisis del Real Instituto Elcano* 105 (2006): 1-7.

Desker, Barry, "The Jemaah Islamiyah Phenomenon in Singapore," *Contemporary Southeast Asia* 3 (2003): 489-507.

Finel, Bernard, "The War on Terrorism: Are We Winning?" *UCF Today* (20 January 2011), *at* http://today.ucf.edu/the-war-on-terrorism-are-we-winning/.

Fink, Naureen Chowdhury, and Ellie B. Hearne, *Beyond Terrorism: Deradicalization and Disengagement from Violent Extremism*, New York: International Peace Institute, 2008.

Foreign Broadcast Information Service of the USA, "Declaration of Jihad Against the Americans Occupying the Land of the Two Holy Mosques," in *Compilation of Usama Bin Ladin Statements 1994 – January 2004*, FBIS Report (January 2004), at http://www.fas.org/irp/world/para/ubl-fbis.pdf.

Forest, James J. F., "Strategic and Tactical Considerations: An Introduction," in *Countering Terrorism and Insurgency in the 21st Century: International Perspectives, Vol.1*, ed. James J. F. Forest, Westport: Praeger, 2007, pp. 1-35.

Ganor, Boaz, *The Counter-Terrorism Puzzle: A Guide for Decision Makers*, New Brunswick and London: Transaction Publishers, 2007.

Guelke, Adrian, *The Age of Terrorism and the International Political System*, London: Taurus Press, 1995.

Gunaratna, Rohan, Jolene Jerard and Lawrence Rubin (eds.), *Terrorist Rehabilitation and Counter-Radicalization: New Approaches to Counter-terrorism*, London and New York: Routledge, 2011.

Haque, M. Shamsul, "Government Responses to Terrorism: Critical Views of their Impacts on People and Public Administration," *Public Administration Review* 62 (2002): 170–180.

Hassan, Mohammad Haniff, *Unlicensed to Kill: Countering Imam Samudra's Justification for the Bali Bombings*, Singapore: Peace Matters, 2006.

Herman, Susan, "The USA Patriot Act and the U.S. Department of Justice: Losing Our Balances," *Jurist* (2001): 5-6.

Hinnen, Todd M., "The Cyber-Front in the War on Terrorism: Curbing Terrorist Use of the Internet," *Columbia Science and Technology Law Review* 5 (2004): 1-42.

HM Government, "Delivering the Prevent Strategy: An updated guide for local partners," August 2009, p. 9, at http://www.dcsf.gov.uk/violentextremism/preventstrategy/downloads/2009%20Updated%20guide%20to%20local%20partners.pdf.

Hoffer, Eric, *The True Believer: Thoughts on the Nature of Mass Movements*, New York: Harper and Row, 1951.

Hoffmann, Stanley, "Clash of Civilizations," *Foreign Affairs* 4 (2002): 104-115.

Holmes, Jennifer S., *Terrorism and Democratic Stability*, Manchester, U.K.: Manchester University Press, 2001.

Horgan, John, "Psychological Factors Related to Disengaging from Terrorism: Some Preliminary Assumptions and Assertions," in *A Future for the Young: Options for Helping Middle Eastern Youth Escape the Trap of Radicalization*, ed. Cheryl Benard, Santa Monica: RAND Corporation, 2005, pp. 65-91.

Horgan, John, "Individual Disengagement: a Psychological Analysis," in *Leaving Terrorism Behind*, ed. Tore Bjørgo and John Horgan, New York: Routledge, 2009, pp. 17-29.

Horgan, John, *Walking Away from Terrorism: Accounts of Disengagement from Radical and Extremist Movements*, London and New York: Routledge, 2009.

Howard, Michael, "What's In A Name? How to Fight Terrorism," *Foreign Affairs* 1 (2002): 8-13.

Institute for Economics and Peace, "The 2012 Global Terrorism Index: Capturing the Impact of Terrorism for the Last Decade," (December 2012), at http://www.visionofhumanity.org/sites/default/files/2012_Global_Terrorism_Index_Report.pdf.

International Centre for the Study of Radicalisation and Political Violence (ICSR), "Prisons and Terrorism: Radicalisation and De-radicalisation in 15 Countries," 2010, p. 2, at http://www.icsr.info/publications/papers/1277699166PrisonsandTerrorismRadicalisationandDeradicalisationin15Countries.pdf.

International Crisis Group, "Jemaah Islamiyah in South East Asia: Damaged but Still Dangerous," Asia Report, 63, (6 August 2003), p. 26, at http://www.crisisgroup.org/~/media/Files/asia/south-east-asia/indonesia/063%20Jemaah%20Islamiyah%20in%20South%20East%20Asia%20Damaged%20but%20Still%20Dangerous.pdf.

International Crisis Group, "Pakistan: Karachi's Madrasas and Violent Extremism," Asia Report, 130, (29 March 2007), at http://www.crisisgroup.org/en/regions/asia/south-asia/pakistan/130-pakistan-karachis-madrasas-and-violent-extremism.aspx.

Jenkins, Brian Michael, *Unconquerable Nation: Knowing Our Enemy, Strengthening Ourselves*, Santa Monica: RAND Corporation, 2006.

Johnson, James Turner, "Just War Thinking in Recent American Religious Debate over Military Force," in *The Price of Peace, Just War in the Twenty-First Century*, ed. Charles Reed and David Ryall, Cambridge: Cambridge University Press, 2007, pp. 76-98.

Kaplan, Eben, "American Muslims and the Threat of Homegrown Terrorism," *Council for Foreign Relations*, (May 2007), at http://www.cfr.org/publication/11509/american_muslims_and_the_threat_of_homegrown_terrorism.html.

Keen, David, *Endless War?: Hidden Functions of the "War on Terror"*, London and Ann Arbur: Pluto/University of Michigan Press, 2006.

Kegley, Chris, "The Characteristics, Causes, and Controls of the New Global Terrorism," in *The New Global Terrorism: Characteristics, Causes, Controls*, ed. Chris Kegley, New York: Prentice Hall, 2003, pp. 1-14

Kiesling, John Brady, "Diplomatic Breakdown," *The Boston Globe Magazine* (27April 2003).

Kilcullen, David J., "Countering Global Insurgency," *The Journal of Strategic Studies* 4 (2005): 597-610.

Kinnane, Derk, "Winning Over the Muslim Mind," The National Interest 75 (2004): 93-99.

Kushner, Harvey, *Holy War on the Home Front: The Secret Islamic Terror*, New York: Sentinel, 2004.

Lasker,John, "Watchdogs Sniff Out Terror Sites," *Wired News*, (25 February 2005), at http://www.wired.com/news/privacy/0,1848,66708,00.html (12 Dec. 2005).

Lovin, Robin W., *Reinhold Niebuhr and Christian Realism*, Cambridge: Cambridge University Press, 1995.

National Commission on Terrorist Attacks Upon the United States, *The 9/11 Commission Report: Final Report of the National Commission on Terrorist Attacks Upon the United States*, Washington, D.C.: U.S. Government Printing Office, 2004.

Lee, Brian Angelo, "Preventive War, Deterrent Retaliation, and Retrospective Disproportionality," *Brigham Young University Law Review* 2 (2009): 254-290.

Lewis, Seth C, and Stephen D Reese, "What is the War on Terror? Framing Through the Eyes of Journalists," *Journalism and Mass Communication Quarterly* 1 (2009): 85-102.

Lord, Carnes, "Psychological-Political Instruments," in *Attacking Terrorism: Elements of a Grand Strategy*, ed. Audrey Kurth Cronin and James M. Ludes, Washington: Georgetown University Press, 2004, pp. 220-237.

Mahathir Mohammad, "Breaking the Muslim Mindset," *The Sunday Times* (Singapore: 28 July 2002).

Mahathir, Muhammad, "U.S. Policy in Iraq, Iran Preclude to 4th World War," *China Daily* (8 June 2006), at http://english.people.com.cn/200606/08/eng20060608_272051.html.

McMillan, Joesph, and Christopher Cavoli, "Countering Global Terrorism," in *Strategic Challenges: America's Global Security Agenda*, ed. Stephen J. Flanagan and James A. Schear, Washington D.C.: National Defence University Press and Potomac Books, 2008, pp. 20-60.

O'Neill, Bard E., and Donald J. Alberts, "Responding to Psychological, Social, Economic and Political Roots of Terrorism," in *Countering Terrorism and Insurgency in the 21st Century, Vol. 2*, ed. James Forest, Westport: Praeger, 2007, pp. 305-324.

Osiel, Mark, *The End of Reciprocity: Terror, Torture and the Law of War*, Cambridge: Cambridge University Press, 2009.

Paddock, Alfred Jr., "Military Psychological Operations," in *Political Warfare and Psychological Operations: Rethinking the US Approach*, ed. Carnes Lord and Frank R. Barnett, Washington, DC: National Defense University Press, 1989, pp. 45-76.

Perl, Raphael F., *International Terrorism: Threat, Policy, and Response*, Darby: DIANE Publishing, 2007.

Pillar, Paul R., "Counter-terrorism after Al Qaeda," *The Washington Quarterly* 3 (2004): 101-113.

Pillar, Paul R., "Terrorism Goes Global," *Brookings Review* 4 (2001): 34-37.

Porges, Marisa L., and Jessica Stern, "Getting Deradicalization Right," Foreign Affairs May/June 2010, acccesible at http://www.foreignaffairs.com/articles/66227/marisa-l-porges-jessica-stern/getting-deradicalization-right.

Post, Jerard M., "The Key Role of Psychological Operations in Countering Terrorism," in *Countering Terrorism and Insurgency in the 21st Century, Vol. 1*, ed. James Forrest, Westport: Praeger, 2007, pp. 380-396.

Rabasa, Angel Stacie L. Pettyjohn, Jeremy J. Ghez, Christopher Boucek et al., *Deradicalizing Islamist Extremists*, Santa Monica: RAND Corporation, 2010.

Ramsey, Paul, *The Just War: Force and Political Responsibility*, Lanham, Maryland: Rowman & Littlefield 1983.

Record, Jeffrey, "Bounding the Global War on Terrorism," *Strategic Studies Institute*, (December 2003), p. 12, at http://www.Globalsecurity.org/military/librar y/report/2003/record_bounding.pdf.

Reese, Stephen D., "Militarized Journalism: Framing Dissent in the Gulf Wars," in *Reporting War: Journalism in Wartime*, ed. Stuart Allan and Barbie Zelizer, New York: Routledge, 2004, pp. 247-265.

Reese, Stephen D., "The Framing Project: A Bridging Model for Media Research Revisited," *Journal of Communication* 1 (2007): 148-154.

Riyadh Al-Jazirah, "Saudi Paper Publishes Study of Saudi Counterterrorism Strategy," 31 December 2005, at http://www.al-jazirah.com.

Rishikof, Harvey, "Morality, Ethics and Law in the Global War on Terrorism (the Long War)," in *Counter Terrorism and Insurgency in the 21st Century, Vol. 1*, ed. James Forest, Westport: Praeger, 2007, pp. 106-132.

Robbins, James S., "Battlefront in the War of Ideas," in *Countering Terrorism and Insurgency in the 21st Century, Vol. 1*, ed. James Forest, Westport: Praeger, 2007, pp. 298-318.

Robison, Kristopher, "Terror's True Nightmare? Reevaluating the Consequences of Terrorism on Democratic Governance," *Terrorism and Political Violence* 1 (2010): 62-86.

Rocheleau, Jordy, "Preventive War and Lawful Constraints on the Use of Force: An Argument Against International Vigilantism," in *Rethinking the Just War Tradition*, ed. Michael W. Brough, John W. Lango, and Harry van der Linden, Albany: State University of New York Press, 2007, pp. 183-204.

Simon, Steven, "The New Terrorism: Securing the Nation against a Messianic Foe," *Brookings Review* 21 (2003), at http: //www.brookings.edu/articles /2003/winter_terrorism_simon.aspx.

Surin, Pitsuwan "Strategic Challenges Facing Islam in Southeast Asia," Lecture delivered at the *Institute of Defence and Strategic Studies and the Centre for Contemporary Islamic Studies*, (Singapore: 5 November 2001).

Telhami, Shibley, "Understanding the Challenge," *The Middle East Journal* 1 (2002): 9-18.

Tellis, Ashley J., "Assessing America's War on Terror: Confronting Insurgency, Cementing Primacy," *NBR Analysis* 4 (2004): 5-100.

The Associated Press, "Cyberattack Wipes Jihadist Forum off the Web," (1 July 2011), at http://www.todayonline.com/World/EDC110701-0000308/Cyberattack-wipes-jihadist-forum-off-the-Web.

Theohary, Catherine A., and John Rollins, "Terrorist Use of the Internet: Information Operations in Cyberspace," Congressional Research Service, R41674, (8 March 2011), p. 8, at http://www.fas.org/sgp/crs/terror/R41674.pdf.

The United Nations, *Counter-Terrorism Implementation Task Force* "Countering Terrorist Use of the Internet – Legal Aspects," Draft (28 November 2010).

The White House, "National Strategy for Combating Terrorism: February 2003," (February 2003), pp. 8-10, at http://www.iwar.org.uk/homesec/resources/counter-terror/counter_terrorism_strategy.pdf.

The White House, "The National Security Strategy 2002," (September 2002), at http://georgewbush-whitehouse.archives.gov/nsc/nss/2002/.

United States Department of Defense, "Dictionary of Military and Associated Terms," (12 April 2001; as Amended Through 19th August 2009), pp. 428 and 432, at http://www.fas.org/irp/doddir/dod/jp1_02.pdf.

United States Department of Defense, "DoD News Briefing: Deputy Secretary Wolfowitz," *News Transcript*, (13 September 2001), at http://www.defenselink.mil/news/Sep2001/t09132001_t0913dsd.html.

US Today, "Rumsfeld's war-on-terror memo," 16 October 2003, at http://www.usatoday.com/news/washington/executive/rumsfeld-memo.htm.

Walzer, Michael, *Just and Unjust Wars: A Moral Argument with Historical Illustrations*, New York: Basic Books, 1977.

Wedgwood, Ruth, "Al Qaeda, Terrorism, and Military Commissions," *The American Journal of International Law* 2 (2002): 328-337.

Wee, Chow-How, *Sun Zi: Art of War*, Singapore: Prentice Hall, 2003.

Weigel, George, "The Development of Just War Thinking in the Post-Cold War World: an American Perspective," in *The Price of Peace: Just War in the 21st Century*, ed. Charles Reed and David Ryall, Cambridge: Cambridge University Press, 2007, pp. 19-36.

Weinberg, Leonard B., William L. Eubank, and Elizabeth A. Francis, "The Cost of Terrorism: The Relationship Between International Terrorism and Democratic Governance," *Terrorism and Political Violence* (2008): 257- 270.

Wilkinson, Paul, *Terrorism versus Democracy: The Liberal State Response*, London: Frank Cass, 2001.

Wilkinson, Paul, "Maintaining the Democratic Process and Public Support," in *The Future of Political Violence: Destablization, Disorder and Terrorism*, ed. Richard Clutterbuck, New York: Palgrave Macmillan, 1986, pp. 177-178.

Zellen, Barry, "Whither Victory in the War on Terror?," *Strategic Insights* 2 (2007), at http://www.nps.edu/Academics/centers/ccc/publications/OnlineJournal/2007/Mar/zellenMar07.pdf.

# Fighting Terrorism with Smart Power: The Role of Community Engagement and Terrorist Rehabilitation

*Rohan Gunaratna*

## *A. Introduction*

Today, terrorism presents a tier one national security threat to most countries. Both hard power and soft power are essential to fight terrorism and its precursor, ideological extremism. The use of hard power by itself will not produce the desired outcome. To be effective, hard power must be integrated with soft power. This combination, smart power, is the game changer in combating downstream terrorism and upstream extremism. This paper aims to expound the concept of smart power by explaining the role of community engagement to prevent extremism and rehabilitation to cure terrorism. Drawing from the strategic counterterrorism experiences of various countries, this paper underscore the need for investing in both counter-radicalization and de-radicalization programs.

As a vicious by-product of politico-religious extremism, terrorism today is shaped by a digitally interconnected human terrain with ethnic and religious fault lines. If they remain unengaged a growing number of individuals from vulnerable communities will fall into the hands of the extremists. Last one decade's experience shows that ideological extremism is no longer confined to conflict zones. The spillover effect is rapid and it is often manifested in migrant and community support for terrorism. Migrant and diaspora pockets often identify themselves with developments in conflict zones. The phenomenon of self-radicalized cells and individuals in North America, Europe, Singapore and Australia demonstrates the impact of such extremist propaganda. With attacks by such cells and individuals, entire communities may be demonized threatening communal relations. The accumulation of prejudices often results in reciprocal violence against the group conducting terrorist actions, through either newly formed right wing groups or the violent reaction of individuals like Anders Behring

Breivik.[1] Disharmony can weaken and damage the social fabric of any, particularly any multicultural society. As extremists strive to tear societies apart, governments must be steadfast in their response and make the best use of smart power. The paper emphasizes on the centrality of the human terrain – the community in fighting terrorism.

## *B. The Context*

Traditionally most governments use kinetic and lethal methods to fight terrorism. They employ their intelligence services to uncover terrorist attacks during the early stages of planning and preparation, their law enforcement to investigate and charge terrorists at home, and their military to combat terrorism abroad. The traditional criminal justice and prison systems in most countries are designed for a reactive response in the form of deterrence and punishment, not prevention and rehabilitation.

Kinetic and lethal responses by governments are often effective as a preliminary response especially in terms of weakening the operational capability of highly organized terrorist groups. But such responses cannot stem the tide of ideological extremism. I suggest, that the latter can be fought efficiently by smart power which combines both hard and soft power. I also argue that for rehabilitation and community engagement to be successful, it has to be multifaceted, a long term public-private sector partnership, and led by creative and innovative leaders. For custodial rehabilitation to be successful, it has to be followed by community rehabilitation. In parallel with rehabilitation in detention centers and prison settings, it is paramount for engagement programs to prepare the ground for successful reintegration of the rehabilitated beneficiary.

An efficient fight against terrorism must attend three areas simultaneously. It must prevent its citizens from embracing extremist ideologies and becoming terrorists; rehabilitate terrorists and extremists, and address issues exploited by terrorists and extremists to build its membership and support base. Counter-radicalization by community engagement and deradicalization by rehabilitation are two crucial pillars of a contemporary counter terrorism strategy. The first part of this paper (C.) will deal with

1 Angered by Norway's position on multiculturalism, Breivik, a 32 years right wing terrorist, bombed a government building killing 8 and shot 69 at a political youth camp on July 22, 2011.

Community Engagement and the second part of this paper (D.) will deal with de-radicalization.

## *C. Community Engagement*

Community engagement refers to the process by which community benefit organizations and individuals build ongoing, permanent relationships for the purpose of applying a collective vision for the benefit of a community. Engaging community in countering ideological extremism is a key component of soft power. A few governments built partnerships with trusted members of the community and organizations supporting ad hoc and structured community engagement programs. Although community engagement is a promising strategy to counter extremism, most governments are yet to create partnerships, build platforms, allocate budgets, and to train personnel.

Governments in the past did build capabilities to engage communities to fight crime particularly when law enforcement authorities, especially the police, realized the value of community support. In the West, engaging communities as a strategy against ideological extremism has its roots in September 11, 2001. As opposed to paid informants, community sources became the eyes and ears of the communities vulnerable to terrorist penetration through both infiltration and recruitment. As opposed to police initiated community engagement, the leaders and elite of the community initiated engagements with the police. Such engagements led to partnerships where trusted networks were built. As success of counter-terrorism depends on secrecy, the sharing of counter-terrorism information is sensitive. However, there is strategic information that can be shared without compromising ongoing and future counter terrorism operations. When trusted, community members felt that they are stakeholders in maintaining security. That sense of ownership led community members to bring to the attention of the police suspicious activities. Rather than arrest, police developed community solutions. By arranging community elders to counsel, the police facilitated those affected by extremist ideology to re-enter the mainstream. Community participation to counter-extremism including violent extremism grew over time. As opposed to an engaged community, a disengaged community unaware of the threat was likely to view counter-terrorism operations as targeting the community.

Terrorist organizations operate through front, cover and sympathetic organizations. These organizations target communities for recruitment, funding, intelligence and other forms of support. Minority communities, politically and economically marginalized are particularly susceptible to extremist indoctrination and terrorist recruitment. Governments today engage community support in order to prevent terrorism. By building community partnerships and promoting moderation, toleration and co-existence, the logical thinking was that the community could be immunized from extremism. By building a norm and an ethic against extremist ideology, the community could be protected from extremist influence.

Military, law enforcement and intelligence measures are insufficient to end support for politically motivated violence. As terrorist organizations present a multidimensional threat, it requires confronting the threat both militarily and non-militarily. While the terrorists and guerrillas have to be confronted through military and law enforcement means, resiliency against extremist ideology has to be built by engaging the community politically, ideologically, and socially. The approaches in engagement and partnership were developed by trial and error in the first decade after 9/11. As a result of a segment of the press stereotyping and stigmatizing Muslims as terrorists, government saw the increase in number of inter-communal incidents including insults and hate crime. One single incident could have sparked a riot. Rather than blindly implement the law, enforcement and intelligence services became more sensitive to community perceptions.

To counter the perception that the members of a particular community were being targeted, the relevant agencies briefed community elite and at times gave them access to arrested terrorists. Furthermore, they prepared and released reports to the public. Engagement led to increasing community awareness and understanding of their problems. As some community organizations were infiltrated by extremists and terrorists, government and their partners entrusted with engagement had to be selective. While they engaged everyone, they empowered community organizations selectively. Unfortunately, in the spirit of assisting communities, many well intentioned governments in Canada, the United Kingdom (UK) and Australia empowered community organizations that actually promoted an extremist agenda. The UK admitted and Canada stopped support but only after a decade of supporting such groups, perhaps thinking that they could influence them to embrace harmony. In addition to empowering communities to resolve their own problems, law enforcement authorities and intelligence agencies started to work with schools, clergy and the media to influence the general population.

Government not only engaged the communities but also the private sector. As the terrorists exploited hospitality, financial and other sectors, governments engaged these trusted stakeholders in building their understanding to detect pre-attack indicators. With an increase in government investment, the community and private sector became partners in the fight against extremism and terrorism. By sharing the burden of security, they felt a sense of ownership to protect their own community and businesses. A few enlightened political leaders and senior bureaucrats provided guidance and local government, private sector and community institutions provided leadership.

Most community engagement programs worldwide were triggered by an event or a series of events. Over time, these unstructured and ad hoc programs become structured and streamlined with national policies with a clear activity plan, objectives and goals. With institutionalization, the sustainability of the program is guaranteed. Nonetheless, for such programs to be effective, they must adopt a bottom-up approach in which community engagement projects are led by community leaders involving different strata of society with the government providing some general guidelines. Rather than waiting for the government to initiate programs, anyone who desires future peace and stability should work for it. The strata of society are: first, government, second, community, third, private sector, and fourth, civil society. These four principal sectors should contribute within a coordinating body. The visionary leaders in government, political parties, business community, education sector, religious establishment, media, the arts, youth organizations, NGOs and diaspora should build common platforms to promote the ideals of moderation, toleration and coexistence.

### *I. Global Programs*

Community engagement programs to counter extremism can be ranked as developed, developing and emerging. The developed programs are in the UK, Saudi Arabia and Singapore; the developing programs are in Europe, Australia and North America; and the emerging programs are in South Asia (India, Pakistan, Bangladesh, etc.), in the Middle East (Yemen, Jordan, Morocco, etc.) and in Africa (South Africa and Sahel). The impetus for almost all the community engagement programs was often a successful, failed or aborted terrorist attack.

While the UK, Singapore and Saudi Arabia have structured and institutionalized programs to counter extremism, most of the programs in other countries are unstructured and ad hoc. The British, with its long history of fighting terrorism in Northern Ireland and elsewhere, realized the value of engaging the Muslim community after 9/11. Police community engagement aimed at building relations with the Muslim community was initiated by the Muslim Contact Unit of New Scotland Yard in 2002. Although CONTEST, a strategy by the UK Home Office, was launched to engage communities in early 2003, community engagement programs took off in earnest only after the London bombings of July 2005.[2] With government and private funding, several programs emerged including STREET (Strategy to Reach, Empower and Educate), UK; Channel, Supporting Individuals Vulnerable to Recruitment by Violent Extremists, UK; and Cached Quilliam, Challenging Extremism, Promoting Pluralism, and Inspiring Change. A counter-extremism think tank, Quilliam notes: "Challenging extremism is the duty of all responsible members of society. Not least because cultural insularity and extremism are products of the failures of wider society to foster a shared sense of belonging and to advance liberal democratic values."[3]

Radical Middle Way, founded in the wake of the 9/11 attacks, promote(s) a mainstream, moderate understanding of Islam that young people can relate to. Radical Middle Way is a safe place for people to ask difficult questions and explore challenging issues. Since 2005, Radical Middle Way has delivered over 230 programs and events in the UK, Pakistan, Sudan, Indonesia, Mali and Morocco. In the UK alone, over 75.000 people have participated. Tens of thousands more have participated (in the other regions).[4]

To engage the community further, the UK police started to work with the local councils in 2011 under Prevent II. The developing programs are

2 See http://www.homeoffice.gov.uk/counter-terrorism/review-of-prevent-strategy/; latest accessed September 18, 2016.

3 Http://www.quilliamfoundation.org/about/, latest accessed September 18, 2016.

4 See http://www.radicalmiddleway.org/page/about-us, latest accessed February 14, 2012.

in continental Europe, North America, and Australia.[5] Although the Madrid train bombing on March 11, 2004, killed 191 and wounded 1.800 people and an official investigation revealed that it was perpetrated by European born or raised Muslims, it was not until Mohammed Bouyeri, a Dutch Moroccan Muslim, killed, Theodoor "Theo" van Gogh, on 2nd November, that the Europeans realized that the threat from community radicalization had to be tackled. Not all governments thought likewise. In France, for instance, the government did not invest in community engagement programs.

Community approach means there is a problem between communities. The word is dangerous. In France, there are no communities. In contrast to the UK, where they respect and empower communities, we want to integrate everyone into the French society. Such a program will not work in France for social and historical reasons.[6]

A few European NGOs responded to community radicalization even before the contemporary wave of politico-religious radicalization. Among the programs created were the EXIT program, Sweden;[7] Violence Prevention Network, Germany; CoPPRa (Community Policing and the Prevention of Radicalisation), Belgium; Centre for Equal Opportunities and Opposition to Racism project to tackle hate speech on the internet, Belgium. In the Netherlands, the Ministry of Justice launched a series of programs to engage the Muslim diaspora, for example, through the local councils.

Although Canada and Australia did not suffer from terrorism on its own soil, they hosted diaspora and migrant communities that actively supported terrorism elsewhere. If not for effective intelligence and law enforcement operations, both Canada and Australia would have suffered from terrorism by homegrown groups. Their community engagement strategies were deeply influenced by UK CONTEST. To promote government-community collaboration, Cross-Cultural Roundtable on Security, jointly supported by Public Safety Canada and the Department of Justice, brought together the leaders of various communities. They engaged with the government by raising social and cultural issues. National Security Community Outreach, a local initiative of the Royal Canadian Mounted Police Force,

5 See Hanniman, "Canadian Muslims, Islamophobia and National Security Royal Canadian Mounted Police," 2008, pp. 271-285.

6 Interview, Jean-Louis Bruguiere, counter-terrorism advisor to the French Government, February 12, 2012.

7 Exit Program was established to assist Neo-Nazi's to join the mainstream.

engaged radicalized segments of Canadian migrant and diaspora communities especially in Toronto and Montreal. Like the Chaplains in the UK came under government scrutiny, the government encouraged and enabled universities to engage imams to promote moderation. In Australia, the Australian Federal Police (AFP) built Community Liaison Teams to strengthen community relationships. To increase awareness of diverse communities, the AFP hosted annual Iftar/Eid dinners, sporting events including football matches, Muslim women's camps and education initiatives aimed at resisting extremist narratives. In addition to developing a Community Integration Support Program, the AFP also created a parole program for those currently incarcerated. AFP's three-pronged approach was religious education, practical support and community relations. In addition to government initiatives, national security hotlines, that were of exceptional value, several community and civil society organizations contributed to the change in the Australian threat landscape. For instance, the Lebanese, Somali, Pakistani and other high risk communities were engaged. From Queensland to Victoria and New South Wales, projects supported by the Office of the Attorney General of Australia were developed to "counter narrative messages to challenge Islamic militancy propaganda."[8]

The programs in North America, continental Europe and Australia demonstrated early attempts to educate the host communities about Islam and Muslims but with limited success. Compared to the Europeans, Americans are resilient to extremist and terrorist propaganda, which aims to draw a distinction between Muslims and non-Muslims. As American ideals include equality, more than most others, Americans are more receptive to differences in religion, ethnicity, and place of birth. However, the US government focused on fighting terrorism, and as a result, did not invest heavily in engaging the Muslim communities on US soil until the Obama Administration. With President Obama determined to develop a comprehensive strategy, the US authorities started some major community engagement initiatives in 2011. Several US-supported NGOs are active both on US soil and overseas. For example, the Zaytuna Institute in California is headed by Hamza Yusuf Hanson, an American convert to Islam, who worked on both sides of the Atlantic. He invites mainstream speakers who

8 See http://www.resilientcommunities.gov.au/getinvolved/Pages/qld.aspx.

distinguished between fundamentalism and extremism to speak to the community, with the aim of engaging the young generation.

Community engagement to counter extremism is a relatively new tool in most of Middle East, Asia and Africa. Traditionally, diverse communities have lived in peace. For instance, Jewish communities lived throughout the Middle East and in Asia including in Iraq and Afghanistan. With ethnicity and religion assuming salience at the end of the 20$^{th}$ century, both governments and civil society organizations have invested in some community engagement initiatives. Although governments in the Middle East and in Muslim Asia have been fighting Muslim extremism and terrorism prior to 9/11, they did not perceive it as a community problem. While these governments initially tolerated the presence of violent extremists, they used force and detention as tools when the problem became significant. However, after 9/11, the rulers and religious establishment of most Middle Eastern and Asian Muslim governments realized that law enforcement and intelligence services alone cannot fight this battle. To influence the communities, both secular and religious leaders made statements promoting moderation. Some leaders such as the King of Jordan, Morocco and Brunei took the lead in espousing religious moderation. Furthermore, religious institutions were encouraged to vet the Friday sermons in some countries. Although not collectively for all mosques, these sermons advised Muslims not to overreact to developments in Iraq, Afghanistan, Palestine, and Kashmir. Education curricula and recommended readings were reviewed in a few countries. In a small number of countries, both civil society and community organizations built a partnership with governments beginning to counter extremism.

Australia, the UK and US authorities have openly, and discreetly, funded some projects in Indonesia to promote community engagement initiatives. Together with the Government of Indonesia, the U.S. Department of Justice's International Criminal Investigative Training Assistance Program (ICITAP) began a Countering Violent Extremism Project in 2010 to assess "community perspectives of enablers of community destabilization, with a focus on building strategies to counter violent extremism through community-based derived initiatives and interventions."[9] Similarly, NGOs in Indonesia produced films, books and cartoons for school children. Both the Lazuardi Birru and the International Institute of Peace Building in Jakarta

9 Gerald H. Heuett Jr, personal communication, September 21, 2011.

made efforts to engage university students and former radicals through films, comics and cartoons. The law enforcement agencies, such as the National Counter Terrorism Agency (BNPT) in Indonesia and the Special Task Force (Operations and Counter Terrorism) of the Malaysian police, responded to invitation to address schools and universities.

In South Asia, programs emerged only after a terrorist event resulted in an ethnic or religious riot. For example, thousands of Sikhs were killed after Prime Minister Indira Gandhi was assassinated in 1984. Likewise, hundreds of Tamils were killed by mobs after the Liberation Tigers of Tamil Ealam (LTTE) attacked an army patrol in northern Sri Lanka in 1983. In India, Pakistan, Sri Lanka and Bangladesh, community engagement programs took the shape of reconciliation initiatives.[10] At the end of the conflict in Sri Lanka in May 2009, the Sri Lankan military transformed rapidly from a war fighting force to a nation building force.

The military and police have developed community engagement programs in the Philippines and Thailand to varying degrees of success. In the Philippines, both the US Embassy and Special Operations worked closely with the Philippines military to shore up civil military operations capability. In active conflict zones, civil military operations and community engagement initiatives overlapped.

With the penetration of extremist ideologies, Africa is emerging as a new stage for terrorist operations. Following the spillover effects of the revolution in Libya, AFRICOM has planned to develop community engagement capacity in the Sahel. The South African government, working with civil societies and community organizations, has developed several community engagement initiatives to tackle non-traditional security issues. The development of extremism in West Africa (Nigeria), North Africa (Algeria) and East Africa (Somalia) can be resisted and contained through community engagement efforts.

## *II. Challenges and Opportunities*

A common challenge was to identify charismatic religious practitioners who could reach the masses and converse both inside and outside the

10 See http://www.kadirgamarinstitute.lk/events/video.htm, latest accessed February 14, 2012.

mosque. To influence the Muslim community, they had to work through not only the religious institutions (mosque) but the educational establishment (madrasah), and the mainstream and social media. To build bonds by enhancing the interaction between Muslim and non-Muslim communities, they also had to engage the non-Muslims. To negate the impression that community engagement programs are targeting Muslims, programs to promote religious harmony should reach out to the main-stream.

Political will at the highest level is required to develop and implement community engagement programs. Like rehabilitation programs, community engagement programs need sustained support and steadfast backing from the country's top leadership. Visionary leaders like then Minister of Endowments and Guidance, Judge Hamoud Al-Hittar of Yemen, helped to develop a program for mainstream both detainees and the community from the late 2002s to the mid-2006. However, support for Yemen's Religious Dialogue program was disrupted mid-way. As the program did not receive the support required from the President, the program had to be discontinued.[11] Some activities such as sermons and books continued to be published but they did not make a significant impact to stabilize the situation. Furthermore, the success of the program was dependent on the authorities understanding the cultural context. While Saudi Arabia and Singapore developed state-of-the-art rehabilitation initiatives, the UK met with partial success on rehabilitating terrorist offenders.[12]

Any country committed to maintaining a cohesive society should invest in a multifaceted community engagement program. Creating community engagement programs is essential to bridge the disconnection between the people and government. Community engagement is also a tool to hold the diverse communities in a society together – especially during times of crisis. "Community engagement should be for nation building. Effective community engagement has the necessary infrastructure to not only counter terrorism but also manage other national crises."[13] Common security can be advanced only by social inclusion and not leaving any commu-

---

11 Interview, Judge Hammoud Al Hittar, Sana'a, Yemen, 21 July 2010.

12 Compared to Saudi Arabia and Singapore where the programs were developed to meet the cultural context, the program in the UK was a partial success because the Muslim communities were diverse. On many occasions, the imams and the inmates engaged in a "shouting match" where they would argue citing verses from the Koran and the Hadith.

13 Interview, Salim bin Mohamed Nasir, February 13, 2012.

nity behind. If any individual is marginalized and alienated from the mainstream – either within that community or from outside –, extremist and subversive elements will succeed in their personal and political goals.

## D. Terrorist Rehabilitation

Communities should be protected not only from extremist ideologies but also from detained and convicted terrorists released from prisons. In parallel with their work to engaging communities towards reducing the immediate threat stemming from terrorist infrastructure, a concerted strategy should be launched to de-radicalize detainees and inmates in prison settings. The involvement of diverse partnerships is necessary to create a dedicated and robust rehabilitation program for de-radicalizing terrorists and extremists.

We must rehabilitate terrorists and their supporters in custody to avoid them posing a threat to public safety and security. Terrorists aim to contaminate society and increase the pool of supporters and sympathizers. They may form a part of the terrorist iconography earning the status of heroes worthy of respect and emulation by the next generation of terrorist recruits.

To rehabilitate terrorists, governments and their partners have developed several modes of rehabilitation. To restore normalcy, the modes of rehabilitation developed include, first, religious and spiritual, second, educational and vocational, third, psychological, fourth, family, social, and cultural, fifth, recreational and, sixth, creative arts components.[14] Although the origins of rehabilitation can be traced to Greece, British Malaya and British Kenya in the mid-20th century, it has assumed a new dimension in the early 21st century. The historical and contemporary programs, both ad hoc and structured, provide some insight.

### I. The Origins of Rehabilitation

During the Greek Civil War (1946-1949), communists – mostly left wing political dissidents – were dispatched to the barren island of Makronisos

---

14 See Gunaratna, "Terrorist Rehabilitation: A Global Imperative," 2011, pp. 65-82.

for indoctrinating and re-educating them into the national dogmas.[15] The same communists were part of the resistance against Nazis, but after the defeat of Germany, they were regarded as enemies of the state and traitors.

In the island, still known as 'The New Parthenon', the 'redeemed' inmates were encouraged to build replicas of classical monuments, and the regime's discourse emphasized the perceived incompatibility of the inmates' 'destiny' (as descendants of ancient Greeks) with left-wing ideologies. Paradoxically, many of the counter-discourses of the Makronisos inmates and their supporters also subscribed to the essentialist discourse of continuity and ancestral glory.[16]

The Greek government rehabilitated them as well as some military personnel into becoming model citizens.[17]

In response to the communist insurgency spearheaded by the Communist Party of Malaya (CPM), the British High Commissioner to Malaysia Sir Henry Gurney (October 1948 – October 1951) and his successor Field Marshall Sir Gerard Templar (January 1952 to May 1954) conceived, developed and implemented a counter-insurgency strategy.[18] Although rehabilitation of detained terrorists started during Gurney's period, Templar formalized and built a systematic and a comprehensive winning hearts and minds campaign. After a comprehensive assessment of the threat, Templar built a new village aftercare program corresponding to his new understanding of the importance of the propaganda of the deed, also called "realistic or materialist propaganda."[19]

---

15 See Voglis, *Becoming a Subject: Political Prisoners During the Greek Civil War*, 2002.

16 See Hamilakis, "The Other 'ParthenonAntiquity and National Memory at Makronisos," 2002, pp. 307-338.

17 See "Makronesos (Makronisos)," in *Guide to the Greek Pamphlet Collection at the Firestone Library, Princeton University*, comp. Alexandros K. Kyrou, Princeton University 1997, item #6, n.p., n.d. 33 p.: illustrations. Image reproductions, captions, and descriptive text of the April 1949 photographic exhibit on Makronisos political detention center/island. Greek state-sponsored propaganda on the rehabilitation of ideologically disloyal military personnel.

18 See Jambi, *The Failure of Communist Ideology (Malaysia)*, Marine Corps University Command and Staff College, 1997. The thesis described how the Government of Malaya exploited the communists' own ideology and theories to successfully counter the potential for an insurgency.

19 Ramakrishna, *Emergency Propaganda: The Winning of Malayan Hearts and Minds 1948-1958*, 2002, p. 128. Ramakrishna credits Yong Shook Lin of the Malaysian Chinese Association for using this term.

The Malaya program had an indigenous component, such as the Taiping Rehabilitation Camp, where knowledge was developed by trial and error as well as practical methods introduced from outside.[20] The British experiment in Malaya drew inspiration from the Makronisos experience but the British approach was more humane.[21]

> The work in the camps was inextricably linked to rural development and social reform measures in the Emergency Villages. Those who suffered from Communist intimidation – and those who escaped the notice of the police – needed relief and reform. Moreover, future homes and employment opportunities had to be created for ex-detainees.[22]

The British approach became a model for many other countries suffering from terrorism and insurgency. This includes Singapore in the early 1970s after it became independent in 1965 but still faced a threat from communism. As a part of Malaya, Singapore had its own rehabilitation program.[23]

The Mau Mau Uprising (1952-1960) was an insurgency by members of Kenya's Kikuyu ethnic community against the British colonial rule. One year after its beginning, the Kenyan government built a full scale rehabilitation program called "the pipeline" transforming Mau Mau men and women into progressive citizens.[24] In June 1953, the British Governor Charles Evelyn Baring of Kenya (1952 to 1959) sought the direct assistance of General Templar and the Federation of Malaya agreed to train a civil servant from Kenya to assist with rehabilitation of the detainees.[25] In August 1953, Thomas Askwith, who organized the rehabilitation of detainees in Kenya visited Templar and crafted the official rehabilitation policy in Kenya.[26] Appointed commissioner for community development and

---

20 See Rhodes House, Oxford, Mss. Afr. S. 596, Papers of the EU and EEMO, Box 42, File 2, K. J. Hendersen, "Extracts from the Experiment at the Taiping Rehabilitation Camp," 20 July 1953, pp. 8-9.

21 Interview, Kumar Ramakrishna, March 19, 2010.

22 Elkins, "The Struggle for Mau Mau Rehabilitation in Late Colonial Kenya," 2000, p. 35.

23 See "Rehabilitation in Singapore," *The Times*, 3 March 1953.

24 See Elkins, "Mau Mau Rehabilitation," p. 25.

25 See Public Record Office, London, Colonial Office 822/703/1, Baring to Lyttleton, 24 June 1953 and Public Record Office, London, Colonial Office 822/703/3, Lyttlelon to Templar, 10 July 1953.

26 See Kenya National Archives, MAA 8/154/2, "Detention and Rehabilitation," Report submitted by T.G. Askwith to Henry Potter, Chief Secretary, 27 August 1953.

rehabilitation in October 1953, Askwith understood from his tour of Malaya the interrelated concepts of "rehabilitation and resettlement." Askwith argued that rehabilitation is a "waste of time, money and effort" unless there was "resettlement or employment, not rehabilitation alone."[27] Askwith also found the methods adopted by the Greek government useful with its emphasis on "moral and civic re-education classes, employment training opportunities, and a routine work discipline" that had already provided Malaya government some guidance.[28] Like every rehabilitation program that is unique, the Kenyan program drew from its indigenous traditions and rituals. Askwith working with the famed archeologist L.S. B. Leakey built a method for the Mau Mau to confess that they had taken an oath. To remove the spell of the oath, they were cleansed with a traditional ceremony.[29] Although the program in Kenya identified practical lessons from the other programs, the early and subsequent attempts to rehabilitate political detainees demonstrate that the core of each program was local.

### *II. The Contemporary Wave of Rehabilitation*

With the beginning of the contemporary wave of international terrorism in the Middle East in 1968, a number of politico-religious groups in Egypt turned violent. Consequently, the very first program for the rehabilitation of terrorist groups was created in Egypt, the fountain of political Islam.[30] Although the Muslim Brotherhood (MB) started as a "peaceful, faith-based, character-building movement", it took a violent trajectory.[31] The movement's "secret apparatus" appeared in thc 1940s and took part in political violence which included the assassination of the Prime Minister of Egypt in 1948 and possibly an attempt to assassinate Gamal Abdel Nasser in 1954. While the movement officially renounced violence in the 1970s, the momentum and expectations the MB generated contributed to the formation of radical groups such as the Egyptian Islamic Jihad (EIJ) and the Islamic Group (IG) in Egypt. With the Soviet invasion of Afghanistan in

27 Askwith, *From Mau Mau to Harambee*, 1995, pp. 100-109.
28 See Elkins, "Mau Mau Rehabilitation," p. 36.
29 See Elkins, "Mau Mau Rehabilitation, " p. 37.
30 See Gunaratna and Ali, "'De-Radicalization Initiatives in Egypt: A Preliminary Insight," 2009, pp. 277-291.
31 See Ibrahim, "Foreword," 2009, p. ix.

December 1979, and the resultant anti-Soviet multi-national Afghan campaign (1979-1989), the political ideology of Islamism steadfastly spread and spawned like-minded but more violent groups globally. With its leadership drawn from highly experienced Egyptian groups, al Qaeda influenced the contemporary wave of global extremism and terrorism. After ideologues and operatives of EIJ and IG were detained by their security services, both EIJ and IG revised their ideologies and called their members to abandon violence.

Egypt engaged the incarcerated leadership of these threat groups and successfully dismantled their structures and ideologies in the country. Although the program has ceased, Egypt is the best early example of a multifaceted rehabilitation program where clerics and scholars, political leaders and bureaucrats, as well as security and intelligence leaders came together to address a multi-dimensional threat. Operating globally, EIJ and IG acted as a template for multiple groups in the 1990s. Except for one single faction all of EIJ in 2001 integrated to al Qaeda, which is driving the contemporary wave of ideology and violence globally. However, the Egyptian government has successfully disrupted the threat and contained its ideology within its country.[32]

Egyptian success spawned the Algerian group the Islamic Salvation Front (FIS) to dismantle its militant wing Islamic Salvation Army (AIS) but not to give up its ideology. The twin approaches of opportunities for dialogue and a sustained counter terrorism response produced results. Although the national security strategy of Algeria created the conditions for key surviving leaders and factions of a few other groups to de-radicalize, the hardline groups continued the fight. While the Armed Islamic Group (GIA) was militarily dismantled, the Salafist Group for Call and Combat (GSPC) evolved into al Qaeda in the Islamic Maghreb (AQIM). Like the Egyptian case, the Algerian case demonstrates that not all groups, factions and leaders were willing to abandon violence.

The most comprehensive rehabilitation programs are the Saudi and Singapore programs. Created in response to the post 9/11 threat, both these programs were crafted to correct the misunderstanding of Islam among the terrorists in custody and their supporters and sympathizers in the community. The Saudi and Singapore programs had independent origins. They

32 For details see Rubin, Gunaratna, Jerard (eds.), *Terrorist Rehabilitation and Counter-radicalisation: New Approaches to Counter-terrorism, Routledge,* 2011.

developed mostly by trial and error. Nonetheless, considerable contact and communication exist between security and intelligence officials, clerics and the academics of the two programs. The Singapore program is written by Ustaz Mohamed Feisal Bin Mohamed Hassan, Secretariat Member of the Religious Rehabilitation Group of Singapore (RRG), a Singapore academic. The RRG, a voluntary body of Muslims, mostly clerics and scholars, conduct religious counseling of detainees and community engagement in Singapore. In addition to counseling several detainees, Ustaz Feisal, a Muslim cleric, also wrote the religious manual used for counseling the detainees. At the forefront of terrorist rehabilitation is Singapore's Internal Security Department responsible for managing the rehabilitation program and the Ministry of Home Affairs for coordinating the community engagement program. A compact, robust and a systematic national program, its leaders emphasizes on one-to-one counseling, aftercare, community participation and security. Unlike many other cases, the Singapore program has no cases of recidivism.

Like the Singapore program, the Saudi program is a multifaceted program and is led by Prince Muhammed bin Nayef, the Deputy Minister of the Interior of Saudi Arabia. One of the world's largest rehabilitation programs, the Saudi program has three components – the program in prisons, the aftercare centre, immediately before release, and the community engagement program. With royal patronage, the Saudi program is also one of the best funded programs. The Saudi program is extended to the beneficiary and his family and includes post-release benefits. Although this unique approach has been criticized by the West, it works. The recidivism in Saudi Arabia, though highlighted in the Western media, is much lower than in the U.S. Dr. Abdulrahman Al-Hadlaq, Director-General, Ideological Security Directorate of the Interior Ministry of Saudi Arabia, provides the philosophy, structure and the direction of the program. An academic from the U.S., Dr. Christopher Boucek, who has studied the Saudi approach, provides an assessment of the Saudi program. Both the Singapore and Saudi programs provided practical lessons for the Iraqi Program during the early and formative phases.

The largest ever rehabilitation program in the world, the Iraqi program was built and operated by the US military from 2006-2010. As a huge population of Iraqi insurgent and terrorist suspects had to be detained, the program was designed and developed to prevent further radicalization in custody. The program also developed a wide-ranging vocational rehabilitation component not witnessed in other programs. The religious rehabilitation component was introduced from Singapore and the art therapy component was introduced from Saudi Arabia. The architect of the Iraq program, Major General Douglas Stone, the former Commanding General of the Detainee Task Force 134 authored the study on the Iraqi program. Beginning 2010, the US operated Iraqi program started to hand over the responsibility to rehabilitate detainees to the Iraqis. Although its continuity is debatable, the Iraqi program provided a template for the US run Afghanistan Program that began in 2010. In preparation, specialist teams from TF-134 from Iraq and General Stone himself visited Afghanistan, and conducted a detailed assessment and assisted JTF 435 in Afghanistan to develop a blue print for launching a rehabilitation program. The fact that it took U.S. eight long years to embark on a rehabilitation program shows that only a minority of the US commanders believes in rehabilitation. With the appointment of Vice Admiral Robert Harward as the Commander of the Joint Task Force 435 in December 2009, the U.S. embarked on building a rehabilitation program in 2010.

With renewed U.S. interest in Pakistan's tribal region, the global epicenter of terrorism, the US has supported the creation of a rehabilitation program in Pakistan. Pakistani leaders have been discussing building a rehabilitation program for a few years but it remained an idea only. Whilst the civilian bureaucracy and the political leadership were still discussing, the Pakistani Army moved rapidly and built a centre for rehabilitating captured terrorists in 2009. Although it was an ad hoc attempt to de-radicalize Pakistani terrorists, the first centre was established in Malakhand in September 2009. After a review of the Singapore and the Saudi programs in 2008-9, Pakistan's political leaders approved the idea of building a national rehabilitation program in December 2009. The proposal by the National Counter Terrorism Authority (NACTA) led by General Tariq Pervez was to build two rehabilitation centres in Peshawar and in Rawalpindi. However, there was no progress until USAID allocated funds to develop a policy on rehabilitation and reintegration of terrorists in Pakistan.[33] Working together with the Federally Administered Tribal Area (FATA) Secretariat, USAID planned to host the first strategic meeting in Peshawar in April 2010, but it was postponed due to a double suicide attack targeting the US Consulate in Peshawar on April 6, 2010. The '1st Strategic Work-

33 See Aziz, Brig. (ret.) Iqbal and Col. (ret.) Shapiro, *Concept for 1st Strategic Workshop on Rehabilitation and Deradicalization of Militants and Extremists*, FATA Capacity Building Program (CBP), March 15, 2010.

shop on Rehabilitation and De-Radicalization of Militants and Extremists' was held on May 18-19, 2010. The Pakistan case demonstrates the bureaucratic, resource and security challenges developing nations face in building new institutions to manage their threats. Today, the US are also keen to revive Yemen's government-run rehabilitation program that existed from 2002 to 2005. According to the head of the Yemeni Program Judge Hamoud Al Hitar, the Yemeni program focused on Islamic dialogue. There was no socio-economic reintegration. Like in the Saudi case, the impetus for the program was several thousand Yemenis who travelled to Afghanistan to train and fight with al Qaeda. Upon their return, inspired to fight against the Yemeni regime and the West, some of them participated in attacks including the bombing of the US warship, the U.S.S. Cole in October 2000. Furthermore, the Yemeni's played a role in coordinating the 9/11 attacks.

The rehabilitation program emerged from within the government that faced considerable pressure from the West. Nevertheless, Western governments were unwilling to support it financially. Although the judge claimed that 340 terrorists were rehabilitated, the program was seen as ineffective by the West.[34] The Yemeni Program collapsed because of the lack of government interest and funding. The US invasion of Iraq in 2003 increased the threat manifold. Several hundred Yemenis traveled to Iraq to fight and many planned attacks against Western targets in Yemen. The poorest Arab country, Yemen lacked the resources to contain the threat. Although those detained, counseled and released pledged an oath of not returning to violence against Yemen, there was no emphasis to prevent them from traveling to Iraq or attacking Western targets in Yemen. Nonetheless, the US was keen to handover 91 Yemeni detainees in the U.S. Detention Centre, Guantanamo Bay to Yemen. With US support, the Yemeni program needs to be revived, enhanced and sustained. To be effective, it must be accompanied by a successful community engagement program supported by Yemen's mainstream politicians and moderate clerics.

Away from the glare of the international media, Sri Lanka built a state-of-the-art program to rehabilitate the former leaders and members of the Liberation Tigers of Tamil Eelam (LTTE). After a bloody battle on the banks of the Nandikadal lagoon in Mullaitivu in May of 2009, the Sri

34 See Coker and Levinson, "Yemenis Consider Sending al Qaeda to Rehab: Government Seeks Funds to Use Quran to Pacify Extremist Militants – but the Money, for Now, Goes to Military Effort," 2010.

Lankan security forces defeated the LTTE. The Sri Lankan security forces breached a LTTE-controlled human shield of nearly 300,000 Tamil civilians and LTTE cadres. The government created welfare centres to house the Tamil civilians and rehabilitation centres. Although the government had a civilian led rehabilitation authority for a few hundred LTTE cadres captured or surrendered, it failed to cope with the influx of over ten thousand LTTE surrendees.

To meet the challenge, Sri Lanka built a program for rehabilitating the surrendered cadres and cadres identified by civilians in welfare centres housing the Internally Displaced Persons (IDPs). As the LTTE recruited its cadres by force in the final phase and also threatened and shot civilians that wished to leave the LTTE controlled area, it was the IDPs that identified most LTTE cadres who were masquerading as civilians. Rather than punishing them, government decided to offer rehabilitation to the LTTE cadres identified in IDP welfare centres. As of May 2013, the Bureau of the Commissioner General of Rehabilitation (BCGR) has reintegrated to society just over 11,696 cadres that surrendered or were identified after the defeat of the LTTE in 2009.

The LTTE cadres rehabilitated were classified into three categories – children, adult male and female cadres. As the LTTE developed a policy according to which one member of each family should serve in the LTTE, the group recruited several thousand children fighters, most forcibly. Of 594 children rehabilitated, 363 were boys and 231 were girls. The child beneficiaries were given a choice of continuing studies or learning vocational skills at the Protective Accommodation Centre in Ambepussa or study at Colombo Hindu College, Ratmalana.

The two Protective Accommodation and Rehabilitation Centres (PARC) set up in Ambepussa and in Poonthottam in Vavuniya are for children, accommodating a total of 535 former child soldiers. Of child beneficiaries, 373 wished to study and some have entered universities including medical schools. Afterwards they were transferred to Jaffna and Vavuniya. The others were taken to Ambepussa and given vocational training. The Ambepussa centre was started in March 2008, mainly to rehabilitate children who were freed from the clutches of a breakaway group of the LTTE led by Karuna which fought in the Eastern province. Karuna was invited and joined government as a cabinet Minister. Of the surrendees, 1170 were disabled persons having lost limbs in the war. They were released and reunited with their families. These included some hardcore leaders and members. Persons over the ages of 50 were also released. Among the surrendees were 148 university students from Jaffna. Initially these undergrads were given leadership positions among the detainees and used to instill disciplinary norms. The future success of the program depends on the ability and willingness of the government and community to continue to treat those reintegrated as good citizens. They also need to be protected from misguided ideas and extremist ideologies articulated by LTTE factions operating in the West.

Rehabilitation programs in Egypt, Algeria, Libya and Yemen are now defunct, and the programs in Iraq, Uzbekistan, Colombia, Spain and Indonesia are ad-hoc. Structured programs are present in Saudi Arabia, Pakistan, Sri Lanka, Malaysia and Singapore. The programs in Afghanistan, Philippines, Thailand, India and Bangladesh did not take off because of lack of leadership. There is a need for ad-hoc programs to evolve into structured programs and for structured programs to be sustained in the long term. Some of the more crucial challenges faced by current rehabilitation programs include monitoring recidivism, managing the transition for detainees ready to be reintegrated back into society, and staying on top of the ever-changing terrorist narratives to counter them effectively when attempting to de-radicalize detainees.

## *E. Conclusion*

The key to successfully countering terrorism and extremism is to develop smart power, a combination of hard and soft power. The latter includes terrorist rehabilitation and community engagement. But for this approach to be successful, it has to be multifaceted, facilitated by a long term public-private partnership, and led by creative and innovative individuals. There is a growing awereness among governments of the need to invest in creating new terrorist rehabilitation and community engagement programs and in sustaining existing ones. With the failures of Western nations in Iraq and Afghanistan to end terrorism predominately using kinetic and lethal means, more governments including those of the West are likely to consider the smart approach by the integration of community engagement and rehabilitation to their fighting strategy. With support from governments, NGOs, community organizations, and the private and academic sectors, terrorist rehabilitation and community engagement programs are likely to double worldwide in the coming decade.[35]

## Bibliography


Askwith, Thomas, *From Mau Mau to Harambee, Memoirs and Memoranda of Colonial Kenya*, Cambridge: Cambridge University Press, 1995.

Aziz, Khalid, Javed Iqbal, and Barry Shapiro, "Concept for 1st Strategic Workshop on Rehabilitation and Deradicalization of Militants and Extremists," FATA Capacity Building Program (CBP), March 15, 2010.

Coker, Margaret, and Charles Levinson, "Yemenis Consider Sending al Qaeda to Rehab: Government Seeks Funds to Use Quran to Pacify Extremist Militants – but the Money, for Now, Goes to Military Effort," *The Wall Street Journal* (9 January 2010), at http://www.wsj.com/articles/SB126299677407522423.

Elkins, Caroline, "The Struggle for Mau Mau Rehabilitation in Late Colonial Kenya," *International Journal of African Historical Studies* 1 (2000): 25-57.

Government of the United Kingdom, "Counter-terrorism," at http://www.homeoffice.gov.uk/counter-terrorism/review-of-prevent-strategy/.

Gunaratna, Rohan, "Terrorist Rehabilitation: A Global Imperative," *Journal of Policing, Intelligence and Counter Terrorism* 1 (2011): 65-82.

Gunaratna, Rohan, "Terrorist Rehabilitation and Community Engagement: New Frontiers in Combating Terrorism," *Counter Terrorist Trends and Analysis* 4 (2013): 2-4.

Gunaratna, Rohan and Mohamed Bin Ali, "'De-Radicalization Initiatives in Egypt: A Preliminary Insight," *Studies in Conflict & Terrorism* 4 (2009): 277-291.

Gunaratna, Rohan, Interview with Jean-Louis Bruguiere, February 12, 2012.

Gunaratna, Rohan, Interview with Judge Hammoud Al Hittar, Sana'a, Yemen, 21 July 2010.

Gunaratna, Rohan, Interview with Kumar Ramakrishna, March 19, 2010.

Gunatratna, Rohan, Interview with Salim bin Mohamed Nasir, February 13, 2012.

Gunaratna, Rohan, Personal communication with Gerald H. Heuett Jr., September 21, 2011.

Hamilakis, Yannis, "The Other 'Parthenon Antiquity and National Memory at Makronisos," *Journal of Modern Greek Studies* 2 (2002): 307-338.

Hanniman, Wayne, "Canadian Muslims, Islamophobia and National Security Royal Canadian Mounted Police," *International Journal of Law, Crime and Justice* 4 (2008): 271-285.


35 See Gunaratna, "Terrorist Rehabilitation and Community Engagement: New Frontiers in Combating Terrorism," 2013, pp. 2-4.

Hendersen, K. J., "Extracts from the Experiment at the Taiping Rehabilitation Camp," 20 July 1953, Rhodes House, Oxford, Mss. Afr. S. 596, Papers of the EU and EEMO, Box 42, File 2, pp. 8-9.

Ibrahim, Saad Eddine, "Foreword," in *The De-Radicalization of Jihadists: Transforming Armed Islamist Movements*, ed. Omar Ashour, London: Routledge, 2009, pp. viii-xii.

Jambi, Major Jamaluddin, "The Failure of Communist Ideology (Malaysia)," *GlobalSecurity.org* 1997, at http://www.globalsecurity.org/military/library/report/1997/Jambi.htm.

Kenya National Archives, MAA 8/154/2, "Detention and Rehabilitation," Report submitted by T.G. Askwith to Henry Potter, Chief Secretary, 27 August 1953.

K. Kyrou, Alexandros, "Makronesos (Makronisos)," in *Guide to the Greek Pamphlet Collection at the Firestone Library, Princeton University*, Princeton University 1997, item #6, n.p., n.d. 33 p.: illustrations. Image reproductions, captions, and descriptive text of the April 1949 photographic exhibit on Makronisos political detention center/island.

Public Record Office, London, Colonial Office 822/703/1, Baring to Lyttleton, 24 June 1953 and Public Record Office, London, Colonial Office 822/703/3, Lyttlelon to Templar, 10 July 1953.

Ramakrishna, Kumar, *Emergency Propaganda: The Winning of Malayan Hearts and Minds 1948-1958*, Richmond, Surrey: Curzon Press, 2002.

"Rehabilitation in Singapore," *The Times* (3 March 1953).

Rubin, Lawrence, Gunaratna, Rohan an Jerard, Jolene Anne R. (eds.), *Terrorist Rehabilitation and Counter-radicalisation: New Approaches to Counter-terrorism,* New York: Routledge, 2011.

Voglis, Polymeris, *Becoming a Subject: Political Prisoners During the Greek Civil War*, New York: Berghahn Books, 2002.

# Counter-Terrorism Measures and De-radicalization Efforts in Southeast Asia: A View from the Philippines*

*Rommel C. Banlaoi*

## *A. Introduction*

Southeast Asia has been confronting the threats of terrorism long before the September 11, 2001 (9/11) terrorist attacks on the United States. Prior to 9/11, however, terrorist threats in the region were merely viewed as local phenomena falling under the domestic affairs of the respective states.[1] Because of the already established connection of prominent local terrorist groups in Southeast Asia with Al-Qaeda, the 9/11 experience led to the acknowledgement of the terrorist threats in Southeast Asia as a global security problem. This has prompted the US to describe the region as the "second front" in the global campaign against terrorism.[2]

To counter terrorism, governments in Southeast Asia have implemented various measures from hard to soft approaches. One of the soft approaches is de-radicalization. This paper aims to describe de-radicalization programs with a focus on the Philippines, particularly with a view on Muslim detainees accused of various crimes associated with terrorism.

---

* Updated version of a paper presented at the International Conference on Deradicalization and Disengagement and its Implications for National Counter-Terrorism Strategies organized by German-Southeast Asian Center of Excellence for Public Policy and Governance, Centre for the Study of Terrorism and Political Violence and Human Development Forum Foundation at Rembrandt Hotel, Bangkok, Thailand on 21 June 2011.

1 For the author's detailed discussions on this topic, see Banlaoi, *War on Terrorism in Southeast Asia*, 2004. For a sequel and updated analysis of the issue; also see Banlaoi, *Counter-Terrorism Measures in Southeast Asia: How Effective Are They?*, 2009.

2 See Tan, "Southeast Asia as the Second Front in the War Against Terrorism: Evaluating the Threat and Responses," 2003, pp. 112-138. For a more recent analysis of the issue, see Acharya and Acharya, "The Myth of the Second Front: Localizing the War on Terror in Southeast Asia," 2007, pp. 75-90.

### B. The Contested Concept of De-radicalization

De-radicalization as a soft approach to counter terrorist threats is based on the premise that classical military and police approaches cannot completely defeat terrorism, particularly if threats are emanating from Islamist extremists. In order to nip terrorism in its buds, there has been a call "to go beyond security and intelligence measures, taking proactive measures to prevent vulnerable individuals from radicalizing and rehabilitating those who have already embraced extremism."[3] This soft proactive measure is generally called de-radicalization, exemplary programs which have been implemented in Algeria, Egypt, Indonesia, Jordan, Malaysia, Saudi Arabia, Singapore, Tajikistan, United Kingdom, and Yemen, among others.

Although de-radicalization is now widely accepted as an innovative counter-terrorism measure, the concept, however, has been poorly defined and remains less studied, under-theorized and is still even not really well understood by some of the relevant scholars, experts, journalists, practitioners and policy-makers. Despite a number of de-radicalization programs in various countries, we still know little about the subject. De-radicalization remains a contested concept which is viewed by some to be problematic as it "carries with it equally troubling expectations."[4]

There is a tendency to define de-radicalization as a reverse process of radicalization, which is broadly defined as "the process of adopting an extremist belief system, including the willingness to use, support, or facilitate violence, as a method to effect societal change."[5] Based on this definition, de-radicalization is understood, on the other hand, as "the process of abandoning an extremist worldview and concluding that it is not acceptable to use violence to effect social change."[6]

In other words, de-radicalization is a process that aims to remove the reasons for violent extremism. It is also a process that leads an individual

---

3 Rabasa, Pettyjohn, Ghez and Boucek, *Deradicalizing Islamist Extremists*, 2010, p. xiii.

4 See Horgan, *Walking Away from Terrorism: Accounts of Disengagement from Radical and Extremist Movements*, 2009, p. 17.

5 Quoted in Rabasa, Pettyjohn, Ghez and Boucek, *Deradicalizing Islamist Extremists*, p. 1. from the written testimony of Charles E. Allen to U.S. Senate Committee on Homeland Security and Governmental Affairs "Threat of Islamic Radicalization to the Homeland", p. 4.

6 Quoted in Rabasa, Pettyjohn, Ghez and Boucek., *Deradicalizing Islamist Extremists*, p. 1 from Allen, "Threat of Islamic Radicalization to the Homeland", pp. 1-2.

or group to change extreme ideas and attitudes about violence – particularly about the use of violence against civilians.[7] While de-radicalization appears to focus more on the ideological approach, de-radicalization also pays attention to the behavioral approach. While ideological de-radicalization results from a change in belief behavioral de-radicalization emphasizes a change in attitude and action.[8]

De-radicalization is not synonymous with counter-radicalization, which attempts "to dissuade individuals at risk of radicalization – usually young people" by preventing exposure to radical ideas that glorify acts of violence.[9] De-radicalization aims to convince already radical individuals to abandon their radical beliefs and leave the use of violence behind.

Another concept associated with de-radicalization is rehabilitation. While the rehabilitation of terrorists became a buzzword after 9/11, initial thoughts on rehabilitation were already conveyed as early as the 1980s.[10] Usually implemented in prison, rehabilitation puts individuals in a therapy session that involves other related "cleansing" processes of trust building, psychological counseling, religious dialogue, community involvement, and after-care programs such as family support and post-rehabilitation employment. Existing literature indicates that terrorist rehabilitation is an essential program to complement the de-radicalization process.[11]

Finally, de-radicalization is sometimes being confused with the concept of disengagement. If de-radicalization entails the abandonment of radical ideas that endorse violence, disengagement refers to decision of individuals to leave the use of violence behind or to relinquish their ties to groups or movements engaged in violent acts. While de-radicalization may lead to disengagement, disengagement does not necessarily lead to de-radicaliza-

---

7 See Ashour, "Lions Tamed: An Inquiry Into the Causes of Deradicalization of Armed Islamist Movements: The Case of the Egyptian Islamic Groups," 2007, pp. 596-624.

8 See Ashour, "Lions Tamed," p. 599.

9 See Rabasa, Pettyjohn, Ghez and Boucek, *Deradicalizing Islamist Extremists*, pp. 1-2.

10 See Hoffman, *The Prevention of Terrorism and Rehabilitation of Terrorists: Some Preliminary Thoughts*, 1985.

11 See Barrett and Bokhari, "Deradicalization and Rehabilitation Programmes Targetin Religious Terrorists and Extremists in the Muslim World: An Overview," 2009, pp. 170-180.

tion. There are disengaged individuals who retain their radical ideas while opting to traverse the path of peace.[12]

### *C. Exemplary Practices of De-radicalization in Southeast Asia as a Means for Counter-Terrorism*

As mentioned above, de-radicalization programs in Southeast Asia have been notably implemented in Indonesia, Malaysia, and Singapore. These programs aimed to counter in particular terrorist threats emanating from Muslim individuals associated with Jemaah Islamiyah (JI).[13]

In Indonesia, de-radicalization programs concentrated on Muslim prisoners involved in 'Jihadi crimes' such as bombings, murders, and homicides. The Indonesian police spearheaded the implementation of de-radicalization programs through a special branch called Detachment 88.[14] The programs involved religious counseling, ideological dialogues and material inducements. Through de-radicalization programs, more than 150 Jihadi detainees have been released and reunited with their families.

Malaysia, the other predominantly Islamic state in this region, has developed another de-radicalization program which is characterized by some unique features compared with the Indonesian one. Target of the Malaysian program are especially detainees under the Internal Security Act (ISA) with the program implemented through the combined efforts of the police and various state agencies with the assistance of religious institutions like the Department of Islamic Advancement of Malaysia. The de-radicalization programs adopted a three-stage approach designed for: the pre-detainment period, the detainment period and the post-detainment period.[15]

Probably, the most discussed de-radicalization and rehabilitation program in the region is the one applied in Singapore. It focuses predominantly on the rehabilitation of JI detainees and their families. Endorsed by the

---

12 See Horgan, "Individual Disengagement: A Psychological Analysis," 2008, p. 27.

13 For a detailed preliminary discussion, see Abuza, "The Rehabilitation of Jemaah Islamiyah Detainees in Southeast Asia: A Preliminary Assessment," 2009, pp. 193-211.

14 See International Crisis Group, "Deradicalization and Indonesian Prisons," Asia Reports, No. 142 (19 November 2007).

15 For detailed discussion see Harun, "Rising Up to the Challenges of Islamic Extremism and Militancy in Malaysia," 2011, pp. 93-106.

Singaporean government as part of its soft counter-terrorism measures, the rehabilitation program is implemented by the Religious Rehabilitation Group (RRG) that aims to implement an understanding of Islam as a religion of peace. The rehabilitation program involves counseling and "counter-ideological" activities, based on the four principal modes of rehabilitation: first religious rehabilitation, second psychological rehabilitation third, social rehabilitation, and fourth vocational rehabilitation.[16] As a result, around 40 terrorists have been released from jail with a positive prognosis concerning their non-violent attitude.

### *D. De-radicalization Efforts in the Philippines: The Case of Muslim Detainees Accused of Various Crimes Associated Witch Terrorism*

The Philippines is home to some Jihadi groups engaged in terrorism and other acts of political violence. These are the Abu Sayyaf Group (ASG), the rouge factions of the Moro National Liberation Front (MNLF), the lawless elements of the Moro Islamic Liberation Front (MILF), the Rajah Solaiman Islamic Movement (RSIM), the Al Khobar Group (AKG) and other more recently emerging groups such as the Bangsamoro Islamic Freedom Movement (BIFM) and the Awliyah Group of Freedom Fighters.[17] With the reported success of de-radicalization programs abroad, the Philippine government also explored the possibility of implementing similar programs to counter threats of terrorism in the country.

Though the Philippine government recognizes the importance of de-radicalization as a soft counter-terrorism measure, it, however, has failed to implement a coherent and systematic de-radicalization program that can approximate exemplary programs implemented in Indonesia, Malaysia and Singapore.

The 16-point Counter-Terrorism Program of the Philippine government in 2003 identified "inter-faith dialogues" (point 9) and "special development programs" (point 10) as cornerstones of its de-radicalization and counter radicalization policy. Interfaith Dialogue involved seminars, workshops, conferences and meetings in the Southern Philippines as well as in-

---

16 For further discussion see Gunaratna, "The Battlefield of the Mind: Rehabilitating Muslim Terrorists," 2009.

17 For a brief overview of these groups, see Banlaoi, "Current Landscape of Terrorist Threats," 2012.

ter-faith discussions in radio programs and civil action activities. Special development programs included poverty reduction, hunger mitigation, employment generation, livelihood program, and social integration program implemented by the different agencies of the national government. While these programs could contribute to the process of de-radicalization, they were, however, not de-radicalization programs in strictest terms. The Philippine government was just "forcing these issues" to be part of de-radicalization efforts.

In 2007, the Philippine government enacted into law the Human Security Act, which serves as its national anti-terrorism law. This law recognizes the need to protect human rights in countering terrorism and to address the root causes of radicalism in the Philippines. The National Anti-Terrorism Strategy released in 2009 also urges all agencies of the Philippine government and all sectors of the Philippine society to address the "factors that can lead to radicalization and recruitment" of individuals to join terrorist groups. However, the Philippine government did not actually implement de-radicalization programs as understood abroad.

The Anti Terrorism Council (ATC) through the National Intelligence Coordinating Agency (NICA) and the National Counter Terrorism Action Group (NACTAG), renamed as National Counter Terrorism Unit (NCTU), was tasked to lead the development and implementation of de-radicalization programs in the Philippines. But activities towards this end were limited to the training of wardens and jails guards and not actually to detainees. The Armed Forces of the Philippines (AFP) conducted the Sala'am Project in the conflict-affected areas in Mindanao. But the Sala'am Project was nothing but the usual civil-military operations implemented in the Southern Philippines. The Philippine National Police (PNP) used the Sala'am Police to induce Muslims to become police officers in order to promote peace and order in the Muslim communities. But the Sala'am Police was not really involved in de-radicalization programs as practiced in other countries.

In short, there has been no actual implementation of programs of the Philippine government focusing on the de-radicalization and rehabilitation of Muslim detainees. De-radicalization and rehabilitation plans remain in the conceptual and preparatory stage.

To examine "de-radicalization" efforts in the Philippines, the Philippine Institute for Peace, Violence and Terrorism Research (PIPVTR), an independent, non-government think-tank, conducted in 2008 a study of Muslim detainees accused of various crimes associated with terrorism. The study was conducted in the High Risk Detention Cell at Camp Bagong Diwa, Taguig City. This cell is officially called "Special Intensive Care Area" or SICA. At the time of the study, there were 136 Muslim detainees in SICA. Aim of the study was to find ways to de-radicalize these detainees by encouraging them to renounce ideologies that venerate the use of violence and to leave behind violent acts associated with terrorism. PIPVTR conducted a profiling of the detainees that yielded the following results:

Age Profile: At the time of the study, 60% of the detainees belonged to age bracket 20 to 30 years old; 30% belonged to age bracket 31 to 40 years old; and, only 10% belonged to age bracket 41 years old and above. This profile indicated that the majority of the detainees in SICA were young. There were even juvenile detainees who were locked in jail when they were only 14 to 16 years old.

Religious Profile: Almost all or 93% of the Muslim detainees at the time of study were born Muslims. Only 7% were Muslim converts. Interestingly, however, all Muslim converts in SICA were accused of bombings, thus activists at the very rough end of the spectrum of suspected delinquencye.

Years of Detention: When the study was conducted in 2008, 88% of the Muslim detainees have been in jail for more than six years. Only 12% of the detainees have been in jail for less than five years.

All detainees were only accused and have not been found guilty yet. Their years of detention have created many uncertainties that made them highly vulnerable to self-radicalization in prison.

Organizational affiliation: Almost all or 96% of the Muslim detainees were accused of being members of the ASG, 2% were accused of being members of RSIM and the remaining 2% were associated with the MILF or JI respectively.

Case Profile: PIPVTR found out that 90% of the Muslim detainees were accused of kidnapping cases; 4% multiple murder; 4% bombing; and, 2% rebellion. In a related study made by PIPVTR, 95% of the financial resources of the ASG were mobilized through kidnap-for-ransom activities. Thus, the case profile of most of the detainees was consistent with the resource mobilization activities of the ASG.

## E. Challenges in Implementing De-radicalization Programs as Counter-Terrorism Measures

Since 2008, PIPVTR has been conducting occasional visits to Muslim detainees in SICA. Visits to Muslim detainees in Bicutan Jail for the past three years have raised awareness on the need to develop a coherent and systematic counter-radicalization and de-radicalization program in the Philippines. The Philippine government can draw valuable lessons from the exemplary practices in Singapore, Indonesia and Saudi Arabia, among others.

But instead of replicating all these exemplary practices abroad the peculiar situation of Muslim detainees in the Philippines must be taken into account. Since all Muslim detainees in Bicutan Jail are only "accused" not "convicted", they cannot be subjected yet to "rehabilitation" programs in the strict sense of the term. Some of them who acknowledge to be "radical" maintain that they are not 'guilty'. PIPVTR discovered that each detainee had unique stories to tell about the circumstances that led to their imprisonment. Most of the detainees claimed to be "victims of harsh circumstances." Some of them claimed that they were "victims of mistaken identity". Few of them admitted that they were in prison because they wage "jihad" or rebellion against the government but they did not feel "guilty" about it.

Existing Philippine government efforts related to de-radicalization and rehabilitation programs have to contend with enormous conceptual and operational challenges. Most of the Muslim detainees joined "terrorist" groups because of circumstantial and behavioral reasons rather than ideological conviction.

Thus, understanding the experiences of Muslim detainees on how they got into their present situation is crucial in convincing them to change their attitudes about political violence and terrorism. Though de-radicalization programs may have exhibited exemplary practices abroad, there is a need to address the problem of recidivism. In Indonesia, for example, individuals who underwent de-radicalization programs returned to violent activities upon release.[18]

---

18 See Arianti, "Jihadi Recidivism: The Case of Indonesia," 2011, available at https://www.rsis.edu.sg/wp-content/uploads/2014/07/CO11018.pdf.

## *F. Towards a De-radicalization Program for the Philippines*

Based on PIPVTR findings, the Philippine government has to adopt a coherent de-radicalization program that shall involve the following phases:

- Visitation
- Counseling
- Legal Assistance
- Social and Economic Assistance
- After Care

### *I. Visitation*

This is an important step in the de-radicalization program. Through frequent visitations, inmates will be familiarized with the people implementing the de-radicalization project. Visitations also allow detainees to socialize with project proponents, thus creating trust and confidence among the people involved in the process including jail wardens and guards. Through visitations, detainees can share their experiences on how they came to be in their present situation. The sharing process not only allows the project proponent to understand the context of their detention but also provides the detainees an outlet to speak their minds and air their grievances.

The sharing process during visitation can build personal bridges between the detainees and the project proponent to forge mutual understanding among all people involved in the de-radicalization program. Building personal relationships with the detainees can ease the de-radicalization process. Research has demonstrated that personal transformations of radicals from violence to peace "hinges on a relationship with a mentor or friend who supports and affirms peaceful behavior."[19]

For research and policy development purposes, the visitation process will also allow the project coordinator to acquire the personal profile of all detainees involved in the de-radicalization program. Their profile will allow the project coordinator to identify the most appropriate intervention for counseling purposes.

---

19 Garfinkel, "Personal Transformations: Moving from Violence to Peace," 2007, p. 1.

## *II. Counseling*

This process will involve the intervention of Muslim clerics who will engage detainees in a religious dialogue. In Saudi Arabia, Muslim clerics formed a group called Advisory Committee with the Religious Sub-committee composed of 150 clerics, scholars and university professors.[20] Members of the Religious Subcommittee speak to detainees like with siblings in order to guide them in the proper interpretation of Islamic faith.[21]In Singapore, these above mentioned Religious Rehabilitation Group (RRG) provides counseling to JI detainees. Composed of Islamic teachers and scholars working on a voluntary basis, it aims to counter the ideological misunderstanding of the JI members through counseling.[22]

The Philippines needs to create a similar group of Muslim scholars, teachers and clerics who will provide counseling work to Muslim detainees. This group shall undergo a short training to prepare them for the counseling process. Counseling is an essential aspect of the de-radicalization program. It is during this process where religious counselors share with the detainees that they have been misguided by the distorted interpretations of Islam.

## *III. Legal Assistance*

It has been shown that in jail radical ideas flourish. A RAND study, for example, has observed, "Imprisonment may increase a prisoner's susceptibility to adopting new and radicalized ideas or beliefs."[23] This particularly applies to young detainees. RAND underscores that "placing young Muslims (who may already be vulnerable to radicalizing influences) in a prison environment, with all its accompanying psychological and physical dangers may well compound their vulnerability to radicalization."[24] The

20 See Boucek, *Deradicalizing Islamist Extremists,* 2010, p. 11.

21 See Boucek, *Deradicalizing Islamist Extremists,* p. 11: also Boucek, "The Counseling Program: Extremist Rehabilitation in Saudi Arabia," 2008.

22 See Religious Rehabilitation Group at http://www.rrg.sg/subindex.asp?id=A033_07.

23 Hannah, Clutterbuck, Rubin, *Radicalization or Rehabilitation: Understanding the Challenge of Extremist and Radicalized Prisoners*, 2008, p. x.

24 Hannah, Clutterbuck, Rubin, *Radicalization or Rehabilitation*, p. x.

longer young detainees stay in prison without proper counseling, the greater the possibility of radicalization.

Thus, it is an important outcome of de-radicalization to expedite the release of the detainees from prison. In Saudi Arabia, Yemen and Singapore, around 700, 300 and 3 detainees, respectively, have been released as a result of the de-radicalization program.[25] Providing detainees with legal assistance serves to offer them hope for prison release. This process particularly applies to detainees who viewed themselves as "political prisoners" or victims of "mistaken identity" and "false accusations". Legal assistance can also be a good inducement for detainees to support the de-radicalization program and participate in the counseling process.

### *IV. Social and Economic Assistance*

A practical aspect of de-radicalization program is the provision of financial incentives and support to detainees and their families. This scheme has been effectively applied in Indonesia. The Indonesian government not only fed and clothed the family of detainees but also gave greater family access to visit the detainees. The Indonesian government even supplemented the travel expenses of families to allow them to visit their loved ones in jail.[26] This form of economic inducements can encourage detainees to join the de-radicalization program. For the Saudi Arabian de-radicalization program it has actually found that one of the keys to success of de-radicalization program is "the extensive social support given to a detainee and his family, intended to offset hardship and short circuit further de-radicalization within a family."[27]

### *V. After Care*

Another exemplary de-radicalization measure in the Saudi-Arabian program is its after care process. It prepares the "de-radicalized" detainees to

---

25 See Hannah, Clutterbuck, Rubin, *Radicalization or Rehabilitation*, p. xi.

26 See Fink and Hearne, *Beyond Terrorism: Deradicalization and Disengagement from Violent Extremism*, 2008.

27 Boucek, "Counter-Terrorism from Within: Assessing Saudi Arabia's Religious Rehabilitation and Disengagement Programme," 2008, p. 60.

go back to society and become productive citizens. The Saudi government has established a care center that provides detainees transitory exposure to life outside the custody of jail officials. Successful detainees will be released from the care center to rejoin their families.

Upon detainees' release, social and economic support is continued to prevent recidivism. Support can be given in form of government allowances and even a modest apartment. Job assistance is also offered to demonstrate that there is a better life in de-radicalization.

## G. Conclusion

There is no doubt that de-radicalization programs as soft counter-terrorism measures have yielded positive results in Southeast Asia. Though implementation of these programs has faced some challenges abroad, these programs provide valuable lessons for the Philippines to develop its own de-radicalization programs.

To this day, the Philippine government has not yet implemented a de-radicalization program as understood abroad. However, the Philippine government intends to implement similar programs soon. This paper elucidated, why in the development of such program, the following phases should be considered: visitation, counseling, legal assistance, social and economic assistance, and after care.

## Bibliography

Abuza, Zachary, "The Rehabilitation of Jemaah Islamiyah Detainees in Southeast Asia: A Preliminary Assessment," in *Leaving Terrorism Behind: Individual and Collective Disengagement*, ed. Tore Bjorgo and John Horgan, New York: Routledge, 2009, pp. 193-211.

Acharya, Amitav, "The Myth of the Second Front: Localizing the War on Terror in Southeast Asia," *The Washington Quaterly* 4 (2007): 75-90.

Arianti, V., "Jihadi Recidivism: The Case of Indonesia," *RSIS Commentaries* 08/2011 (14 February 2011), at https://www.rsis.edu.sg/wp-content/uploads/2014/07/CO11018.pdf.

Ashour, Omar, "Lions Tamed: An Inquiry Into the Causes of Deradicalization of Armed Islamist Movements: The Case of the Egyptian Islamic Groups," *Middle East Journal* 4 (2007): 596-624.

Banlaoi, Rommel C., "Current Landscape of Terrorist Threats," *Rappler* (13 January 2012), at http://www.rappler.com/thought-leaders/824-current-landscape-of-terrorist-threats.

Banlaoi, Rommel C., *Counter-Terrorism Measures in Southeast Asia: How Effective Are They?*, Manila: Yuchengco Center, De La Salle University, 2009.

Banlaoi, Rommel C., *War on Terrorism in Southeast Asia*, Quezon City: Rex Book Store International, 2004.

Barrett, Richard and Laila Bokhari, "Deradicalization and rehabilitation programmes targeting religious terrorists and extremists in the Muslim world. An overview," in *Leaving Terrorism Behind: Individual and Collective Disengagement*, ed. John Horgan and Tore Bjorgo, London: Routledge, 2008, pp.170-180.

Boucek, Christopher, "Counter-Terrorism from Within: Assessing Saudi Arabia's Religious Rehabilitation and Disengagement Programme," *Royal United Service Institute Journal* 6 (2008): 60-65.

Boucek, Christopher, "The Counseling Program: Extremist Rehabilitation in Saudi Arabia," in *Leaving Terrorism Behind: Disengagement from Political Violence*, ed. Tore Bjorgo and John Horgan, New York: Routledge, 2008.

Boucker, Richard, "Saudi Arabia's 'Soft' Counterterrorism Strategy;" *Carnegie Papers* 97 (2008): 1-25.

Fink, Naureen Chowdhury and Ellie B. Hearne, *Beyond Terrorism: Deradicalization and Disengagement from Violent Extremism*, New York: International Peace Institute, 2008.

Garfinkel, Renee, "Personal Transformations: Moving from Violence to Peace," *United States Institute of Peace Special Report* 186 (2007): 1-16.

Gunaratna, Rohan, "The Battlefield of the Mind: Rehabilitating Muslim Terrorists," *UNISCI Discussion Papers* 21 (2009): 148-163.

Hannah, Greg, Lindsay Clutterbuck and Jennifer Rubin, *Radicalization or Rehabilitation: Understanding the Challenge of Extremist and Radicalized Prisoners*, Cambridge: Rand Europe, 2008.

Harun, Ruhanas, "Rising Up to the Challenges of Islamic Extremism and Militancy in Malaysia," 2011, pp. 93-106, at http://www.searcct.gov.my/featured-articles/47-rising-up-to-the-challenges-of-islamic-extremism-and-militancy-in-malaysia.

Hoffman, Bruce, *The Prevention of Terrorism and Rehabilitation of Terrorists: Some Preliminary Thoughts*, Santa Monica: Rand, 1985.

Horgan, John, "Individual Disengagement: A Psychological Analysis," in *Leaving Terrorism Behind: Individual and Collective Disengagement*, ed. John Horgan and Tore Bjorgo, New York: Routledge, 2008, p. 17-29.

Horgan, John, *Walking Away from Terrorism: Accounts of Disengagement from Radical and Extremist Movements*, New York: Routledge, 2009.

International Crisis Group, "Deradicalization and Indonesian Prisons", *Asia Reports*, No. 142, 2007, at https://www.ciaonet.org/attachments/3943/uploads.

Rabasa, Angel, Stacie Pettyjohn, Jeremy Ghez, and Christopher Boucek, *Deradicalizing Islamist Extremists*, Santa Monica: RAND, 2010.

Tan, Andrew, "Southeast Asia as the Second Front in the War Against Terrorism: Evaluating the Threat and Responses," *Terrorism and Political Violence* 2 (2003): 112-138.

# Terrorist Action, Radicalism, and the Normalcy of Extremism: A Conceptual Framework and Implications for De-radicalization*

*Michael Fischer and Eva-Maria Reh*

## *A. Introduction*

Understanding de-radicalization presupposes conceptual and theoretical clarity about the nature of extremism and radicalization, and about how these concepts relate to terrorist violence. Since the 2005 London bombings, the term 'radicalization' has increasingly drawn public attention in Europe. With it came an interest in so called 'homegrown-terrorism' and the question how seemingly well integrated members of society could turn to terrorism.[1]

Commonly, 'radicalization' is rather vaguely understood as a process leading to extremism and/or terrorism. It is "at present the standard term used to describe 'what goes on before the bomb goes off'."[2] There is no consensus among social scientists or policy makers on the exact definition of the terms 'extremist', 'radical', or 'radicalization'. Looking at the vast amount of literature and research concerned with these issues,[3] the terms are in fact conspicuously under-defined.[4] Often, the terms 'radical' and

---

* This paper is based on a presentation given at the international conference on "De-Radicalization and Disengagement in Counter-Terrorism Strategies" in Bangkok, 2011, and resulted from the research project "Technical Prevention of Low-Cost-Terrorism" funded by the German Federal Ministry of Education and Research (BMBF). The authors wish to thank Martin Carrillo Aravena and Sebastian Scheerer for valuable comments and Norbert Fabritius for graphic software support.

1 Sedgwick, "The Concept of Radicalization as a Source of Confusion," 2010, pp. 479-494.

2 Sedgwick, "Concept of Radicalization," p. 479.

3 For an overview see Schmid and Price, "Selected Literature on radicalization and de-radicalization of terrorists: Monographs, Edited Volumes, Grey Literature and Prime Articles published since the 1960s," 2011, pp. 337-348.

4 Neumann, "Radikalisierung, Deradikalisierung und Extremismus," 2013, pp. 3-10.

'extreme' are used interchangeably.[5] Extremism is understood to exist in basically two variants: as 'cognitive extremism' and as 'violent extremism'. Cognitive extremist refers to a person whose political ideas or goals fundamentally oppose the basic values of a given society, whereas violent extremist refers to a person who pursues political goals by violent means.[6] As a third type (usually conflated with the second), but a subcategory, 'violence-prone' extremism is regularly mentioned. 'Radicalization' would thus describe a process leading to either cognitive extremism, a 'violence-prone' state or violence itself. Some authors specifically focus on the issue of violence and the preparation for conflict: "Functionally, political radicalization is increased preparation for and commitment to intergroup conflict. Descriptively, radicalization means change in beliefs, feelings, and behaviors in directions that increasingly justify intergroup violence and demand sacrifice in defense of the group."[7]

However, this employed definition of the terms 'extremism' and 'radicalization' is not apt (and sometimes not intended) to grasp the nature of terrorism or terrorists specifically. On the one hand, the relationship between cognitive extremism and political violence is disputed: Cognitive extremism does not always lead to violent extremism, some violent extremists might not be particularly cognitive extremist, and cognitive extremists may even play a useful role in de-radicalizing violent extremists.[8] On the other hand, definitions relating to violence and conflict capture far more than the case of terrorism: Joining a regular army also involves a socialization into violence-prone behavior; every intergroup bar fight requires a change in beliefs and feelings in a direction that justifies intergroup violence. Every state could be called a violent extremist actor if all that was required is to pursue political goals by violent means.

The discourse about extremism and radicalization does point out various relevant concepts for the study of terrorism and de-radicalization, which, in our view, all need to be taken into account, but need to be separated analytically and should not be confused as one concept. Important dimensions that are incorporated to varying degrees in definitions of extremism and radicalization are:

---

5 Sedgwick, "Concept of Radicalization," p. 483.

6 Neumann, "Radikalisierung".

7 McCauley and Moskalenko, "Mechanisms of Political Radicalization: Pathways Toward Terrorism," 2008, pp. 415-433.

8 See, e.g., Neumann, "Radikalisierung,".

a dimension relating to relative positions in a distribution of political ideas or values (extremism);

a dimension regarding attitudes and modes of action that prepare for or tend to induce conflict (radicalism);

a behavioral dimension relating to militancy and the use of violence.

In this paper, we provide a conceptual and theoretical framework for the understanding of extremism and radicalism based on a general theory of action and a macro-sociological view on the normalcy of deviance. We thereby take into account and distinguish between the distributional, the attitude- and habitus-related, and the behavioral aspects of terrorism. Based on this analysis we will then outline implications for de-radicalization.

## *B. Terrorist Action as Rational Action*

The discourse about extremism and radicalization focuses on the question about the difference between terrorists and normal, mainstream individuals. Terrorist actors obviously do not act normal in a statistical sense. However, it is important to not exclusively consider the differences, but to also take into account in which regards terrorist action is action by normal agents. The view that terrorists suffer from any peculiar psychological disorders has been refuted time and again. "What limited data we have on individual terrorists", Crenshaw already concluded in 1981, "suggest that the outstanding common characteristic of terrorists is their normality."[9] Since then, numerous studies have demonstrated that persons accused of or convicted for terrorist activities show no significant mental pathologies that could offer an explanation of terrorism.[10] In fact, many terrorist organizations carefully pick their recruits and try to avoid granting membership to anyone with a somewhat deranged personality.[11] As action of psychologically normal agents, terrorist action can be described in a general

9 Crenshaw, "The Causes of Terrorism," 1981, pp. 379-399; idem, "The Psychology of Political Terrorism," 1986, pp. 379-413.

10 See, e.g., Richardson, *What Terrorists Want. Understanding the Terrorist Threat*, 2007, p. 14.

11 Richardson, *What Terrorists Want*, p. 15.

framework of action theory.[12] Like most action, it can follow different rationalities on a norm-regulated (following values and normative prescriptions), an instrumental (achieving ends through means), as well as a dramaturgical and expressive (presenting and expressing oneself) dimension.[13]

Terrorist action (here in the case of sub-state, revolt-directed terrorism)[14] is fundamentally norm-regulated. Subjectively, it follows the logic of social control.[15] Based on an alternative value system – or at least on alternative judgments about right and wrong – terrorists observe large-scale, permanent, and collective deviance and, typically, injustice. Based on the concept of collective liability,[16] terrorism reacts to the observed deviance with negative sanctions. Like in more conventional forms of punishment, the topoi of revenge and retaliation play a major role: "The most powerful theme in any conversation with terrorists past or present, leader or follower, religious or secular, left wing or right wing, male or female, young or old, is revenge."[17] The enemy is seen as responsible for starting the conflict and own deeds are framed as reactions to previous attacks or wrongs. Research on terrorist careers shows that references to revenge are an important tool for convincing and recruiting supporters, followers, and comrades.[18] The call to revenge can build on personal experiences like cases of cruelty toward or killings of individuals personally known. It may also rely on reports, pictures or movies depicting the cruelties committed by the adversary and build on an association with a more or less abstract collective or "imagined community" that the 'recruit' associates with.[19] Retribution can be demanded for specific events or for the antagonist's

12 Fischer, "Terrorismus und staatliches Strafen: Figurationen der sozialen Kontrolle," 2014.

13 Habermas, *Theorie des kommunikativen Handelns*, 1988.

14 Hess, "Terrorismus: Quo vadis? Kurzfristige Prognosen und mittelfristige Orientierungen," 2006, pp. 105-150.

15 Black, "The Geometry of Terrorism," 2004, pp. 14-25; Black, "Terrorism as Social Control," pp. 9-18; Fischer, "Terrorismus und staatliches Strafen".

16 Roche, "Collective Violence as Social Control," 1996, pp. 97-128; Black, "The Geometry of Terrorism," 2004a, pp. 14-25.

17 Richardson, *What Terrorists Want*.

18 McCauly and Moskalenko, "Mechanisms of Political Radicalization: Pathways Toward Terrorism," 2008.

19 Anderson, *Imagined Communities. Reflections on the Origins and Spread of Nationalism*, 1983.

overall wickedness. Escalations of terrorism and counter-terrorism continually provide new reasons prompting new retributive reactions.[20]

On an expressive level, terrorism always and fundamentally is an expression of disapproval. The terrorist attack draws attention to perceived injustice, distinguishes between good and evil, and demonstrates the claim for validity of the terrorists' normative stance. This expressive dimension will typically be mixed with other motivations, but can also stand on its own. To sharply shown disapproval with grave injustice can be perceived as important in itself, as cathartic liberation or as a personal duty, even if political success is improbable. Dramaturgically, the terrorist attack draws attention to the perpetrators who can demonstrate their moral qualities and their heroism through the strong expression of disapproval and their commitment to the just cause. As one ideal result, the terrorist may expect celebration as a martyr.

In the instrumental dimension, terrorist action may serve several strategic purposes. Applying the basic logic of instrumental violence and de-terrence[21], terrorist groups make demands and threaten further violence in case these are not met; they try to mobilize followers and to incite resistance – be it by means of demonstrating the possibility of resistance or through provoking the state to act suppressive against specific groups, thereby creating resentment and cohesion; they try to produce media coverage and attention for grievances that will otherwise be less noticed; they may try to physically weaken the enemy (even though the psychological effect is the primary one); and they try to undermine the state's legitimacy through demonstrating that it cannot protect its citizens.[22]

There has been a frequent discussion on the question whether terrorist action is 'rational' or not. In the framework of an action theory based approach, terrorist action can generally be considered to be as rational or irrational as non-terrorist action. If by 'rational' we only refer to instrumen-

---

20 Richardson, *What Terrorists Want;* Scheerer, "Agonaler Autismus und diskrepante Interpunktion. Zwei Restriktionen im Umgang mit terroristischer Gewalt," 2011, at http://www.wiso.uni-hamburg.de/fileadmin/sowi/kriminologie/Workin_Paper_Series/IKS_WPS_002_Scheerer.pdf.

21 Arendt, *On Violence*, 1970; Popitz, *Phänomene der Macht*, 1992.

22 Crenshaw, "The Causes of Terrorism," 1981, pp. 379-399; Hoffman and McCormick, "Terrorism, Signaling, and Suicide Attack," 2004; Münkler, *Die neuen Kriege*, 2003; Richardson, *What Terrorists Want*, pp. 77 f.; Scheerer, *Die Zukunft des Terrorismus: Drei Szenarien*, 2002; Waldmann, *Terrorismus: Provokation der Macht,* 1998.

tal or strategic rationality and expect actors to thoroughly think through a given problem based on extensive and unbiased considerations regarding all possible circumstances and outcomes, then terrorist action will not always be rational in that sense. Like other actors, terrorists will sometimes follow more or less routinized scripts based on their definition of the situation. When no suitable routines exist, terrorist action will try to more or less reflectively maximize subjective expected utility on a normative, instrumental, dramaturgical and expressive level (whereby actors in different positions in terrorist organizations may follow differing typical rationalities). The rationality of terrorist actors is bounded, multi-dimensional, and influenced by pre-formed scripts and group dynamics just like the rationality of action generally is.

## C. Terrorist Action as Radical Action

Terrorist action displays a certain attitude and a mode of action that we may call 'radicalism'. Radicalism is a set of principles which relate and guide individual perceptions and actions. Intellectually, radicalism is characterized by the search for uncompromising truth and purity of teachings. On the level of action, radicalism is characterized by certainty, deep engagement, and strong determination. Individuals may display a radical attitude or act radically occasionally; they may also develop a more stable radical habitus.[23] Terrorist action is radical action within the framework of a collective conflict. It implements the principles of radicalism on instrumental, normative, dramaturgical, and expressive dimensions of action.

On the normative level, radical (conflict-related) action implies a highly certain distinction between good and evil, a 'manichean' worldview. This is accompanied by the observation of grave injustice, certainty in the ascription of responsibility for grievances and the feeling of a personal duty to fight for the just cause. Where collective conflicts are observed, this often comes with a tendency for the ascription of collective liability and a rigid distinction between in- and out-group. Radical actors may show strong altruistic feelings towards the in-group while suspending empathy when it comes to out-group-members. On the instrumental level, radical

23 Crossley, "From Reproduction to Transformation: Social Movement Fields and the Radical Habitus," 2003; Vertigans, *The Sociology of Terrorism. People, Places and Processes*, 2011.

action implies the ascription of very high subjective utility to reaching one's goals, a strong determination to achieve, and a readiness to accept large risks and costs. On the dramaturgical level, radical action implies a demonstration of consistency of beliefs and authenticity of convictions as well as an orientation towards self-sacrifice. The radical actor demonstrates that her action is consequent and that the cause at issue is more important than herself. In collective conflicts, this induces a tendency for the perception of moral superiority, for heroism, and for martyrdom, which may be complemented by strong forms of 'othering' and the devaluation of opponents. On the expressive level, radical action prefers drastic forms of expression.[24]

Overall, the radical mode of action incorporates an unquestionable definition of the situation, strong commitment, and a determination to succeed. It describes the opposite of ambivalence, detachment, and apathy. The radical actor strongly believes (or: 'knows' – in the sense of a sociology of knowledge) that every sane and truthful person of goodwill would have to acknowledge the correctness of one's own perception of the situation, the rightfulness of one's own judgment, and the respectability of one's own self. From the perspective of the radical, critics must be evil, delusional, or both.

Radicalism does not in itself make violence unavoidable, but it may induce a tendency towards the use of violent means. Violence, we may assume, will be employed either when there is a routinized violent script fitting the definition of the situation, or once the subjective expected utility of an action (on the instrumental, normative, dramaturgical, and expressive level) using violent means exceeds the utility of non-violent alternatives. There is no cause specific to violence, it is merely a matter of a threshold.

A radical pacifist will become ever more peaceful, the more radical she gets. Her sacrifice and martyrdom will consist in even enduring violence without retribution; her strong value-orientation and determination will let her try to stay peaceful at all costs. If non-violence is not a major part of the radical's ideology, radicalism typically facilitates violence through strong distinctions between in-group and out-group, through the very high

24 See Fischer, "Terrorismus und staatliches Strafen," pp. 187-202; also, e.g., Richardson, *What Terrorists Want*; Schmidtchen, "Terroristische Karrieren," 1981, pp. 13-77; Jäger and Böllinger, "Studien zur Sozialisation von Terroristen," 1981, pp. 117-243; de la Roche, "Collective Violence as Social Control," 97-128.

utility that is ascribed to reaching one's goals, through the readiness to accept high risks and high costs, through the concept of sacrifice and heroism, and through the preference for drastic forms of expression. All of this widens the scope of acceptable means worth trying out if nothing else helps, while at the same time making violence a potentially attractive way of expressing and presenting oneself – even if it is not likely that instrumental goals will be reached.

The example of the radical pacifist has already pointed to another consequence of this analytic perspective: While we have referred to the field of terrorism to describe the radical mode of action, it is not only political conflicts, in which individuals may act radically, and it is not only terrorists who may be radical. People from the societal mainstream and also the state itself may get radically involved in certain issues or conflicts. In fact, counter-terrorism itself is often executed in a radical manner[25]: as a war between good and evil that must be won no matter what even using violence if necessary. Radicalism is reciprocally inter-related with conflict: It contributes to the escalation of and tends to be induced by conflicts.

## D. The Normalcy of the Extreme

What distinguishes a deviant political radical from a mainstream, conformist radical is not the general habitus, nor necessarily the use of violence, but his relatively extreme position in a particular continuum. Sedgwick has drawn attention to the fact that when using such a relative understanding of extremism (in Sedgwick's terminology: of radicalism), we must not simply assume that some sort of 'continuum of opinions' exists, but must specify the continuum we refer to.[26] Moreover, it is questionable if 'opinion' in itself and on its own is a useful category for understanding political extremism at all. The idea of the 'opinion' typically concentrates on the individual level and assumes that each individual can be assigned a specific and relatively stable one of these opinions – which is a problematic assumption, as we will illustrate. Even more important, it ignores emotion, communication, and action and thereby psychological and sociologi-

25 Schmid and Price, "Selected Literature," 2011.

26 Sedgwick, "Concept of Radicalization," pp. 490 ff.

cal dimensions which are vital for the understanding of political extremism.

For a fundamental conceptualization of extremism, we need a more complex approach. Instead of thinking in terms of a continuum of opinions, it is more useful to start from a societal distribution of value judgments regarding single or several moral and/or political issues. We can think of moral judgments being operative on cognitive, emotional, communicative, and pragmatic levels. Both cognitive and communicative instances of value judgments are mediated through language. The moral extreme is an immanent possibility of language-mediated moral thought and communication. About any action or person X, it is possible to think or say that X is good or X is bad, that X equals moral perfection or that X signifies the worst possible evil. These are objective and absolute extreme positions in the sense of maxima of positive or negative evaluation. They are possibilities of what can be said or thought, independently of the question of whether somebody actually says or thinks them.

It is, for example, possible to think or say that abortion is a moral duty to minimize the number of human beings and to thereby reduce human suffering. It is also possible to think or say that abortion is murder and needs to be punished by death.

Even if such extreme attitudes are not present in a given social system, there always is a probability $> 0$ that the thinkable will be thought and that the effable will be said. On an emotional level, moral judgments will correlate to stronger or weaker positive or negative emotions, depending on how important values are and how much the state of the world is conform to or contradicts the value judgments. Typical feelings may be praise, awe, honor, or anger, outrage, aggression, depression. On the pragmatic level, moral judgments will show as a tendency to act in a way as to uphold or reach a normatively satisfying state of the world. The more a desired and actualized state is threatened, or the more the actual state contradicts the desired state, the stronger the tendency to act will be.

Based on these four levels, we can conceptualize a continuum from the worst possible to the best possible evaluation of a given empirical state of the world in a social system. The worst possible state of the world will be characterized by its maximum condemnation in thought and communication, maximum negative emotions, and either a maximum tendency to change the state of affairs or apathetic resignation. The best possible state of the world will be characterized by its maximum praise in thought and communication, maximum positive emotions, and a maximum tendency to preserve the current state of affairs.

Empirically, in a given social system (and in psychological systems), there will be a distribution of more or less positive or negative value judgments regarding particular moral and political issues. If we speak of a distribution of value judgments, this is an abbreviation for saying that there are distributions of moral thought and beliefs, of moral emotions, of moral communication, and of normative tendencies to act. Analytically, we are at this stage not speaking of a distribution of individuals and 'their' value judgments. Individuals may be affected by differing thoughts and e-motions, and may be involved in differing communications and interactions. The position of an individual may be a different one in each underlying distribution and may be seen as inconsistent: E.g., the judgment on the cognitive level might mismatch the judgment on the emotional, communicative, or pragmatic level. People may think differently from how they feel, feel differently from how they talk, talk differently from what they tend to do. Regarding the same issue, they can be extreme on one level, and mainstream on another. Moreover: They can be (i.e.: think, feel, talk, or prefer) extreme in one moment and mainstream in the next. Individuals can fluctuate in the spectrum of value judgments and will not always stabilize in one position. As a further abbreviation, we can speak of 'extreme' individuals, indicating that individuals can be pushed and pulled into extreme (and sometimes more consistent) positions in the spectrum of value judgments and can stabilize there for a certain amount of time.

Empirical distributions of moral judgments regarding a particular issue in a given social system need not (and typically will not) cover the whole range from maximum possible negative to maximum possible positive evaluation. However, even if nobody holds absolutely extreme positions, there will be relative extremes (as long as not all individuals are the same).

E.g., there will be people condemning or supporting abortion more than others, even if their positions are pretty close together.

As a general assumption, we can suppose that moral judgments regarding particular issues will often be roughly normally distributed. There will be less social positions that show relatively strong positive and relatively strong negative evaluations, while the majority of judgments will be around the median judgment of the social system. Persons affected by relatively extreme judgments may be called 'extremist' regarding the issue in question.[27] Every pluralist social system produces extremists in this general and statistical sense on many issues of evaluation. Moral judgments regarding single issues will thereby not be all independent, but will build clusters around political ideologies and worldviews. Consequentially, individuals may get into extreme positions regarding not only single issues, but clusters of issues. Many such instances of extremism will be temporary – an individual may show an extreme judgment one day or for a limited period of time, and then float back into the realm of more average judgments. Other individuals will be pulled and/or pushed to the fringes of distributions for prolonged periods of time.

If the laws and procedures of a society are more or less in line with average moral beliefs, then observing society from a relatively extreme point of view enhances the chance that societal conditions will be judged as wrong and unjust. Normalcy may appear deviant from the standpoint of extreme moral judgments.

E.g., in a society that has legalized abortion the person who absolutely condemns abortion and equates it with murder will observe an ongoing process of what amounts to mass murder.

Once societal conditions are judged as deviant and unjust, this observation introduces relative deprivation (of the unjustly treated) and a culture conflict (with those who do not observe the injustice) at the same time. Large variance in the distribution of moral judgments may tend to induce larger conflicts, and conflicts have a tendency to enlarge the variance through processes of escalation.

Statistical moral extremism does not necessarily lead to the development of radical forms of action. The 'extremist' may react with fatalism or cynicism. He may want to change social conditions but not know how. He may not be able to develop sufficient heroism or to identify a clearly responsible enemy. He may feel that there is not enough support for his case, etc. pp. There is a variety of reasons why statistical extremism may remain on the level of mere factual communication or pure solitary thought. However, given adequate social conditions and a suitable opportunity structure for radicalization, statistical extremism will typically in-crease the chance of radical action, since the observation of injustice provides a potentially

27 It thereby is a somewhat arbitrary – and not analytically but only politically interesting – decision, where to draw the line; since in political discourse, 'extremist' is a pejorative term, it is itself a value judgment to tell which judgments are considered to be 'extreme'.

fruitful basis for the emergence of strong determination, clear in-group-out-group-distinctions, a feeling of duty, and a role for heroes.

Figure 1 gives an illustration of the distribution of extremism and radicalism in a given society. Here we assume a normal distribution of value judgments regarding some moral or political issue (which includes the dimensions of thought and beliefs, emotions, communication, and tendencies for action). Radicalism will also be distributed unevenly in society. For simplification, we show three levels of radicalism. There may be individuals in the mainstream of the distribution of value judgments showing a radical attitude (and/or act radically) regarding the question at issue, just as there may be radical extremists. Other individuals will show a medium level of radicalism, while yet others will be particularly non-radical.

*Figure 1: Distributions of Extremism and Radicalism*

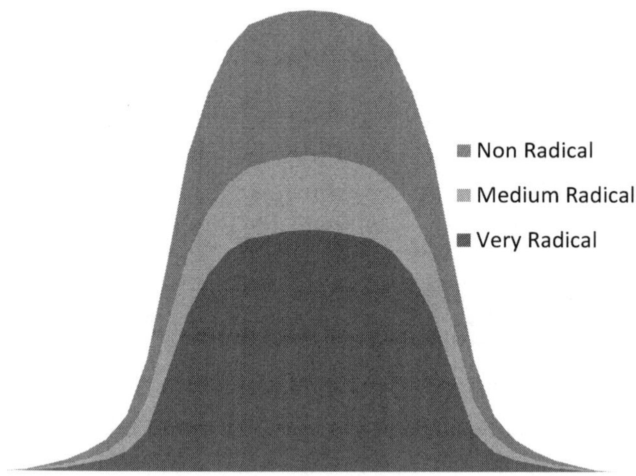


Due to the mutual interrelation of extremism, radicalism, and conflict, we can expect that a radical mode of action is more common among extremists than among more mainstream individuals. This is also because mainstream individuals – in a state where the laws are more or less in line with average judgments – can delegate the actual conflict procedure to state agents and are rarely personally involved. Relative extremism, radical attitudes and conflict orientation form a mechanism that has a tendency to escalate in a positive feedback loop and enhances the chance of violence.

Under peaceful conditions, this tendency to escalate is permanently counteracted through processes of (often: informal) social control. It is difficult and exhausting to develop into a stabilized extremist and radical since the display of extremism combined with a radical habitus will be met by all sorts of sanctions: ridicule, gossip, rejection, exclusion, police intervention, punishment.

Once the dynamics of relative extremism, radical action, and conflict regarding a particular issue or a perceived syndrome of issues become strong enough to form a milieu of more or less radical (not necessarily: violent) activists in extreme positions, this milieu can pull people in (who are at the same time pushed by the sanctions of mainstream society), start to build identities of resistance, and begin to successfully sanction normalcy (again: through ridicule, rejection, exclusion, devaluation, punishment). Now, while it is still difficult to become a stabilized extremist and radical, it is also difficult to de-extremize and de-radicalize.

## *E. Implications for De-radicalization*

Counter-radicalization programs (which in our terminology relate to extremism, radicalism, and associated violence) are usually terminologically divided into de-radicalization measures which seek the abandonment of extreme views and violence (if already occurred), disengagement measures which seek the abandonment of the involvement in terrorist activities only, and radicalization prevention measures which are generally directed at a segment of society seen to be vulnerable to radicalization.[28] It has been noted that the success of de-radicalization programs is very difficult to evaluate. There is some uncertainty about what exactly should define the success of a de-radicalization program in the first place. Within the common dichotomy of extremist opinions vs. 'extremist' (i.e. violent) behavior, either a cognitive shift towards less extreme opinions or a behavioral change towards non-violent means could be counted as a marker of success. The former alternative raises the question as to exactly how mainstream beliefs have to get before a person should be called de-radical-

28 Vidino and Brandon, "Countering Radicalization in Europe," 2012, p. 9; in practice, measures for de-radicalization, disengagement, and prevention will show oftentimes overlapping approaches.

ized.[29] Moreover, recidivism rates can only be measured after many years; some programs will not allow the most radical militants to participate, making their success rates higher than that of programs with a wider eligibility; and programs focusing on individuals will be dependent upon local and political circumstances, so that the same program may work (or seem to work) better under one set of circumstances and worse under another.[30]

Since measuring overall success is difficult, it will be useful to have a conceptual framework that allows us to observe the effects of de-radicalization programs in more detail while at the same time sharpening the view for their limitations. Moreover, recognizing the normalcy of extremism has implications for possible ways of integrating individual de-radicalization programs with societal approaches towards reducing the variance of moral judgments.

### *I. De-Radicalization Programs: Possible Effects on Extremism, Radicalism, and Terrorist Motives*

De-radicalization programs considered to be effective will typically encompass several approaches.[31] Counter-ideology will attempt to show the contradictions and factual errors in radical ideologies and establish and foster moderate belief systems. This is pursued either via impeding the spread of ideology (i.e. propaganda) or through promoting narratives that contradict those spread by terrorist ideologues.[32] Skills training will try to provide radical individuals with competencies that enable them to cope and be successful in a conform way of life; this may encompass vocational skills to enable a professional career as well as emotional skills to cope with negative feelings like anger, stress, shame, and fear.[33] Changing ref-

---

29 Neumann, "Radikalisierung,"; Horgan and Braddock, "Rehabilitating the Terrorists? Challenges in Assessing the Effectiveness of De-radicalization Programs," 2010, p. 268.

30 Neumann, "Prisons and Terrorism. Radicalisation and De-radicalisation in 15 Countries," 2010, p. 49.

31 Neumann, "Prisons and Terrorism".

32 Sedgwick, "Jihadist ideology, Western counter-ideology, and the ABC model. Critical Studies on Terrorism," 2012, pp. 359 f.; Horgan and Braddock, "Rehabilitating the Terrorists?," p. 280.

33 Stern, "Mind over Martyr: How to Deradicalize Islamist Extremists," 2010, pp. 95-108; Stern, "Deradicalization or Disengagement of Terrorists: Is it Possible?,"

erence groups and significant others will involve separating individuals from the influence of extremist groups and milieus and strengthening involvement in and inducing commitments to mainstream social groups and milieus like families, communities, tribes, or workplace.[34] Rewards may provide direct incentives to abandon terrorism, be it financially or through early release from prison or amnesty.[35] On the level of criminal law, repression may incapacitate radical individuals and deter others from engaging in violent activism.[36] On a political level, dialogue, negotiation, political reform, and reconciliation may enable processes of collective de-radicalization.[37]

For analyzing effects of de-radicalization programs within our conceptual approach, we can distinguish 1. between dimensions of the motivation of terrorist action as rational action (norm-regulated, instrumental, dramaturgical, and expressive), 2. between extremism, radicalism, and violence, while separating 3. the cognitive, emotional, communicative, and pragmatic dimensions of extremism and 4. implementations of radicalism in norm-regulated, instrumental, dramaturgical, and expressive action. It is beyond the scope of this article to provide a systematic analysis of individual de-radicalization programs in this framework. Here, we can only draw a rough outline on how de-radicalization measures generally affect statistical extremism, radicalism, and terrorist motives.

Counter-ideology is intended to move individuals' or groups' beliefs from statistically extreme to more mainstream positions. This will probably be most effective in cases, where ideology was a factor of medium strength in the radicalization process, i.e. for individuals who are impressed by but not experts in ideology.[38] For individuals, on the other

---

2010, at http://www.hoover.org/sites/default/files/research/docs/futurechallenges_stern.pdf; Boucek, "Saudi Arabia's 'Soft' Counterterrorism Strategy. Prevention, Rehabilitation, and Aftercare," 2008, p. 7.

34 Richardson, *What Terrorists Want*, pp. 215 f.; Horgan and Braddock, "Rehabilitating the Terrorists?," p. 280.

35 Horgan and Braddock, "Rehabilitating the Terrorists?," p. 280.

36 LaFree and Dugan, "Research on Terrorism and Countering Terrorism," 2009, pp. 423-427.

37 Scheerer, "Agonaler Autismus,"; Dudouet et al., "From Combatants to Peacebuilders. A case for inclusive, participatory and holistic security transitions," 2012.

38 On the different role ideology may play for different types of members in terrorist groups cf. Nesser, "Profiles of Jihadist Terrorists in Europe," 2006; Richardson, *What Terrorists Want*, p. 81.

hand, who engaged in political radicalism as followers and for reasons primarily other than ideology (like group dynamics or other psychological reasons), we can expect counter-ideology to be less effective. Also, for ideological experts and radical intellectuals, counter-ideology may be a difficult approach, since experts can often rely on sophisticated systems of arguments that may be tough to prove to be false or more contradictory than mainstream ideology typically is itself. Since counter-ideology against expert ideologues requires expert counter-ideologues, there also is the practical problem of finding and hiring qualified de-radicalization staff in sufficient quantities.

Regarding radicalism, effective counter-ideology should work against the certainty of the definition of situations in all dimensions of actions by introducing ambivalence through counter-narratives. Strong distinctions between in- and out-group can be challenged through presenting a more complex picture of the assumed enemy while introducing doubts about the pure victim- and hero-status of the in-group.[39] Moreover, distinctions between in-group and out-group can be confused through emphasizing different affiliations. Strong determination and high risk behavior can be mitigated through questioning the superiority of the desired social order and advocating mainstream values.[40] Concepts of heroism can be eroded by confronting militants with victims of terrorism.[41]

In the case of the religious Jihadi ideology, counter-ideology will address the question as to what the Islamic god supposedly demands and/or prohibits, and will present more moderate theological interpretations.[42]

---

39 E.g., the US-led Information Operations Task Force (IOTF), a unit which operated in Iraq in 2005–2006, broadcasted TV documentaries and radio shows that focused on the flaws and contradictions within Jihadi narratives and emphasized capital crimes or attacks committed against Iraqis by Jihadists (cf. Sedgwick, "Jihadist ideology," p. 369).

40 For example, the German "Violence Prevention Network" (VPN) addresses right-wing extremists in prisons by frequently challenging the detainees' xenophobic or nationalist views by talking about personal experiences in discussion groups and leading participants to articulate and analyze existing problems and perceptions. Instead of confronting participants with dogmatic moral lectures, a dialogue is established, as program leaders point out (Violence Prevention Network 11/06/2013).

41 Horgan and Braddock, "Rehabilitating the Terrorists?," p. 281.

42 For example, Saudi Arabian approaches to de-radicalize convicted terrorists rely on cooperation with Islamic clerics who meet and discuss with detainees in order to promote moderate aspects of Islam and also point out why terrorist activities ac-

Counter-ideology should be presented by interlocutors who appear authentic and authoritative. A counter-ideologue who does not express truthfulness will be perceived as manipulative and not trustworthy. More generally speaking, the problem of counter-ideology is that it is a strategic endeavor designed to manipulate individuals' beliefs while having to pretend to be a coercion-free discourse interested only in the truth. It must pretend that the better argument will win, while at the same time the framework of the de-radicalization program prohibits that the radical argument may ever emerge as the winning one.[43] Counter-ideology may backfire, if this trick becomes too obvious.[44]

---

tually contradict Islam. Other such examples are the Yemenite program which initiated religious dialogues between prisoners and clerics or the Singaporean Religious Rehabilitation Group with religious re-education as a core aspect. European countries such as France, the Netherlands, and the UK have started to introduce prison imams within their penitentiary staff (cf. Neumann, "Prisons and Terrorism," pp. 50 f. and 33 f.).

43 E.g. in Yemen, clerics challenged prisoners "to enter into a 'dialogue of equals', with both sides pledging to accept the other side's arguments if they were seen as more plausible and convincing. (Needless to say, the government's clerics won all rounds of this 'competition'.)" (Neumann, "Prisons and Terrorism," p. 52.).

44 As opposed to counter-ideology after the fact, *impeding propaganda* aims at hampering the spread of terrorist ideology in the first place. This may downsize the spread of extremist value judgments and elements of a radical habitus, and lead to a relative increase in counter-terrorist propaganda promoting mainstream values. Impeding propaganda can be accomplished by tackling means of communication (especially the Internet), places of recruitment, or main propagandists. E.g., Dutch policies seek to impede propaganda by removing extremist content from the web as well as – when possible – deporting preachers considered to spread radical ideas (cf. Vidino and Brandon, "Countering Radicalization in Europe," p. 56). In accounting for the major role the Internet plays in spreading propaganda (cf. e.g. Steinberg "Jihadistische Radikalisierung im Internet und mögliche Gegenmaßnahmen," 2013, pp. 17-25), Great Britain introduced a special 'Counter Terrorism Internet Referral Unit' (CTIU) which has the task of shutting down 'suspicious websites' and which calls on citizens to report any such web content. Similarly, the British *Prevent* strategy suggests 'disrupting propagandists' (Home Office 2011, "Prevent Strategy," p. 49, available at https://www.gov.uk/government/uploads/system/uploads/attachment_data/file/97976/prevent-strategy-review.pdf.). Although stopping the flow of propaganda material might complicate recruitment (especially of 'lone wolf' terrorists) and bind resources of propagandists trying to skirt the restrictions, it may on the other hand drain a valuable source of information for intelligence services (cf. El Difraoui, "Jihad.de. Jihadistische Online-Propaganda: Empfehlungen für Gegenmaßnahmen in Deutschland," 2012, p.19) and is an infringement on the freedom of speech.

Skills training will primarily address militants with problematic early biographies, a lack of approval and/or educational deficits. Establishing vocational skills (or even basic skills like reading and writing) may reduce the need for heroism through pointing out viable options for recognized careers and providing alternative role models. Skills training also constitutes a general device for diversion, since perpetuating a radical habitus in an extreme position takes time and attention which are now partially invested in training. Emotional skill training for coping with negative emotions may reduce the benefits of aggressive expression by reducing anger towards the out-group, reducing emotional dependency upon an extremist milieu in-group, providing alternative and less costly means for dealing with stressful situations, and showing ways of preserving self-respect other than the destruction of some enemy.[45] Emotional skill training requires an interlocutor who is capable of building relationships of trust, which is aided by independence from prosecuting and penal institutions.

Vocational skill training will obviously be less effective in cases of middle- and upper-class terrorism. Emotional skill training will probably be less effective where a radical ideology is not primarily a pretext for dealing with personal problems but rooted in social emotions like altruism and a desire for justice.

Changing reference groups, and building involvement in and commitment to them, is designed to switch the mechanics of social control from deviance to moderation. Involvement in mainstream groups should break the isolation in communicative islands of extremist views that is typically one element in processes of radicalization.[46] The involvement in normal

45 E.g., the German "Violence Prevention Network" tries to provide help at the stage of prison release by offering vocational training as well as emotional training like conflict and anger management (see Korn and Weilnböck, "Der lange Abschied von Hass und Gewalt," 2013). The Dutch "Polarisation and Radicalisation Action Plan 2007-2011" seeks to reduce sources of frustration by improving access to the labor market via education, traineeships and personal development mentoring (see Vidino and Brandon, "Countering Radicalization in Europe," p. 29). In Afghanistan, one developing program is trying to alter role models and opportunities of convicted Taliban via education such as reading and writing classes (see Neumann, "Prisons and Terrorism," p. 52).

46 Elwert, "Weder irrational noch traditionalistisch: Charismatische Mobilisierung und Gewaltmärkte als Basis der Attentäter des 11. September," 2003. For example, STREET (Strategy to Reach, Empower and Educate), an initiative by a south London Muslim community, aims at integrating youths who are drifting away from the moderate mainstream or may be vulnerable to extremist propaganda by providing

reference groups influences normative, instrumental, and dramaturgical motives of (potential) terrorism. It produces enhanced exposition to normalcy and to the expectation of normalcy, including the informal social controls that sanction deviance. It establishes new goals through obligations and opportunities in the family and in the workplace. And it strengthens the commitment to average social roles. At the same time, investment and success in normal roles make deviance more and more costly.

Changing reference groups may fail as a de-radicalization approach if the radical individual succeeds in radicalizing his new surroundings. While unlikely in a normal community setting, this aspect is especially a problem in prisons, where extremists may find a population of vulnerable targets for propaganda.[47]

Rewards are a simple short term influence on the instrumental level.[48] They can work as additional incentives, but cannot be assumed to work on their own.[49]

Repression, as has often been noted, is an ambivalent strategy. While it will incapacitate some individuals and deter others, it reinforces the desire for revenge, it introduces new goals to fight for (e.g. in the form of campaigns for freeing prisoners), and it creates martyrs. Repression may (tem-

---

a range of leisure activities and after school programs (see Briggs, "Tackling Extremism: Deradicalisation and Disengagement," 2012, pp. 11 f.). Re-integration through enhancing contact with moderate or mainstream groups is also emphasized by the Saudi PRAC program (Prevention Rehabilitation and After Care) that encourages family members of detained terrorists to visit them in prison by providing accommodation and financial support for visits. Additionally, 'family leave' is granted to detainees in order for them to feel an obligation to employ moderate value judgments (see El-Said and Harrigan, *Deradicalizing Violent Extremist: Counter-Radicalization and Deradicalization Programmes and Their Impact in Muslim Majority States*, 2013, p. 215.).

47 Neumann, "Prisons and Terrorism," p. 16; see Stern, "Deradicalization or Disengagement of Terrorists: Is it Possible?," 2010, pp. 1-18.

48 E.g., in Indonesia, Saudi Arabia, and Singapore, detained terrorists are offered incentives such as financial support of their families and also material support after release (e.g. through providing housing, cars or TVs; cf. Neumann, "Prisons and Terrorism," p. 53). In Northern Ireland, IRA prisoners could on certain conditions partake in the so called 'Early Release Scheme' to promote de-escalation. This reward though was combined with deterrent measures, since the alleviation was coupled with the threat of having to serve the full sentence in addition, in case the detainee was convicted again for a related offense (see Horgan and Braddock, "Rehabilitating the Terrorists?," p. 269).

49 Neumann, "Prisons and Terrorism".

porarily) end conflicts, but it may also contribute to processes of escalation that provide an optimal social climate for increased extremism and radical responses.[50] Waves of strong and violent repression can go on for decades without terminally ending conflicts.

### *II. De-radicalization and Distributions of Extremism*

Measures for de-radicalization are targeted specifically towards milieus and groups with extremist political judgments and radical habitus. They try to identify individuals who are in stabilized positions at the extremes of the distribution at issue. De-radicalization aims at pulling or pushing individuals back into what is considered to be mainstream.

Approaching the issue from the perspective of a distribution of moral judgments illustrates that we cannot expect to cleanly cut off a range of judgments in a society: A sudden end of values at some specified point considered to be the border of the acceptable mainstream is too improbable to be expected. We will have to expect that the more extreme the judgments, the fewer individuals will be affected by them or even stabilize in that position – yet without a sudden drop to zero occurring. Even if we managed to de-radicalize or incapacitate all of the extreme and radical individuals at a certain societal moment, we might – from a structural and macro-sociological point of view – expect, that other individuals can fill the free space of radical positions. There is terrorism, because there are terrorists. But there are also terrorists, because there is terrorism.[51] Almost no individual decides to become a terrorist, if the terrorist movement in question is not already established. Once established, however, it can pull individuals into terrorist positions in social space. It is therefore possible, that de-radicalizing some individuals will just open these terrorist positions for new applicants. If, e.g., a terrorist organization has more applicants than it can organizationally handle, the de-radicalization of some applicants will hardly reduce overall terrorism. Thus, even an exact measure of recidivism rates of individuals may not be able to prove the success of de-radicalization on a macro-level.

---

50 Sack, "Staat, Gesellschaft und politische Gewalt: Zur 'Pathologie' politischer Konflikte," 1984, pp. 17-386; LaFree and Drugan, "Research on Terrorism and Countering Terrorism," pp. 424 f.; Richardson, *What Terrorists Want,* p. 217.

51 Scheerer, *Die Zukunft des Terrorismus*; Waldmann, *Terrorismus*.

From a distributional perspective, what are realistic options to reduce or eliminate extreme and at the same time radical values?

1. De-radicalization may be (and typically is) combined with the prevention of radicalization so that the field of individuals in positions that have a tendency towards developing into violent radicalism is more broadly reduced. This may reduce the variance of the distribution without presupposing a sudden and abrupt end of values, and diminish the pool of potential recruits that may substitute de-radicalized individuals.
2. In a two-sided approach, de-radicalization and prevention of radicalization can be applied at both ends of the political spectrum (regarding the issue in question). E.g. programs against left-wing-radicalization are complemented by programs against right-wing-radicalization, programs against Jihadism with programs against the discrimination of Muslims.[52] This may reduce conflicts that not only arise from opposition to societal mainstream politics, but that can be enhanced by the confrontation with strongly opposing political groups.
3. A different approach to de-radicalization would take its starting point in the mainstream of society instead of (only) focusing on extremist views. If the variance within positions considered to be mainstream is reduced, it might become less probable that far out extreme positions can find enough individuals to support them. E.g., if a resentment against foreigners is reduced within mainstream positions, right-wing extremists will have less communicative connectivity, fewer options for interactions with like-minded individuals, and a reduced plausibility for the claim of representing the silent majority. 'Mainstreaming the mainstream', however, will probably only work on the basis of actual agreement and conflict resolution – when based on the ignorance of conflicts or on the exclusion of larger segments of society, it may stimulate extremist deviance rather than diminish it.
4. De-radicalization may focus on radical conflict only, leaving extremists in extreme, but non-radical positions. On a collective level, negotiation, compromise, and political integration may primarily address the mode of conflict, rather than political and moral judgments. On

52 E.g., the German Violence Prevention Network started with targeting white supremacy/right-wing radical youth and in 2006 expanded the program to include radical Islamist youth as well (cf. Violence Prevention Network, at http://www.violence-prevention-network.de/de/).

both sides of the conflict, it may also be redefined what sorts of demands are considered to be 'extremist' and which are acceptable, thereby lowering the radicalism of extremists as well as that of the mainstream.

## *F. Conclusion*

Terrorist action is rational action in that it follows specific rationalities on norm-regulated, dramaturgical, expressive, and instrumental dimensions. Understanding the careers through which normal agents become terrorists, as well as their de-radicalization, requires a conceptual approach to 'extremism' and 'radicalism' that allows us to observe relevant factors regarding societal distributions of individual social positions and guiding principles of action. Terrorist action implements the principles of radicalism in the framework of a collective conflict. It is guided by certainty, deep engagement, and strong determination, implying clear distinctions between good and evil, strong separation between in- and out-group, the ascription of high subjective utility to achieving goals, a feeling of personal duty, and an inclination for heroism. Extremism, on the other hand, describes positions in a distribution of value judgments regarding moral or political issues. It encompasses cognitive, emotional, communicative, and pragmatic levels. The deviant and violent political radical operates from a position in this distribution which makes normalcy itself appear deviant. However, it is important not to conceptually conflate extremism, radicalism, and violence. There are extremist radicals, mainstream radicals, extremist non-radicals, and mainstream non-radicals; and violence may be employed by mainstream individuals and in a non-radical mode of action as well. While conceptually independent, extremism, radicalism, conflict, and violence are causally interrelated and may escalate in a positive feedback loop which de-radicalization (in the usual sense of the term) needs to tackle. While the success of de-radicalization is hard to measure, a differentiated conceptual framework distinguishing terrorist motives, extremism, radicalism, and violence should allow us to observe effects and limitations of de-radicalization measures in more detail. At the same time, the distributional perspective indicates that de-radicalization should not focus on the individual level only. Counter-terrorism needs to consider realistic options for reshaping societal distributions of moral and political judgments overall.

## *Bibliography*

Arendt, Hannah, *On Violence*, London: Penguin, 1970.

Anderson, Benedict, *Imagined Communities: Reflections on the Origins and Spread of Nationalism*, London: Verso, 1983.

Black, Donald, "The Geometry of Terrorism," *Sociological Theory* 1 (2004): 14-25.

Black, Donald, "Terrorism as Social Control," in *Terrorism and Counter-Terrorism: Criminological Perspectives, Sociology of Crime, Law and Deviance, Vol. 5*, ed. Mathieu Deflem, Oxford: JAI, 2004, pp. 9-18.

Briggs, Rachel, "Tackling Extremism: Deradicalisation and Disengagement," Institute for Strategic Dialogue policy briefing, London, 2012.

Boucek, Christopher, "Saudi Arabia's 'Soft' Counterterrorism Strategy: Prevention, Rehabilitation, and Aftercare," *Carnegie Endowment for International Peace paper* 97 (2008): 1-27.

Crenshaw, Martha, "The Causes of Terrorism," *Comparative Politics* 4 (1981): 379-399.

Crenshaw, Martha, "The Psychology of Political Terrorism," in *Political Psychology: Contemporary Problems and Issues*, ed. Margaret G. Hermann, San Francisco: Jossey-Bass-Publ, 1986, pp. 379-413.

Crossley, Nick, "From Reproduction to Transformation: Social Movement Fields and the Radical Habitus," *Theory, Culture & Society* 20 (2003): 43-68.

Dudouet, Véronique, Hans J. Giessmann, and Katrin Planta, *From Combatants to Peacebuilders. A Case for Inclusive, Participatory and Holistic Security Transitions*, Policy Report, Berlin: Berghoff Foundation, 2012.

El Difraoui, Asiem, "Jihad.de. Jihadistische Online-Propaganda: Empfehlungen für Gegenmaßnahmen in Deutschland," *Stiftung Wissenschaft und Politik publication*, Berlin, 2012.

El-Said, Hamid, and Jane Harrigan, *Deradicalizing Violent Extremist: Counter-Radicalization and Deradicalization Programmes and Their Impact in Muslim Majority States*, New York: Routledge, 2013.

Elwert, Georg, "Weder irrational noch traditionalistisch: Charismatische Mobilisierung und Gewaltmärkte als Basis der Attentäter des 11. September," in *Entsetzliche Soziale Prozesse: Theorie und Empirie der Katastrophen*, ed. Lars Clausen, Elke M. Geenen and Elisio Macamo, Münster: Lit 2003, pp. 95-123.

Fischer, Michael, "Terrorismus und staatliches Strafen: Figurationen der sozialen Kontrolle," in *Die Sinnprovinz der Kriminalität*, ed. Henner Hess and Henning Schmidt-Semisch, Wiesbaden: Verlag für Sozialwissenschaften, 2014, pp. 187-202.

Habermas, Jürgen, *Theorie des kommunikativen Handelns. Band I: Handlungsrationalität und gesellschaftliche Rationalisierung*, Frankfurt a.M.: Suhrkamp, 1998.

Hess, Henner, "Terrorismus: Quo vadis? Kurzfristige Prognosen und mittelfristige Orientierungen," in *Terrorismus und Extremismus: Der Zukunft auf der Spur. Polizei und Forschung, Vol. 3*, ed. Uwe E. Kemmesies, München: Luchterhand, 2006, pp. 105-150.

Hoffman, Bruce, and Gordon H. McCormick, "Terrorism, Signaling, and Suicide Attack," *Studies in Conflict & Terrorism* 4 (2004): 243-281.

Horgan, John; and Kurt Braddock, "Rehabilitating the Terrorists? Challenges in Assessing the Effectiveness of De-radicalization Programs," *Terrorism and Political Violence* 2 (2010): 267-291.

Jäger, Herbert, and Lorenz Böllinger, "Studien zur Sozialisation von Terroristen," in *Lebenslaufanalysen. Analysen zum Terrorismus,Vol. 2*, ed. Bundesministerium des Innern, Opladen: Westdeutscher Verlag, 1981, pp. 117-243.

Korn, Judy, and Harald Weilnböck, "Der lange Abschied von Hass und Gewalt, " *Aus Politik und Zeitgeschichte* (2013): 32-39.

LaFree, Gary and Laura Dugan, "Research on Terrorism and Countering Terrorism," *Crime and Justice* 1 (2009): 413-477.

McCauley, Clark and Sophia Moskalenko, "Mechanisms of Political Radicalization: Pathways toward Terrorism," *Terrorism and Political Violence* 3 (2008): 415-433.

Münkler, Herfried, *Die neuen Kriege*, Reinbek bei Hamburg: Rowohlt, 5th ed., 2003.

Neumann, Peter R., "Prisons and Terrorism. Radicalisation and De-radicalisation in 15 Countries," *International Centre for the Study of Radicalisation and Political Violence publication*, London, 2010, pp. 1-68.

Neumann, Peter R.,"Radikalisierung, Deradikalisierung und Extremismus," *Aus Politik und Zeitgeschichte* (2013): 3-10.

Nesser, Petter, "Profiles of Jihadist Terrorists in Europe," in *A Future for the Young, Options for helping Middle Eastern Youth Escape the Trap of Radicalization*, ed. Cheryl Bernard, Wahington: RAND, 2006, pp. 31-49.

Popitz, Heinrich, *Phänomene der Macht*, Tübingen: Mohr, 2nd ed., 1992.

Porges, Marisa, "Getting Deradicalization Right," *Foreign Affairs* 3 (2011): 155-157.

Richardson, Louise, *What Terrorists Want: Understanding the Terrorist Threat*, New York: Random House, 2007.

Sack, Fritz, "Staat, Gesellschaft und politische Gewalt: Zur 'Pathologie' politischer Konflikte," in *Protest und Reaktion. Analysen zum Terrorismus, Vol. 4/2*, ed. Bundesministerium des Innern, Opladen: Westdeutscher Verlag, 1984, pp. 17-386.

Scheerer, Sebastian, "Ein theoretisches Modell zur Erklärung sozialrevolutionärer Gewalt," in *Angriff auf das Herz des Staates: Soziale Entwicklung und Terrorismus, Vol. 1*, ed. Henner Hess, Martin Moerings, Dieter Paas, and Sebastian Scheerer, Frankfurt: Suhrkamp, 1988, pp. 75-189.

Scheerer, Sebastian, *Die Zukunft des Terrorismus: Drei Szenarien*, Lüneburg: Zu Klampen, 2002.

Scheerer, Sebastian, "Agonaler Autismus und diskrepante Interpunktion. Zwei Restriktionen im Umgang mit terroristischer Gewalt," *IKS Working Paper Series* 2 (2011): 4-18.

Schmid, Alex P., and Eric Price, "Selected Literature on radicalization and de-radicalization of terrorists: Monographs, Edited Volumes, Grey Literature and Prime Articles published since the 1960s," *Crime, Law and Social Change* 55 (2011): 337-348.

Schmidtchen, Gerhard, "Terroristische Karrieren," in *Lebenslaufanalysen. Analysen zum Terrorismus, Vol. 2*, ed. Bundesministerium des Innern, Opladen: Westdeutscher Verlag, 1981, pp. 13-77.

Sedgwick, Mark, "The Concept of Radicalization as a Source of Confusion," *Terrorism and Political Violence* 4 (2010): 479-494.

Sedgwick, Mark, "Jihadist ideology, Western counter-ideology, and the ABC model," *Critical Studies on Terrorism* 3 (2012): 359-372.

Senechal de la Roche, Roberta, "Collective Violence as Social Control," *Sociological Forum* 1(1996): 97-128.

Steinberg, Guido, "Jihadistische Radikalisierung im Internet und mögliche Gegenmaßnahmen," *Aus Politik und Zeitgeschichte* (2013): 17-25.

Stern, Jessica, "Mind over Martyr. How to Deradicalize Islamist Extremists," *Foreign Affairs* 3 (2010): 95-108.

Stern, Jessica, "Deradicalization or Disengagement of Terrorists: Is it Possible?," in *Future Challenges in National Security and Law*, ed. Peter Berkowitz, Stanford, CA: Hoover Institution Press, 2010, pp. 1-18.

Vidino, Lorenzo, and James Brandon, *Countering Radicalization in Europe*, International Centre for the Study of Radicalisation and Political Violence (ICSR) policy report, London: International Center for the Study of Radicalisation and Political Violence, 2012.

Waldmann, Peter, *Terrorismus: Provokation der Macht*, München: Gerling 1998.

# Youth: The Challenge of Extremism and Terrorism

*Thomas Koruth Samuel*

## *A. Introduction*

It always starts with a story. Indoctrination, radicalization, recruitment and terrorism all have their roots in a narrative; that of the terrorists.

Given this simple yet profound truth, we have to ask ourselves a few questions:

> What is the story of the enemy?
>
> How have they presented this story?
>
> And why has it gained traction, particularly among young people?

Perhaps, in our efforts to eliminate the terrorist threat, we have forgotten that behind the particular individual lies a story that, unfortunately, continues to remain long after the terrorist has fallen. And I would argue that it is this story that we need to study, target and to counter.

Given this, I hope to distill in this paper some of the arguments put forth by terrorists and extremists in the Southeast Asian region and to suggest some ways to counter their story. In this regard, it is interesting to note that while there have been numerous attempts to classify and categorize terrorists based on their ideology and strategy, there are some general characteristics which interestingly cuts across the various groups. So, while there will always be differences between these groups this study would like to consider certain shared characteristics.

On that note, of equal importance is the need to develop our own tailored narrative, simply because debunking something without providing an alternative is of little use. I also aim to share some challenges that we will face and the lessons that we have learned in the sphere of youth and terrorism.

## B. Youth and Extremism

### I. The Danger Signs

> "Oh, East is East, and West is West, and never the twain shall meet."
> (Rudyard Kipling)

Is there a connection between young people and violence and, by extension, terrorism?

In Peter Singer's book, 'Children at War', he states that 300.000 boys and girls under the age of 18 are combatants fighting in almost 75% of the world's conflicts. It is sad to note that 80% of these conflicts where children are present include fighters under the age of 15 and approximately 40% of the armed organizations in the world (157 of 366) use child soldiers.[1] The vast majority of them have been forced to participate and in a sense are victims themselves.

What do the experts say?

Professor Joseph Liow from Singapore warned that militants often target youth, ranging in age from early teens to young adults[2] while Professor Kumar Ramakrishna postulated that youths, particularly males between the ages of 18 and 35, have always been the focus of terrorist organizations, citing the Japanese Red Army and the Italian Red Brigade as examples.[3] Noor Huda Ismail, a counter-terrorism expert based in Indonesia,[4] highlighted that in Indonesia, since the Darul Islam (DI) era, terrorist organizations have targeted people as young as 16 to 17 years old.

The corresponding assumption that young age is a common thread of a broad range of very different terrorist movements is reflected by the facts. The Mumbai attacks in November 2008 that left 165 civilians and security personnel dead, for instance, was a series of coordinated attacks orchestrated by ten individuals – all of them below 30 years of age. The eldest terrorist, Nazir/Abu Umer, was only 28 years old while the average age of

---

1 See Singer, *Children at War,* 2005.

2 Joseph Liow, interview by author, S. Rajaratnam School of International Studies (RSIS), Nanyang Technological University, Singapore, 10 March 2011.

3 Kumar Ramakrishna (Professor), interview by author, S. Rajaratnam School of International Studies (RSIS), Nanyang Technological University, 9 March 2011.

4 Noor Huda Ismail, interview by author, Semarang, Indonesia, 5 April 2011.

the other nine terrorists was only 23 years. The leader, Ismail Khan, was just 25 years old.

Accordingly, the extent of the involvement of youth in terrorists activities was particularly highlighted by the UK's MI5 Chief, Jonathan Evans, when he stated that 'extremists were methodically and intentionally targeting young people and children in the UK,' and that groups like Al-Qaeda were recruiting children as young as 15 to wage 'a deliberate campaign of terror' in Britain. In his first speech since taking over MI5, Evans warned that extremists were "radicalizing, indoctrinating and grooming young, vulnerable people to carry out acts of terrorism" and that urgent action was required on the part of the UK government to "protect its children from exploitation by violent extremists."[5] This risk is addressed by the present paper.

## *II. The Root of the Problem*

Often, when we see the tragic face of terrorism, be it in form of a suicide bomber at a place of worship or a car bomb exploding at a popular night spot, we forget that what we see is only the culmination of the work of the terrorist. The incident is only the final result of a process that took both time and effort to develop.[6]

If this act of violence is the result of a process, how and why did this process begin and succeed and in how far are our efforts to counter this process actually working?

Most studies indicate that violent action is a possible consequence of radical thought. At this juncture, it is pertinent to note that the author does not suggest that all radical thoughts lead to violent action but rather that most terrorist violent action has its beginnings in radical thought.

That being the case, it is pertinent for us to ask if we can actually counter radical thought through the sole use of hard power:

5 Johnston, "MI5: Al-Qaeda Recruiting U.K. Children for Terror," http://www.telegraph.co.uk/news/uknews/1568363/MI5-Al-Qaeda-recruiting-UK-children-for-terror.html, 7 November 2007.

6 Samuel, *Reaching the Youth: Countering the Terrorist Narrative*, 2012.

Can ideology be defeated solely through kinetic force? Or to phrase it in another way, can we defeat an idea with a bullet?

This is a significant question, for the reality on the ground is that the majority of counter-terrorist efforts at the strategic, tactical and operational level depend a great deal on the use of force. While it is possible to understand the role of force when actively countering violent action, it might be presumptuous to assume that kinetic force could have the same level of success when dealing with an idea or thought.

So where does that leave us? While a great deal of thinking and resources have rightfully gone into developing an effective counter-terrorism strategy against the terrorist use of force, too little has gone into developing parallel strategies in countering the idea or narrative of the terrorist.

Simply put, we have allowed radical ideas to develop into violent action without doing enough about it. This 'intervention-at-a-later-stage' strategy has allowed the terrorists a distinct advantage in capturing the 'hearts and minds' of young people.[7]

Perhaps it is time to change.

## *C. The Narrative of the Terrorist*

### *I. The Premise of the Terrorist*

What then is the story of the terrorist?

I would like to postulate that the main rhetoric of the terrorist comprises a simple three-step progression, which is formed as follows.[8]

> There are injustices occurring in many parts of the world against members of the own group;
>
> there is a need to act; and
>
> violence is the only possible response.

These straightforward assumptions particularly appeal to idealistic and simplistic youths and have the added advantage of being partially true. Firstly, it is reiterated and reinforced by the terrorist narrative that there

---

7 See Samuel, *Reaching the Youth.*

8 See Samuel, *Reaching the Youth.*

are tremendous acts of injustice, cruelty and discrimination, causing incredible misery, suffering and anguish to numerous innocent people all around the world. According to Roy Anthony Rodgers from University Malaya, terrorists are very adept at exploiting and manipulating such grievances.[9] Reports, images and life-witness accounts, authentic or manipulated, are all skillfully deployed to bear witness to this worldwide suffering, and the message is subsequently conveyed by the terrorists to any interested individual through any available means.

Secondly, the gauntlet is thrown in the form of a question:

> What are you going to do about this?
>
> What is your response to this tragedy?

Harry Setyo R,[10] a former terrorist in Indonesia, relates from his own experience, how terrorist recruiters would draw the youths' attention to the plight of suffering Muslims, and subsequently question them on their response to such tragedies. Very similarly, Marhmudi Hariano alias Yusuf highlights how as a young man he felt compelled to defend his fellow Muslims, whom he perceived as suffering, wherever they were, after being exposed to the rhetoric of the terrorists.[11] Sydney Jones reiterates that in the Indonesian case, the premise that 'this is the way that you can actively help your fellow Muslims', functions as a strong and effective recruiting strategy for the terrorists.[12]

Given the usual degree of emotional volatility, the perceived need for action and the high sense of idealism among young people, the need to act upon these diligently presented injustices would naturally be very great. Indeed, young people often wonder how it is possible for such terrible injustices to have continued all this time without anyone taking action to counter them. This, then, very much motivates the youth to act and correct what appears as inacceptable injustice of terrible scale.

It is significant to note that, with the corresponding narratives, the terrorist often has not strayed far from the truth: there are numerous cases of severe wrongdoing happening all around the world causing great pain and

---

9 Roy Anthony Rodgers, interview by author, University Malaya, 26 January 2010.

10 Harry Setyo R., interview by author, Semarang, Indonesia, 5 April 2011.

11 Marhmudi Hariano alias Yusuf, interview by author, Semarang, Indonesia, 5 April 2011.

12 Sydney Jones, interview by author, Jakarta, Indonesia, 6 April 2011.

misery to the innocent. Also, acting to counter these flagrant abuses is not only morally correct; it is also the right thing to do.

Young people not only are able to both identify with and comprehend these two premises but they are also drawn by idealism and altruism to wholeheartedly support these ideas. It is however here that the terrorists slip in the third premise, innocuously, as the most natural progression from the initial two premises: violence is the only possible response. In an interview, Roy Anthony Rodgers[13] highlights that the assumption that there was 'no other way' and that extreme action was 'the only recourse left', was a very important triggering factor for youths to embrace violence.

Therefore, the young people are shown visual and graphic evidence of the first premise – that injustice is thriving and causing tremendous misery. Once their conscience is seared and their idealism evoked, they are confronted with the second premise: that they now have to act. In this excited state, where emotions are stirred and passions are running high, the third premise, that violence is the sole alternative, is offered. Often, it is blindly accepted, with little critical evaluation or thinking on the part of the young person. Hence, critical thinking, logic and reason are abandoned.

In the book *A Force More Powerful: A Century of Non-Violent Conflict*, Ackerman and DuVall has this to say,

> But calls to arms leave little time for thought […] the avatars of violence never developed a systematic understanding of how their chosen sanctions – firefights, bombing, street battles or terror – were supposed to replace old forms of authority with new opportunities for freedom […]. Instead, they wove a vague but seductive mythology around the putative power of violence.[14]

Thus, it is significant to note that in the hands of terrorists, the youths do not just arrive at the conclusion that violence is a possible alternative; rather, they are carefully, methodically and systematically led through various stages involving their mental and emotional faculties, passing from intellectual analysis to a stirred conscience and finally to a perceived undeniable conclusion that violence is the sole alternative[15] to resolve the then most crucial issue for them.

---

13 Roy Anthony Rodgers, interview by author, University Malaya, 26 January 2010.

14 Ackerman and DuVall, *A Force More Powerful: A Century of Non-Violent Conflict*, 2000.

15 See Samuel, *Reaching the Youth.*

### *II. The Narrative of the Terrorist and its Inconsistencies*

We have looked at the method the terrorists use to reach out to the young, but what is the message that they wish to convey?

Or in other words, what is the narrative of the terrorist?

I would argue, that like all good lies, the story the terrorists put forward contains many elements of the truth, providing the terrorists' message with a great deal of credibility and believability. These half-truths then dominate the terrorist narrative.

**Myth # 1:** 'Violence is the Only Way'

It is important to note that the violence of the terrorists that the author speaks of here does not refer to the act of self-defense but rather to indiscriminate and deliberate attacks on civilians and properties with the express purpose to hurt, kill and destroy.

The first myth that is propagated by the terrorist is that this form of violence is the only possible way. The audience, particularly the youth, is made to believe that the world that they dream of can only be shaped through violence. Violence is seen as a cleansing force to rid the world of the evil that thrives on inequality, injustice and discrimination. In this light, violence is seen as both permissible and justifiable.

Also, the use of force is touted as an operational and strategic option that will propel the terrorists group towards success and the accomplishing of their objectives and goals. Violence, then, is branded both as the morally justifiable and tactically superior option that will in due time ensure complete victory. The Islamic State (IS) has been superb in developing this premise and continues to draw many captured by such a notion. In terms of recruitment, in May 2015, Ban Ki-moon, the United Nations Secretary-General warned that the flow of Foreign Terrorist Fighters (FTFs) into IS and other extremist groups had increased from 15,000 fighters from 80 countries in November 2014 to 25,000 fighters from 100 countries at present. This translates to a staggering 70% increase.[16] Said and

16 'At debate, UN and Security Council Renew Pledge to Counter Foreign Terrorist Fighters', UN News Centre, 29 May 2015, http://www.un.org/apps/news/story.asp?NewsID=51005#.VXcikU2Jhdg.

done, their affinity to extreme violence is said to be one of the reason for their apparent success.

It is significant to note that youths having a comparatively strong disposition for rebelling against all forms of authority and questioning all its assumptions, are surprisingly meek and often seem to tamely accept the premises of the terrorists with shocking ease. This lack of critical thinking on the part of the youths, according to Roy Anthony Rodgers,[17] is the result of a deficient education system which makes youths susceptible to radical teachings.

At this particular juncture, the authorities could emulate the terrorists, who have been very successful in getting the youths to question authority. Perhaps, the time has come to give the terrorists a dose of their own medicine. While the questioning and potentially rebellious nature of the youth is probably what led them to get involved with terrorism, there is also considerable potential to use those very same traits to get them to question and possibly rebel against their own terrorist groups. This possibility of disengagement, according to Kumar Ramakrishna, often comes when young people gradually mature and develop the ability to critically think about and evaluate the situation.[18]

When dealing with young people who often 'reprimand' the author for his ignorance and proceed to inform him that the terrorists are using violence because that is the only alternative, the author than challenges them to examine the rhetoric used by the terrorists.

The author then proceeds to ask these young people to list for him groups that have used violence and, through violence, successfully achieved their objectives. Usually, what follows is dead silence. Saying this, the author does have to caution that there are some instances where there is empirical evidence of groups that have utilized violence and achieved some short-term goals. This being said, groups that have had considerable long-term success as a result of their use of violence are relatively few.

The idea then is to challenge the young people to do three things:

- Firstly, for them to show the objectives of these terrorists groups (which in most cases focus on the liberation of a certain group of peo-

17 Roy Anthony Rodgers, interview by author, University Malaya, 26 January 2010.

18 Kumar Ramakrishna, interview by author, Nanyang technological University (NTU), 9 March 2011.

ple from foreign invaders, the end of discrimination, the need for justice and equality etc.);
- Secondly, to compare these objectives with the actions that have been taken by the terrorists (indiscriminate bombings, beheadings of prisoners, killing of civilians through suicide attacks); and
- Thirdly, to analyze if any of their actions have helped them achieve their objectives.

The purpose of this exercise is to show the young people that strategically speaking, the tactic of terrorism via violence is an inferior one. This is important, because thus far, most counter-narratives (if any) against the terrorists focus on the moral argument that violence is both illegal and immoral. While this is true, the argument loses its potency when it is shown that the enemies of the terrorists are themselves at times extremely violent, evil people and therefore the presumption is that violence against such an enemy is permissible as it is simply an act of self-defense against the more malevolent authorities.

Therefore, at present, most of our arguments that emphasizes the immorality of violence fall on the deaf ears of a generation who are very well aware of the injustices and cruelty perpetrated by 'legitimate' authorities and states and who therefore consider it hypocritical that these actors be spared from the violence that they themselves seem so freely to dispense. Therefore, a counter-narrative that focuses on the immorality of the violence perpetrated by the 'perceived aggressors' gains very little traction in the hearts and minds of the young.

However, should we be able to challenge the effectiveness of the strategy that is being employed by the terrorists, we need not waste time defending the 'wickedness of the regime in power', but can focus instead on how, tactically, the terrorists are using a strategy that – statistically and historically speaking – has very little chance of success.

Hence, the author's question to the young people is, 'why would you suggest a strategy that has so little chance of success to a group that you actually support and sympathize with?'.

The author tries to show the young people that, by first looking at what the terrorists proclaim to do through their manifestos, and then considering their actions and analyzing their subsequent impact, two main conclusions can be derived:

At best, violence is a tactically inferior strategy; and at worst, terrorists are aware of this but have their own vested interests which have very little to do with their stated objectives of helping the people.

Besides showcasing the tactical inferiority of violence, there is also the need to document the inherent weaknesses and dangers that come from using the strategy of violence.

Firstly, there is the ironic possibility of the victim becoming the aggressor when violence is used. By definition, the term victim suggests an individual or group that is marginalized physically, mentally or even emotionally. When such victims resort to acts of violence such as indiscriminate bombing to deliberately hurt and kill civilians or to destroy property, the idea that they are victims no longer seems tenable and instead they now take on the mantle of the aggressors. This does little to further their cause.

Secondly, when violence is used, we are, figuratively speaking, on a very slippery slope. Violence signifies the end of any effort to reconcile differences through other means such as negotiations or compromise. It means that there is no longer room for discourse or discussion to solve the problem or disagreement. Should this be the perception, then we must not be surprised when violence is therefore seen as the only way to deal with a dispute or a disagreement. Indeed, history has shown us that leaders, who achieve power through violence, are just as often overthrown through violence. As remarked by a very perceptive man, "All who draw the sword will die by the sword."

Also, this could explain why terrorist groups often break into splinter groups, each preferring to go their own way or at times even turning their weapons on each other, when a disagreement arises. This is due to violence being seen as the only option to solve a problem. Hence, terrorist groups who engage in violence lay the seed for the younger generation, particularly for those born and raised in conflict situations, to see things solely through the lenses of force and aggression. Simply put, the language of violence will be the only language spoken.

Is that the legacy that we are willing to let the terrorist leave behind for a community that we sympathize with?

These ideas should be presented to the young people to allow them the chance to study the issue from a different perspective.

**Myth # 2:** 'We are doing it for the People'

Most, if not all terrorist groups proclaim that all their actions, particularly the ones that raise concerns in terms of morality and legitimacy, are done 'for the people.' Hence, following their line of argument, violence is but a natural response on behalf of a marginalized group of people against an unjust authority. The late leader of the Liberation Tigers of Tamil Eelam (LTTE), Vellupillai Prabakharan, echoed this thought when he said,

> It is the plight of the Tamil people that compelled me to take up arms. I felt outrage at the inhuman atrocities perpetrated against an innocent people. The ruthless manner, in which our people were murdered, massacred, maimed [...].[19]

Hence, terrorists have been able to shift attention from their insidious use of violence by characterizing it as the justifiable need for self-defense on behalf of a suffering and victimized people-group.

In the author's engagement with students, he mentions how the late Osama bin Laden often reiterated his passion for defending the rights of the oppressed people. The author then asks the students how the late Osama came into the position of representing the people he claimed to be fighting for.

> Who elected Osama to take this role?
>
> Did he get a mandate from the people that he claimed to be fighting for?
>
> Why could he not go through more conventional means, such as trying to get elected as the leader of the people he claimed to be fighting for? At the very least, did the majority of the people-group that he purportedly represented join his organization?

To bring this argument to the level of the young people, there is a need to question them on whether they would allow themselves to be ruled and spoken for by a group or an individual whom they did not choose.

There is a need to ask the young people to consider if there are any differences between a terrorist organization, which claims to speak and act on behalf of a group and a malevolent dictator who decides, unilaterally and with impunity, what is good for the people he forcibly rules.

---

19 Tamil National Leader Hon. V. Prabakharan's interview, *The Week (India)*, March 23, 1986 as quoted by Richardson, *What Terrorists Want: Understanding the Terrorist Threat*, 2006.

The question must be asked why people are aghast when authorities come to power through force, yet treat as legitimate the actions of terrorist groups which have not even been legally chosen to represent the people they claim to be fighting for.

Is it justifiable for a terrorist group to claim that they are representatives of a suffering group of people simply because they are fighting for them? If that is the case, hypothetically, can a Malaysian who is angry with what is going on in Palestine and intends to fight for the rights of the Palestinian people, immediately assume the role of the representative of the Palestinians, simply because he has decided to fight for them?

Is this method acceptable?

Ironically, this is what is claimed by the terrorist. The premise of the terrorist in this situation is very simple;

> We claim that you are marginalized.
>
> Because of that, we will fight for you.
>
> This very act of fighting on your behalf is sufficient to give us the right to represent you and your interest.

The author challenges the young people to consider the logic of the terrorist, which implies that a people-group that is suffering from some form of oppression by an unjust authority no longer has the right to choose who should represent them and by default has no choice but to accept these terrorists as their representatives.

During the author's sessions with young people, he often puts up a slideshow of pictures featuring the two planes crashing into the World Trade Centre Towers on 11 September 2001. He then asks the students to ponder the statement of the terrorist perpetrators that this was purportedly done for the people, and after that, to consider these two questions:

> Firstly, who are the people that this was done for?
>
> The people in Afghanistan?
>
> The people in Palestine?
>
> The marginalized Muslims in different parts of the world?
>
> Secondly, what good has it done them or any other group of people?
>
> In fact, what do we actually see happening?

The country and the people of Afghanistan suffered tremendously after the 11 September bombings in the United States.

The plight of the Palestinians has altered little since the New York World Trade Centre bombings.

Muslims in many parts of the world have suffered both directly and indirectly after the attacks in the United States.

So who has benefited from all this? Certainly not the people that these terrorist groups claim to be fighting for.

Often, in our engagements with young people, when these questions are asked, there is no clear consensus as to who 'benefited' from the 9/11 atrocities. This is quite astounding, for Al-Qaeda has categorically stated, over and over again, that it is fighting for the people. We are, however, still unclear on whom they are fighting for, and how this action has brought any benefit to these people.

We need to let the young people know that while injustice and discrimination by authorities often cause great suffering and pain to innocent people, there is also a need to be wary of any individual or organization that takes it upon themselves to represent the victimized group without going through any due process, particularly when the manner in which they hope to achieve their objectives involves indiscriminate and arbitrary violence.

Often when the author points these ideas out to the young people, he finds a few angry ones, launching into a tirade on how the terrorists are up against an evil enemy that has shown little mercy and has cruelly wronged many. It is at these moments that the author relates to the young people the story of the famous Kurdish General Saladin. Legend has it that his soldiers brought to him prisoners of war during the crusades and were waiting to torture them. What instead transpired was that General Saladin instructed that they be treated with the greatest care and respect. His astonished and angry soldiers then recounted what the enemy had done to their captured comrades and how this was the opportune time for them to get their revenge. General Saladin's response to the outbursts that came from his soldiers is worth remembering: "Since when did your enemies become your teachers?"

While we acknowledge that numerous authorities and people in power have made cruel and evil decisions that have caused great pain and misery to many, we also have to put forth to the young people that this by no means makes terrorism or the act of killing, hurting, and destroying innocent civilians and their properties justifiable.

Simply put, two wrongs will never make a right.

**Myth # 3:** 'We have No Choice'

Terrorists, when confronted about their use of violence against the innocent, often claim that they had very little choice in the matter. They feel as if their hands were forced and that they had no alternative but violence. The late LTTE leader Vellupillai Prabakharan stated:

> The Tamil people have been expressing their grievances in parliament for more than three decades. Their voices went unheard like cries in the wilderness. In Sri Lanka there is no parliamentary democracy where our people could effectively represent their aspirations. What passes as parliament in Sri Lanka is an authoritarian rule founded on the tyranny of the majority.[20]

Hence, following this logic, the choice of violence was not taken by them but was rather forced upon them through the various actions of the authorities.

The question that the author poses to the youths is, 'what is the justification for killing the innocent?'

Have they exhausted all other means before they have come to the conclusion that they have no choice but to turn to violence, or is violence seen as the less difficult path to take in wanting to achieve their objectives?

Does it make sense in rational, moral or religious terms to take the life of another due to the pain and misery brought about by a third party, solely on the basis that the aggressor and the victim of terrorism had some things in common, such as their nationality, race or religion?

As mentioned earlier, does that not make the victim the new aggressor?

Is it not logical to conclude that using violence against a stronger opponent (as is in the case of terrorism) would in most cases further enrage the aggressor, causing greater violence to be unleashed on the victims?

Will the act of terrorism not alienate the victims from the mainstream and will they not now lose support when they engage in acts of violence?

Is this a good strategy?

Should violence be used, will it not mean that the victim has to give up the moral high ground which is often the only advantage he or she possesses?

Given the doubtful effectiveness of the tactic of violence, is that trade-off a wise one?

---

20 Tamil National Leader Hon. V. Prabakharan's interview, *The Week (India)*, March 23, 1986.

Will it not ensure that the possibility of compromise is less tenable and further justifying the authorities in question to continue their unjust ways?

Given all these questions, we need to highlight to our young people that the premise of the terrorist – 'that they have no choice', is ill conceived.

**Myth # 4:** 'We are Representing the Oppressed'

Almost all terrorist groups claim to be fighting for the oppressed and marginalized of society.

It is pertinent for us to ask the youth whether these terrorists are the best candidates to take up that job and what qualities and attributes they have that allow them the right to do so.

It is also significant to ponder whether terrorists have a vested interest in ensuring that the conflict continues, irrespective of whether it is detrimental to the people they claim to represent. In many cases, where conflicts are passed from one generation to another, terrorism is seen as an industry that provides a vocation, security and status. In such a situation, should peace occur, what would happen to terrorist group members, who owe their power, position and strength to the conflict?

In such situations, would it be likely that terrorists would give up their position of power and strength, and instead take the course that, while being detrimental to their position, would bring about greater benefit to the people they claim to be fighting for?

Should they not wish to do so, what then can the people do?

And as mentioned earlier, what good have they brought the oppressed people that they claim to be fighting for?

What are the tangible and concrete benefits that have brought to the already suffering masses?

In terms of economic, social, health, culture and welfare, how have the oppressed benefited from the actions of the terrorists?

Indeed, have they not in fact suffered more due to the actions taken by the terrorists?

Arguably, this being the case, the actions of the terrorists, which in most cases further deprive and marginalize the community, ironically ensure that the community in question never reaches a stage where it is educationally and economically able to challenge the power of the malevolent authority.

Also, should the day come when these terrorists actually wield power, would it be possible, should the populace wish it, for them to be turned out of power?

Would Indonesians be able to dismiss Jemaah Islamiyah and elect another party to power?

Would the people of Afghanistan be able to do the same with the Taliban?

Essentially, while terrorists justify their actions to wield power in order to represent the peoples true wishes, they seem to care very little of the peoples wishes when it does not suite their agenda to stay in power.

**Myth # 5:** Our Recruits are Committed to the Cause and Victory Will be Ours

Terrorists are also adept at giving the impression that it is simply a matter of time before they attain success as a result of their struggles. While the reality on the ground may be far different, the terrorists successfully convince the potential youth recruits that it is just a matter of time before they are victorious. They do so for two distinct purposes. Firstly, to show-case and exaggerate the strength and advantages they have over the enemy, be it in terms of the dedication and skill of their recruits, their brilliant and courageous leaders, divine assistance, or the sheer potency of their tactical, operational and strategic plans. They seek to convince the young people that though they may appear to be the weaker party, they are in actual fact going to emerge triumphant.

Hence, terrorists place great emphasis upon the dissemination of rhetoric on the quality of their recruits. They thus seek to balance the equation when dealing with a numerically superior adversary by inspiring more potential recruits to join them. In cases of religious-based terrorist groups, God, as the all-powerful force, is also prominently highlighted. The assurance of divine intervention not only gives credence and legitimacy to their struggle, but also provides reassurance to the youth and instills perseverance when things are not going well for the terrorist organization. Terrorists are also very well aware that including the divine equation not only increases hope in young people but ensures their loyalty, as the young individual is no longer fighting for just a group, but for a group that is perceived to be carrying out the will of God.

In non-religious terrorist based groups, the leaders of terrorist groups are also often highlighted as beacons of hope and inspiration. Terrorist organizations constantly work on the image of such leaders, making them appear like heroic and courageous legendary figures, so as to inspire awe and devotion on the part of the followers, sympathy on the part of the population and even fear on the part of the enemy. Stories are circulated about the brilliance of the leadership in inflicting crushing defeats on the enemy and the absolute fear on the part of the adversary when dealing with these leaders. All these efforts are carefully designed to give the impression that despite what is being said by the media or regardless of the situation on the ground, the terrorist organization is on the path to victory.

Terrorists also often seek to discredit the authorities by painting them as being incompetent, corrupt and lacking the mandate and goodwill of the population. As again mentioned by the late LTTE leader Vellupillai Prabakharan, "[I]n Sri Lanka there is no parliamentary democracy where our people could effectively represent their aspirations. What passes as parliament in Sri Lanka is an authoritarian rule founded on the tyranny of the majority."[21]

Hence, while possibly acknowledging the superiority of the enemy in terms of strength of numbers and military might, terrorist organizations constantly portray the enemy as being on the brink of collapse due to the intrinsic and extrinsic problems that it faces as a result of its own corruption or illegitimacy. Any positive development on the part of the adversary is simply seen as mere propaganda to shore up support for a dying regime and any setback on the part of the terrorist group is seen as a small, temporary setback that will have little effect on the final outcome of the conflict. This unrealistic assessment of the proceedings of war is often uncritically accepted by the young people, who have been indoctrinated to accept the rhetoric of their leaders.

**Myth # 6:** Our Enemy Knows Only the Language of Violence

With this premise, the terrorists seek to depict the enemy (most often the ruling authority) as a party that acts and reacts only through the lens of violence. Hence, compromise, negotiations and discussions with such an enemy will simply be pointless, not because these strategies have not been attempted, or because of a lack of effort by the 'victims', but rather because of the inherent nature of the 'enemy' that refuses to use or recognize

21 Tamil National Leader Hon. V. Prabakharan's interview, *The Week (India)*, March 23, 1986.

any form of interaction but violence. When Al Qaeda launched its English-language online terror magazine called "Resurgence", there was a brief video combining audio from a 1965 Malcolm X speech justifying violence, including the quote "talk the language that they understand", with images of both U.S. soldiers and Islamic militants in a purported attack on a U.S. base in Afghanistan and the Boston Marathon bombings.[22] Simply put, the enemies' are thought to understand only the language of blood[23], that is, terrorist violence.

Given this scenario, the option of violence is therefore forced upon the 'victims' as, they are told, no other forms of interaction with the authorities will be successful. By using this line of thought, the terrorists again try to show that the option of violence has been forced upon them.

In the author's engagements with undergraduates, this is often the refrain that he hears. 'How else can one deal with an enemy that only knows the language of violence?'

This premise has some underlying assumptions that need to be examined closely. Firstly, there is the assumption that the enemy is homogeneous and that violence is accepted by all on the other side. This is seldom the case. Even when the Nazi atrocities were at their height, there were numerous Germans and people of other nationalities who refused to 'simply follow orders' and courageously chose to take a different path. If this is the case, is it then justifiable to label everyone on the other side as the enemy and even worse, to target and terrorize them?

Secondly, assuming that the authorities are indeed unjust and violent, there is the assumption that there is nothing that can be done through non-violent ways to change their ways and mindset. This assumption runs contrary to what we see in reality, when we consider statesmen such as Nelson Mandela who was labeled a terrorist in South Africa, but later went to become the President of the rainbow nation and a force for unification, earning the respect and admiration of many who, prior to that, condoned and practiced the apartheid system of governance.

---

22 Cole and Windrem, "Al Qaeda Announces New English-Language Terror Magazine," *NBC News*, 9 March 2014, http://www.nbcnews.com/news/investigations/al-qaeda-announces-new-english-language-terror-magazine-n48531.

23 O' Balance, *Language of Violence: The Blood Politics of Terrorism San Rafael*, 1979.

Often times, the author has found that this question gets young people to seriously rethink their previous conviction that terrorist use of violence would bring about positive change.

The reality on the ground suggests that very rarely is it seen that lasting peace, which is acceptable to both sides, can be achieved when aggression and violence are used to resolve the conflict. While it is probable that short-term peace might be possible, it is at times simply the lull before the storm. Hence, one might be able to win the war through use of force, but unless one achieves peace, it is simply a matter of placing one's self between the end of World War One and the beginning of World War Two.

Mahatma Gandhi, who in his lifetime confronted hatred, prejudice and suffering without resorting to violence, once remarked, "an eye for an eye, and in the end, the world will grow blind."

## *III. Challenging the Myths: The Actors*

It is pertinent to note that the terrorist rhetoric mentioned earlier, particularly their justification for the use of violence, finds tremendous traction with young people. In this regard, the author would argue that authorities, in their counter-terrorism strategies, need to pay more attention to debunking and developing an 'alternative' or counter-narrative to that of the terrorists.[24] While great attention is paid to countering the terrorists mainly via hard power and kinetic force, scant attention is given to the fact that much ground has been lost, particularly in tackling the youth at the mental, emotional and intellectual planes. In this regard, hard and searching questions need to be asked[25], among them being:

When a youth is confronted with the terrorists' rhetoric and propaganda, does he possess the ability to critically analyze the assumptions and presuppositions of the terrorists and is he equipped to counter the narrative of violence subscribed to by the terrorists?,

Should not the authorities have a more active role in challenging the myths of the terrorists? and

Do the current counter-terrorism efforts take into account the need for developing a counter-narrative to the terrorists' own narrative?

---

24 Saifudeen, interview by author, Home Team Academy, Singapore, 8 March 2011.
25 Samuel, *Reaching the Youth.*

### 1. The Audience

Who would be the target audience of such a counter-narrative programme?

One would think that the individuals that should be targeted in such a counter-narrative programme should be those that have displayed signs of radicalization, belong to susceptible or vulnerable groups already on the radar screen of the terrorists as potential recruits.

The rationale would be that we identify such individuals by perhaps profiling them and then focus our resources on debunking the terrorist's arguments as well as providing them with working non-violent alternatives to address grievances and resolve conflicts.

I would however, beg to differ.

While it might certainly be good to ensure that those who are radicalized or are in the path to be radicalized are exposed to some form of counter-radicalization program. Focusing our attention solely on this specific group might be detrimental in the long run.

Firstly, how do we identify those that are cognitively or mentally radicalized?

While there are some youth, who might publicly demonstrate through their words or actions that they support terrorism, it would be naïve to imagine that this is the case for all.

When the Islamic State (IS) threat initially surfaced, there were numerous public declarations of support from various individuals, particularly over the Internet. However, over a period of time, when it was evident that the security and law enforcement agencies were closely monitoring the cyber-space, such public pronouncements (without hiding their identity) were less visible.

The point being there is the possibility that there are numerous recruits, sympathizers and supporters, who at varying degrees might support terrorism, but choose not to reveal so for the obvious reasons. That being the case, a counter-narrative program that focuses only on those who have publicly pronounced their sympathy, passive and active support, might actually miss out numerous other individuals who might harbor secret support and sympathy to such groups.

Secondly, to identify those that could be at risk to radicalization, how do we profile those that are susceptible and vulnerable to the pull of the terrorist rhetoric and propaganda?

While many, who belong to such susceptible and vulnerable groups have fallen for the terrorist spell; time and time again, we see, individuals, particularly the youth, who do not fit the profile being indoctrinated and radicalized by terrorists. Hence, if we focus solely on those that are deemed susceptible and vulnerable, we run the risk of missing a sizable number not falling under that particular cohort group, who might nevertheless be lured into passively or actively joining a terrorist group.

What then could be our course of action?

I would like to propose that the counter-narrative for the youth be targeted and disseminated to all young people.

Given that it is difficult to identify specific profiles of young people who are targeted by terrorists and the reality that young people (like any other age-group of people) might at later stages in their lives undergo changes to their personality, environment and circumstances that could make them vulnerable to the terrorist influence, it would therefore be better to ensure that all young people are exposed to the counter-narrative of terrorism.

Would it be a wise decision to expose the youth to the counter-narrative, even if they have yet to be exposed to the narrative of the terrorist?

Given the finite resources available, would it then be advisable to target the whole group of young people?

While there are rightfully such challenges to the strategy of targeting all young people, I would like to argue that we have little choice in this matter but to do so.

Given that we do not know when the youth will be exposed to the rhetoric of the terrorist as well as their narrative, it would then be essential that we have the possibility of being the first in line to have a chance to frame their minds and 'set' the 'agenda' on how the issue of resolving a conflict or addressing grievances using violence should be seen.

This idea of building a 'mental firewall' to prevent terrorists from getting a mental foothold in the minds of the young people would mean that regardless of the propensity of an individual to be radicalized, he or she nevertheless goes through a process of equipping themselves with the necessary knowledge and critical thinking should they be exposed to terrorists rhetoric and propaganda.

An example of this form of reasoning can be found in the public health sphere. The idea of vaccination or mass immunization does not take into account the possibility of an individual to contract a certain disease but rather assumes that the cost to deal with the disease is far higher than that of preventing it. For example, in 1988, there were 350,000 people affected by Polio. However, in 2013, the figure dropped to 416 cases, a dramatic reduction of more than 99%.[26] The reason this came about to be was the aggressive efforts by national and international health authorities and agencies to vaccinate the masses. Little effort was taken to identify who were the vulnerable or susceptible groups but rather more effort was placed in ensuring that every individual was indeed vaccinated.

Given this, the author would like to propose that all efforts be undertaken to ensure that all youths are exposed to programs where they are shown in very persuasive and tangible ways on both the futility and immorality of the terrorists' indiscriminate use of violence as well as the possible non-violent alternatives to resolve conflict and address grievances.

This would mean that all channels, be it educational, community, religious and social platforms, utilizing various actors, such as teachers, parents, religious leaders, community leaders, role models and even celebrities be trained, equipped and fully exploited to spread the word to the young people.

### 2. *The Facilitator*

Given the nature of this audience made up of youth, who would be the best facilitator to deliver such a counter-narrative?

What would the criteria of such a facilitator look like?

Essentially, the messenger must have two essential components. Firstly, the facilitator must know the audience well and, secondly have the skill set to both debunk the terrorist narrative as well as to provide a compelling alternative.

#### a) Knowing the Audience

The facilitator of the program must be one who is able to understand both the rational (thinking) and emotional (feeling) mechanisms driving young people. He or she must be able to sympathize and empathize with the aspirations and idealism of the youth. Without understanding the emphasis that these young people place on the desire to 'make a difference' he or she will not be able to communicate and understand the youth.

26 World Health Organisation (WHO), http://www.who.int/mediacentre/factsheets/fs114/en/.

b) Knowing the Subject

Besides listening to them, the facilitator must be able to slip through the mental 'defenses' of some of the young people in getting them to see and subsequently question the justification of the terrorists in using indiscriminate violence. He or she must also be able to make them think out-of-the-box in finding alternative ways to that of the terrorists in resolving conflicts and addressing grievances.

In essence, the facilitator needs to be able to guide the youth in finding convincing alternatives to real problems and issues of injustice, inequality and conflict happening in different parts of the world. This would involve showcasing and exploring together with the youth, the various non-violent alternatives and real-life case studies that have been used to resolve conflicts and fight injustice. The campaign against the slave trade by William Wilberforce, the movement for female suffrage by Susan B. Anthony, Carrie Chapman Catt and numerous others, the Gandhian philosophy of 'satyagraha' (devotion to truth), Nelson Mandela's struggle to overcome apartheid in South Africa and Martin Luther King Jr's part in the American Civil Rights movement are excellent case studies of non-violent strategies that have been carried out and have achieved considerable success despite tremendous opposition.

The facilitator must also be able to use both the intellectual component to rationalize the futility of indiscriminate violence as well as the emotional component to highlight the barbarity of killing innocents to defend the innocent. Should the terrorists attempt to use religious justification to sanction their acts, the facilitator must also be well-versed and qualified enough to debunk the pseudo-religious points as well as to show how the religious texts have been manipulated, exploited and taken out of context by the terrorists to suite their own agenda.

## *IV. The Challenges of the Counter-Discourses*

A young man in a discussion with the Author once remarked, "All Governments in the world have taken part in NATO exercises". By NATO, he did not mean the North Atlantic Treaty Organization but rather "No Action, Talk Only'. There has been a lot of talk with regards to counter-discourses and counter-narratives, but very little substantial work has been done in this particular area, especially when it comes to young people.

This has created a 'content-imbalance' very much in favor of the terrorist rhetoric and propaganda. It is therefore, imperative that we address this situation through the following steps.

### *1. Start Listening*

One of the attractions that the extremists seem to offer the young people is the belief that their opinions matter and that they are being listened too. Whether true or otherwise, these extremist/terrorists groups have been able to cultivate the idea that they are the mouthpiece of the people in general and the youth in particular.

It is however sad to note that in many parts of the world, the authorities do not hold such a place in the hearts of the young people or do not enable opportunities. The only way to rectify this problem for the authorities in question is to really start listening to the young people, or no longer can we go, meet them and 'present them facts and truths' for them to listen and obey. This model does not work and often does more harm than good. Instead, we need to engage them by listening to them, understanding their challenges, taking into account their aspirations and subsequently partnering with them in developing a possible future.

The young must be given a platform to express their views and opinions, particularly on matters affecting them and the authorities must both interact and engage with them in a substantive and sustainable manner. Simply put, if we do not lend our ears, they will not lend theirs.

### *2. Understand and Counter the Message of the Enemy*

The extremists seem to have the uncanny ability to nurture a narrative that resonates with the young people because, firstly, they have developed a message that is appealing and, secondly, they have understood the psyche of their audience. Simply put, the extremists have mastered their craft at both ends.

Therefore, it is imperative that we attempt to understand the narrative of the extremists for two reasons. Firstly, to attempt to identify weaknesses and deconstruct the narrative, and secondly (and ironically), to see if there is anything that we can learn from the extremists when we craft our counter-narrative massage.

In developing a counter-narrative, our aim would be to craft a robust message that would act as a 'mental firewall' in the event that an individual is exposed to the extremist rhetoric. This theological and ideological firewall[27] could help 'immunize' young people against violent action. Like a vaccine, the aim would be to inoculate as many young people as possible by getting them to carefully identify the weaknesses of the extremist arguments as well as to understand existing mechanisms that would allow them to bring about change in a manner that does not involve violence. In doing so, there is an urgent need to develop viable alternatives to non-violence that have the capacity and capability to address the grievances of the young people. In this particular matter, instead of solely developing techniques of non-violence as an alternative, emphasis could also be put on personalities in the past who have successfully demonstrated the potential of peaceful methods to solve issues. Young people (as with their older counterparts) may identify better with a person rather than a technique.

We also need to develop ways to extend the reach and the depth of our counter narrative message. Not only do we need to find creative ways to reach out to a wider audience, we also need to do so in a way that is able to penetrate their minds and if possible modify their behavior. Hence, utilizing technology like the internet or even utilizing traditional platforms such as schools, civil societies and religious institutions to reach out to audiences previously not thought possible via creative avenues such as dance, song and film making may better our chances in winning the young people of this current generation.

For example, in Pakistan, young people have reacted very positively to the 'Burka Avenger'[28], a cartoon that depicts a female superhero battling villains such as Baba Bandooq, a Taliban-like figure who attempts to close her school down. With eye-catching computer animation, fast paced action, flashes of humor coupled with a catchy theme song entitled "Don't Mess with the Lady in Black', the message of the dangers of extremism is conveyed in a way that is both appreciated and enjoyed by young people.[29] It is therefore important to realize that while content of our counter

---

27 Ramakrishna, *Self-Radicalization and the Awlaki Connection*, 2010.

28 Masood and Walsh, "Burka Avenger to the Rescue," *Guardian News Media*, 2013.

29 Clark, "Don't Mess With the Lady in Black: Pakistan's Burka Avenger", *NBC News*, 31 July 2013, retrieved on 15 August 2013: http://worldnews.nbcnews.com/

narrative is important, the delivery of this message must be equally emphasized, particularly when focusing on the youth of today.

### 3. *Learning from Models of Youth Radicalization to Develop Modules of Counter-Radicalization*

How is the youth being radicalized?

What age-groups are specifically vulnerable to extremist ideology?

What are the trigger factors and catalysts that promote young people to walk the path of radicalization?

How and why does radical thinking in certain young people transform into violent action?

To answer these questions, we may need to develop models of radicalization that might defer from existing ones as the available models might not take into consideration the various factors that determine how a youth reacts in the current environment.

Understanding the pathways of radicalization for the young and developing models that explain the phenomenon should be the precursor to developing a counter-narrative module. In other words, such models of radicalization should form the basis when crafting modules of counter-radicalization for the young people. These modules must address the terrorist rhetoric as well as the concerns of the young people in their efforts to achieve change. These modules must also be fashioned in such a manner that is both, interesting to the young audience as well as easily understood and disseminated by the potential facilitators.

Creating counter-radicalization modules without understanding radicalization models might prove to be a costly mistake and developing radicalization models without subsequent efforts to facilitate counter-radicalization modules constitutes a luxury we can ill afford.

---

_news/2013/07/31/19796587-dont-mess-with-the-lady-in-black-pakistans-burka-avenger?lite.

### *4. Developing Tools to Measure Effectiveness of the Counter-Narrative Mechanisms*

While it is very much possible to develop a counter-narrative and subsequently deliver the program, there is also a compelling need to develop a mechanism to measure the effectiveness of the program. Indicators must be set in place to gauge the value and efficacy of implemented programs. From having pre and post surveys of a program to other more sophisticated means of analysis such as the triangulation of both quantitative and qualitative data, we need to create and develop techniques to measure strengths as well as weaknesses.

Only then we would be able to craft interventions that now have the capacity and capability to target specific groups or niche audiences within the youth demography. This is necessary not just to justify the existence of our intervention programs but more importantly to develop best practices and lessons learned to ensure that future endeavors have lesser pitfalls and a higher probability of success. Such feedback mechanisms could also guard against the possibility of replicating modules that do not fit a specific, targeted audience. Given the importance of such a mechanism, it is pertinent to ask from whom should we get back feedback from and how do we do so.

Firstly, we need to identify our target audience. Educated young people, unemployed young people, religious young people, misguided young people, bored young people, young people seeking adventure, young people seeking an identity or any other group of young people requiring a specific tailored response. To craft such a response needs us to intimately know our target audience. Subsequently, after we conduct our intervention programs, we must 'go on the ground' and assess and evaluate the effectiveness of our efforts. This evaluation will be greatly heightened if we are able to work with the 'gate-keepers' or other interested parties that are already on one ground with our targeted audience. Teachers, lecturers, youth workers, civil organizations, youth organizations, youth clubs might not be directly involved in counter-terrorism, but by virtue of being on the ground and working with a specific youth demography, they are able to offer valuable insight on the efficacy of our intervention programs. It is also significant to note that because of their close proximity with the targeted youth group, they are able to detect subtle shifts in thinking and behavior, which could be valuable input for both, crafting and assessing counter-terrorism interventions.

## D. Lessons Learned

Georg Wilhelm Friedrich Hegel once remarked, "We learn from history that we do not learn from history." It is hoped that the following observations, with regards to the radicalization of young people shall not suffer the same fate.

### I. Hear Things you do not like to Hear

Young people are both passionate and idealistic. However, at times this passion and idealism could lead to expressions that are not very endearing and are more often than not, directed to the authorities and the way they are conducting their jobs. This could lead to situations wherein the authorities shy away from engaging in honest interactions with the youth. This is something that we cannot afford. We need to learn how to hear things we do not like being spoken, particularly from the youth, for two very important reasons.

Firstly, if they are expressing their thoughts and opinions to you and subsequently the authorities are deemed to be both listening and addressing these grievances, there is little need for these young people to then take their message to extremists. Secondly, having an audience of young people that is not on your side and critical to your every action and words does at least indicate that the authorities have at least succeeded in targeting the right audience. For this is precisely the group that is targeted by extremist groups: young, vocal and critical of the government's policies. For too long, we have been preaching to a group that is either on our side or too fearful to voice their true opinions and thoughts. This defeats the purpose of interacting with young people; which is to engage them and if possible initiate behavior modification on issues such as the propensity to use violence. If we are not listening to things that we do not like to hear, it could possibly mean that we are 'preaching to the converted' which is a waste of precious resources. So, there is a need to search out, interact and debate with the young people who have a 'bone to pick' with the authorities.

### *II. Make Mistakes Fast and Rectifications Faster*

In combatting terrorism, making a mistake might have disastrous consequences. That being said, mistakes are nevertheless made. The reality of the matter is that in any field, regardless of the consequences and impact of a mistake, they are nevertheless often times made. In this regard, policy and delivery programs on counter-terrorism, particularly targeting the youth, need careful thought, planning and consideration. While numerous programs to reach out and 'educate' the young people have been implemented, there has been little attempt to study the impact and efficacy of such interventions. Often times, the content and delivery of such programs do not take in to account the youth make-up, psychology and emotions, rendering them less effective and powerful.

While much has been rightly said about reducing the possibility of making mistakes in the first place, little has been said about developing mechanisms to identify already made mistakes and to subsequently rectifying them. Given that mistakes are inevitable, we need to find ways to 'allow for these' mistakes at the very onset of the process, identify these errors, rectify them and subsequently 'roll out' the 'upgraded' versions faster. The further down the line the mistake is allowed to continue, the more crushing the impact and the consequences. It is important to note that the worst case scenario is not that a mistake is made but rather, a mistake is allowed to continue.

Business models have understood this very well and have both developed and engineered creative mechanisms to gather feedback quickly and to make the subsequent changes to improve the product or the service. A case in point would be the manner in which software companies launch their new programs. In the event a glitch is detected, it is immediately identified, rectified and the amended program is rolled-out once again. While this entire process might not be fully applicable by those developing counter-narrative programs, there is still much that could be emulated.

### *III. Be Humble, Seek Help and Form Alliances*

James Bond in all his exploits exudes an air of arrogance, never seeks assistance and in almost all instances, saves the world from utter destruction by himself. This is of course why Mr. Bond remains a fictional character.

For developing an effective counter-narrative that targets the young people, there is a need to recognize that we cannot do it on our own. It is highly unlikely that any single entity would possess the knowledge, experience, technical know-how, resources, expertise, skill-set, audience and delivery mechanism to initiate, deliver and evaluate a sufficiently successful counter-narrative program in a sustainable manner over an extended period of time.

This recognition needs to be accompanied by a humble spirit that acknowledges the need to seek help and in certain cases form alliances. Hence, while counter-terrorist authorities are the leading agencies when it comes to matters involving terrorism; in developing counter-narratives for young people there is a need to involve youth leaders, behavioral psychologists, youth experts, social workers, teachers, lecturers, policy makers, communication specialists, media specialists, rehabilitated terrorists and also parents.

Forming alliances allows entities to focus on their areas of expertise and avoid duplication of efforts. For example, in Malaysia, the coordinated efforts of the Royal Malaysian Police (the leading agency), the Prison Department and the Religious Department in rehabilitating former terrorists has proven to be quite successful. This highlights the dictum that 'the whole is greater than the sum of its parts.'

### *IV. Focus on What Can Be Done*

While on one spectrum, particularly amongst those who are directly involved in countering terrorism, there are those who believe that they are able to do everything, there are also those on the opposite end, normally involving those who are not directly involved in counter-terrorism, who are of the opinion that the problem is simply insurmountable and that there is little or nothing that they can do. While countering terrorism and extremism and redressing the influence it has on the young is certainly challenging, a sense of helplessness will certainly not aid the situation. The idea therefore, can be beautifully summed up through the words of Theodore Roosevelt, "Do what you can, with what you have, where you are."

There are numerous things that we can do to both dispel the myth of violence as well as to address the grievances of the youth. From providing them a platform to express their ideas to teaching them to critically examine violent propaganda to channeling their energy via constructive outlets, many things can be achieved both in a formal and informal manner by various parties to help the young people turn away from violence.

### *V. Building Programs Around an Institution or Alliance and not as an Individual*

While utilizing charismatic individuals with a flair for reaching young people would certainly be a bonus, it must be clear that the bulk of the work will be done by ordinary individuals with average skills. Hence, the focus must be placed on building and improving the collective skills and expertise of the majority of the people that make up the institution that is involved in countering radical violent ideology.

Leaving the job of reaching the youth to a few gifted individuals would mean that their ability to reach a wider audience would be greatly hampered by their individual limitations of time and space. Hence, it would be worthwhile to consider these gifted individuals to be involved not only in delivering the counter narrative to the youth but to also be involved in training and building the skill-set of the institution, so as to widen the pool of potential experts to reach out to the young people.

### *VI. Treating the Youth as Part of the Solution and not Part of the Problem*

Young people are sensitive enough to realize if they are seen as a 'part of the problem' or are viewed as 'partners' to solve the problem. Treating them as a 'part of the problem' would be counter-productive and would result in a greater 'trust deficit' which would only act to make an already hard task even harder. Instead, we have to make them stakeholders and work with them to get the best results. Therefore, the method of delivery, the terms used and the techniques utilized to reach out to the young people must be designed in a way that while not being impotent, does also not 'punish' the young for choosing to give 'us' a chance. They must feel that they have been equipped and empowered in having a say on what happens to them.

## E. Conclusion

Young people make up only 18% of the global population but 100% of our future.[30] Extremists, at times, seem to have a better understanding of this than we do. To ensure that the youth do not fall prey to the ideology that political violence is both legitimate and advantageous, authorities need to develop and deliver a counter-narrative that appeals and resonates with the young people. Doing so would firstly require a deeper understanding of their psyche and aspirations coupled with creative and strategic ways of reaching out to them and secondly a long hard appraisal on what has been done and how to subsequently make it better.

## Bibliography

Ackerman, Peter, and Jack DuVall, *A Force More Powerful: A Century of Non-Violent Conflict*, New York: Palgrave Macmillan, 2000.

Barrelle, Kate, "Individual Psychology & Behaviour Make-Up of a Violent Extremist," paper presented at the *Countering Violent Extremism Workshop*, Petaling Jaya, Selangor, 28-30 September 2012.

Clark, Mandy, "Don't Mess With the Lady in Black: Pakistan's Burka Avenger", *NBC News* (31 July 2013), at http://worldnews.nbcnews.com/_news/2013/07/31/19796587-dont-mess-with-the-lady-in-black-pakistans-burka-avenger?lite

Cole, Matthew, and Robert Windrem, "Al Qaeda Announces New English-Language Terror Magazine," *NBC News* (9 March 2014), at http://www.nbcnews.com/news/investigations/al-qaeda-announces-new-english-language-terror-magazine-n48531.

Johnston, Philip, "MI5: Al-Qaeda Recruiting U.K. Children for Terror," The Telegraph (7 November 2007), at http://www.telegraph.co.uk/news/uknews/1568363/MI5-Al-Qaeda-recruiting-UK-children-for-terror.html.

Masood, S., and D. Walsh, "Burka Avenger to the Rescue," *Guardian News Media*, 2013.

Ramakrishna, Kumar, "*Self-Radicalization and the Awlaki Connection*", *RSIS Commentaries* 2010, at https://www.rsis.edu.sg/wp-content/uploads/2014/07/CO10075.pdf.

Richardson, Louise, *What Terrorists Want: Understanding the Terrorist Threat*, London: John Murray Publishers, 2006.

30 Barrelle, "Individual Psychology & Behaviour Make-Up of a Violent Extremist," paper presented at the *Countering Violent Extremism Workshop*, Petaling Jaya, Selangor, 28-30 September 2012.

Samuel, Thomas Koruth, *Reaching the Youth: Countering the Terrorist Narrative*, Southeast Asia Regional Centre for Counter-Terrorism (SEARCCT), 2012.

Samuel, Thomas Koruth, Interview with Roy Anthony Rodgers, University Malaya, 26 January 2010.

Samuel, Thomas Koruth, Interview with Omer Ali Saifudeen, Home Team Academy, Singapore, 8 March 2011.

Samuel, Thomas Koruth, Interview with Kumar Ramakrishna, S. Rajaratnam School of International Studies (RSIS), Nanyang Technological University, 9 March 2011.

Samuel, Thomas Koruth, Interview with Joseph Liow, S. Rajaratnam School of International Studies (RSIS), Nanyang Technological University, Singapore, 10 March 2011.

Samuel, Thomas Koruth, Interview with Harry Setyo R., Semarang, Indonesia, 5 April 2011.

Samuel, Thomas Koruth, Interview with Noor Huda Ismail, Semarang, Indonesia, 5 April 2011.

Samuel, Thomas Koruth, Interview with Marhmudi Hariano alias Yusuf, Semarang, Indonesia, 5 April 2011.

Samuel, Thomas Koruth, Interview with Sydney Jones, Jakarta, Indonesia, 6 April 2011.Singer, Peter W., *Children at War*, New York: Pantheon, 2005.

O' Balance, Edgar, *Language of Violence: The Blood Politics of Terrorism San Rafael*, California: Presidio Press, 1979.

World Health Organisation, "Poliomyelitis," April 2016, at http://www.who.int/mediacentre/factsheets/fs114/en/.

United Nations News Centre, "At debate, UN and Security Council Renew Pledge to Counter Foreign Terrorist Fighters", 29 May 2015, at http://www.un.org/apps/news/story.asp?NewsID=51005#.VXcikU2Jhdg.

# Radicalization and De-Radicalization: Trip to Hell and Back? Appreciation and Purpose of Dropout Programs for Political and Religious Fanatics and Alternatives – a German and European Perspective

*Oliver Gerson*

## *A. Introduction*

"Fanaticism is the only 'will strength' the weak and unsafe can have"
(Friedrich Wilhelm Nietzsche)

Radicalization is not a process which appears overnight.[1] The urge to consider things and circumstances in black and white schemes[2] and stereotypes[3] rendering opinion in terms of absolutes,[4] dominates individual be-

1 See Silke, "Holy Warriors – Exploring the Psychological Processes of Jihadi Radicalization," 2008, pp. 118 f.; Borum, "Radicalization Into Violent Extremism I: A Review of Social Science Theories," 2011, pp. 14 ff.; McCauley and Moskalenko, "Mechanisms of Political Radicalization," 2008, pp. 419 ff.; Hess, "Netzwerke des Terrors – Netzwerke gegen den Terror," 2005, p. 123; OSCE, "Preventing Terrorism and Countering Violent Extremism and Radicalization that Lead to Terrorism: A Community-Policing Approach," 2014, p. 36; Neumann, "Radikalisierung, DeRadikalisierung und Extremismus," 2013, p. 3.

2 See Richardson, *Was Terroristen wollen, die Ursachen der Gewalt und wie wir sie bekämpfen können*, 2007, p. 72.

3 See EXIT-Germany, "We provide the way out: De-Radicalization and Disengagement," 2014 p. 3; Buschbom et al., "Rechtspopulismus, Argumente und pädagogische Annäherung," 2008, p. 4; Geschke, "Vorurteile, Differenzierung und Diskriminierung – sozialpsychologische Erklärungsansätze," 2012, p. 34; Puschnerat, "Zur Bedeutung ideologischer und sozialer Faktoren in islamistischen Radikalisierungsprozesses – eine Skizze," 2006, p. 225.

4 See Briggs and Feve, "Review of Programs to Counter Narratives of Violent Extremism: What works and what are the implications for Government?," 2013, p. 9; Groß et al., "Von der Ungleichwertigkeit zur Ungleichheit: Gruppenbezogene Menschenfeindlichkeit," 2012, p. 11; Schroeder, *Rechtsextremismus und Jugendgewalt in Deutschland, Ein Ost-West-Vergleich*, 2003, p. 107; Dovermann, "Narrative und Gegen-Narrative im Prozess von Radikalisierung und DeRadikalisierung," 2013, p. 44; Zöller, *Terrorismusstrafrecht. Ein Handbuch*, 2009, p. 85.

havior more and more, finally destroying tolerance like a slow poison.[5] This essay hereafter wants to reveal several adequate "antidotes". Therefore it comments on the phenomenon of "opt-out-programs" and rehabilitation organizations for radical and fanatic individuals. Paradigmatically, two types of extremist groups will be examined: at first, political extremists with nationalist and racist bias and secondly, religious and ideological groups. Afterwards the essay will show the efforts taken to re-integrate refugees and escapists of those groups. The third part will consider social and legal implications of such reintegration and will bring to attention underrated ramifications of failed and miscarried rehabilitation.

## *I. Starting with "Roots"*

The adjective "radical" is derived from the Latin word radix and describes the aspiration to attack social and political problems "at the root"[6] and to solve them there very extensively, completely and with lasting effect.[7] In radical thinking, prejudices and resentments become deeply anchored in the fanatic's head,[8] while the personal view concerning questions of tolerance and empathy is blurred by simple truths[9] and dangerous pre-varications. The long process of radical isolation often finds its starting point in

5 See Cross and Snow, "Radicalism within the Context of Social Movements: Processes and Types," 2011, p. 118; OSCE, "Preventing Terrorism," p. 39; see Neumann, "Radikalisierung, DeRadikalisierung und Extremismus," p. 7.

6 See Cross and Snow, "Radicalism Within," p. 119, citing Angela Davis.

7 See Neumann, "Radikalisierung," p. 3; see also Horgan, "From Profiles to Pathways and Roots to Routes: Perspectives from Psychology on Radicalization Into Terrorism," 2008, pp. 82 ff.; see also Cross and Snow, "Radicalism Within," pp. 116, 118 using a more "political" approach; resembling McCauley and Moskalenko, "Mechanisms of Political Radicalization," p. 416. In the usage of the state protection authorities of the Federal Republic of Germany the word "radicalism" was removed since 1975 finally by the concept "Extremism", see Neugebauer, "Einfach war gestern. Zur Strukturierung der politischen Realität in einer modernen Gesellschaft," 2010, p. 5; Mudde, "Radikale Parteien in Europa," 2008, p. 12. For this essay, both words will be used rather similarly; an attempt to clarify those terms by Schroeder, *Rechtsextremismus und Jugendgewalt*, p. 15.

8 See Korn and Weilnböck, "Der lange Abschied von Hass und Gewalt," 2013, p. 36; Groß et al., "Gruppenbezogene Menschenfeindlichkeit," p. 13.

9 See Buschbom et al., "Rechtspopulismus," p. 4; Neumann, "Radikalisierung," p. 7; Korn and Weilnböck, "Der lange Abschied," p. 38; Sirseloudi et al., "Radikalisierung von europäischen Muslimen: Zwei Erklärungsansätze," 2010, p. 46.

individual strokes of fate.[10] Bad experiences with groups or behaviors are perceived as rivalry or threat to the individual's persuasion of being "against" the system.[11] Sometimes also stupefying disasters such as wars or massacres[12] lead to extreme disinhibition.[13] The maelstrom of brutalization determines the further behavior and radical thinking takes on a life of its own. Extremism is the impetus, which moves Europe into turmoil.[14] The brutal assassinations in Paris[15] and Copenhagen[16] are recent shocking signs of a seemingly menacing development. The fear of further assassinations paralyzes social life.[17] Terrorism and extremist violence have a lock on Europe.[18] The consequences as well as shape and form of appearance diverge: whereas some individuals seclude themselves to reside absolutely

10 See Neubacher, "Terrorismus – Was haben »Rote Armee Fraktion« und »Jihadisten« gemeinsam?" 2010, p. 749; see for several more and different theories of radicalization Borum, "Radicalization Into Violent Extremism I," pp. 16 ff.

11 OSCE, "Preventing Terrorism," p. 36; deeper to those attempts of explanation see Schroeder, *Rechtsextremismus und Jugendgewalt*, pp. 94 ff. with more proofs; also Böllinger, "Die Entwicklung zu terroristischem Handeln als psychosozialer Prozess," 2008, p. 4.

12 See the examples of Richardson, "Was Terroristen wollen," pp. 107 ff.

13 See McCauley and Moskalenko, "Mechanisms of Political Radicalization," pp. 427 f.; Hoffmann-Plesch, "Deutsche IS-Dschihadisten, Kriminalätiologische und kriminalpräventive Analyse des Radikalisierungsprozesses, Teil 2: Kriminalpsychologische Aspekte," 2015, p. 10; Eckert, "Radikalisierung – Eine soziologische Perspektive," 2013, p. 17; Richardson, "Was Terroristen wollen," pp. 68 ff.; Neumann, "Radikalisierung," p. 7.

14 See Ramalingam, "Old Threat, New Approach: Tackling the Far Right Across Europe, Guide for Policy Makers," 2014, p. 1; Vidino, "DeRadikalisierung durch gezielte Interventionen," 2013, p. 25. The terms of radicalism, extremism and terrorism do not have an exactly equal meaning, but are used too often as synonyms; for an attempt to clarify the term "terrorism" see Richardson, "Was Terroristen wollen," pp. 27 ff.: She concludes that terrorism requires violence and a message, and that its assassinations conduct symbolic impact.

15 See "The Charlie Hebdo Massacre in Paris," *New York Times*, 7 Jan. 2015.

16 See "Copenhagen Shooting Suspect Shot Dead After 2 Killed In 2 Attacks In Denmark," The Huffington Post, 15 Feb. 2015.

17 See Carnival processions in Germany and the Netherlands have been quitted, see http://www.welt.de/videos/article137495157/Terrorwarnung-ueberschattet-Karnevalsumzuege.html.

18 See http://www.spiegel.de/politik/ausland/giftgas-pocken-festnahmen-furcht-vor-dem-terror-hat-europa-im-griff-a-223221.html; Eckes, *EU Counter-Terrorist Policies and Fundamental Rights, The Case of Inndividual Sanctions*, 2009, pp. 64 ff.

cut off from the outside world,[19] others tend to develop verbal aggressions, arming their vocabulary in order to attack the "enemies"[20] located in the nearer or farther surrounding[21] ("hate crimes"[22]). Some even go further down this road: support and endorsement of violence against different-minded groups entraps these people in becoming outlaws.[23] They oppose minorities, religious opinions, statutory structures or political interdependences. At the last stage, some individuals will decide to join a group of like-minded persons.[24] Then, the brain-washing system, used by radical demagogues and fundamental sophists, unleashes its omnipresent power. The moral concepts of the later ideology have to be internalized, while thinking becomes contaminated with new and more "fitting" components of one-sided propaganda. The community, the leading peer group, and the new spirit of camaraderie instill ideas of allegedly necessary fights.[25] There are different types of such groups to be distinguished, depending on their reasons and motivation for being created. The spreading hostility toward foreigners feeds the number of pure racists, flocking together in na-

19 See Waldmann, "Islamistischer Terrorismus: Ideologie, Organisation und Unterstützungspotential," 2005, p. 39; Böllinger, "Die Entwicklung zu terroristischem Handeln," p. 63.

20 Böllinger, "Die Entwicklung zu terroristischem Handeln," p. 62; Bundesamt für Verfassungsschutz (BFV), "Islamismus: Entstehung und Erscheinungsformen," 2013, p. 16; Neubacher, "Terrorismus," p. 745; Identification with like-minders and sympathie for the alleged "victims" are an essential feature of the extremists thinking, Richardson, "Was Terroristen wollen," p. 72; another specific phenomenon is the reversing of rules of aggressor and defendant, pp. 75 f.; see also Neubacher, "Terrorismus," p. 746.

21 See Sirseloudi et al., "Radikalisierung von europäischen Muslimen," p. 40.

22 Korn and Weilnböck, "Der lange Abschied," p. 32; Ramalingam, "Old Threat, New Approach," p. 7.

23 See Ramalingam, "Old Threat, New Approach," p. 7; for several others models see Neumann, "Radikalisierung," p. 3; Silke, "Holy Warriors," p. 117; McCauley and Moskalenko, "Mechanisms of Political Radicalization," p. 421.

24 See McCauley and Moskalenko, "Mechanisms of Political Radicalization," pp. 422 f.; Richardson, "Was Terroristen wollen," p. 76; Böllinger, "Die Entwicklung zu terroristischem Handeln," p. 64; Neumann, "Radikalisierung," p. 7.

25 See Steinberg, "Jihadistische Radikalisierung im Internet und mögliche Gegenmaßnahmen," 2013, p. 21; Silke, "Holy Warriors," pp. 111 ff; Möller and Schuhmacher, "Ein- und Ausstiegsprozesse rechtsextremistischer Skinheads," 2007, p. 21.

tionalist[26], far-right or xenophobic groups and parties.[27] In addition to this, religious fanatics exaggerate and superelevate the importance and the global validity of their own (to some extent singular) interpretation of what should be considered as right and adequate behavior.[28] Permanent contact with like-minded, but rather non self-reflexive devotees of a self-righteous world distorts the boundaries of sentiments, into becoming both reasonable and virtuous.[29]

Some people find a new ideological home in those quagmires of bogus values and permanent inflations of one's self-evaluations by separating themselves from "others".[30] For others, the new experiences fill a gap, carved by the burden of loneliness and often conditioned by a bad childhood.[31] But the new satisfaction factors, i.e. feelings of being important and needed and the conceit of suddenly being "someone"[32], will not last too long. Whatever had been the reason for pulling the emergency brake (there are intrinsic and extrinsic motives, see below), some people suddenly want to exit their peer group. But escaping from a herd is not the easiest endeavor. Most fanatic squads have specific codes-of-conduct and codes-of-honor[33] that do not allow members to leave the community without serious consequences. As a sudden dissident, one's internal world focus flips. The former friend-or-foe scheme[34] used to identify oneself with the chosen peer group goes into reverse: former pals have become enemies.[35] The long term of socialization in the peer group hampers the willingness to take a step back to normality, returning to family and the indigenous so-

26 See "Revolutionary Nationalism instead of global Capitalism," *Deutsche Stimme*, July 2003.
27 See Schroeder, *Rechtsextremismus und Jugendgewalt*, p. 15.
28 See Schroeder, *Rechtsextremismus und Jugendgewalt*, p. 96; Richardson, "Was Terroristen wollen," pp. 138 ff.
29 OSCE, "Preventing Terrorism," p. 37.
30 Böllinger, "Die Entwicklung zu terroristischem Handeln," p. 63; Silke, "Holy Warriors," p. 116.
31 See Korn and Weilnböck, "Der lange Abschied," p. 37.
32 Rommelspacher, "Warum steigen Aussteiger aus? Und tun sie es tatsächlich?," 2008, p. 1.
33 See Hoffmann-Plesch, "Deutsche IS-Dschihadisten Teil 2," p. 12.
34 See Eckert, "Radikalisierung," p. 11.
35 See Eckert, "Radikalisierung," p. 15; Möller and Schuhmacher, "Ein- und Ausstiegsprozesse," p. 22.

cial environment.[36] To facilitate this long path back to society, several state and non-governmental organizations offer programs to rehabilitate those "returnees". At first blush, this seems a sensible, proper and necessary approach. But there are lots of hurdles to over-come, starting with psychological and social frictions, up to severe legal and criminal issues.

### *II. Thesis: Radicalization of Human Beings Done by Human Beings*

Broaching the topic "Radicalization and De-Radicalization" at an early stage, possible solutions have to be identified. Such a complex and nearly overwhelming issue like "de-radicalization" could generally be treated and addressed in two ways. One method might be to sum up all specific details of the topic, weigh the subtle differences and portray the individual processes meticulously. The other way is to reveal and demonstrate existing similarities of occurrences in order to find practical solutions for a huge number of cases and individual fates. The first method could be described as "approximation through atomization". This essay instead prefers a "reduction of complexity" (in the sense and mental legacy of Niklas Luhmann and Talcot Parsons on the one and Ernst von Glasersfeld and Paul Watzlawick on the other hand) creating an "approximation by comparison". Unfortunately, while contemplating social and psychological phenomena necessary simple truths have often gone missing.[37] But human beings are wired analogically; they "work" appropriately to the same patterns and mindsets. Therefore, all means to facilitate de-radicalization processes have to be measured against their applicability on human beings done by human beings. This philosophy does not exonerate the requirement for a scrupulously precise approach.[38] However, the results of such an approach, to some extent, will seem more "evident" or "trivial". But triviality cannot be condemned as amiss, as long the facts and means appear trivial because of being sensible.

36 See the brochure EXIT-Germany, "De-Radicalization and Disengagement," p. 11; Vidino, "DeRadikalisierung durch gezielte Interventionen," pp. 26, 28; Rommelspacher, "Warum steigen Aussteiger aus?", p. 1.

37 See differently Savage, "Four Lessons From the Study of Fundamentalism and Psychology of Religion," 2011, pp. 134 f.

38 To much generalization remains dangerous, see Savage, "Four Lessons," p. 133.

Hereafter, the different terms and used topoi for radicalization processes will be clarified and explained. Radicalization, Extremism and Terrorism are based on comparable principles, but they differ in various areas (B). Then, two types of radicalization, the political right-wing movement and religious extremism (using one specific manifestation of Islamism) will be portrayed (B.I.-II.). Subsequently, the structure and work of four drop-out programs for political and religious fanatics in Germany and the European Union will be shown and prescribed (C.). Afterwards the critical involvement begins: fanatic thoughts are embedded very deeply in the person's head and therefore cannot be deleted absolutely and with lasting effect (C.II.). Hence, the work of opt-out programs might be supported by different alternatives and additive means (E.). Banning of extremist groups and enactment of legal sanctions both compete with psychological interdependences and legal infringements (E.I.-V.). Especially, criminal law is often brought into position to achieve social goals (E.VI.). In the final analyses, it will be proven that, of course, none of these measures used separately will solve the demonstrated problems. Consequently the author will develop a combined three-step-model that merges all shown positive effects to the largest possible extent (F.). Finally, the conclusion will bundle the thoughts once again (G.).

## *B. Defining Phenomena and Measures*

To be able to develop a sensible strategy with the complicated topic of de-radicalization in general, four different phenomena among three blocs have to be distinguished: radicalization, cognitive and ready-to-use-violence extremism together with terrorism. Radicalization means the progressive process of independence of a "fixed idea" as an ideology.[39] Extremism describes the upper concept for every form of forcible radicalization;[40] it derives from "extremus" (edge).[41] Within extremism one can dis-

39 For further definition see Borum, "Radicalization Into Violent Extremism I," pp. 8 ff., 12 f.

40 See Neubacher, "Terrorismus," p. 746; see also RAN Charta, 1; Neumann, "Radikalisierung," p. 4.

41 See Neugebauer, "Einfach war gestern," p. 3; extremism also can be the antonym for democratic, see Jesse, "'Extremistische Parteien' – worin besteht der Erkenntniszugewinn?," 2008, p. 8; Mudde, "Radikale Parteien," p. 12; see also Borum, "Radicalization Into Violent Extremism I," p. 10.

tinguish again between the cognitive and the ready-to-use-violence manifestation.[42] Cognitive extremists have escalated their individual point of view; in other words, their points of view are radicalized to a certain extent.[43] However, they abstain from using violence and remain "tame", except for verbal aggressions.[44] The ready-to-use-violence or concrete violent extremists regard their radicalization as only demonstrated by ostensible actions, e.g. in property damage, inflammatory demonstrations or thuggish attacks to the point of seditious and governmental-toppling encroachments.[45] These manifestations of extremism can be mostly relegated to the term "terrorism".[46] The special role of the cognitive extremist in the process of de-radicalization will be discussed later (see below). The word "fanaticism" will be used as a synonym for all forms of mental fixations such as bigotry, pathologic narrow-mindedness, intolerance and obsession. There is no commonly recognized definition for the term "terrorism",[47] however, it can be understood as the penal-juridical and security-juridical perceptible result of radicalization, in other (shortened) words the concrete assault.

---

42 See Ressembling Jesse, "'Extremistische Parteien'," p. 8: active, parliamental, oriented to discussion; see also Borum, "Radicalization Into Violent Extremism II: A Review of Conceptual Models and Empirical Research," 2011, p. 38; Özerdem and Podder, "Disarming Youth Combatants: Mitigating Youth Radicalization and Violent Extremism," 2011, p. 64.

43 See Neumann, "Radikalisierung," p. 4.

44 See Ressembling Dovermann and Güvercin, "Auf Fragen von Extremisten reagieren können: Eren Güvercin im Gespräch mit Ulrich Dovermann," 2010, p. 17.

45 See Neumann, "Radikalisierung," p. 5.

46 While not every violence is political and not every extremist must act violently, see Dovermann and Güvercin, "Fragen von Extremisten," p. 19; see also Borum, "Radicalization Into Violent Extremism II: A Review of Conceptual Models and Empirical Research," p. 58.

47 Sambei et al., *Counter-Terrorism Law and Practice: An International Handbook*, 2009, pp. 1 para 1.06 ff.; Silke, "Holy Warriors," p. 100; Neubacher, "Terrorismus," p. 745; Proposal at Zöller, *Terrorismusstrafrecht*, p. 213; for several approaches Barisch, *Die Bekämpfung des internationalen Terrorismus durch § 129b StGB, Verfassungswidrig politisiertes symbolisches Feindstrafrecht zum Schutze eines Scheinrechtsgutes oder sinnvolles Strafanwendungsrecht eines streitbaren demokratischen Rechtsstaates in der Weltgesellschaft?*, 2009, pp. 30 ff.; Holley, *Das Recht der internationalen Terrorismusbekämpfung, Asset Freezing, UN- und FATF-Vorgaben, US-Recht, EuGH-Judikatur, Grundrechte*, 2010, pp. 11 ff.

Concerning those manifestations on a fictional time line,[48] a progression follows: the first step is the period of radicalization. The individual gets in contact with the impinging influences and develops a personal persuasion. From that moment, radicalization has become an ineluctable meaning and spirit of his daily life, the person is entrapped in extremist thinking. Patterns of reasoning shift and the behavior keeps him in line. Committing crimes in line with the internalized ideology hence may indicate a step over the edge of terrorism.[49] Bearing this chronological and qualitative order[50] in mind, the measures to be taken have to be understood as methods in different stages: "early", "pressing" and "afterwards". Another possible categorization would be "preventive" and "repressive".[51] Violence by terrorists displaces the borders of inner and outer security.[52] That has to be kept in mind when searching for solutions to this immersive threat.

---

48 Or an "assembly belt of radicalization", see Neumann, "Radikalisierung," p. 6; Borum, "Rethinking Radicalization," 2011, p. 2; Borum, "Radicalization Into Violent Extremism II: A Review of Conceptual Models and Empirical Research," pp. 39 f.; against those linear models Neugebauer, "Einfach war gestern," p. 4.

49 See Neumann, "Radikalisierung," p. 5. Of course, escalation is a very individual process, depending mostly on unique characteristics of the concerned human being. The shown straight-forward evolution thus only describes one possible course of events; see also Silke, "Holy Warriors," pp. 105 f.

50 "Pathways", see Borum, "Radicalization Into Violent Extremism I," p. 9.

51 Vidino, "DeRadikalisierung durch gezielte Interventionen," p. 26 uses the terms "prevention" and "intervention".

52 See Holley, *Das Recht der internationalen Terrorismusbekämpfung*, p. 2; Pitschas, "Innere Sicherheit in 'guter Verfassung'? Zur Terrorismusbekämpfung im präventiven Gewährleistungsstaat," 2008, p. 241; Zöller, "Der Rechtsrahmen der Nachrichtendienste bei der 'Bekämpfung' des internationalen Terrorismus," 2007, pp. 767 f.; Denkowski, "Gesetz zur Abwehr von Gefahren des internationalen Terrorismus durch das BKA, Kritische Anmerkungen zum zweiten Referentenentwurf," 2008, p. 413; Möllers and van Ooyen, "Bundeskriminalamt, Bundespolizei und 'neue Sicherheit'," 2008, p. 27.

## C. *The Types of Radicalization: Political and Religious Fanaticism as pars pro toto*

"Fanaticism means doubling the strain if the aim is forgotten"
(George de Santayana)

It is not possible to describe all conceivable types of fanatic and extremist streams that have spread all over the world. Just trying to count all splinter groups would cause more problems than bring solutions, because singularity is one of the most important distinctive features for extremist groups.[53] They all fight for their values and they do it, in general, for higher aims or out of deep creed. More important (and more helpful) than getting lost in details would be summarizing the similarities.[54] Therefore, it would be more fair to randomly choose two "associations", to illustrate the long way to radicalization and the even longer and harder path back to a normal life in a democratic society. As pars pro toto for a highly stable and established political group we hereafter examine the actions of the far-right[55] German National-Democratic Party (NPD). As an example for religious fanaticism, the Islamist or Salafist movement should serve as illustrative material to explain the structure of bigotry.[56]

### I. *The National Democratic Party of Germany: Old Wine in new Bottles*

At first sight, it might seem uncommon to select a German Party (also represented in several state parliaments) in order to enlighten the peculiarities of right-wing political extremism. Anyhow, the NPD constitutes a paradigm of institutional political extremism, the so-called "party-linked" extremism.[57] Under its democratic fig-leaf, several anti-democratic and re-

53 See Steinberg, "Jihadistische Radikalisierung," p. 17; that is also the fact for moderate religions groups, see Vidino, "DeRadikalisierung durch gezielte Interventionen," p. 30.

54 Differently Savage, "Four Lessons," pp. 133 ff.

55 An overview for the far-left extremism at Mletzko, "Gewalthandeln linker und rechter militanter Szenen," 2010, pp. 10 ff.

56 Bearing in mind, that especially the IS forms a conglomerate of very different and specific types of religious extremism.

57 See Stöß, "Zur Entwicklung des Rechtsextremismus in Deutschland," 2015, p. 1, available at http://www.bpb.de/politik/extremismus/rechtsextremismus/198940/zur-entwicklung-des-rechtsextremismus-in-deutschland.

visionist powers live like a bee in clover. This mixture between legal and illegal currents among one single political movement predestines the NPD to be examined as an especial German form of right-wing extremism. While in the year 2013, a total of about 21,700 German individuals[58] could be classified with right-wing extremism, about one third of them were listed members in one of the following political parties:

**Numbers of right-wing extremists in parties**

| | 2011 | 2012 | 2013 |
|---|---|---|---|
| **Total** | 7.300 | 7.150 | 7.000 |
| **NPD** | 6.300 | 6.000 | 5.500 |
| **"DIE RECHTE"** | - | 150 | 500 |

**Numbers of right-wing extremists in parties**

| | 2011 | 2012 | 2013 |
|---|---|---|---|
| **"Bürgerbewegung pro NRW" ("pro NRW")** | - | 1,000 | 1,000 |
| **"Deutsche Volksunion" (DVU)** | 1,000 | - | |

Source: http://www.verfassungsschutz.de/de/arbeitsfelder/af-rechtsextremismus/zahlen-und-fakten-rechtsextremismus/zuf-re-2013-parteien.html#tableComment1.

That table shows that right-wing extremism in Germany is mostly related to political parties. One of the biggest parties is the NPD. The National Democratic Party of Germany (German: Nationaldemokratische Partei Deutschlands, NPD), is, as mentioned above, a right-wing extremist political party in Germany.[59] It was founded in 1964, as the successor to the German Reich Party (German: Deutsche Reichspartei, DRP). Its own party statements also self-identify the party as Germany's "only significant patriotic force".[60] The party is usually described as a neo-Nazi organization and has been referred to as the most significant neo-Nazi party to emerge since 1945. Neo-Nazi is the term used for individuals who build their political and social persuasions mostly on a national-socialist mind-

58 See Ministry for the Protection of the Constitution, http://www.verfassungsschutz.de/de/arbeitsfelder/af-rechtsextremismus/zahlen-und-fakten-rechtsextremismus/zuf-re-2013-gesamtuebersicht.html.

59 See their homepage on http://npd.de/teil-1-gruendung-und-erste-erfolge/; instructive for the European right-wing movement Ramalingam, "Old Threat, New Approach," pp. 5 ff.

60 Http://npd.de/was-versteht-die-npd-unter-nationalismus; Dovermann, "Narrative und Gegen-Narrative," p. 43; Priester, "Fließende Grenzen zwischen Rechtsextremismus und Rechtspopulismus in Europa?," 2010, p. 35.

set. Admittedly, the NPD has changed the "socialists" element in its name into a "democratic" one. All the same, the NPD's political philosophy coincides with the notion of a third political position, an idea created among criticism of both liberal capitalism and communism.[61] Moreover, the NPD favors certain beliefs about human nature. The philosophy of the NPD differs from both communism and social liberalism in that it acknowledges people as unequal products of their societies and environments, largely governed by what is called natural law: "The uppermost reference point of national-democratic politics is the responsibility for survival and continuity of the German people in its hereditary Central European living space."[62] The party is also influenced by the views of modern ethnologists such as Konrad Lorenz[63] and Irenäus Eibl-Eibesfeldt.[64] The NPD asserts that Germany is larger than the present-day Federal Republic, and calls for a return of German territory lost after World War II,[65] a foreign policy position definitely abandoned by the German government in 1990. All these views can be classified as revisionist,[66] racist and extremist.[67]

Besides the political party, the NPD is organized in several subgroups and squads. The party continues to pursue a "people's front" of nationalists consisting of the NPD, DVU and forces not attached to any political party, supposed to develop into a base for an encompassing "German people's movement".[68] The aggressive agitation of the NPD blatantly aims to abolish parliamentary democracy and the democratic constitutional state, although the use of violence is currently officially rejected for tactical rea-

---

61 See http://www.bpb.de/politik/extremismus/rechtsextremismus/198941/was-denkt-die-npd.

62 Http://npd.de/thema/identitaet/; Eckert, "Kulturelle Homogenität und aggressive Intoleranz. Eine Kritik der Neuen Rechten," 2010, p. 27.

63 To its impact see Eckert, "Kulturelle Homogenität," p. 27.

64 See his institute for human-ethnological studies in Frankfurt (Main), http://www.humanetho.de/; ideas of superiority of races and species is typical for right-wing extremism, see Neugebauer, "Einfach war gestern," p. 7.

65 The legacies of the Second World War are a problem for the whole European Union; Ramalingam, "Old Threat, New Approach," p. 10.

66 See http://npd.de/wie-steht-die-npd-zum-grundgesetz/.

67 See German Ministry of the Interior, at http://www.bmi.bund.de/DE/Themen/Sicherheit/Extremismusbekaempfung/Rechtsextremismus/rechtsextremismus_node.html;jsessionid=66113F04B2883D645E30513CAB785AEB.2_cid373.

68 BFV, "Die 'Nationaldemokratische Partei Deutschlands' (NPD) als Gravitationsfeld im Rechtsextremismus," 2006, p. 4.

sons.[69] Statements of the NPD bear witness to an essential affinity with National Socialism; its agitation is racist, anti-Semitic[70] and revisionist, and intends to disparage the democratic and lawful order of the constitution.[71] The very dangerous side effects of the NPD are its thuggish and rowdy members[72], executing the filthy job of spreading fear and terror[73] demarcating "no-go-areas"[74] and "German quarters".[75] The active networking of the NPD among these militant groups started in the 1990s. The party was searching contact to right-wing extremist subcultures trying to serve as a housekeeping "leader".[76] Especially after banning several smaller groups of violent gangs, the unruly powers in the German right-wing extremism scene became an inherent part of the NPD.[77] The NPD does not officially admit any connection to these groups of skinheads,[78] fraternities[79] and biker gangs.[80] But as a matter of fact, those entities create the breeding ground for racist and xenophobic thinking.[81]

---

69 See BfV, "NPD als Gravitationsfeld," p. 7; Schedler, "Autonome Nationalisten," 2010, p 25; BfV, "Autonome Nationalisten – Rechtsextremistische Militanz," 2009, p. 7; that's a difference to lots of others extremist and extremist groups, see OSCE, "Preventing Terrorism," p. 37.

70 See BfV, "Argumentationsmuster im rechtsextremistischen Antisemitismus. Aktuelle Entwicklungen," 2005, pp. 7 ff.

71 See http://npd.de/wie-steht-die-npd-zum-grundgesetz/.

72 For example "Autonom Nationalist", see Bundesamt für Verfassungsschutz, "Autonome Nationalisten," p. 1; Mletzko, "Gewalthandeln," p. 11; instructive also Schedler, "Autonome Nationalisten," pp. 20 ff.

73 BfV, "NPD als Gravitationsfeld," p. 5.

74 Frindte and Preiser, "Präventionsansätze gegen Rechtsextremismus," 2007, p. 33.

75 Bundschuh, "Die braune Seite der Zivilgesellschaft: rechtsextreme Sozialraumstrategien," 2012, p. 31.

76 Stöß, "Entwicklung des Rechtsextremismus," p. 1.

77 See Stöß, "Entwicklung des Rechtsextremismus," p. 1.

78 See Schroeder, *Rechtsextremismus und Jugendgewalt*, pp. 40 ff.; Mletzko, "Gewalthandeln," p. 11.

79 See Mletzko, "Gewalthandeln," p. 11.

80 To understand the Europe-wide spreading see Ramalingam, "Old Threat, New Approach," p. 7.

81 See Backes, "Interdependenzen und Interaktionen zwischen gewaltlosen und gewaltorientierten extremistischen Akteuren am Beispiel von 'Autonomen', 'Neonationalsozialisten' und 'Skinheads' in der Bundesrepublik Deutschland," 2006, p. 51.

The recruitment for future members of the NPD or its subgroups starts at a very early stage. Public youth work[82] in deprived areas[83] (rural regions without any job prospects, high relative poverty[84] and high rate of "foreign domination"[85]) attracts predominantly young men, often with lower education and income, to find an alleged new sense in demarcating their way of life from those they call "system menials"[86] or "vassals".[87] The neo-nationalists try to get in contact with young adolescents and want to spread their opinions, at first glance, in a rather harmless way. On the surface, the nationalists give answers to fervent questions: developments on the job market, security in nearby neighborhoods, a future for the upcoming generation.[88] The right-wing extremists use vague formulations and indistinct allusions: "For many years the social problems are incalculable in the federal republic. Bit by bit the social state is hollowed out, proven standards are lowered. The gap between poor and rich is widening more and more"; "In the public space of the Federal Republic of Germany the security, the right on intactness and rule of law erode in an increasing manner."[89] Once decoyed by these hot spots of social and political life, the nationalists begin to infiltrate their policies with subtle or not so subtle allusions and propaganda.[90] The bogeyman soon will be identified concretely: the democratic and pluralistic society allows too many "foreigners" not willing to integrate and assimilate the indigenous manners and behaviors,

82 See BfV, "Autonome Nationalisten," p. 8; That is the method of the far-right all over Europe, see Ramalingam, "Old Threat, New Approach," p. 10.

83 See Schroeder, *Rechtsextremismus und Jugendgewalt*, p. 21.

84 Poverty and fear for the future are the best hotbed for radicalization Richardson, "Was Terroristen wollen," pp. 89 f.

85 Typical nationalist narrative, see Dovermann, "Narrative und Gegen-Narrative," p. 43; Schroeder, *Rechtsextremismus und Jugendgewalt*, p. 117; EXIT-Germany, "De-Radicalization and Disengagement," p. 3; see the two exemplifying case studies by Mansour, "Salafistische Radikalisierung – und was man dagegen tun kann," avaible at http://www.bpb.de/politik/extremismus/islamismus/193521/salafistische-Radikalisierung-und-was-man-dagegen-tun-kann; it derives by the idea of the necessity of a "clash of cultures", see Eckert, "Kulturelle Homogenität," p. 29.

86 Dovermann, "Narrative und Gegen-Narrative," p. 43.

87 For citation see BfV, "Autonome Nationalisten," p. 5.

88 Ramalingam, "Old Threat, New Approach," p. 12; BfV, "NPD als Gravitationsfeld," p. 6; see also the homepage of the NPD http://npd.de/themen/.

89 See the homepage of the NPD: http://npd.de/themen/.

90 See Buschbom et al., "Rechtspopulismus," p. 2; OSCE, "Preventing Terrorism," p. 37.

destroying the concept of values and virtues of the occidental societies.[91] The plurality of contact points facilitates the feigned certainties: foreigners capture jobs, women, cultural identity and social security.[92] The topo "foreign" becomes the battle cry.[93] Anything not common and not known has to be degraded as inferior and debased.[94] Propaganda and ideology are spread by tattoos, merchandise[95] and by infiltrating the internet.[96] Another frequently used platform is music.[97] While doing so, the particular German History of the first half of the 20th century builds an obtrusive connection.[98] The idea of being superior to other races and ethnic groups justifies vilification of strangers and minorities.[99] The hatred is based on an interaction of racism,[100] nationalism, foggy fears for the future[101] and the feeling of being left far behind other members of society, who are regard-

---

91 See Schroeder, *Rechtsextremismus und Jugendgewalt*, pp. 96 f.

92 See Geschke, "Vorurteile," p. 35; EXIT-Germany, "De-Radicalization and Disengagement," p. 3; Buschbom et al., "Rechtspopulismus," p. 8; Eckert, "Radikalisierung," p. 13.

93 See Schroeder, *Rechtsextremismus und Jugendgewalt*, p. 96; EXIT-Germany, "De-Radicalization and Disengagement," p. 3; Eckert, "Radikalisierung," p. 13.

94 See Sitzer and Heitmeyer, "Rechtsextremistische Gewalt von Jugendlichen," 2007, p. 3; Ramalingam, "Old Threat, New Approach," p. 7; Groß et al., "Gruppenbezogene Menschenfeindlichkeit," pp. 12 ff.

95 See Ramalingam, "Old Threat, New Approach," p. 10; Steinberg, "Jihadistische Radikalisierung," p. 19.

96 Instructive with a listing of several hompages Steinberg, "Jihadistische Radikalisierung," pp.18 ff.; Glaser and Schneider, "Zielgruppe Jugend: Rechtsextreme im Social Web," 2012, pp. 40 ff.; Briggs and Feve, "Counter Narratives of Violent Extremism?," p. 9; BfV, "Jugend und 'Jihad'," 2014, p. 2; Priester, "Fließende Grenzen?," p. 37; Eckert, "Radikalisierung," p. 14.

97 See Dovermann, "Narrative und Gegen-Narrative," p. 43; Mletzko, "Gewalthandeln" p. 11; Priester, "Fließende Grenzen zwischen Rechtsextremismus und Rechtspopulismus in Europa?," p. 37; Möller and Schuhmacher, "Ein- und Ausstiegsprozesse," p. 22.

98 Schroeder, *Rechtsextremismus und Jugendgewalt*, pp. 25 ff.

99 Schroeder, *Rechtsextremismus und Jugendgewalt*, p. 16; Dovermann, "Narrative und Gegen-Narrative," p. 43; Groß et al., "Gruppenbezogene Menschenfeindlichkeit," p. 11; Wenzel, "Betrachtungen zum Islamistischen Terrorismus – die arabische Perspektive," 2005, p. 68; Eckert, "Radikalisierung," p. 13; Sitzer and Heitmeyer, "Gewalt von Jugendlichen," p.3.

100 See Schroeder, *Rechtsextremismus und Jugendgewalt*, p. 17.

101 See BfV, "NPD als Gravitationsfeld," p. 6; Heitmeyer, "Rechtsextremismus und gesellschaftliche Selbstentlastung," 2012, p. 24; Richardson, "Was Terroristen wollen," p. 89; Groß et al., "Gruppenbezogene Menschenfeindlichkeit," p. 17.

ed as wealthy and powerful.[102] The ruling "class of the elites" has forgotten its roots[103] and does not care about the needs and requirements of the man-on-the-street.[104] Those "abandoned" adolescents now searching for solidarity and companionship[105] become addicted to the power they get by admitting their hatred and their aggressions.[106] The feeling of not being bound to social rules imparts personal strength and self-confidence.[107]

> We understand 'right-wing extremism' as a totality of settings, behavioral patterns and actions (organized or not) which ground themselves on an alleged inequality of social conditioned ethnics or races of people, that requires ethnic homogeneity of people and rejects the equality order of the declaration of human rights, which stresses the priority of the community before the individual based on subordination of citizens and rejects the value of pluralism of a liberal democracy and therefore wants to cancel democratization.[108]

The spiral of radicalization leads to continual identification with the peer group and its codes-of-conduct.[109] The hidden string-pullers in the background exploit this creeping process by solidifying the ties through rites and oaths.[110] The team spirit,[111] or esprit de corps, must (at least up to the string-puller's opinion) be the most important fact of life, determining all thought and decisions of the individual.[112] The single person will be in-

---

102 See OSCE, "Preventing Terrorism," p. 37.

103 See Buschbom et al., "Rechtspopulismus," p. 4.

104 See Schroeder, *Rechtsextremismus und Jugendgewalt*, p. 96; BfV, *NPD als Gravitationsfeld im Rechtsextremismus*, p. 6; the "man-in-the-street" is also a typical argumentation pattern of far-right populism, see Buschbom et al., "Rechtspopulismus," p. 2; Priester, "Fließende Grenzen zwischen Rechtsextremismus und Rechtspopulismus in Europa?," p. 38; but also in the Islamist thinking, the feeling of being left behind is widespread, Wenzel, "Arabische Perspektive," p. 63; also known as "theory of disintegration", Sitzer and Heitmeyer, "Gewalt von Jugendlichen," p. 10.

105 See Möller and Schuhmacher, "Ein- und Ausstiegsprozesse," p. 19; Richardson, "Was Terroristen wollen," pp. 80, 304; Eckert, "Radikalisierung," p. 14.

106 See OSCE, "Preventing Terrorism," p. 37.

107 See Sitzer and Heitmeyer, "Gewalt von Jugendlichen," p. 8.

108 Jaschke, *Rechtsextremismus*, p. 31.

109 See Neubacher, "Terrorismus," p. 748; Möller and Schuhmacher, "Ein- und Ausstiegsprozesse," pp. 21, 22 f.

110 See Richardson, "Was Terroristen wollen," p. 79; Hoffmann-Plesch, "Deutsche IS-Dschihadisten Teil 2," p. 12; Waldmann, "Islamistischer Terrorismus," p.35; Sirseloudi et al., "Radikalisierung von europäischen Muslimen," p. 44.

111 See Korn and Weilnböck, "Der lange Abschied," p. 34.

112 See OSCE, "Preventing Terrorism," p. 38.

strumentalized to undergird the impact of the party and its sympathizers. The step into relevant criminal responsibility hence is taken rapidly. The verbal lapse occurs: anti-foreign slogans, hate speeches,[113] denials of commonly known historical facts (existence and extent of the Holocaust,[114] the war guilt of Germany,[115] the new borders in Europe after the unconditional surrender and the rearrangement of the political systems by the Allies[116]). The threshold[117] to physical violence turns out as expected.[118] Continuous criminal property damage and vandalism[119] diminish inhibitions while the omnipresent attendance of the inculcated propaganda blurs the consciousness for the effected injustices.[120] Hence, the individual continuously dulls his or her scruples. Out of obedience and internalized persuasion, the physical integrity of third persons becomes a declining factor.[121] The concerned individual handles life through a new ideology and aligns the surroundings in appropriate manners.[122] As soon as the whole life has been infiltrated by the propaganda and hate, the unalloyed view on social conditions moves over to a far range.

---

113 See Buschbom et al., "Rechtspopulismus," p. 3; Dovermann, "Narrative und Gegen-Narrative," p. 40; Korn and Weilnböck, "Der lange Abschied," p. 32.

114 See NPD-Parteivorstand (ed.), *Argumente für Kandidaten und Funktionsträger. Eine Handreichung für die öffentliche Auseinandersetzung. NPD. Die Nationalen Argumente für Kandidaten und Funktionsträger*, 2006, p. 10; also the statements on the party homepage http://npd.de/ist-die-npd-eine-antisemitische-partei/; BfV, "Argumentationsmuster im rechtsextremistischen Antisemitismus," pp.18 ff.

115 See Dovermann, "Narrative und Gegen-Narrative," p. 43; Eckert, "Kulturelle Homogenität," p. 32.

116 See Eckert, "Kulturelle Homogenität," p. 27.

117 For the different models of escalation, see Sitzer and Heitmeyer, "Gewalt von Jugendlichen," p. 9.

118 See Briggs and Feve, "Counter Narratives of Violent Extremism?," p. 9; Eckert, "Radikalisierung," p. 13.

119 See Neumann, "Radikalisierung," p. 5; Korn and Weilnböck, "Der lange Abschied," p. 32.

120 See OSCE, "Preventing Terrorism," p. 37; several more forms of far right-extremist activities by Ramalingam, "Old Threat, New Approach," p. 9; Neumann, "Radikalisierung," p 5.

121 See Schroeder, *Rechtsextremismus und Jugendgewalt*, p. 98; EXIT-Germany, "De-Radicalization and Disengagement," p. 4; OSCE, "Preventing Terrorism," p. 37; Mletzko, "Gewalthandeln," p. 13.

122 See Böllinger, "Die Entwicklung zu terroristischem Handeln," pp. 65 ff.

### II. The Religious Fanaticism: Islamism, Salafism, Wahhabism

The connection between religion and extremism is very old.[123] Moreover, religious motives have been one of the most important hotbeds for extremism in recent decades.[124] Religious fundamentalism is characterized by several features: the base ideology contains the perception of the necessity of a "holy war"[125] against different-minders, requesting blind obedience from its members while declaring an absolute claim of truth for all its dogmas.[126] The "good old times" have to be recovered and re-installed, while the present world of degrading and forgotten values needs to rid itself of nonbelievers to reset itself. One of the biggest threats emanating from this conglomerate of distortion is the fundamental-Islamic movement.[127] The variety of existing Muslim-fundamentalism movements is not easy to grasp any more.[128] By the end of the year 2013 about 30 active Islamic

---

123 See Waldmann, "Islamistischer Terrorismus," p. 43; See Richardson, "Was Terroristen wollen," pp. 50 ff. for a historical overview of its roots in ancient times; instructive Zöller, *Terrorismusstrafrecht*, pp. 11 ff.

124 See Richardson, "Was Terroristen wollen," pp. 95 ff.; Vidino, "DeRadikalisierung durch gezielte Interventionen," p. 25.

125 Neubacher, "Terrorismus," p. 744; Silke, "Holy Warriors," p. 100; Hoffmann-Plesch, "Deutsche IS-Dschihadisten, Kriminalätiologische und kriminalpräventive Analyse des Radikalisierungsprozesses, Teil 1: Religionskriminologische und psychopolitische Aspekte," 2014, pp. 701, 702 f.; Dovermann, "Narrative und Gegen-Narrative," p. 42; Sirseloudi et al., "Radikalisierung von europäischen Muslimen," p. 42; the fight against different-minded individuals is not unique to Islamist extremism, but can be found in several fundamental ideologies.

126 See Sirseloudi et al., "Radikalisierung von europäischen Muslimen," p. 41; Zöller, *Terrorismusstrafrecht*, p. 85; Dovermann, "Narrative und Gegen-Narrative," pp. 42 ff.

127 See Werthebach, "Deutsche Sicherheitsstrukturen im 21. Jahrhundert," 2004, p. 8.

128 See Ende, "Gerechtigkeit," p. 19; Neubacher, "Terrorismus," p. 746; Brettfeld and Wetzels, *Muslime in Deutschland, Integration, Integrationsbarrieren, Religion und Einstellungen zu Demokratie, Rechtsstaat und politisch-religiös motivierter Gewalt, Ergebnisse von Befragungen im Rahmen einer multizentrischen Studie in städtischen Lebensräumen,* 2007, pp. 15 ff.; Steinberg, "Jihadistische Radikalisierung," p. 17; the most popular are the Hamas, Hisbollah, Ansar als-Islam, Al-Quaida, Boko Haram, Al Nusra, IS etc; for an overwiew of the biggest currents see Sirseloudi et al., "Radikalisierung von europäischen Muslimen," pp. 40 ff. and Hoffmann-Plesch, "Deutsche IS-Dschihadisten Teil 1," p. 700; for a historical overview see Ouaissa, "Aufstieg islamistischer Parteien," 2008, pp. 40, 41 ff.

organizations existed all over the country. The total number of Islamic extremists in Germany has risen from 42,550 (2012) to 43,190. This increase is particularly based on the steady growth of members and adherents of Salafist movements in Germany.

**Numbers of persons in extremist organizations in Germany**

| | 2011 | 2012 | 2013 |
|---|---|---|---|
| **Name of Organization** | | | |
| **"Al-Qaida" and similar terroristic groups** | No valid numbers | No valid numbers | No valid numbers |
| **Islamist-Kurdish Network/"Ansar al-Islam" (AAI)** | No valid numbers | No valid numbers | No valid numbers |
| **"Islamist Movement Usbekistans" (IBU)** | No valid numbers | No valid numbers | No valid numbers |
| **Salafist Movement** | 3,800 | 4,500 | 5,500 |
| **"Hizb Allah"** | 950 | 950 | 950 |
| **"Harakat al-Muqawama al-Islamiya" (HAMAS)** | 300 | 300 | 300 |
| **"Northern-Kaukasien Separatists" (NKSB)** | 500 | 500 | 250 |
| **"Turkish Hizbullah" (TH)** | 350 | 350 | 350 |
| **"Hezb-e Islami-ye Afghanistan" (HIA)** | 200 | 200 | 200 |
| **"Hizb ut-Tahrir"** | 300 | 300 | 300 |
| **"Muslim Brotherhood" (MB)** | 1,300 | 1,300 | 1,300 |
| **"Tablighi Jama'at" (TJ)** | 700 | 700 | 700 |
| **"Islamist Community Millî Görüş e.V." (IGMG)** | 31,000 | 31,000 | 31,000 |
| **Others** | 2,480 | 2,450 | 2,340 |
| **Total** | 38,080 | 42,550 | 43,190 |

Source: http://www.verfassungsschutz.de/de/arbeitsfelder/af-islamismus-und-islamistischer-terrorismus/zahlen-und-fakten-islamismus/zuf-is-2013-gesamtuebersicht.html.

Compared to the 21,000 right-wing extremists above (C.1.), the Islamic extremists outnumber the right-wing extremists by 50%. Of course, the exact number may be much higher, as there are many undocumented cases. This essay does not want to fix and expose a concrete demarcation of only one single form of religious extremism. Rather, common characteristics of all forms of radicalization should be highlighted in the religious sector. Moreover, as the most extreme form of radicalization, "civil war tourism" is to be evaluated, i.e. that European citizens convert to radical

Islam[129] with the intention to travel to civil war regions such as Syria or North Africa in order to actively take part in the Jihad[130] against the "enemies"[131] (home-grown terrorists[132]).[133] The decision to travel voluntarily into a crisis area shows on one hand a great deal of internal conviction, but on the other hand is a high degree of estrangement toward western values.[134]

A closer look at the atrocities[135] (decapitation, crucifixion, live mutilation, eating brains and hearts of victims, etc.)[136] of the "Islamic State" and a careful examination of its approaches and motives, reveals that the brutalization and dehumanization of its members occurs in a frightening way.[137] Shared thinking and persuasion is set above the value of life of others, the self-righteous interpretation of supposed dogmas is used as a pseudo rational justification for all criminal border-crossings.[138] Whereas Islam represents one of the three big monotheistic world religions, Islamism describes a form of political extremism.[139] Islamists abuse the ideas of peaceful Islam for their own political purposes interpreting new, all-embracing set of rules for everybody that implement social, juridical,

129 See Vidino, "DeRadikalisierung durch gezielte Interventionen," p. 25; Sirseloudi et al., "Radikalisierung von europäischen Muslimen," p. 39.

130 See Heine, *Terror in Allahs Name: Extremistische Kräfte im Islam*, 2004, 17 ff. describes the principle of the jihad; see also Silke, "Holy Warriors," pp. 100 f.

131 Neubacher, "Terrorismus," p. 746; BfV, "Islamismus: Entstehung und Erscheinungsformen," 2013, pp. 27, 30 ff.; Puschnerat, "Ideologische und soziale Faktoren," p. 222.

132 See Sirseloudi et al., "Radikalisierung von europäischen Muslimen," p. 43.

133 See Hoffmann-Plesch, "Deutsche IS-Dschihadisten Teil 1," p. 700.

134 See Richardson, "Was Terroristen wollen," p. 104; Dovermann, "Narrative und Gegen-Narrative," p. 41; Information about 378 people who have left up to the 30th of June, 2014 from Germany with Islamic motivation in the direction of Syria is given to the security services. 89 percent of these left people are men, 11 percent are women. The left are between 15 and 63 years old. The from 15 to 30-year-old show the numerically biggest age group, see BT- Drucksache 18/2865 of 14. Oct 2014, 6.

135 See also Silke, "Holy Warriors," pp. 103 ff.

136 See Hoffmann-Plesch, "Deutsche IS-Dschihadisten Teil 2," pp. 13, 14.

137 See for more information Hoffmann-Plesch, "Deutsche IS-Dschihadisten Teil 1," pp. 700 ff.

138 See Schroeder, *Rechtsextremismus und Jugendgewalt*, p. 42.

139 See Zöller, *Terrorismusstrafrecht*, pp. 45, 48.

economic and political dimensions.[140] Furthermore, they regard Islam as a sort of ideal, universal world order[141] reckoning the religion as a divine order of society and state.[142] An example of this philosophy is the application of a strictly and literally interpreted[143] sharia law (Islamic legal apprenticeship).[144]

Although all Islamist appeal to Islam, they draw a clear distinction from each other.[145] Differences appear in the chosen means used to achieve individual aims. Especially radical Islamists, the political "Jihadist", tend to use violence.[146] According to their opinion, violence does not only represent a means among others, but it describes the only allowed means to achieve any aim.[147] Other groups act more moderately.[148] Their political activities penetrate Islamic positions in social life.[149] By stressing their own Muslim identity while concurrently rejecting the "immoral and debauched Western culture",[150] (da-al-harab: "House of Hostility"[151] "Field

140 See Richardson, "Was Terroristen wollen," p. 102; BfV, "Islamismus: Entstehung und Erscheinungsformen," p. 10; Wenzel, "Arabische Perspektive," p. 68.

141 See BfV, "Islamismus: Entstehung und Erscheinungsformen," p. 10; Puschnerat, "Ideologische und soziale Faktoren," p. 224.

142 See Richardson, "Was Terroristen wollen," p. 103; Zöller, *Terrorismusstrafrecht*, p. 49.

143 That is especially the request of the Salafists, see Zöller, *Terrorismusstrafrecht*, p. 52; Hoffmann-Plesch, "Deutsche IS-Dschihadisten Teil 1," p. 702.

144 See Puschnerat, "Ideologische und soziale Faktoren," p. 224; Dovermann, "Narrative und Gegen-Narrative," p. 41; See for the infringement of religion and state in Islamic societies Abdillah, *Verfassungsgebung in muslimischen Ländern*, pp. 55 ff.; a short overview of the interpretation of the sharia by Ende, "Gerechtigkeit," p. 20.

145 See Zöller, *Terrorismusstrafrecht*, pp. 47 f.

146 See BfV, "Islamismus: Entstehung und Erscheinungsformen," p. 12; Puschnerat, "Ideologische und soziale Faktoren," p. 227.

147 See BfV, "Islamismus: Entstehung und Erscheinungsformen," Puschnerat, "Ideologische und soziale Faktoren," p. 219; Eckert, "Radikalisierung," p. 12; there occurs a similarity to the "autonom nationalists", see Schedler, "Autonome Nationalisten," p. 22.

148 See BfV, "Islamismus: Entstehung und Erscheinungsformen," pp. 19 ff.; Eckert, "Radikalisierung," p. 16.

149 For example the salafist, BfV, "Islamismus: Entstehung und Erscheinungsformen," p. 10.

150 Wenzel, "Arabische Perspektive," p. 67; Heine, *Terror in Allahs Namen*, p. 93; Dovermann, "Narrative und Gegen-Narrative," p. 41.

151 Hoffmann-Plesch, "Deutsche IS-Dschihadisten Teil 1," p. 702; opposite "dar-al-islam" = House of Islam; see also Heine, *Terror in Allahs Namen*, p. 23.

of War"[152]) these organizations thus promote the building and strengthening of parallel societies.[153] To ease their spreading and their impact range, those organizations transform their ideology into suitable social and cultural offerings, especially shaped for young[154] adolescents.

The reasons for adolescents' radicalization processes are various. For a large part, suffering military oppression, typically after wars or conflicts, demoralizes the personal habitude and lead to an aggressive attitude against the former occupation power.[155] This phenomenon can be regarded in the Israel/Palestine Conflict,[156] in Iraq during the occupation and after the withdrawal of the "coalition of the willing"[157] and in many parts of the world that are former colonies of the European powers.[158] Increasing discontentment with economic and social surroundings, the fear of poverty and famines as well as permanent civil riots continuously destabilize whole regions. Victimization becomes an important part of life.[159] Moreover, the Muslim world feels especially left-behind concerning the distri-

152 Heine, *Terror in Allahs Namen*, p. 23.

153 See Hoffmann-Plesch, "Deutsche IS-Dschihadisten Teil 1," p. 700; Vidino, "De-Radikalisierung durch gezielte Interventionen," p. 31.

154 See for the special impact of age and gender Silke, "Holy Warriors," pp. 105 ff.

155 See Zöller, *Terrorismusstrafrecht*, p. 79; Neumann, "Radikalisierung," p. 7; Silke, "Holy Warriors," pp. 113 ff.; see Borum, "Radicalization Into Violent Extremism I," pp. 22 ff. for more information on those "conversion theories of radicalization".

156 Instructive Heine, *Terror in Allahs Namen*, pp. 132 ff.; Neubacher, "Terrorismus," p. 749; Priester, "Fließende Grenzen zwischen Rechtsextremismus und Rechtspopulismus in Europa?," p. 38.

157 Silke, "Holy Warriors," p. 114; Neubacher, "Terrorismus," p. 749; initial ignition for huge propaganda efforts in the Muslim world, see Steinberg, "Jihadistische Radikalisierung," p. 19; initial ignition for the western world to start the "war against terrorism", Dombrowsky, "Terrorismus und die Verteidigung des Zivilen," 2004, p. 37; this was the ignition for lots of radical individuals to escalate, see Hoffmann-Plesch, "Deutsche IS-Dschihadisten Teil 2," p. 11.

158 See Sirseloudi et al., "Radikalisierung von europäischen Muslimen," p. 41; Heine, *Terror in Allahs Namen*, pp. 74 ff; a similar ethnical-national conflict exists in Ireland, in Spain, in Turkey etc.

159 See Horgan, "From Profiles to Pathways," p. 85; McCauley and Moskalenko, "Mechanisms of Political Radicalization," pp. 418 ff.; Eckert, "Radikalisierung," p. 14; Hoffmann-Plesch, "Deutsche IS-Dschihadisten Teil 1," p. 700; Sirseloudi et al., "Radikalisierung von europäischen Muslimen," p. 42.

bution of goods and wealth.[160] The “Western” world[161] strengthens this misbalance by acquiescing to despotic tyrannies as a quid pro quo for mineral resources and trade routes. In this way, the Islamic world sees itself being exploited as a “cheap cash cow” by decadent and immoral occidental societies.[162] So, many Islamic regions have triggered violent resistance against this quasi self-evident exploitation[163], humiliation[164] and deprivation.[165]

The radicalization of youngsters often carries very individual traits.[166] There is no typical “jihadist” profile,[167] even though a quite specific trend occurs. The real form of radicalization arises as a mixture of social and ideological factors of influences.[168] Surely, one prerequisite is the existence of an age-conditioned disorientation, often strengthened by or resulting from the search for right values, a real community and putative “justice”. Another reason for the susceptibility of future radicals is a special sort of feeling of superiority,[169] developing because one perceives himself situated on the part of the “good”.[170] The way to “Jihadism” mostly is

160 See Eckert, “Radikalisierung,” pp. 14 f.; Silke, “Holy Warriors,” p. 112; Özerdem and Podder, “Disarming Youth Combatants,” p. 66.

161 Typical narrative of the Islamic propaganda, see Dovermann, “Narrative und Gegen-Narrative,” p. 41.

162 See Zöller, *Terrorismusstrafrecht*, p. 82; Eckert, “Radikalisierung,” p. 14.

163 See Neubacher, “Terrorismus,” p. 746; Dovermann, “Narrative und Gegen-Narrative,” p. 42.

164 See Steinberg, “Jihadistische Radikalisierung,” p. 18; Dovermann, “Narrative und Gegen-Narrative,” p. 42; Sirseloudi et al., “Radikalisierung von europäischen Muslimen,” p. 41.

165 See Sirseloudi et al., “Radikalisierung von europäischen Muslimen,” p. 44; Silke, “Holy Warriors,” pp. 112 ff.

166 See Puschnerat, “Ideologische und soziale Faktoren,” p. 221; Neumann, “Radikalisierung,” p. 7.

167 See BT-Drucksache 18/2865 of 14. Oct 2014, 7.

168 See Silke, “Holy Warriors,” pp. 107 ff.; Özerdem and Podder, “Disarming Youth Combatants,” pp. 66 ff.; Puschnerat, “Ideologische und soziale Faktoren,” p. 222; Neubacher, “Terrorismus,” p. 747.

169 Dovermann, “Narrative und Gegen-Narrative,” p. 43; Eckert, “Kulturelle Homogenität,” p. 30.

170 See Eckert, “Radikalisierung,” p. 12.

guided by the internet[171] or is based in the personal sphere (friendship or cliques, charismatic leaders in mosques or Islamic organizations).[172]

Up-and-coming jihadists get recruited from different sources. However, a high-powered element of the radicalization process is permanent contact with the same-aged peers with similar ideas. Individual radicalization often expresses particular behaviors and features. Bearing in mind a comprehensive consideration of each individual case (to avoid unnecessary misinterpretation), there are many signs of radicalization: changes in external appearance (clothes, hairstyle), changes in life-style (eating and sleeping habits), construction of a new social sphere, higher importance of religion in the person's own life, and permanent consumption of Islamic content.[173]

### *III. Effects of Radicalization*

"Fanaticism is the highly explosive mixture of narrow-mindedness and energy"
(Herbert von Karajan)

The individual is trapped in a spiral of self-evidential demonstrations of power.[174] The feeling of superiority, no longer accepting one's fate but actively trying to change the environment, determines the point of view of the extremist.[175] His obedience has gone head over heels as an end in itself, while becoming victim to his own radicalization. He loses ground, because the awareness of an ineluctable violence intimidates and paralyzes daily life.[176] The upcoming existential anguish and the cognition of per-

171 There exists an extreme machinery of propaganda videos, platforms, chatrooms and further infiltration spreading all over the world with myriad sources and agitators, see Steinberg, "Jihadistische Radikalisierung," pp. 20 ff.

172 See BfV, *Islamismus: Entstehung und Erscheinungsformen*, pp. 28 ff.; Neubacher, "Terrorismus," p. 749; BT-Drucksache 18/2865 of 14. Oct 2014, p. 7; Sirseloudi et al., "Radikalisierung von europäischen Muslimen," p. 42.

173 See Puschnerat, "Ideologische und soziale Faktoren," p. 222. See the list by BfV, "Jugend und 'Jihad'," p. 2.

174 See Neubacher, "Terrorismus," p.748.

175 See Dovermann, "Narrative und Gegen-Narrative," p. 43.

176 See Neumann, "Radikalisierung," p. 8.

manent life endangerment sharpen the recognition of one's own mortality.[177]

### *C. Drop-out Organizations and Their Work (stages "early"/"preventive")*

For some, the turning point appears out of the blue. A personal calamity alters the perception. Good experiences with the former "enemy" changes an individual's point of view. A new stage of reflections emerges, and the previous way of life does not fit any longer with the recent propensities. Drop-outs often are "switchers of mental position".[178] The way back commences by stating new goals. But leaving the vicious cycle is not as easy as entering it. Specific opt-out programs try to help those individuals on their way back to society. An effective intervention is one of the most important and powerful ways to have an impact on existing movements, although it is often left out of national strategies and action plans against violent far-right extremism.[179] Intervention includes de-radicalization programs aimed to re-integrate dropouts back into society, or at least to dissuade them from violence.[180] These programs also aim to reverse the radicalization process for those partly or already radicalized.[181] The opt-out organizations try to accompany the dropout back to a normal life.[182] The most important means for extremists and terrorists is subtle certainty of insecurity. This special form of pressure works well, as long as the user may handle its consequences. But then, immunity against radicalization vanish-

---

177 This applies to the extremists as well as to the victims, Zöller, *Terrorismusstrafrecht*, p. 84.

178 Schoelermann, "Der Weg aus der Szene ist steinig," 2008, p. 1, available on http://www.bpb.de/politik/extremismus/rechtsextremismus/41374/der-weg-aus-der-szene-ist-steinig.

179 See Vidino, "DeRadikalisierung durch gezielte Interventionen," p. 26.

180 See Vidino, "DeRadikalisierung durch gezielte Interventionen," p. 29; see the good practice guidelines and principles at Korn and Weilnböck, "Der lange Abschied," p. 34.

181 See Ramalingam, "Old Threat, New Approach," p. 19; Neumann, "Radikalisierung," p. 10.

182 See EXIT-Germany, "De-Radicalization and Disengagement," p. 2; Ramalingam, "Old Threat, New Approach," p. 20.

es: the walls close in and the individual needs to escape from its own glided cage of self-righteous suicidal disaster.[183]

### *I. The German drop-out Program EXIT*

In Germany, a non-governmental organization was created to fight against radicalization. It is called EXIT, and is an initiative helping people who want to break away from right-wing extremism and to start a new life.[184] EXIT Germany was founded by certified criminologist and former criminal commissioner Bernd Wagner and Ex-Nazi leader Ingo Hassel, both providing assistance for self-help since the summer of 2000 for dropouts from the radical right-wing scene. At the same time, they try to argue against the world-image and behaviors of right-wing extremists to reduce xenophobic and racist prejudices. EXIT Germany admittedly works politically but this subject is nonpartisan. They do not work under orders from statutory authorities, police or the German Ministry for the Protection of the Constitution and Justice. As such, they guarantee data protection since collected personal information is not transmitted to any of those authorities. EXIT Germany wants to help dropouts to develop new perspectives beyond the radical right-wing scene. Moreover, they provide contact to public agencies and offer practical aid. The organization answers frequent questions about security and of social and personal processing. They explicitly do not offer economic or social security[185] and also do not protect against criminal persecution.[186] A successful dropout is described by EXIT as follows:

> An 'exit' is considered completed by us when a critical reflection, reassessment as well as successful challenge of the old ideology have taken place. Thus, 'exit' to us means more than simply leaving a party or group. It also goes beyond changing the aesthetics of expression or refraining from vio-

183 See this psychological spiral described by Hoffmann-Plesch, "Deutsche IS-Dschihadisten Teil 2," pp. 10 f.

184 See http://www.exit-deutschland.de/start/; EXIT-Germany, "De-Radicalization and Disengagement," p. 2.

185 But so do many others, see Vidino, "DeRadikalisierung durch gezielte Interventionen," p. 28.

186 See http://www.exit-deutschland.de/exit/?c=ueber-uns.

> lence. An exit is successful when the fundamental ideologies and purposes of the previous actions have been resolved.[187]

The organization stands for the long-term and would like to achieve lasting success. In addition they use successful dropouts as advisers and street workers,[188] openly or in the background.[189] Their therapy involves a five-step-model:

| | |
|---|---|
| 1st step: | The drop-out expresses doubts in long conversations with co-workers. EXIT encourages the extremists by showing possibilities and plans for the future (motivation). |
| 2nd step: | A climbing out phase, as the dropout must quit contact with the radical right-wing scene. Depending on circumstances, a security draft is compiled to avoid revenge acts against the dropout. |
| 3rd step: | An establishment phase, exploring future social, economic, and employment perspectives (establishment). |
| 4th step: | A reflective phase, where the dropouts excogitate their past, their former ideology and committed actions (reflecting). |
| 5th step: | In ideal cases (see above), former extremists successfully exit and have found new social groups, secured their financial future, and represent humanistic values (stabilization). |

EXIT trusts in self-organization and has installed some action circles to improve their efforts. An action circle wants to appeal to former companions and publicly clear up which ideas and theories form the background of ideologies of the extreme right. The former extremists, mostly with national-socialist background, co-operating in the action circle, observe very thoroughly what happens in the country, what their previous "friends" and fellow combatants do and how the scenes develop.

Many people who want to dissociate themselves from the radical right-wing scene search for a new beginning without person-despising propaganda. Apart from the mental processing of their political position, quite a number of dropouts are confronted with relics engraved under their skin: their tattoos of national-socialist emblems which regularly constitute criminal offences. The clearing of the tattoos, also offered by Exit, aims to al-

187 EXIT-Germany, "De-Radicalization and Disengagement," p. 9.

188 See Korn and Weilnböck, "Der lange Abschied," p. 34.

189 See EXIT-Germany, "De-Radicalization and Disengagement," p. 12; Ramalingam, "Old Threat, New Approach," p. 20.

low a visible dimension of the dropping out process, which is also absolutely necessary in many cases.[190]

## II. HATIF

Under the name HATIF, the German Federal Office for Protection of the Constitution pursued a dropout's program for people who wanted to free themselves of Islamism and Islamic terrorism, from 2010 to 2014. The name HATIF is an acronym from "Out from terrorism and Islamic fanaticism". As well, it corresponds to the Latin spelling for the Arabic word for "phone". The program offers assistance to former extremists, who want to free themselves from a fanatical and radical sphere. For this purpose a hotline was established, which was constantly accessible from July 2010 to September 2014. The phone calls were accepted by professional staff of the Federal Office for Protection of the Constitution. Phone calls were also possible in Turkish and Arabian language. The aim of the program was to help people free themselves from a sphere, in which fanatical recommendations of the use of force is preached and lived. Apart from talks and advice, HATIF offered help in contacting authorities, support in situations of threats, mediation of qualification measures and, in particular cases, material help.

HATIF was not ended for financial reasons. Rather the program was not being used sufficiently. The uptake remained low. The telephone often didn't ring for weeks.[191] Therefore, the program was stopped in September 2014. The Federal Office for Protection of the Constitution refers, instead, to the "advice center of radicalization" of the Federal Office for Migration and Refugees.[192] The Federal Office for Migration and Refugees (BAMF) is well known by citizens with and without migration backgrounds. In particular, it is well received for its activities in the area of integration and the yearly German Islam conference. Hence, many people searching advice relating to security services do not have as many inhibitions relating to BAMF.[193]

190 See http://www.exit-deutschland.de/ausstieg/?c=ex-it.

191 The resonance was absurd: less than seven calls of concerned in almost four years, see BT- Drucksache 18/2865 of 14. Oct 2014, 2.

192 Available at http://www.bamf.de/DE/DasBAMF/Beratung/beratung-node.html.

193 See BT-Drucksache 18/2865 of 14. Oct 2014, 3.

### *III. Radicalization Awareness Network (RAN)*

In order to help the first-line local practitioners and to facilitate the exchange of experiences and best practices between them, the European Commission set up the EU-wide Radicalization Awareness Network (RAN), which was officially launched on 9 Sept, 2011 by EU-Commissioner Malmström.[194] The Radicalization Awareness Network is an umbrella network connecting people involved in preventing radicalization and violent extremism throughout Europe.[195] In RAN, first liners[196] (i.e. individuals in concrete contact with the extremists such as street workers, teachers, guides, social workers etc.) from different member states can meet, each in their area of expertise, in order to exchange ideas, knowledge and experiences on countering radicalization and violent extremism. It is a "network of networks".[197]

RAN is organized in thematic working groups, driven by a Steering Committee and chaired by the Commission.[198] The Committee includes the leaders of the working groups and the Committee of Regions. RAN connects first-line practitioners, field experts, social workers, teachers, NGOs, civil society organizations, victims' groups, local law authorities, academics and others. There are eight RAN Working Groups, each with its own topic.[199] The results of RAN's work are reported back to policy makers both at the EU and Member States' levels.[200]

---

194 See Part of COM [2010]673; see homepage http://ec.europa.eu/dgs/home-affairs/what-we-do/networks/radicalisation_awareness_network/index_en.htm; Rules of procedure available at http://ec.europa.eu/dgs/home-affairs/what-we-do/networks/radicalisation_awareness_network/docs/ran_rules_of_procedures_en.pdf.

195 See RAN Charta, p. 1.

196 See Korn and Weilnböck, "Der lange Abschied," p. 34; critically concerning the effectiveness of frontliners Vidino, "DeRadikalisierung durch gezielte Interventionen," p. 27.

197 RAN Charta, p. 2.

198 See RAN Charta, p. 3.

199 For example RAN POL (the possible role of local and community police in preventing radicalization leading to violent extremism and/or to terrorism); RAN PREVENT (early interventions with individuals and groups most vulnerable to radicalization leading to violent extremism and/or to terrorism); RAN INT/EXT (from radicalization to foreign fighters/what role can the diaspora play in the fight against radicalization?).

200 Another important opt-out programm is "PREVENT" acting in the United Kingdom, see https://www.gov.uk/government/policies/protecting-the-uk-against-terr

### IV. European Network of Deradicalization (ENoD)

The European Network of Deradicalization (ENoD)[201] is an interactive platform of NGO-practitioners, taking on face-to-face de-radicalization work. The practitioners exchange methodologies, target groups, good practices, challenges, needs, institutional standing and support with respective member states. There are plans to widen activities, for example, to encompass cross-training and capacity building among facilitators from different fields and countries. The project is run by the Violence Prevention Network (Berlin), a non-profit organization of academics and professional first-line-practitioners, who combine practical experience and social research expertise.[202] The European Network of Deradicalization started in January 2012. It is closely connected with the EU Radicalization Awareness Network (RAN, see above). The main working field of the European Network of Deradicalization is to promote European exchange of practices and to cross-fertilize different regions with practical approaches. In the long run, these methods and experiences may lead to an analysis of key impact factors and general guidelines for successful first-line deradicalization interventions. At the end of the day, the development of evidence-based training programs for practitioners is planned.[203]

## D. Problems of De-Radicalization (stage "early" / "preventive")

The actions to fight radicalization are multifaceted. Moreover, various issues have to be considered:

---

orism/supporting-pages/prevent; or Radical Middle Way see http://www.radicalmiddleway.org/.

201 See http://www.european-network-of-deradicalisation.eu/.

202 See http://www.violence-prevention-network.de/; Korn and Weilnböck, "Der lange Abschied," p. 34.

203 See http://www.european-network-of-deradicalisation.eu/objectives.

### I. Vengeance and Group Pressure

"Fanaticism is the paradise for a sect"
(John Keats)

In general, groups and communities with totalitarian patterns of behavior do not tolerate the exit of a member. For one, the member had access to secret procedures and structures of power within the association.[204] Thus, he might serve as a suitable whistleblower, revealing sensitive information which can cause great damage to the organization as a whole.[205] Detecting and disclosing their highly complex and well-structured clandestine networks[206] is one of the biggest worries of all extremist groups.[207] Their impact and operation depend massively on tainted entanglements with politicians, high-ranking officials and external funding. Therefore, the United Nations Security Council issued several resolutions to stem and drain terroristic sources of income.[208] The unveiling of hidden structures is often linked to drastic consequences for dropouts.

Therefore, an information leakage constitutes the worst case scenario for every association situated in legal grey areas. Hence, the potential informer has to be muzzled. This aim can be reached by permanent intimidation, threatening behavior as well as permanent hostilities.[209] Fanning fear prevents most potential dropouts from leaving their association. The anxiety for retribution paralyses the decision making process,[210] while the

---

204 See Neubacher, "Terrorismus," p. 749.

205 See Neumann, "Radikalisierung," p. 10.

206 For example the world-wide network of the Al Quaida, see Zöller, *Terrorismusstrafrecht*, p. 71; therefore a counter-network of police and security agencies is required by many experts, see Stegmaier and Feltes, "Vernetzung – neuer Effektivitätsmythos für die innere Sicherheit," 2007, pp. 19 ff.; 23 f.; Werthebach, "Deutsche Sicherheitsstrukturen," p. 12.

207 Sometimes, the own adherents "prattle way", see the examples at Steinberg, "Jihadistische Radikalisierung," p. 22.

208 For example, Resolution 1267 (1999) against Osama bin Laden; Resolution 1373 (2001) against money funds for terrorists; see also Eckes, *EU Counter-Terrorist Policies*, pp. 24 ff., 73 ff.; Sambei et al., *Counter-Terrorism Law and Practice,* pp. 1 para 1.03; 6 para 624 ff; an overview of the UN Counter-Terrorism Instruments in 2 para 2.23.

209 See Neumann, "Radikalisierung," p. 10; http://www.exit-deutschland.de/ausstieg/; differently BT- Drucksache 18/2865 of 14. Oct 2014, 6.

210 See EXIT-Germany, "De-Radicalization and Disengagement," p. 11.

machinery of brainwashing attempts to reconvert the "sinner".[211] The only way to save and shelter the dropout effectively would be to cut off all existing connections to the group and its members.[212] The more intensive and deep the affiliation, the harder is the unbundling.[213] If the dropout, beyond the fact of being infiltrated, also founded a family life and social connections with another member, the situation becomes desperate to the greatest possible extent. In that case, the integration reached a level of intensity[214] that could only be ripped apart by making enormous, painful sacrifices.[215] Hence, the partner has to join the exit, or he or she must be left behind. In the following, professional witness protection programs are able to conceal the concerned dropouts by allowing them to change their places of residence and their identities.[216]

## *II. Embedding of Racist or Fanatic Thoughts (stage "early")*

> "A fanatic is a person who cannot change his view and does not want to change the subject"
> (Sir Winston Churchill)

Some of the reasons that lead to racist or fanatic opinions have already been mentioned. Social and private conditions that generate feelings of inferiority and problems of self-discovery increase the risk of being misled to extremist ideas.[217] The search for an exit can stumble on the last hurdle, if the dropout did not renounce his or her former views. In general, it is not correct to rate extremists, fanatics and terrorists as insane or mentally disturbed.[218] The obeyed behaviors and followed patterns were rational

---

211 Eckert, "Radikalisierung," p. 15; Sirseloudi et al., "Radikalisierung von europäischen Muslimen," p. 45.
212 See EXIT-Germany, "De-Radicalization and Disengagement," p. 2.
213 See EXIT-Germany, "De-Radicalization and Disengagement," p. 10.
214 For the special impact of relationships on the progress of radicalization see Möller and Schuhmacher, "Ein- und Ausstiegsprozesse," p. 21; the role of family and friends is examined by Rieker, "Fremdenfeindlichkeit," 2007, pp. 31 ff.
215 See Neumann, "Radikalisierung," p. 10.
216 See EXIT-Germany, "De-Radicalization and Disengagement," p. 3.
217 See Schroeder, *Rechtsextremismus und Jugendgewalt*, pp. 129 ff., 144 ff.; for further information; an short overview of all theories on pp. 155 f.
218 See Richardson, "Was Terroristen wollen," p. 40; Silke, "Holy Warriors," pp. 103 ff., 119; Borum, "Radicalization Into Violent Extremism I," p. 14; Entdorf,

and carefully considered.[219] Several further reasons may be contemplated; they mainly depend on the sort of fanaticism and its surroundings.[220] Moreover, social factors have an important and influential impact.[221] To understand the intricate phases of this reformation process, it is necessary to consider the generation of prejudices:[222] "Ultimately, ordinary psychological processes and small group dynamics play a major role in understanding Islamist radicalization."[223] Every judgment begins with a pre-judgment. Every decision is deducted from a biased decision-making procedure. The process of perception in the subconscious mind is characterized by its individuality. Schematically, cognition does not follow a straightforward path, but rather can be described as a never-ending pigeonholing process.[224] The incoming stimulus is perceived by the exterior sensatory organs. Those transfer the "clean" stimulus into the center of perception, the human brain. There, the stimulus is correlated to different factors: new or known, comfortable or dangerous, helpful or amendable. For this purpose, the human brain uses patterns and structures already acquainted and stored. The comparison of new stimuli is thus determined by the existence of established structures and schemes.[225] In the space of a

---

*Islamistischer Terrorismus*, p. 87; Neubacher, "Terrorismus," p. 745; but there exists an exception for some of the extremely sadistic killers of the jihadist movement, see Hoffmann-Plesch, "Deutsche IS-Dschihadisten Teil 2," pp. 14 f.

219 Those narratives serve as substitutes for real arguments and combine often ideology and facts into a persuasive basis for discussion, see Dovermann, "Narrative und Gegen-Narrative," pp. 42 f.

220 See Böllinger, "Die Entwicklung zu terroristischem Handeln," p. 59; the placate triad of "Revenge, Fame, Reaction" fits in the most cases, see Richardson, "Was Terroristen wollen," pp. 117 and 126 ff.

221 See Schroeder, *Rechtsextremismus und Jugendgewalt*, pp. 123 ff.; the importance of identy and social group building factors is described by Geschke, "Vorurteile," p. 36.

222 See Silke, "Holy Warriors," pp. 119 ff.

223 See Silke, "Holy Warriors," p. 119; see also Horgan, "From Profiles to Pathways," pp. 81 ff.; Borum, "Radicalization Into Violent Extremism I," pp. 20 ff.; Özerdem and Podder, "Disarming Youth Combatants," p. 67; McCauley and Moskalenko, "Mechanisms of Political Radicalization," p. 417.

224 See Pendry, "Soziale Kognition," 2007, pp. 111 ff.

225 See Blum, "Mögliche Auswirkungen der Ermittlungsakte auf die Informationsverarbeitung und die Entscheidungsbildung im Strafverfahren," 2012, pp. 242 ff.; Studies showed that people search for patterns and schemes even if they are told that these schemes do not exist, see Geipel, *Handbuch der Beweiswürdigung*, 2013, Chap. 13 para. 18 with further evidence.

few seconds, perception creates the first prejudice, becoming a binding classification of the perceived stimulus. This process passes subconsciously and hardly cannot be affected or controlled. The comparisons depend on various factors, for example personal experiences, mood at the time of perception, stated conditions and further aspects.[226] The created "pre"-judgment then impinges all following actions.[227]

Because of the subliminal cycle, rational reflections first counteract only after having noticed the prejudgment.[228] So the necessary counter-balancing element is only set in motion, when the emotion already has reached a perceptible intensity.[229] In the long run, experiences, environmental influences and permanent subconscious comparisons of stimuli and occurrences modify the way of perceiving and discerning the world.[230]

The influence of subliminal stimuli processing are well explored.[231] For example, first impressions may extremely vary the judgment of events. It has been verified by studies that the words used to describe a still unknown person are so powerful in their impact, that any further interaction with this human being will be preshaped. If a still unknown person is described with very positive characteristics like pleasant, friendly and caring and is introduced afterwards as a teacher holding a trial lesson, the interviewed students will describe him as a good and qualified academic. Exactly the same lesson will be characterized as boring, inadequate or inflexible if the teacher was introduced with negative or neutral characteristics like clinical, severe, uncommunicative or incompetent. The teacher's chances to persuade the class of his own abilities and skills will be coun-

---

226 See Bender et al., *Tatsachenfeststellung vor Gericht, Glaubwürdigkeits- und Beweislehre, Vernehmungslehre*, 2007, para. 40 ff.

227 See for example, Murphy and Zajonc, "Affect, Cognition, and Awareness: Affective Priming With Optimal and Suboptimal Stimulus Exposures," 1993, pp. 723 ff.

228 See Dustdar, "Demokratie und die Macht der Gefühle," 2008, p. 34.

229 See Geipel, *Handbuch der Beweiswürdigung*, Chap. 22 para. 51 ff.; Bender et al., *Tatsachenfeststellung vor Gericht*, para. 17; Kühne, *Strafprozessrecht*, § 20, para. 318; Wendler and Hoffmann, *Technik und Taktik der Befragung im Gerichtsverfahren, Urteile begründen, Urteile prüfen. Lüge und Irrtum aufdecken*, 2009, 8 para. 6.

230 See for this model of "active kognition" von Glasersfeld, *Radical Constructivism*, p. 1.

231 See for example, Murphy and Zajonc, "Affect, Cognition, and Awareness," pp. 723 ff.

teracted by the extremely negative predisposition.[232] The once-adopted opinions could not be changed easily.

This phenomenon is described in the theory of cognitive dissonance.[233] This thesis specifies the cementing of preconceived opinions. Every individual aspires to balance his or her thoughts and opinions. This balance is guaranteed if accepted assumptions are not attacked too often by intrinsic or extrinsic doubts. But from the very moment an embosomed idea is confronted with contradictory statements or facts, the balance is at risk.[234] Thus, the concerned person is forced to compensate for the misbalance. One possibility would be to ignore the contradictory fact by searching for new endorsements that strengthen one's own opinion. Another possibility could be to incriminate the new fact as being wrong or fallacious. The last possibility would be to adopt the new fact by changing former opinions and ideas. While the first and the second method of regaining balance do not require much effort, the holistic change required in accepting an opposing fact can spiral into a mammoth task. It seems to cause almost supernatural strain to reshape once-hardened views.[235]

---

232 See Higgins et al., "Category Accessibility and Impression Formation," 1977, pp. 141 ff.; Nisbett and Wilson, "The Halo Effect: Evidence for Unconscious Alteration of Judgments," 1977, pp. 250 ff.; Blum, "Auswirkungen der Ermittlungsakte," p. 251 with further references; Habschick, *Erfolgreich Vernehmen, Kompetenz in der Kommunikations-, Gesprächs- und Vernehmungspraxis*, 2010, p. 91; Gerding, *Trial by Jury. Die Bewährung des englischen und des US-amerikanischen Jury-Systems. Eine Idee im verfassungsrechtlichen und gesellschaftlichen Wandel*, 2007, p. 338 with further references. The *Recency* Effect describes the impact of the "recent word", Gerding, *Trial by Jury*, p. 338; Neumann, "Radikalisierung," p. 8.

233 See Festinger, *Theorie der kognitiven Dissonanz*, 1978; Borum, "Radicalization Into Violent Extremism I," pp. 29 f.; also Blum, "Auswirkungen der Ermittlungsakte," pp. 254 f.; Geipel, *Handbuch der Beweiswürdigung*, Chap. 16 para. 75; Bender et al., *Tatsachenfeststellung vor Gericht*, para. 158 ff.; Jansen, *Zeuge und Aussagepsychologie*, para. 368 ff.; for the generation of acceptance see Luhmann, *Legitimation durch Verfahren*, 1978, pp. 33 f.; for the linked phenomenon of „primacy", see Anderson, "Primacy Effects in Personality Impression Formation Using a Generalized Order Effect Paradigm," 1965, pp. 1 ff.

234 This phenomen can also be contemplated in bigger social processes, see Geschke, "Vorurteile, Differenzierung und Diskriminierung – sozialpsychologische Erklärungsansätze," p. 37.

235 See Sommer, *Effektive Strafverteidigung, Recht-Psychologie-Überzeugungsarbeit der Verteidigung*, 2013, Chap. 3 para. 49.

Therefore, prejudgments persist. The concerned person is bound and the narrow one-way street becomes a dead end. The vicious cycle closes in. Which effects does this have on the question of the rehabilitation of the former extremists? The answer to this question is as remarkable as it is sobering: The actual likelihood of an effective "re-education" is extremely low. Most dropouts only feign renouncement of their previously celebrated ideology.[236] Consequently, the efforts of most of the dropout programs resemble a fight against windmills. The idea of superiority of races or other clearly racist and xenophobic opinions are hardened in the heads of the ordinary "man-on-the-street".[237] Indeed, EXIT boasts in its informational material about 500 successful dropouts with a recidivism rate of only 3%.[238] The Violence Prevention Network states 700 program participants with a recidivism rate of 13%.[239] But the high numbers which are shown in the statistics of extremist violence show that the quote of "Once a Nazi, always a Nazi" cannot be denied too easily.[240] Many states are only recently transitioning from the assumption that far-right extremism is not a serious problem or that it is just a normal male youth issue.[241] That is a dangerous fallacy.[242]

### *III. Interim Findings: Opt-out Programs are not Enough*

The demonstrated embedding of fanatic thoughts and the problem of vengeance and group pressure disclose that effective de-radicalization

---

236 See Neumann, "Radikalisierung," p. 8; Möller and Schuhmacher, "Ein- und Ausstiegsprozesse," p. 20; see for example the experiences with the terrorist Mohammed Ai Hamadi, Mückenberger, "Zum Profil eines Terroristen (Mohammed Ali Hamadi)," 2014, pp. 232 ff.

237 Buschbom et al., "Rechtspopulismus," p. 2; Dovermann, "Narrative und Gegen-Narrative," p. 43; Neubacher, "Terrorismus," p. 748; Korn and Weilnböck, "Der lange Abschied," p. 36.

238 See EXIT-Germany, "De-Radicalization and Disengagement," p. 2.

239 See Korn and Weilnböck, "Der lange Abschied," p. 33.

240 See EXIT-Germany, "De-Radicalization and Disengagement," p. 12; Vidino, "DeRadikalisierung durch gezielte Interventionen," p. 29.

241 See Ramalingam, "Old Threat, New Approach," p. 13.

242 Evidently, the countries fail in collecting data completely, see Ramalingam, "Old Threat, New Approach," p. 36.

cannot be achieved in a monocausal way.[243] The opt-out programs are a sensitive shelter and may offer reasonable advice.[244] But they can only help those concerned, who are willing to change their way of life. Voluntary returnees will succeed by experiencing help from professional coaches and psychologists, street workers and therapy groups.[245] What about the process of radicalization itself? What about the structures of extremism and the quagmires of prejudices? They have to be "drained" as an alternative measure,[246] in addition to the work of the opt-out organizations. The different sectors of implementation will now be portrayed.

## *E. Alternatives and Additions*

### *I. Banning Extremist Groups and Associations (stage "repressive")*

The relatively good statistics of the dropout programs may not reflect the fact that in many cases radicalization continues after the official exit.[247] In particular, the theory of cognitive dissonance sends a reminder.[248] Better than trusting in a full-extensive purification,[249] multifunctional measures should be taken to fight against radicalization before it gains a foothold. One way of combatting radicalization could lie in banning far-right parties and organizations. As mentioned above, criminal associations in legal grey areas massively depend on internal contacts and the complex intra-organic structures which they have perfected over years. Forbidding the umbrella organizations can weaken the sub-groups so severely that resting becomes virtually impossible. Constant influxes of human and financial capital are

243 See Neumann, "Radikalisierung," p. 8; Vidino, "DeRadikalisierung durch gezielte Interventionen," p. 26.

244 See Vidino, "DeRadikalisierung durch gezielte Interventionen," p. 27.

245 See Vidino, "DeRadikalisierung durch gezielte Interventionen," pp. 28 ff.; Korn and Weilnböck, "Der lange Abschied," p. 36.

246 See Vidino, "DeRadikalisierung durch gezielte Interventionen," pp. 27 ff.; The European Union is interested in it reducing financing possibly by oil shops, see http://www.dw.de/bessere-kooperation-gegen-den-terror/a-18201212.

247 See Vidino, "DeRadikalisierung durch gezielte Interventionen," p. 27.

248 See Neumann, "Radikalisierung," p. 8; another one is the NSU process in Germany that demonstrated the blindness of the German authorities concerning right-wing terrorism for decades.

249 Which is very hard to achieve, see Korn and Weilnböck, "Der lange Abschied," p. 37.

indispensable in most of the cases, because small sub-groups often suffer from a lack of organization and decompose without a leading authority.[250] Draining the swamp kills the frogs.

In Germany, there already had been several attempts to ban the NPD, unfortunately none of them succeeded. For special reasons lying in the German Constitution, banning political parties follows severe rules.[251] According to article 21 § 2 of the German Constitution, political parties, provided that they are based and founded on democratic principles, enjoy the so called "party privilege".[252] This principle protects parties from being dissolved on the grounds of the imputation of their radicalism by a statutory authority. The right to dissolve or ban a political party is incumbent solely upon the German Federal Constitutional Court, Art. 21 § 2 Sentence 2 of the German Constitution. Thus, the NPD uses the means of democracy against democracy itself. Although the party would like to abolish the pluralistic order, this position, however, only is demonstrated rudimentarily and subtly, so there does not exist enough usable evidence which could carry a ban procedure.[253]

Therefore the NPD, as a consciously anti-democratic organization, can enjoy the democratic protection of the German Constitution (and partake in state-financing of political parties[254]). The banning of radicals and extremists, however, turns out to be easier.[255] Party privilege only applies to

250 See Volkmann, "Kampf gegen die Hydra? Der Staat und der Rechtsextremismus," 2012, p. 18; Hetzer, "Europäische Strategien gegen Geldwäsche und Terror," 2004, p. 31.

251 See Kluth, in *Beck'scher Online-Kommentar GG*, 2014, Art. 21 para. 206; instructive Volkmann, "Dilemmata des Parteiverbots," 2007, pp. 577 ff.; Backes, "NPD-Verbot: Pro und Contra," 2012, p. 10.

252 Kluth, in *Beck'scher Online-Kommentar GG*, Art. 21 para. 211 f.

253 Further information to this subject, just see Ipsen, "Rechtsfragen des NPD-Verbots," 2002, p. 866; Hufen, "Neues Parteiverbotsverfahren gegen die NPD? Verfassungsrechtliche Voraussetzungen vor dem Hintergrund der NSU-Taten," 2012, p. 202; Volkmann, "Dilemmata des Parteiverbots," pp. 577 ff.; Volkmann, "Kampf gegen die Hydra," p. 16.

254 See Backes, "NPD-Verbot: Pro und Contra," p. 14; Volkmann, "Kampf gegen die Hydra," p. 18.

255 See Several subgroups and extremist associations have been banned final in Germany, see BfV, *Rechtsextremismus: Symbole, Zeichen und verbotene Organisationen,* 2015, pp. 20 ff.; http://www.verfassungsschutz.de/de/arbeitsfelder/af-rechtsextremismus/verbotene-organisationen-rechtsextremismus; but it is not as effective as banning the party, see Volkmann, "Kampf gegen die Hydra," p. 17.

political parties within the meaning of the Party Act, a federal law. So, subgroups, associations[256] and biker gangs that break the rules of democratic society may be banned, based on less severe restrictions of the Act Regulating Clubs and Associations. The permanent opposition against the elementary constitutional principles of freedom and democracy, partly with violent means, is enough reason for a ban.[257]

With regard to the banning of Islamic groups, the pointlessness of this proposal becomes manifest. Admittedly, Germany already decided to ban the "Arbeiterpartei Kurdistan" (PKK, Kurdistan Worker's Party), "AL AQSA e.V.", "Internationale Humanitäre Hilfsorganisation e.V." and the Salafist movement "Millatu Ibrahim".[258] Moreover, the Federal Minister of Internal Affairs ordered on the 12th of September, 2014 that all activities of the so-called "Islamic state" are forbidden in Germany. In the estimation of the Ministry, the IS opposes the constitutional order as well as the ideal of understanding among nations. The ban is connected with the prohibition to use signs of the "Islamic state" in public.[259]

But this method remains rather inflexible: The first hurdle to clear is freedom of worship. The exercise of a religion cannot be prohibited with the argument that some followers pervert the ideas and use them for criminal purposes. Islam enjoys the same level of protection of any other religion, forbidding Islam would be no less than an inexcusable intervention in guaranteed civil rights.

Moreover, the umbrella organizations of the Islamic extremism are rarely situated in just the country where the members act. The global movement of Islamism has centers but no capital, it has leaders but no universally accepted guiding figure. For one "beheaded" terrorist, ten new ones will appear.[260] Draining the swamp in the face of a global movement is both a ridiculous and dangerous enterprise. It is ridiculous because the wide-spread network will not miss one single association as long as the world-wide infringement stays safe. Moreover, it is dangerous because it underestimates the power of extremism and radicalization to resist: you

---

256 See Mletzko, "Gewalthandeln," p. 11.

257 Volkmann, "Kampf gegen die Hydra," p. 17.

258 Http://www.bmi.bund.de/DE/Themen/Sicherheit/Extremismusbekaempfung/Vereinsverbote/vereinsverbote_node.html.

259 See http://www.bundesregierung.de/Content/DE/Artikel/2014/09/2014-09-12-is-verbot.html.

260 Differently Steinberg, "Jihadistische Radikalisierung," p. 23.

can ban a party, but you cannot ban the idea behind it.[261] Making martyrs[262] is counterproductive.[263]

Therefore, in order to ameliorate the level of de-radicalization, banning groups is just a superficial measure with symbolic consequences. As long as the national states may not offer an alternative, such as discussions at eye level with the ideological leaders of the extremist groups, the intellectual instigation of future adherents will continue.

### *II. Legal Sanctions against Extremists (stage "repressive")*

The basic problem in fighting radicalization is the mixture of concepts. Extremism, radicalization and terrorism are connected with each other; nevertheless, they are not identical. While dropout programs can stem radicalization, the criminal law, according to its very nature, only intervenes afterwards. For some experts, legal frameworks should form the bedrock to any governmental approach to extremism.[264] But as a repressive instrument, criminal law punishes the "results" of radicalization.[265] Therefore, criminal law can only be one measure out of a great bundle, trying to decrease the threat.[266] Criminal law represents a statutory regulation system that impacts a relative relationship, namely between the state authority and a delinquent. Its actual suitability for prevention and guidance of social streaming is restricted. It is a fragmented order, edging the ultima ratio of sanctioning systems in a democracy.[267] Nonetheless, a deeper look at the criminal efforts and counter-terrorism acts in Germany and Europe remains valuable, because criminal law can offer good insight into the consciousness of the affected states and societies, representing a measuring gauge on social developments.

---

261 See Klein, in *Grundgesetz-Kommentar*, ed. Theodor Maunz and Günter Dürig, 2014, Art. 21 para. 487; Backes, "NPD-Verbot: Pro und Contra," p. 12; Heitmeyer, "Rechtsextremismus und gesellschaftliche Selbstentlastung," p. 26.

262 To this phenomenon Heine, *Terror in Allahs Name*, pp. 30 ff.

263 Differently the opponents of the banning, see the citations at Backes, "NPD-Verbot: Pro und Contra," 2012, p. 14.

264 See Ramalingam, "Old Threat, New Approach," pp. 16 ff.; OSCE, "Preventing Terrorism," pp. 42 ff.

265 See Zöller, *Terrorismusstrafrecht*, p. 216.

266 See Volkmann, "Kampf gegen die Hydra," p. 19.

267 See Zöller, *Terrorismusstrafrecht*, p. 223.

### III. Counter-Terrorism Legislation in Germany

German criminal law already knows several criminal elements of offences that try to handle the upcoming threat of radicalization. Special sections of anti-terrorism legislation and political criminal law sentence delinquents for special types of background motives. For example, the German criminal code, sections 129a and b StGB, punish the contribution and involvement of an individual in a terroristic association. The sanctions can be pronounced for participation in Germany as well as for acting on a transnational level. We observe enormous dogmatic flaws in those offences. There is no definition for the exact form of criminal "terrorism", moreover the starting point for assignable action leading to a criminal responsibility is antedated to a very early point[268] while the assessment whether the action was terroristic or not is based on the intensity and not (what would be more sensible) on the concrete mens rea of the delinquent.[269] This way, the inherent structures and purpose of criminal law are ignored.

The principle of clarity and certainty laid down in the German Constitution in Art. 103 § 2 of the Basic Law requires clear and unequivocal needs for the appearance and system of law. Certainty of legal norms also figures as a human right. Certainty in this context means that the law should be sufficiently clear to allow individuals to govern their future behavior. Thus, a law had to be formulated with sufficient precision to enable the citizen to regulate his or her conduct. The person must be able to foresee (up to a reasonable degree) the circumstances and consequences which a certain action may entail.[270] Those norms that predominantly try to effect and influence political or social processes overstretch the request for a predictable and understandable legal system. Legally protected goods (German Rechtsgut) have to be defended against interventions and impairments. The development of a "conviction criminal law" would thus be

268 See BGHSt 28, 116; Wasser and Piaszek, "Staatsschutzstrafrecht in Bewegung?," 2008, p. 319; to the resembling section 89a StPO see Mitsch, "Vorbeugende Strafbarkeit zur Abwehr terroristischer Gewalttaten," 2015, p. 211; instructive to the problem of "antedating", Sinn, "Vorverlagerung der Strafbarkeit am Beispiel der Organisierten Kriminalität und des Terrorismus," 2013, pp. 149 ff.; see especially Jakobs, "Kriminalisierung im Vorfeld einer Rechtsgutverletzung," 1985, pp. 756 f. (also below).

269 See for broad critic Zöller, *Terrorismusstrafrecht*, pp. 145 ff.

270 See ECtHR Sunday Times v. The United Kingdom, judgment of 26.4.1979 – 6538/74, § 49.

both actionist and against state-of-law.[271] Therefore, those regulations mentioned above are to be considered as political criminal law[272] full of symbolic values[273] which do not fit the regular order of a legal system.[274]

Apart from generating criminal offences, the Federal Government also wants to strengthen prevention. By now, it is possible to take away a passport from a suspect and thus prevent crossing the border from Germany.[275] Some lower Courts already had to decide such cases. For example, the Administrative Court in Arnsberg judged on the 23rd of January, 2015[276] that the ordered confiscation of a passport against a German Moroccan was lawful, because the person was suspected of deliberate participation in the civil war (Jihad) in Syria on part of the radical Islamists. In its decision the court recurred on the integration of the accused in a Salafist network. This was shown by a video published on the internet where the accused appeals for crossing a border to Syria. Moreover the man is accused in preliminary proceedings to be a member of a gang united to support the Jihad. The accused had already once travelled to the Turkish-Syrian border area and has presumably stayed for several weeks in Syria. Especially for such cases, the Ministry of Internal Affairs plans to also take away ordinary identity cards from suspects and to substitute them with other cards, thus hampering leaving the country.[277] This idea is also being discussed among the European ministries of security and justice.[278]

271 See Hirsch, "Die subjektive Versuchstheorie, ein Wegbereiter der NS-Strafrechtsdoktrin," 2007, p. 494.

272 See Wasser and Piaszek, "Staatsschutzstrafrecht in Bewegung?," p. 319.

273 See Barisch, *Bekämpfung des internationalen Terrorismus durch § 129b StGB*, pp.79 ff.

274 See Montag, "Strafbarkeit des Besuchs terroristischer Ausbildungslager – von der Vorfeldstrafbarkeit einer Vorfeldstrafnorm," 2008, p. 141.

275 See instructive Daum, "Anforderungen an Ausreisebeschränkungen von Islamisten," 2014, pp. 526 ff.

276 VG Arnsberg, Judgement of 23 Jan 2015 -12 K 2036/13 (not final).

277 See http://www.faz.net/aktuell/politik/inland/deutsche-islamisten-gelangten-auch-ohne-reisepass-in-kriegsgebiete-13367031.html.

278 See http://www.dw.de/eu-will-terror-söldner-stoppen/a-18226017.

## *IV. Joint Terrorism Defense Centre of Germany (GTAZ)*

The Joint Terrorism Defense Centre[279] was created at the later part of 2004 in Berlin. The GTAZ is not an independent authority but a cooperation and communication platform of 40 national authorities from all areas of internal security. Overarching strategies are the most important and most effective measure to fight extremist and terroristic threats.[280] It was not necessary to enact a specific enabling clause to establish the Centre because no further additional competence were distributed. In lieu thereof, each of the involved authorities takes its measures among their own competences and within the scope of the law applying to them. Hence, there is no "GTAZ leader," rather the representatives of the following facilities cooperate "at eye level":

Federal Office for the Protection of the Constitution

Federal Criminal Police Office

Federal Intelligence Service

General Attorney at the Federal Supreme Court

Federal Police

Customs Criminal Investigation Office

Federal Office for Migration and Refugees

Military Counterintelligence Service

Regional authorities for the protection of the constitution

The installation of GTAZ occurred because of the reinforced menace of Islamic terrorism. The terrorist assaults during the 11th of September, 2001 by "Al Qaida" pointed out a need for strategic rethinking in security policies[281] which strongly affected security structures in both Germany and the international community.

279 See http://www.verfassungsschutz.de/de/arbeitsfelder/af-islamismus-und-islamistischer-terrorismus/gemeinsames-terrorismusabwehrzentrum-gtaz.

280 See Sambei et al., *Counter-Terrorism Law and Practice*, 4 para 4.128.

281 See Sambei et al., *Counter-Terrorism Law and Practice*, 1 para 1.01.

### *V. Counter-Terrorism Legislation in Europe*

At the European level, one has to distinguish between measures of public international law enacted by the Council of Europe, situated in Strasbourg and the specific Union Law of the European Union following the rules of the TFEU (Treaty on the Functioning of the European Union) and the TEU (Treaty on the European Union).[282] The Council of Europe enacted, for example, the Convention on Cybercrime[283], the Convention on Laundering, Search, Seizure and Confiscation of the Proceeds from Crime[284,285] and the Convention on the Prevention of Terrorism.[286]

As a supplement to national anti-terror files[287] the EU has demanded the equipment of a general information system to the radicalization of potential extremists. Suitable drafts to decide upon a standardized, multi-dimensional and part-structured instrument for collecting data and information about radicalization processes in the EU were already presented.[288] In 2009, the EU had dismissed an action conversion plan, requiring the member states to create mechanisms to systematically analyze the main factors in radicalization processes. Besides, the different spheres which generate extremism should be identified and thoroughly examined. Most importantly, the activities of extremist religious "leaders" and other circulators of

282 Instructive for all policies see the doctoral thesis of Eckes, *EU Counter Terrorist Policies and Fundamental Rights*, 2009.

283 See CETS No.: 185, 23/11/2001.

284 See CETS No.: 141, 8/11/1990; see on this subject Hetzer, "Deutsche Umsetzung neuer europäischer Vorgaben zur Bekämpfung der Geldwäsche und der Terrorismusfinanzierung," 2008, pp. 560 ff.

285 See Holley, *Das Recht der internationalen Terrorismusbekämpfung*, p. 30.

286 See CETS No.: 196, 16/5/2005; see also Hetzer, "Europäische Strategien," p. 28; see for more information Eckes, *EU Counter-Terrorist Policies*, pp. 46 ff.; 57 ff.

287 See Zöller, "Rechtsrahmen," pp. 768 f.; Möllers and van Ooyen, "Bundeskriminalamt," p. 32; Normann, *Terrorprävention*, APuZ (2007): 11, 12 ff.; The anti-terror file (ATD) links up knowledge of police and news services of the alliance and the countries from the area of the international terrorism. Such information for the authorities involved in the ATD thereby becomes mutually quickly discoverable, fixed in "Gesetz zur Errichtung einer standardisierten zentralen Anti-terrordatei von Polizeibehörden und Nachrichtendiensten von Bund und Ländern" (Antiterrordateigesetz – ATDG) (ATDG), BGBl I 2006, 3409.

288 The EU-wide transmission of information between police and criminal proceedings authorities for the realization of criminal inquiries or police knowledge production procedures may not be regulated more strictly than the suitable national regulations (so-called «equal treatment principle").

hatred and terror are likely to be exchanged via EUROPOL.[289] The Union wants the member states to use many facets of the suggested instrument to compile data and optimize the exchange of information. EUROPOL should be able to provide suitable lists with people who are involved in radicalization processes or the spreading of extremist messages.[290]

The system should therefore generate warnings which could allow concrete actions such as special supervision or the arrest of suspects. In the area of criminal persecution of terrorist criminal offences, police and judicial cooperation was strengthened. Terrorists can thus be pursued throughout Europe according to consistent criteria, set up by frame decisions on uniform definitions of terrorist criminal offences. They can also be arrested more easily due to the establishment of a European arrest warrant.[291] Since April 2008, certain preparatory actions are in force by a supplement to the frame decision on fighting terrorism.[292] Also EUROJUST takes part in the "fight against terrorism".[293] Moreover, the arrangement of mutual legal assistance in criminal cases allows common inquiry groups of representatives of the judicial authorities to educate themselves, and for police authorities to coordinate inquiries to the EU member states.

289 For the role of EUROPOL in the fight against terrorism see Ruthig, § 20 para. 35 ff.; Esser, "Die Rolle von Europol und Eurojust bei der Bekämpfung von Terrorismus und organisierter Kriminalität," 2013, pp. 61 ff.; Eckes, *EU Counter-Terrorist Policies*, pp. 66 ff.

290 Pitschas, "Innere Sicherheit," pp. 248 f.

291 Framework decision 2002/584/JI, ABl EU L 190 v 18.7.2002, transformed into German Law through Europäisches Haftbefehlsgesetz of 20/7/2006 (BGBl. I 1721) and rule of procedure in §§ 78 IRG.

292 For example the Counter Terrorist Task Force and the First Response Network, see Esser, "Europol und Eurojust," pp. 66 f.

293 See Esser, "Europol und Eurojust," pp. 80 ff.

### VI. Sense of Punishment

> "You have to bear in mind that fanatics are more dangerous than rogues. One can never probably bring a maniac to the reason, but a rogue"
> (Voltaire)

Statutory punishment follows special reasons. It is doubtful if the sanctioning of terrorists and extremists will lead to a real improvement of their re-integration. Therefore, the common sense of punishment has to be described shortly. The improvement or rehabilitation purpose emphasized in the law (Sec 46 paragraph 1 S. 2 of the German criminal code) needs an explanation. The expectations that intensive criminal delinquents would be able to achieve long-lasting socializing effects has not materialized at all.[294] The idea of a chastened ex-criminal remains a chimera, because the inherent will to change one person's behavior cannot be forced with mono-causal means such as lock-ups. The same mechanisms that entrap the "typical radical" in its thoughts might (and do) hamper the "typical criminal" to renounce from deviance. Meanwhile, the perception of an extensive "interchangeability of sanctions" under positively special-preventive aspects prevailed. Above all, a constructive preparation for the life afterwards proves not to be subject to prosecution any more, developed in the confinement of the penal execution was a popular misconception.[295] Protection of the general public from the culprit by penal execution as a special-preventive measure can secure prevention for the duration of the penal execution of criminal offences.[296]

Another purpose of punishment is deterrence.[297] The delinquent should abstain from committing crimes by facing a possible sentence. None of these purposes will unfold their impacts on the deep creed of terrorists.[298] The biggest problem in deterring an extremist (applied to the definition above, see B.) is based in his own ideology.

---

294 See Streng, in *Strafgesetzbuch*, 2013, § 46 para. 34; Kargl, "Friede durch Vergeltung, Über den Zusammenhang von Sache und Zweck im Strafbegriff," 1998, pp. 64 ff.

295 See Streng, in *Strafgesetzbuch*, § 46 para. 34.

296 See Streng, in *Strafgesetzbuch*, § 46 para. 36; Frisch, "Konzepte der Strafe und Entwicklungen des Strafrechts in Europa," 2009, p. 389.

297 See EuGHE 1998, 2965 – Rs 68/88 Rn. 23-25; Frisch, "Konzepte," pp. 402 f.; Kargl, "Strafbegriff," pp. 66 ff.

298 See Neubacher, "Terrorismus," p. 745.

Within the radicalization progress, the individual has adopted the friend-enemy-schema leading him to fight against an "unlawful and unjustified" system.[299] Sentencing a delinquent by this system will affect exactly the wrong symbolic consequences.[300] The wrong stated order has shown its power by subduing its enemy. Successful recanting requires personal awareness of one's own mistakes. Hence, a sentence deepens the feeling of being misunderstood and left behind. Thus, criminal law serves as a protection order to hamper the ongoing menace of the terrorist, albeit the anticipated effects of improvement and reformation fail to materialize.

To sum up: criminal measures are an effective method to save the society from the delinquent's further extremist activities, but will by no means facilitate the de-radicalization progress. On the contrary, the individual might escalate even more while being captured by the "enemy".[301] The assault of September 11th excited the minds[302] and led to more intense discussions about the terrorism criminal law.[303] As a result, terrorism had before been neglected as a "fashionable subject." Since then, the interdisciplinary interests of political scientists, theologians, psychologists, social scientists, journalists and "terrorism experts" have woken up.

However, it cannot be sense and purpose of a legal approach to "understand" Islamic and political terrorism. Such information is mostly managed from knowledge and surmises from second and third hand. Linguistic barriers, but also ethnic and cultural differences create a gap between the nations which are not surmountable by the law. Criminal law is also not able to become the "all-purpose adhesive" for understanding among nations. Anyhow, a criminal approach at a material level is possible. However, up till now this is very incomplete and has occurred sporadically.

---

299 See Neubacher, "Terrorismus," p. 746; Steinberg, "Jihadistische Radikalisierung," p. 21; Savage, "Four Lessons," p. 140.

300 See Zöller, *Terrorismusstrafrecht*, p. 270; Frisch, "Konzepte," p. 392.

301 See Mückenberger, "Profil eines Terroristen," pp. 232 f.

302 See Sambei et al., *Counter-Terrorism Law and Practice*, 1 para 1.03.

303 And of course security as a value itself, see Möllers and van Ooyen, "Bundekriminalamt," pp. 27, 30 ff.; for some it was the end of the "Modern Times", Heine, *Terror in Allahs Name*, p. 7.

## *VII. Special Law for the Enemies of our Values?*

"The enemy of my enemy is my friend"
(Napoleon)

When contemplating the legal system as a peace order, it becomes clear that it is at the same time an expression of a social consensus: the basic rules are accepted by all members of the community as an indispensable value base, while a fundamental canon of human rights protects living together peacefully. But what is going to happen to people positioning themselves consciously and permanently outside this order, breaking intentionally with the dogma of the indispensability of human rights' minimum standards? People who torture others for no reason, who negate other's right to exist, yet actively request the protection of the national law. Those people confront the democratic and peaceful structure of society with a pull test. Does one also have to agree with this trampling of human rights?[304] Or are those individuals situated so far from the "circle of society" that a special "law for others", even a "law for enemies" should be applied to them?

The philosophy of a special enemy criminal law does exist in the German legal doctrine. The most prominent representative is the Law Professor Günter Jakobs.[305] To sum up in a nutshell, according to this (so far purely theoretical!) model there are people who are put beyond the law, because they do not recognize the obligation of the law for themselves or not to a decisive extent.[306] The major group (possibly: the state) then should define who is an "outsider" and whether and when one comes to an arrangement with this, fight against him "punitively" or destroy him.[307]

---

304 Suggestive question asked by the Law Professor *Depenheuer* in a radio interview on SWR on 1 Mar 2008, 8.15 pm; more about the concept of *Depenheuer* see Ruf, "Demokratischer Rechtsstaat und Terrorismus. Ein Feindrecht als Mittel zur Terrorismusabwehr?," 2010, pp. 229 ff.; Hetzer, "Sicherheit durch Ausnahmezustand?," 2008, pp. 93 ff.

305 See Jakobs, "Kriminalisierung im Vorfeld einer Rechtsgutverletzung," pp. 783 ff; see for a historical overview Asholt, "Die Debatte über das 'Feindstrafrecht'," 2011, p. 180.

306 For example Jakobs, "Bürgerstrafrecht und Feindstrafrecht," 2004, p. 95.

307 See Jakobs, "Feindstrafrecht? – Eine Untersuchung zu den Bedingungen von Rechtlichkeit," 2006, p. 290; along the same line (probably involuntary) Steinberg, "Jihadistische Radikalisierung," p. 23 who endorses the killing of charismatic leaders to hamper the spreading of propaganda.

In some newer contributions, his concept also turns to another direction. Jakobs regards his working model of an enemy criminal law at the same time as a description of a right of danger defense or security in a further meaning, as it is already common in German criminal law and criminal proceeding law.[308] The requirement of Jakobs is to isolate the criminal enemy law from the "normal" criminal law for citizens and to sum it up in its own codification.[309] Jakobs concludes that thus, the existence of criminal enemy law should and could no longer be denied.

The lists of critics and opponents of this model are almost infinite[310] and it would lead too far to discuss all aspects which speak for or against this draft. However, it appears sensible to realize the meaning of such thinking for the question of de-radicalization. The idea of an enemy criminal law constructs a sphere "inside" and a sphere "outside". There are the law-abiding citizens following the social conventions and the enemies who negate and fight against them and hence position themselves beyond this order. There arise, of course, many questions if the enemy criminal law is compatible with the German Constitution[311] and if its obvious philosophical approach to some very exponent academic currents[312] in the 1920-1940s might be a fateful aspect.[313] The critical point in this essay is quite a different issue. Facing radicalization and de-radicalization, the demand and requirement for an attitude of "if you're not for us, you're against us" occurs like a slap in the face. The invoking of two camps, one for the "good" and one for the "bad" exactly portrays the first step of the progressing spiral to disinhibition.[314] Stereotypes and simple truth-believers do not solve the problems, even when created by like-minded persons. The dichotomy in the appreciation of people is the biggest failure in the

---

308 See Jakobs, "Feindstrafrecht," pp. 295 ff.; he opposes especially against several sections of the list of pp. 80 ff. StGB (German Criminal Code), the so-called "state security criminal law".

309 See Jakobs, "Bürgerstrafrecht," pp. 92 ff.; Jakobs, "Kriminalisierung," p. 784.

310 Just see Kindhäuser et. al., *Strafgesetzbuch*, before § 32 para. 223 ff.; Greco, *Feindstrafrecht*, 2010, pp. 31 ff.; Zöller, *Terrorismusstrafrecht*, pp. 277 ff.

311 See the analysis of Mahncke, "Bürger oder Feind? Zur Diskussion um das Feindstrafrecht," 2010, pp. 214 ff.

312 See Asholt, "Debatte," pp. 185 ff.

313 See Zöller, *Terrorismusstrafrecht*, p. 278.

314 See Neubacher, "Terrorismus," pp. 746, 749; Eckert, "Radikalisierung," p. 11; Dustdar, "Demokratie und die Macht der Gefühle," p. 38.

concept of the enemy criminal law.[315] There might be a need for a new structure of criminal law, perhaps even for an extensive reform of criminal prevention. But concerning possible solutions for de-radicalization, a planned radicalization of law is the less suitable possibility.

### *F. Tactical Issues (stage preventive)*

The forms of de-radicalization as described above cannot take effect if they are used singularly,[316] and furthermore very often will not be crowned with success. Consequently, the measures of the repressive stage have to be completed by some essential measures of prevention and precaution. Therefore, the "enemy" (used in a metaphorical sense) has to be treated with care. The preferred three-step-model fulfills this premise as follows.

#### *I. Knowing the "Enemy" (1st step)*

"Agree with a fanatic half of it, and you kill him"
(Hans Kasper)

The variety of extremism reveals that the different processes of radicalization do not resemble each other. Hence, precaution also needs purposeful means. The initial step is achieving as much knowledge as possible about the extremist ideology and patterns.[317] Preventative measures taken by states include the development of school curriculae on racism, anti-Semitism and Islamophobia, intercultural and inter-religious learning, citi-

---

315 See Crespo, "Das 'Feindstrafrecht' darf nicht sein!" 2006, pp. 417, 426; Dombrowsky, "Verteidigung des Zivilen," p. 36; Saliger, "Feindstrafrecht: Kritisches oder totalitäres Strafrechtskonzept?," 2006, p. 762; Zöller, *Terrorismusstrafrecht*, p. 285 ff; Eckert, "Radikalisierung," p. 16; Eckert, "Kulturelle Homogenität," p. 31; Schünemann recognizes some circular arguments in the thesis, see Schünemann, "Die deutsche Strafrechtswissenschaft nach der Jahrtausendwende," 2001, p. 212.

316 See Neumann, "Radikalisierung," p. 7; Eckert, "Radikalisierung," p. 17; Vidino, "DeRadikalisierung durch gezielte Interventionen," p. 27.

317 See Richardson, "Was Terroristen wollen," p. 268; see the aims of the EU http://www.dw.de/eu-sucht-im-anti-terror-kampf-nähe-muslimischer-staaten/a-18200294.

zenship, identity, democracy and tolerance education.[318] Not being able to see things from the extremist perspective will nip all efforts of de-escalation in the bud. The friend-or-foe scheme has to be adopted or at least internalized in an "inauthentic" manner: The far-right nationalist plans to save his country from hyperxenesis and assumes nepotism and treason against the people in every nook and corner.[319] The Islamist, on the contrary, feels threatened by an overwhelming and unstoppable spread of Western life, humiliating him and his brothers in faith.[320]

Nevertheless, if stereotypes dominate the opinion, possible solutions recede into the distance. Both groups have fears that have to be appeased.[321] You have to understand the different world view and theoretically "empathize" with the individual existing ideology. Therefore, it is unavoidable to become acquainted with specific rites and oaths as well as with common anxieties and visions.[322] You cannot just pigeonhole through your own biases, but you have to lead the way by sensitively mediating between all concerned.[323] Consequently, overworking the effects of criminal law will mislead, because the imposition of opinions by state authorities does not represent an adequate measure of persuasion. Indeed, the problems of persuading have been demonstrated. One cannot expect a complete catharsis of a staunched adherent.

---

318 See Vidino, "DeRadikalisierung durch gezielte Interventionen," pp. 26 f.; Ramalingam, "Old Threat, New Approach," p. 17; Eckert, "Radikalisierung," pp. 13, 15; Jaschke, "Zur Rolle der Schule bei der Bekämpfung von Rechtsextremismus," 2012, pp. 33 ff.

319 See Dovermann, "Narrative und Gegen-Narrative," p. 44; Priester, "Fließende Grenzen zwischen Rechtsextremismus und Rechtspopulismus in Europa?," p. 34; Stöß, "'Extremistische Parteien' – Worin besteht der Erkenntnisgewinn?," 2008, p. 4.

320 See Neubacher, "Terrorismus," p. 746; Dovermann, "Narrative und Gegen Narrative," p. 41.

321 See Dovermann, "Narrative und Gegen-Narrative," p. 45.

322 See Rohe, *Islam und Recht*, 2011, pp.16 ff.

323 See Neubacher, "Terrorismus," p. 749; Vidino, "DeRadikalisierung durch gezielte Interventionen," pp. 27 ff.; Korn and Weilnböck, "Der lange Abschied," pp. 34 ff.

## II. Finding the "Enemy" (2nd step)

"The enemy is in our walls. Against our own luxury, our own stupidity and our own criminal activity, we must fight"
(Marcus Tullius Cicero)

The fight against radicalization has to start at the earliest possible moment. It appears tempting to expand the competence of the investigating agencies and to infiltrate the typically used platforms[324] of the "rat-catchers" and "gate-keepers":[325] searching the Internet and email, monitoring phones, pursuing bank credit transfers. The more data are collected, the easier it would be to find both the string-puller and the potential victim of the radicalization.[326] Many jurisdictions worldwide rely heavily on these measures.[327] The area of conflict is obvious, because several social fears collide: the fear of becoming a victim of an extremist assassination, the fear of being tracked, observed and shadowed everywhere and the fear of being overwhelmed in face of all the threats of the modern world.[328] The idea of "freedom by guaranteeing security" is as alluring as the concept of "security by guaranteeing freedom".[329] Therefore, it is necessary to browse through the internet to identify critical sites and platforms.[330] The impact of charismatic leaders in the social network world cannot be underestimated.[331] Some experts swear on the targeted removal of single leaders of the extremist community. The "expunging" of important string-pullers

324 See Volkmann, "Kampf gegen die Hydra," p. 21.

325 Sirseloudi et al., "Radikalisierung von europäischen Muslimen," p. 43.

326 See Denkowski, "Gesetz zur Abwehr von Gefahren des internationalen Terrorismus durch das BKA, Kritische Anmerkungen zum zweiten Referentenentwurf,"p. 410.

327 See Sambei et al., *Counter-Terrorism Law and Practice*, 4 para 4.130. ff.

328 See Zöller, "Rechtsrahmen," p. 771.

329 Critical Sommer, "Das Märchen von der Funktionsuntüchtigkeit der Strafrechtspflege," 2014, p. 441; Hassemer, "Sicherheit durch Strafrecht," 2007, p. 18; see for the dangerous relationship between the topics "freedom" and "security" in criminal law policies Ignor, "Die Zukunft des Strafverfahrens – Abschied vom Rechtsstaat?," 2007, p. 934; Crespo, "Das 'Feindstrafrecht' darf nicht sein!" pp. 416, 425.

330 See Glaser and Schneider, "Rechtsextreme im Social Web," p. 46.

331 See Steinberg, "Jihadistische Radikalisierung," p. 24; also Vidino, "DeRadikalisierung durch gezielte Interventionen," p. 27.

may weaken the propaganda machinery so intensively that a propagation of the ideology can be stopped with lasting effect.[332]

Of course, searching extremist leaders by infiltrating the internet or poking about in a fog in order to find some agitators "in the nearer neighborhood" might seem risky at first sight. If surveillance and control enlarge, individual spaces and spheres of freedom are endangered.[333] Augmenting state intervention remains dangerous as long as concrete threats still persist on a low level. Therefore, investigation at least has to be bound to a minimum standard of suspicion. Monitoring social spheres on a grand scale stints and limits the scope of fundamental basic rights such as the general right of personality (Art. 2 § 1 German Basic Law; Art. 8 ECHR [European Convention on Human Rights]) or the freedom of expressions (Art. 5 § 1 German Basic Law and Art. 10 ECHR).

First of all, any provisions that interfere with Convention rights must impose a sufficient element of control over the relevant decision-maker so as to avoid the exercise of arbitrary action. Thus, there must be a measure of legal protection against arbitrary interference by public authorities with the right in Art. 8 ECHR, especially where a power of the executive is exercised in secret and the risk of arbitrariness is evident.[334] It is not enough that the State interfere with the applicant's rights for a legitimate purpose; the restriction of individual rights must be considered necessary in view of the circumstances. The word "necessary" means that there must be a "pressing social need" for the interference.[335] Subsequently, the last hurdle to be cleared is the requirement of proportionality.[336] The principle of proportionality demands that there must be reasonable relationship between a particular objective to be achieved and the means used to achieve that objective. There has to be "a fair balance" between the general and individual interests at stake.[337] Nevertheless, a proper assessment of all different

---

332 See Steinberg, "Jihadistische Radikalisierung," p. 24; Vidino, "DeRadikalisierung durch gezielte Interventionen," p. 27; also the fight against money-laundering and terrorism financing hampers the "work" of clandestine networks.

333 See Sambei et al., *Counter-Terrorism Law and Practice*, 4 para 161 ff.

334 See ECtHR Malone v. The United Kingdom, judgment of 2.8.1984, Serie A No. 82.; see also Sambei et al., *Counter-Terrorism Law and Pratice*, 4 para 4.165 ff.

335 See ECtHR Handyside v. United Kingdom, judgment of 7.12.1976 – 5439/72.

336 See Eckes, *EU Counter-Terrorist Policies*, pp. 408 ff.

337 For example ECtHR Sporrong and Lönnroth v. Sweden, judgment of 23.8.1982 -7151/75, § 69; Sambei et al., *Counter-Terrorism Law and Practice*, 4 para 4.172 ff.

factors of influence in this essay would lead too far. Interdependencies of state investigation and human rights do not represent a specific problem of de-radicalization progressions, but are typical for every coincidence of state and individual interests. Suppose that searching for extremists on the internet, on social platforms and within social spheres took place correctly, the next hurdle is to be taken. Finding of the "enemy" thus entails fighting against him.

### *III. Fighting the "Enemy"*

Fighting the enemy does not mean to kill or injure the extremist's physical integrity. Quite the contrary, the body will stay unhurt, while his or her thinking has to be altered. Radicalization and terrorism have detected the Achilles' heel of our Western societies. By losing religious embedding over the last decades, the pragmatic desire of living without disturbance has become the new dogma. A hostile power choking our way of life and our philosophy of pluralism and tolerance cannot be defeated with known measures.[338] Therefore, it is not too surprising that some politicians and academics try to develop enemy law (see above), counter-terrorism acts (see above) or re-integration camps (see above). The unpredictability of extremism overstrains our imagination. Isolating militant groups is hard, and stigmatization is necessary[339] but almost impossible. The battle against radicalization and terrorism is an unrewarded endeavor. That is why it is even more important to impede and hamper the radicalization of citizens becoming (whatever they hence might be) "opponents, enemies, strangers" before it escalates.[340] A soft but smart measure would be to identify the hotspots of extremism.[341] In this field, the opt-out organizations need help and support. Incidentally, the role of the already mentioned cognitive extremist (see above) has to be enlightened.

---

338 See Hetzer, "Europäische Strategien," p. 32; Dombrowsky, "Verteidigung des Zivilen," p. 34.

339 See Richardson, "Was Terroristen wollen," pp. 262 ff.

340 See Volkmann, "Kampf gegen die Hydra," p. 21; Dombrowsky, "Verteidigung des Zivilen," p. 38.

341 And the charismatic leaders, see Steinberg, "Jihadistische Radikalisierung," p. 25.

The connection between the cognitive and the violent extremist is controversial among experts.[342] It is not common sense that all cognitive extremist will become ready-to-use-violence in a "straightforward" process of radicalization. But looking at flip side, probably all violent extremists are cognitive extremists.[343] Assuming at least the second thesis, the cognitive extremist could play an invaluable role in the process of radicalization. Assuming secondly that it is nearly impossible to force a fanatic to quit its ideology (see the reasons above), it might be possible to persuade him to abstain from using violence (behavioral de-radicalization or "demobilization"[344]). Such a "de-mobilized" person[345] can stay radical and at the same time cognitively extremist, but will not escalate into a terrorist. This way, non-violent extremists who refuse any form of physical conflicts could work as front-liners to ease the de-radicalization of dangerous violent extremists. Those models are discussed and partly field-tested.[346]

Sometimes, those "concerned" have the "common" touch to see into the "heads and hearts" of the up-coming extremists providing experience and advice straight from the horse's mouth.[347] But this "idyllic world" of self-reflection and self-regulation may also backfire. Abstaining from violence could be pleaded out of tactical reasons,[348] while the alleged "good" extremists use their acknowledged benefit of the doubt to aggravate the existing radicalization without disturbance.[349] Nevertheless the integration of drop-outs or "converts" cannot per se be regarded as the wrong way. But this measure has to be used carefully. Only if this form of "therapy" is observed by statutory or non-governmental groups and associations of professional de-radicalization, these means might create a sensible mosaic piece on the long path of de-escalation.

Another option is offered by the mechanism of destabilization. The extremist groups are entrapped in their ideology and tend to believe in con-

---

342 Instructive Neumann, "Radikalisierung," p. 6 with citations.

343 See Neumann, "Radikalisierung," p. 8.

344 Neumann, "Radikalisierung," p. 8.

345 See Neumann, "Radikalisierung," pp. 8 f.

346 See the project STREET (Strategy to Re-Empower and Educate Teenagers), that is run by non-violent Salafist in London; also Vidino, "DeRadikalisierung durch gezielte Interventionen," p. 31.

347 See Resembling Neumann, "Radikalisierung," p. 9.

348 See Neumann, "Radikalisierung," p. 9.

349 See Vidino, "DeRadikalisierung durch gezielte Interventionen," p. 31.

spiracy theories.[350] Typical topoi are "omnipresent state", "others", "Zionist world order", "Western culture", "vassals", "world conspiracy", "capitalism", "communism", "Islamism", "terrorism". The list could be continued infinitively because of the number of "-isms" itself increases rapidly. This very own "permanent paranoia"[351] has to be harnessed. This aim can be achieved through many means.

The abovementioned browsing of the internet could be enhanced by spreading counter-thesis and counter-rumors.[352] The suspiciousness of extremist groups against "the system" can be used as an effective weapon by creating an awareness of being observed, tagged for using the internet and visiting specific homepages.[353] The leading maxim is "spreading disorder".[354] The extremist must have doubts to everything connected to his ideology. The sources of propaganda have to be infiltrated by authorities, the individual persuasion must be distressed by counter-arguments as often as possible. The typical narratives and idioms of the radical world view have to be extracted and examined and a substantial answer for every prejudice and bias has to be formulated and published consistently.[355] The friend-foe-scheme in the extremist head will be over-challenged if the "actual enemy" and the "actual friend" intermingle indissolubly. Mistrust between peer groups, ideologies and battle cries will sooner or later splinter the "extremist front" into its individual members. And without his peer group, the single extremist is lost in his own world of embedded fallacies. Hence, the "prodigal son" comes back to normal life.[356] But how much influence on citizen's opinion and persuasion should be allowed?

Opinion always remains an expression of option and position. Could it be right that with the indisputable higher weight of state influence on society, state authorities could articulate their own opinion unreflectively?[357]

---

350 See Hoffmann-Plesch, "Deutsche IS-Dschihadisten Teil 2," p. 12.

351 Steinberg, "Jihadistische Radikalisierung," p. 25; Hoffmann-Plesch, "Deutsche IS-Dschihadisten Teil 2," pp. 14 f.; Sirseloudi et al., "Radikalisierung von europäischen Muslimen," pp. 41 f.

352 See Horgan, "From Profiles to Pathways," p. 92.

353 See Steinberg, "Jihadistische Radikalisierung," pp. 24 f.

354 Korn and Weilnböck, "Der lange Abschied," p. 38.

355 See Horgan, "From Profiles to Pathways," p. 91; Dovermann, "Narrative und Gegen-Narrative," pp. 44 ff.

356 See Möller and Schuhmacher, "Ein- und Ausstiegsprozesse," p. 22.

357 See for more information to this complex topic *the author* Gerson, "Rolle und Selbstverständnis des Staates im Kommunikationsprozess," 2014, pp. 24 ff.

Paternalistic and pedagogic self-conception of state hence might mislead into totalitarian interpenetration of social and private life.[358] Right here, this topic enfolds its huge philosophical potential: influence by state organs to secure the "good" citizens from the "bad" ones works without metaphorical "frictional losses" as long as the state itself is a "good" one. The leviathan becomes the wolf, if its cage of self-restraint is opened too widely thus the worse comes to worst.

The current examination must stop at this level because of the dire consequences of such perception: philosophically, it is almost impossible to achieve practical concordance (Hesse) in terms of state intervention through pedagogic interventions. Brain-washing (even initiated from state authorities) uncontestably creates an effective measure but would be a door opener to permanent brinkmanship. Freedom of speech and opinion must implicate the right to fend other opinions, even state and democratic ones. As mentioned above: democracy also feeds its own enemies, because the principle of pluralism is guaranteed without restrictions.

As demonstrated, the required measures are situated in the melting pot of individual therapy and social reorganization. But there is much more to alter: reforms bringing young people back into the job market, better education trying to sensitize pluralism and alterity together with a sort of humbleness towards those not benefiting of the advantages of affluence would relieve social tension. Bearing in mind the embedding of prejudices, radicalization starts in the person's head. Following the principle of actus contrarius, it also might end in the head.

## *G. Conclusion*

"A radical is a person who stands with both legs firmly in the air"
(Franklin Delano Roosevelt)

The title of this essay is "Radicalization and De-Radicalization: Trip to Hell and Back? Appreciation and Purpose of Dropout Programs for Political and Religious Fanatics and Alternatives". Due to this title, the whole examination raced like a ride on a roller-coaster. Summing up the results may bundle the thoughts:

358 See Gerson, "Kommunikationsprozess," p. 29.

Radicalization is not a linear or straightforward process. Several intrinsic and extrinsic factors may lead to progressive escalation. The starting point is similar in most of the cases. Feelings of being left behind, bad experiences and contact with fateful peer groups pull vulnerable[359] victims into a spiral of brutalization. Known manifestations diverge, thus not every radicalization will end in a ready-to-use-violence attitude.

The ways out of radicalization must be distinguished between the time of intervention and the anticipated result. Preventive measures trying to prevent radicalization have to start as early as possible and contain social reforms and raise sensibility for hot beds of extremism. Repressive and long-lasting countermeasures compound effective opt-out programs, a severe legal framework and tactical reflections on obtaining the status quo ante bellum.

Separately, the measures are not promising. Opt-out programs are based on willing and voluntary participation. The embedding of ideology and propaganda is too rigorous to bring over every individual extremist. Likewise, banning groups and parties only succeeds if the structure of those associations depends on leading heads. Even arming criminal law will not lead to success. The conversion of criminal law by antedating the point of criminal responsibility and expanding enforcement powers will transform it into a law of safety and hazard defense. Nevertheless, the impact on deradicalization will be negligible. Invoking "enemies" as a solution for unresolved problems of punishment or humiliation, on the other hand, concurrently portrays a vicious circle and an oath of manifestation. Thus, the way back from hell is lined with psychological, social, intercultural and legal measures. Radical, extremist and terrorist individuals have to be treated as human beings and therefore procedures must predominantly consider the "human side". The radical has to be regarded as rooted in extremes and uprooted of confidence and assurance. The best measure, ergo, would be to ground the aloofed.

359 See Horgan, "From Profiles to Pathways," pp. 84 ff.

## *Bibliography*

Abdillah, Masykuri, "Verfassungsgebung in muslimischen Ländern – das Beispiel Indonesien," in *Islam und Rechtsstaat zwischen Scharia und Säkularisierung*, ed. Birgit Krawietz and Helmut Reifeld, Sankt Augustin/Berlin: Konrad-Adenauer-Stiftung e.V, 2008, pp. 55-70.

Anderson, Norman H, "Primacy Effects in Personality Impression Formation Using a Generalized Order Effect Paradigm," *Journal of Personality and Social Psychology* 1 (1965): 1-9.

Asholt, Martin, "Die Debatte über das 'Feindstrafrecht' in Deutschland, Aufleben eines alten Dilemmas am Anfang des 21. Jahrhunderts?," *Zeitschrift für Internationale Strafrechtsdogmatik* (2011): 180-192.

Backes, Uwe, "Interdependenzen und Interaktionen zwischen gewaltlosen und gewaltorientierten extremistischen Akteuren am Beispiel von 'Autonomen', 'Neonationalsozialisten' und 'Skinheads' in der Bundesrepublik Deutschland," in *Terrorismus und Extremismus – der Zukunft auf der Spur, Beiträge zur Entwicklungsdynamik von Terrorismus und Extremismus – Möglichkeiten und Grenzen einer prognostischen Empirie*, ed. Uwe E. Kemmesies, München: Luchterhand Wolters Kluwer, 2006, pp. 41-58.

Backes, Uwe, "NPD-Verbot: Pro und Contra," *Aus Politik und Zeitgeschichte* (2012): 9-15.

Barisch, Kai Thorsten, *Die Bekämpfung des internationalen Terrorismus durch § 129b StGB, Verfassungswidrig politisiertes symbolisches Feindstrafrecht zum Schutze eines Scheinrechtsgutes oder sinnvolles Strafanwendungsrecht eines streitbaren demokratischen Rechtsstaates in der Weltgesellschaft?*, Berlin: Duncker & Humblot 2009.

Bender, Rolf, Armin Nack and Wold-Dieter Treuer, *Tatsachenfeststellung vor Gericht, Glaubwürdigkeits- und Beweislehre, Vernehmungslehre*, München: C.H. Beck, 3rd ed., 2007.

Blum, Barbara, "Mögliche Auswirkungen der Ermittlungsakte auf die Informationsverarbeitung und die Entscheidungsbildung im Strafverfahren," in *Abschied von der Wahrheitssuche?*, Texte und Ergebnisse des 35. Strafverteidigertages Berlin, 25. – 27. 3. 2011, Schriftenreihe der Strafverteidiger-Vereinigungen, Berlin, 2012, pp. 237-262.

Böllinger, Lorenz, "Die Entwicklung zu terroristischem Handeln als psychosozialer Prozess," in *Terrorismus und Extremismus – der Zukunft auf der Spur, Beiträge zur Entwicklungsdynamik von Terrorismus und Extremismus – Möglichkeiten und Grenzen einer prognostischen Empirie*, ed. Uwe E. Kemmesies, München: Luchterhand Wolters Kluwer, 2006, pp. 59-70.

Borum, Randy, "Rethinking Radicalization," *Journal of Strategic Security* 4 (2011): 1-6.

Borum, Randy, "Radicalization into Violent Extremism I: A Review of Social Science Theories," *Journal of Strategic Security* 4 (2011): 7-36.

Borum, Randy, "Radicalization into Violent Extremism II: A Review of Conceptual Models and Empirical Research," *Journal of Strategic Security* 4 (2011): 37-62.

Brettfeld, Katrin, Peter Wetzels and Bundesministerium des Inneren, *Muslime in Deutschland, Integration, Integrationsbarrieren, Religion und Einstellungen zu Demokratie, Rechtsstaat und politisch-religiös motivierter Gewalt, Ergebnisse von Befragungen im Rahmen einer multizentrischen Studie in städtischen Lebensräumen*, Hamburg, 2007.

Briggs, Rachel, and Sebastian Feve, "Review of Programs to Counter Narratives of Violent Extremism: What works and what are the implications for Government?," *Institute for Strategic Dialogue Publication* (July, 2013): 1-63.

Bundesamt für Verfassungsschutz (BfV), *Autonome Nationalisten – Rechtsextremistische Militanz*, (bfv-themenreihe 2009).

Bundesamt für Verfassungsschutz (BfV), *Argumentationsmuster im rechtsextremistischen Antisemitismus. Aktuelle Entwicklungen*, (2005).

Bundesamt für Verfassungsschutz (BfV), *Die 'Nationaldemokratische Partei Deutschlands' (NPD) als Gravitationsfeld im Rechtsextremismus*, (bfv-themenreihe 2006).

Bundesamt für Verfassungsschutz (BfV): *Islamismus: Entstehung und Erscheinungsformen*, (bfv-themenreihe 2013).

Bundesamt für Verfassungsschutz (BfV), *Jugend und 'Jihad'*, (2014).

Bundesamt für Verfassungsschutz (BfV), *Rechtsextremismus: Symbole, Zeichen und verbotene Organisationen*, (bfv-themenreihe 2014).

Bundesministerium des Innern, "Vereinsverbote," at http://www.bmi.bund.de/DE/Themen/Sicherheit/Extremismusbekaempfung/Vereinsverbote/vereinsverbote_node.html.

Bundschuh, Stephan, "Die braune Seite der Zivilgesellschaft: rechtsextreme Sozialraumstrategien," *Aus Politik und Zeitgeschichte* (2012): 28-33.

Buschbom, Jan, Michael Hammerbacher and Gabriel Landgraf, "Rechtspopulismus, Argumente und pädagogische Annäherung," *Violence Prevention Network Publication* (2008): 1-22.

Crespo, Eduardo Demetrio, "Das 'Feindstrafrecht' darf nicht sein!," *Zeitschrift für Internationale Strafrechtsdogmatik* (2006): 413-417.

Cross, Remy, and David A. Snow, "Radicalism within the Context of Social Movements: Processes and Types," *Journal of Strategic Security* 4 (2011): 115-130.

Daum, Oliver, "Anforderungen an Ausreisebeschränkungen von Islamisten," *Die öffentliche Verwaltung* (2014): 526-533.

Denkowski, Charles von, "Gesetz zur Abwehr von Gefahren des internationalen Terrorismus durch das BKA, Kritische Anmerkungen zum zweiten Referentenentwurf," *Kriminalistik* (2008): 410-416.

Deutsche Welle, "EU will Terror-Söldner stoppen," 30 January 2015, at http://www.dw.de/eu-will-terror-söldner-stoppen/a-18226017.

Deutsche Welle, "Bessere Kooperation gegen den Terror," at http://www.dw.de/bessere-kooperation-gegen-den-terror/a-18201212.

Dombrowsky, Wolf R., "Terrorismus und die Verteidigung des Zivilen," *Aus Politik und Zeitgeschichte* (2004): 33-38.

Dovermann, Ulrich, "Narrative und Gegen-Narrative im Prozess von Radikalisierung und Deradikalisierung," *Aus Politik und Zeitgeschichte* (2013): 39-45.

Dovermann, Ulrich, and Eren Güvercin, "Auf Fragen von Extremisten reagieren können: Eren Güvercin im Gespräch mit Ulrich Dovermann," *Aus Politik und Zeitgeschichte* (2010): 17-20.

Dustdar, Farah, "Demokratie und die Macht der Gefühle," *Aus Politik und Zeitgeschichte* (2008): 32-38.

Eckert, Roland, "Radikalisierung – Eine soziologische Perspektive," *Aus Politik und Zeitgeschichte* (2013): 11-17.

Eckert, Roland, "Kulturelle Homogenität und aggressive Intoleranz. Eine Kritik der Neuen Rechten," *Aus Politik und Zeitgeschichte* (2010): 26-33.

Eckes, Christina, *EU Counter-Terrorist Policies and Fundamental Rights, The Case of Inndividual Sanctions*, Oxford: Oxford University Press, 2009.

Ende, Werner, "Gerechtigkeit als politisches Prinzip im Islam," in *Islam und Rechtsstaat zwischen Scharia und Säkularisierung*, ed. Birgit Krawietz and Helmut Reifeld, Sankt Augustin/Berlin: Konrad-Adenauer-Stiftung e.V, 2008, pp. 19-35.

Entdorf, Horst, "Islamistischer Terrorismus: Analysen, Entwicklungen und Anti-Terrorpolitik aus der Sicht ökonomischer Forschung," in *Terrorismus und Extremismus – der Zukunft auf der Spur, Beiträge zur Entwicklungsdynamik von Terrorismus und Extremismus – Möglichkeiten und Grenzen einer prognostischen Empirie*, ed. Uwe E. Kemmesies, München: Luchterhand Wolters Kluwer, 2006, pp. 85-103.

Esser, Robert, "Die Rolle von Europol und Eurojust bei der Bekämpfung von Terrorismus und organisierter Kriminalität," in *Neujustierung des Strafrechts durch Terrorismus und Organisierte Kriminalität*, 2. Deutsch-Taiwanesisches Strafrechtsforum Trier/Osnabrück 2012, ed. Arndt Sinn and Mark A. Zöller, Heidelberg: C.F. Müller, 2013, pp. 61-87.

European Commission, "Radicalisation Awareness Network (RAN)," at

http://ec.europa.eu/dgs/home-affairs/what-we-do/networks/radicalisation_awareness_network/index_en.htm.

European Network of Deradicalisation, "Home," at http://www.european-network-of-deradicalisation.eu/.

Exit Deutschland, at http://www.exit-deutschland.de/exit/?c=ueber-uns.

Festinger, Leon, *Theorie der kognitiven Dissonanz*, Bern: Huber 1978.

Frankfurter Allgemeine Zeitung, "Ohne Reisepass in den Krieg," 13 January 2015, at http://www.faz.net/aktuell/politik/inland/deutsche-islamisten-gelangten-auch-ohne-reisepass-in-kriegsgebiete-13367031.html.

Frindte, Wolfgang, ans Siegfried Preiser, "Präventionsansätze gegen Rechtsextremismus," *Aus Politik und Zeitgeschichte* (2007): 32-38.

Frisch, Wolfgang, "Konzepte der Strafe und Entwicklungen des Strafrechts in Europa," *Goltdammer's Archiv* (2009): 387-405.

Geipel, Andreas, *Handbuch der Beweiswürdigung*, Bonn: ZAP, 2nd ed., 2013.

Gerding, Marc, *Trial by Jury. Die Bewährung des englischen und des US-amerikanischen Jury-Systems. Eine Idee im verfassungsrechtlichen und gesellschaftlichen Wandel*, Osnabrück: Julius Jonscher 2007.

Gerson, Oliver, "Rolle und Selbstverständnis des Staates im Kommunikationsprozess," *Iurratio* (2014): 24-29.

Geschke, Daniel, "Vorurteile, Differenzierung und Diskriminierung – sozialpsychologische Erklärungsansätze," *Aus Politik und Zeitgeschichte* (2012): 33-37.

Glaser, Stefan, and Christiane Schneider, "Zielgruppe Jugend: Rechtsextreme im Social Web," *Aus Politik und Zeitgeschichte* (2012): 40-46.

Glasersfeld, Ernst von, *Radical Constructivism: A Way of Knowing and Learning*, Studies in Mathematics Education Series: 6, Bristol: Falmer Press, 1995.

Government of the United Kingdom, "2010-2015 government policy: counter-terrorism, Updated 8 May 2015," at https://www.gov.uk/government/policies/protecting-the-uk-against-terrorism/supporting-pages/prevent.

Greco, Luís, *Feindstrafrecht*, Baden-Baden: Nomos, 2010.

Groß, Eva, Andreas Zick and Daniela Krause, "Von der Ungleichwertigkeit zur Ungleichheit: Gruppenbezogene Menschenfeindlichkeit," *Aus Politik und Zeitgeschichte* (2012): 11-18.

Habschick, Klaus, *Erfolgreich Vernehmen, Kompetenz in der Kommunikations-, Gesprächs- und Vernehmungspraxis*, Heidelberg: Kriminalistik Verlag Hüthig Jehle Rehm 2010.

Hassemer, Winfried, "Sicherheit durch Strafrecht," in *Wieviel Sicherheit braucht die Freiheit?*, 30. Strafverteidigertag Frankfurt/Main, 2006 (Schriftenreihe der Strafverteidigervereinigungen), Berlin, 2007, pp. 9-38.

Heine, Peter, *Terror in Allahs Namen: Extremistische Kräfte im Islam*, Freiburg im Breisgau: Herder 2004.

Heitmeyer, Wilhelm, "Rechtsextremismus und gesellschaftliche Selbstentlastung," *Aus Politik und Zeitgeschichte* (2012): 22-27.

Hess, Henner, in *Netzwerke des Terrors – Netzwerke gegen den Terror*, ed. Bundeskriminalamt, BKA-Herbsttagung 2004, München: Luchterhand Wolters Kluwer, 2005, p. 123.

Hetzer, Wolfgang: "Sicherheit durch Ausnahmezustand?," *Strafverteidigerforum* (2008): 93-102.

Hetzer, Wolfgang, "Deutsche Umsetzung neuer europäischer Vorgaben zur Bekämpfung der Geldwäsche und der Terrorismusfinanzierung," *Europäische Zeitschrift für Wirtschaftsrecht* (2008): 560-565.

Hetzer, Wolfgang, "Europäische Strategien gegen Geldwäsche und Terror," *Aus Politik und Zeitgeschichte* (2004): 28-32.

Higgins, E. Tory, William S. Rholes and Carl R. Jones, "Category Accessibility and Impression Formation," *Journal of Experimental Social Psychology* 2 (1977): 141-154.

Hirsch, Hans Joachim, "Die subjektive Versuchstheorie, ein Wegbereiter der NS-Strafrechtsdoktrin," *Juristenzeitung* (2007): 494-502.

Hoffmann-Plesch, Roland Christian, "Deutsche IS-Dschihadisten, Kriminalätiologische und kriminalpräventive Analyse des Radikalisierungsprozesses, Teil 1: Religionskriminologische und psychopolitische Aspekte," *Kriminalistik* (2014): 699-704.

Hoffmann-Plesch, Roland Christian, "Deutsche IS-Dschihadisten, Kriminalätiologische und kriminalpräventive Analyse des Radikalisierungsprozesses, Teil 2: Kriminalpsychologische Aspekte," *Kriminalistik* (2015): 10-16.

Holley, Gerhard, *Das Recht der internationalen Terrorismusbekämpfung, Asset Freezing, UN- und FATF-Vorgaben, US-Recht, EuGH-Judikatur, Grundrechte*, Wien: Jan Sramek Verlag 2010.

Horgan, John, "From Profiles to Pathways and Roots to Routes: Perspectives from Psychology on Radicalization into Terrorism," *The Annals of the American Academy of Political and Social Science* 1 (2008): 80-94.

Hufen, Christian, "Neues Parteiverbotsverfahren gegen die NPD? Verfassungsrechtliche Voraussetzungen vor dem Hintergrund der NSU-Taten," *Zeitschrift für Rechtspolitik* (2012): 202-205.

Ignor, Alexander, "Die Zukunft des Strafverfahrens – Abschied vom Rechtsstaat?," *Zeitschrift für die gesamte Strafrechtswissenschaft* (2007): 927-937.

Ipsen, Jörn, "Rechtsfragen des NPD-Verbots," *Neue Juristische Wochenschrift* (2002): 866-868.

Jakobs, Günther, "Bürgerstrafrecht und Feindstrafrecht," *HRRS* (Online-Zeitschrift für Strafrecht) (2004): 88-95.

Jakobs, Günther, "Feind*strafrecht? – Eine Untersuchung zu den Bedingungen von Rechtlichkeit,"* HRRS (Online-Zeitschrift für Strafrecht) (2006): 289-297.

Jakobs, Günther, "Kriminalisierung im Vorfeld einer Rechtsgutverletzung," *Zeitschrift für die gesamte Strafrechtswissenschaft* (1985): 751-785.

Jansen, Gabriele, *Zeuge und Aussagepsychologie*, Heidelberg: C.F. Müller, 2nd ed., 2012.

Jaschke, Hans-Gerd: *Rechtsextremismus und Fremdenfeindlichkeit. Begriffe, Positionen, Praxisfelder*, Opladen: Westdeutscher Verlag 1994.

Jaschke, Hans-Gerd, "Zur Rolle der Schule bei der Bekämpfung von Rechtsextremismus," *Aus Politik und Zeitgeschichte* (2012): 33-39.

Jesse, Eckhard, "'Extremistische Parteien' – worin besteht der Erkenntniszugewinn?," *Aus Politik und Zeitgeschichte* (2008): 7-11.

Kargl, Walter, "Friede durch Vergeltung, Über den Zusammenhang von Sache und Zweck im Strafbegriff," *Goltdammer's Archiv* (1998): 53-77.

Korn, Judy, and Harald Weilnböck, "Der lange Abschied von Hass und Gewalt," *Aus Politik und Zeitgeschichte* (2013): 32-39.

Klein, Hans H., in *Grundgesetz-Kommentar*, ed. Theodor Maunz and Günter Dürig, München: C.H. Beck, 72. Ergänzungslieferung, 2014.

Kluth, Winfried, in *Beck'scher Online-Kommentar GG*, ed. Volker Epping and Christian Hillgruber, 2014, at https://beck-online.beck.de/Modul/1064.

Kühne, Hans-Heiner, *Strafprozessrecht*, Heidelberg: C.F.-Müller, 8th ed., 2010.

Luhmann, Niklas, *Legitimation durch Verfahren*, Darmstadt: Luchterhand, 3rd ed., 1978.

Mahncke, Jakob C., "Bürger oder Feind? Zur Diskussion um das Feindstrafrecht," in *Sicherheit und Freiheit statt Terror und Angst, Perspektiven einer demokratischen Sicherheit*, ed. Gisela Riescher, Baden-Baden: Nomos 2010, pp. 205-227.

Mansour, Ahmad, "Salafistische Radikalisierung – und was man dagegen tun kann," 22 October 2014, at http://www.bpb.de/politik/extremismus/islamismus/193521/salafistische-Radikalisierung-und-was-man-dagegen-tun-kann.

McCauley, Clark, and Sophia Moskalenko, "Mechanisms of Political Radicalization," *Terrorism and Political Violence* 3 (2008): 415-433.

Mitsch, Wolfgang, "Vorbeugende Strafbarkeit zur Abwehr terroristischer Gewalttaten," *Neue Juristische Wochenschrift* (2015): 209-212.

Ministry for the Protection of the Constitution, at http://www.verfassungsschutz.de/de/arbeitsfelder/af-rechtsextremismus/zahlen-und-fakten-rechtsextremismus/zuf-re-2013-gesamtuebersicht.html.

Mletzko, Matthias, "Gewalthandeln linker und rechter militanter Szenen, " *Aus Politik und Zeitgeschichte* (2010): 9-16.

Montag, Jerzy, "Strafbarkeit des Besuchs terroristischer Ausbildungslager – von der Vorfeldstrafbarkeit einer Vorfeldstrafnorm," *Deutsche Richterzeitung* (2008): 141.

Möller, Kurt, and Nils Schuhmacher, "Ein- und Ausstiegsprozesse rechtsextremistischer Skinheads," *Aus Politik und Zeitgeschichte* (2007): 17-23.

Möllers, Martin H.W., and Robert Christian van Ooyen, "Bundekriminalamt, Bundespolizei und 'neue Sicherheit'," *Aus Politik und Zeitgeschichte* (2008): 26-33.

Mudde, Cas, "Radikale Parteien in Europa," *Aus Politik und Zeitgeschichte* (2008): 12-19.

Mückenberger, Heiner, "Zum Profil eines Terroristen (Mohammed Ali Hamadi)," *Monatsschrift für Kriminologie und Strafrechtsreform* (2014): 232-236.

Murphy, Sheila T. and Robert B. Zajonc, "Affect, Cognition, and Awareness: Affective Priming With Optimal and Suboptimal Stimulus Exposures," *Journal of Personality and Social Psychology* 5 (1993): 723-739.

Neubacher, Frank, "Terrorismus – Was haben »Rote Armee Fraktion« und »Jihadisten« gemeinsam? " *Jura* (2010): 744-749.

Neugebauer, Gero, "Einfach war gestern. Zur Strukturierung der politischen Realität in einer modernen Gesellschaft," *Aus Politik und Zeitgeschichte* (2010): 3-9.

Neumann, Peter, "Radikalisierung, Deradikalisierung und Extremismus," *Aus Politik und Zeitgeschichte* (2013): 3-10.

Nisbett, Richard E. and Timothy D. Wilson, "The Halo Effect: Evidence for Unconscious Alteration of Judgments," *Journal of Personality and Social Psychology* 4 (1977): 250-256.

Normann, Lars, "Sicherheitspolitische Reformergebnisse zur Terrorprävention," Aus *Politik und Zeitgeschichte* (2007): 11-17.

NPD-Parteivorstand (ed.), *Argumente für Kandidaten und Funktionsträger. Eine Handreichung für die öffentliche Auseinandersetzung. NPD. Die Nationalen*, Berlin 2006.

Ouaissa, Rachid, "Der Aufstieg islamistischer Parteien," *Aus Politik und Zeitgeschichte* (2008): 40-45.

Özerdem, Alpaslan, and Sukanya Podder, "Disarming Youth Combatants: Mitigating Youth Radicalization and Violent Extremism," *Journal of Strategic Security* 4 (2011): 63-80.

Organization for Security and Co-operation in Europe, "Preventing Terrorism and Countering Violent Extremism and Radicalization that Lead to Terrorism: A Community-Policing Approach," *Organization for Security and Co-operation in Europe publication*, Vienna, 2014.

Paeffgen, Hans-Ullrich, in *Strafgesetzbuch*, ed. Urs Kindhäuser, Ulfrid Neumann and Hans-Ulrich Paeffgen, Baden-Baden: Nomos, 4th ed., 2013, before § 32.

Pendry, Louise, "Soziale Kognition," in *Sozialpsychologie. Eine Einführung*, ed. Miles Hewstone, Klaus Jonas and Wolfgang Stroebe, Heidelberg: Springer, 2007, pp. 111-127.

Pitschas, Rainer, "Innere Sicherheit in 'guter Verfassung'? Zur Terrorismusbekämpfung im präventiven Gewährleistungsstaat," in *Organisation und Verfahren im sozialen Rechtsstaat, Festschrift für Friedrich E. Schnapp zum 70. Geburtstag*, ed. Hermann Butzer, Markus Kaltenborn and Wolfgang Meyer, Berlin: Duncker & Humblodt, 2008, pp. 231-252.

Priester, Karin: "Fließende Grenzen zwischen Rechtsextremismus und Rechtspopulismus in Europa?," *Aus Politik und Zeitgeschichte* (2010): 33-39.

Puschnerat, Tânia, "Zur Bedeutung ideologischer und sozialer Faktoren in islamistischen Radikalisierungsprozesses – eine Skizze," in *Terrorismus und Extremismus – der Zukunft auf der Spur, Beiträge zur Entwicklungsdynamik von Terrorismus und Extremismus – Möglichkeiten und Grenzen einer prognostischen Empirie*, ed. Uew E. Kemmesies, München: Luchterhand Wolters Kluwer 2006, pp. 217-235.

Ramalingam, Vidhya, "Old Threat, New Approach: Tackling the Far Right across Europe, Guide for Policy Makers," *Institute for Strategic Dialogue publication*, London: 2014, at http://www.strategicdialogue.org/ISD_New_Approach_Far_Right_Re port.pdf.

Richardson, Louise, *Was Terroristen wollen, die Ursachen der Gewalt und wie wir sie bekämpfen können*, trans. Hartmut Schickert, Schriftenreihe, Bundeszentrale für politische Bildung, Bonn: 2007.

Rieker, Peter, "Fremdenfeindlichkeit und Sozialisation in Kindheit und Jugend," *Aus Politik und Zeitgeschichte* (2007): 31-38.

Rohe, Mathias, and Bundesministerium der Justiz, *Islam und Recht*, Rechtspolitischer Neujahrsempfang im Bundesministerium der Justiz 2011, Berlin, 2011, pp. 12-23.

Rommelspacher, Birgit, "Warum steigen Aussteiger aus? Und tun sie es tatsächlich?," in *88 Fragen und Antworten zur NPD*, ed. Fabian Virchow and Christian Dornbusch, Schwalbach/Ts.: Wochenschau, 2008, pp. 315-317.

Ruf, Anda, "Demokratischer Rechtsstaat und Terrorismus. Ein Feindrecht als Mittel zur Terrorismusabwehr?," in *Sicherheit und Freiheit statt Terror und Angst, Perspektiven einer demokratischen Sicherheit*, ed. Gisela Riescher, Baden-Baden: Nomos Verlagsgesellschaft 2010, pp. 229-248.

Ruthig, Josef, "Europol," in *Europäisches Strafrecht mit polizeilicher Zusammenarbeit*, ed. Martin Böse, Baden-Baden: Nomos 2013, pp. 749-785.

Saliger, Frank, "Feindstrafrecht: Kritisches oder totalitäres Strafrechtskonzept?," *Juristenzeitung* (2006): 756-762.

Sambei, Arvinder, Anton du Plessis, and Martin Polaine, *Counter-Terrorism Law and Practice: An International Handbook*, Oxford: Oxford University Press 2009.

Savage, Sara, "Four Lessons From the Study of Fundamentalism and Psychology of Religion," *Journal of Strategic Security* 4 (2011): 131-150.

Schedler, Jan, "Autonome Nationalisten," *Aus Politik und Zeitgeschichte* (2010): 20-26.

Schoelermann, Stefan, "Der Weg aus der Szene ist steinig," (2008), at http://www.bpb.de/politik/extremismus/rechtsextremismus/41374/der-weg-aus-der-szene-ist-steinig.

Schroeder, Klaus, *Rechtsextremismus und Jugendgewalt in Deutschland, Ein Ost-West-Vergleich*, Bayerische Landeszentrale für politische Bildungsarbeit, München, 2003.

Schünemann, Bernd, "Die deutsche Strafrechtswissenschaft nach der Jahrtausendwende," *Goltdammer's Archiv* (2001): 205-225.

Silke, Andrew, "Holy Warriors – Exploring the Psychological Processes of Jihadi Radicalization," *European Journal of Criminology* 1 (2008): 99-123.

Sirseloudi, Matenia, Syed Mansoob Murshed and Sara Pavan, "Radikalisierung von europäischen Muslimen: Zwei Erklärungsansätze," *Aus Politik und Zeitgeschichte* (2010): 39-46.

Sinn, Arndt, "Vorverlagerung der Strafbarkeit am Beispiel der Organisierten Kriminalität und des Terrorismus," in *Neujustierung des Strafrechts durch Terrorismus und Organisierte Kriminalität*, 2. Deutsch-Taiwanesisches Strafrechtsforum Trier/ Osnabrück 2012, ed. Arndt Sinn and Mark A. Zöller, Heidelberg: C.F. Müller 2013, pp. 147-165.

Sitzer, Peter, and Wilhelm Heitmeyer, "Rechtsextremistische Gewalt von Jugendlichen," *Aus Politik und Zeitgeschichte* (2007): 3-10.

Sommer, Ulrich, *Effektive Strafverteidigung, Recht-Psychologie-Überzeugungsarbeit der Verteidigung*, Köln: Carl Heymanns. 2nd ed., 2013.

Sommer, Ulrich, "Das Märchen von der Funktionsuntüchtigkeit der Strafrechtspflege," *Strafverteidigerforum* (2014): 441-444.

Spiegel Online, 17 November 2002, at http://www.spiegel.de/politik/ausland/giftgas-pocken-festnahmen-furcht-vor-dem-terror-hat-europa-im-griff-a-223221.html.

Stegmaier, Peter, and Thomas Feltes, "Vernetzung – neuer Effektivitätsmythos für die innere Sicherheit," *Aus Politik und Zeitgeschichte* (2007): 18-25.

Steinberg, Guido, "Jihadistische Radikalisierung im Internet und mögliche Gegenmaßnahmen," Aus Politik und Zeitgeschichte (2013): 17-25.

Stöß, Richard, "'Extremistische Parteien' – Worin besteht der Erkenntnisgewinn?," *Aus Politik und Zeitgeschichte* (2008): 3-7.

Stöß, Richard, "Zur Entwicklung des Rechtsextremismus in Deutschland," (2015), at http://www.bpb.de/politik/extremismus/rechtsextremismus/198940/zur-entwicklung-des-rechtsextremismus-in-deutschland.

Streng, Franz, in *Strafgesetzbuch*, ed. Urs Kindhäuser, Ulfrid Neumann and Hans-Ulrich Paeffgen, Baden-Baden: Nomos, 4th ed. 2013, § 46 para. 34.

Vidino, Lorenzo, "Deradikalisierung durch gezielte Interventionen," *Aus Politik und Zeitgeschichte* (2013): 25-32.

Violence Prevention Network, at http://www.violence-prevention-network.de/.

Volkmann, Uwe, "Dilemmata des Parteiverbots," *Die Öffentliche Verwaltung* (2007): 577-585.

Volkmann, Uwe, "Kampf gegen die Hydra? Der Staat und der Rechtsextremismus," *Aus Politik und Zeitgeschichte* (2012): 15-22.

Waldmann, Peter, "Islamistischer Terrorismus: Ideologie, Organisation und Unterstützungspotential," in *Netzwerke des Terrors – Netzwerke gegen den Terror*, BKA-Herbsttagung 2004, ed. Bundeskriminalamt, München: Luchterhand Wolters Kluwer 2005, pp. 31-44.

Wasser, Detlef, and Alexander Piaszek, "Staatsschutzstrafrecht in Bewegung?," *Deutsche Richterzeitung* (2008): 315-319.

Welt, 16 February 2015, at http://www.welt.de/videos/article137495157/Terrorwarnung-ueberschattet-Karnevalsu mzuege.html.

Wendler, Axel, and Helmut Hoffmann, *Technik und Taktik der Befragung im Gerichtsverfahren, Urteile begründen, Urteile prüfen. Lüge und Irrtum aufdecken*, Stuttgart: W. Kohlhammer, 2nd ed., 2009.

Wenzel, Volkmar, "Betrachtungen zum Islamistischen Terrorismus – die arabische Perspektive," in *Netzwerke des Terrors – Netzwerke gegen den Terror*, BKA-Herbsttagung 2004, ed. Bundeskriminalamt, München: Luchterhand Wolters Kluwer, 2005, pp. 59-74.

Werthebach, Eckart, "Deutsche Sicherheitsstrukturen im 21. Jahrhundert," *Aus Politik und Zeitgeschichte* (2004): 5-13.

Zöller, Mark A., "Der Rechtsrahmen der Nachrichtendienste bei der 'Bekämpfung' des internationalen Terrorismus," *Juristenzeitung* (2007): 763-771.

Zöller, Mark A., *Terrorismusstrafrecht. Ein Handbuch*, Heidelberg: C.F. Müller Heidelberg, 2009.

# Examining the Nexus between Terrorism and Organized Crime: Linkages, Enablers and Policy Implications

*Eelco Kessels and Orla Hennessy*

## *A. Introduction*

Following the end of the Cold War, security threats have grown ever more complex, multidimensional and international. With the decrease in state sponsorship and the rise in globalization of travel and communications structures and networks, terrorist groups increasingly started to look for alternative sources of funding. Some terrorist organizations formed alliances with criminal groups, such as Euzkadi ta Askatasuna's (ETA) cooperation with the Italian mafia and criminal actors in the Balkans to smuggle arms, or Al Qaeda in the Islamic Maghreb (AQIM) providing security to regional criminal networks involved in drug trafficking. Others have appropriated or integrated tactics of the other group, with terrorists developing in-house capacity to launder money and trade in illegal goods, as well as criminal organizations using terror tactics to discredit the government and disrupt counter-operations. In some cases, criminal and terrorist motivations and actions have fully converged within one group, creating hybrid organizations such as the Colombian Fuerzas Armadas Revolucionarias de Colombia (FARC), which principally engages in criminal activities aimed at profit maximization whilst irregularly using political rhetoric as a façade.

Although analysts agree on the existence of such a wide spectrum of links between terrorism and organized crime – ranging from ad-hoc collaborations to appropriation of tactics and even full convergence – opinions differ about the prevalence of these linkages, the underlying motivations and contextual drivers, and how all of this impacts the formulation and implementation of effective counter-measures.

This paper will attempt to shed some more light on these discussions and challenges. Firstly, the paper will provide a brief background into the topic and describe differences and similarities between terrorist and organised crime groups. Subsequently, the various forms of linkages between terrorism and organized crime will be discussed in more detail, looking at both theory and practice. Thirdly, several motivations as well as disincentives to the creation of such linkages will be explored, before the paper turns to some of the contextual drivers and enablers that facilitate the expansion of a crime-terror nexus, often related to situations of bad governance and failed or failing states. Lastly, the effects of the nexus between terrorism and organized crime will be discussed, in addition to various recommendations to prevent and counter its growth.

It is recognized that there is often a fine line between what is characterized as "crime", "organized crime", "criminal group (or "gang")", "terrorism", "terrorist" or "terrorist group". These definitions, as in practice, are often blurred and particularly as the nature of various groups change so will their description. Firstly, it takes the core revised academic consensus definition of terrorism as put forth by Alex P. Schmid:

> Terrorism refers, on the one hand, to a doctrine about the presumed effectiveness of a special form or tactic of fear-generating, coercive political violence and, on the other hand, to a conspiratorial practice of calculated, demonstrative, direct violent action without legal or moral restraints, targeting mainly civilians and non-combatants, performed for its propagandistic and psychological effects on various audiences and conflict parties.[1]

By extension, a terrorist group or terrorist organization is a movement that uses terrorism as a method to achieve its goals. In terms of defining organized criminal group, the paper uses the definition of the Expert Group on Organised Crime of the Council of Europe (as cited in the West Sands Advisory study for the European Union):

> To be considered an organized criminal group, a group must fulfil four mandatory criteria, and at least two of seven optional criteria. The mandatory criteria are that an OCG must (a) consist of a collaboration of at least three people (b) that are gathered for a prolonged or indefinite period of time; (c) be suspected or convicted of committing serious criminal offences; and, (d) have as their objective the pursuit of profit and/or power. Optional criteria include: a specific division of labor; using some form of internal discipline and control; exerting influence on the public and private sectors; using commercial or businesslike structures; engaging in money-laundering; and operating on an international level. Optional criteria include: a specific division of labor; using some form of internal discipline and control; exerting influence on the

1 Schmid, "The Definition of Terrorism," 2011, p. 86.

public and private sectors; using commercial or businesslike structures; engaging in money-laundering; and operating on an international level.[2]

However, it is also accepted that certain examples cited in this paper may not fall into these categories and there may be cases, for example, where criminal groups or activities are not strictly part of an organized syndicate or, equally, where a terrorist group might not be universally accepted and designated as such. Such dilemmas demonstrate the complex nature of the nexus.

### B. *Points of Intersection and Divergence*

It is generally accepted that the crime-terror nexus was solidified during the 1990s, although the term "narco-terrorism" first emerged in the early 80s to describe the involvement of terrorist groups such as the FARC in the drugs trade.[3] The end of the cold war, the decrease in state sponsorship for terrorist organizations, the rise of international transnational crime and the increasing globalisation of travel and communications structures have enabled greater convergence between politically inspired and criminal violence. The end of the cold war period of course brought many changes to the established global architecture. Mary Kaldor argues that recent decades have heralded "new wars", where "old war economies were typically centralized, autarchic and mobilized the population, new wars are part of an open globalized decentralized economy in which participation is low and revenue depends on continued violence."[4] New wars (including, for example, the Global War on Terror) further involve a variety of actors whose roles are increasingly blurred away from the traditional. The crime-terrorism nexus fits within this theory as there is an increasing blurring of lines between what is terrorist, criminal, cybercrime or cyber terrorist to name but a few.

---

2 West Sands Advisory LLP, "Europe's Crime-Terror Nexus: Links between terrorist and organised crime groups in the European Union," 2012, p. 10.

3 See for instance Makarenko, "The Crime–Terror Continuum: Tracing the Interplay between Transnational Organised Crime and Terrorism," 2004, pp. 129-145; Rollins and Wyler, "Terrorism and Transnational Crime," 2013, pp. 1-39; Forest, "Criminals and Terrorists: An Introduction to the Special Issue," 2012, pp. 171-179.

4 Kaldor, "In Defence of New Wars," 2013, pp. 1-16.

In one of the first articles on the nexus between organized crime and terrorism, Alex P. Schmid argues in 1996 that "[a]lthough they are distinct phenomena that should not be confused [...] there are links [...and...] there is some common ground."[5] A few years later, in his book *The New Terrorism*, Walter Laqueur devoted an entire chapter on the intersection between the two, arguing that "more recently this line has become blurred, and in some cases a symbiosis between terrorism and organized crime has occurred that did not exist before."[6] In the end, both kinds of organizations will primarily be driven by strategic concerns, despite having different goals. As Loretta Napoloeoni argues

> [c]riminal organizations operate very much like legitimate private corporations, the ultimate goal being profit and accumulation. Their monetary flows are, therefore, managed through an accountancy system regulated by balance sheets, as in corporate enterprises. Terror groups, however, are politically motivated. Thus, their ultimate aim is not monetary but political: to substitute one form of government with another, for example.[7]

These, and other analysts, have described both differences and similarities between organized crime and terrorist organizations.[8] Points of intersection include: both are generally rational actors; they oppose the state and defy the rule of law; they mostly operate secretly; they use extreme violence to harm individuals; they make use of similar tactics (Kidnapping for ransom, extortion, targeted assassinations, etc.); both are highly adaptive, innovative and resilient; both have provided certain social services; and leaving either type of group is rare and often fatal for a member.

However, there are also clear points of divergence. For instance, no organized crime group is fundamentally based on religious or ideological beliefs and motivations: they are principally driven by economics. Terrorists want to change the status quo, seeking a redress of grievances, political inclusion or a change of leadership, whilst organized crime groups are looking to optimize their profit, often through manipulating or bribing governmental actors. Terrorists often seek out media coverage and claim

---

5 Schmid, "The Links between Transnational Organized Crime and Terrorist Crimes," 2013, p. 40.

6 Lacqueur, *The New Terrorism*, 1999, p. 211. taucht in "Works cited" nicht auf

7 Napoleoni, "The New Economy of Terror: How Terrorism is Financed," 2004, p. 32.

8 The following is based on a helpful overview provided by Sanderson, who has used multiple sources to compile his lists, "Transnational Terror and Organized Crime: Blurring the Lines," 2004, pp. 53-56.

responsibility for attacks, whilst organized crime syndicates avoid publicity as much as possible. Connected to this is that terrorist organizations are far less discriminating in their target choice (the target audience of their actions is generally not the direct victim) in contrast to organized crime. Lastly, terrorists are often far more integrated in a certain community and more likely to provide social services in direct competition with the government.

Most analysts thus seem to agree that terrorism and organized crime share a number of common traits and, in particular, similar tactics. However, when it comes to primary motivational factors, publicity and target selection, there are obvious differences between the two. Defining, then, the groups and individuals engaged in this nexus – especially those that have only fleeting, ad-hoc connections or that alternate between roles – is very difficult. Often relationships will be fluid and opportunistic, happening in the space where terrorists and criminals see mutual benefits. The next section will attempt to provide a brief overview of the types of linkages that exist between terrorism and organized crime.

## *C. Types of Linkages*

There exists a broad spectrum of ways in which linkages between terrorism and organized crime play out in practice. The interactions can be "one off", based on certain needs of one party and capabilities or resources of the other. For instance, terrorist groups might need to engage with organized crime syndicates to obtain forged passports or gain access to established illicit trafficking routes. But linkages could also be more long term with mutually beneficial relationships forming between organized crime and terrorist organizations and/or tactics, sometimes leading to full convergence.

One of the most used models is the crime-terror nexus model developed by Makarenko, first published in 2003[9] and re-developed in 2009.[10] It involves an insightful scale or "continuum", moving from the formation of an alliance between two groups to the appropriation of tactics, a convergence between the two (either the integration of one group into the other

9 See Makarenko, "A Model of Terrorist-Criminal Relations," 2003, pp. 6-11.

10 See Makarenko, "Terrorist Use of Organized Crime: Operational Tool or Exacerbating the Threat?," 2009, pp. 180-193.

or a merger leading to the formation of a hybrid entity that "simultaneously displays ideological and economic motivations by perpetrating acts of politically motivated terrorism and engaging in [organized crime] for profit maximization") and, at the end of the line, a "transformation of the tactics and motivations of one entity into another".[11]

It is important to note here that, although this offers a very helpful theoretical framework, it is in practice very difficult to neatly categorize the linkages between organized crime groups and terrorist organizations. The type of linkage is time and place sensitive, and a group might move back and forward on the continuum for a variety of reasons. Additionally, there may be conflicting approaches to collaboration and the use of the other side's tactics on a local or individual level, as compared to the leadership or overall group level. Moreover, there is a frustrating lack of empirical evidence on the extent and specifics of the crime-terror nexus, which makes the testing of assumption and sound categorization difficult. Nevertheless, Makarenko's classification framework provides a helpful structure and some useful insights.

The first type of linkage are alliances between criminal groups and terrorist organizations, which may vary in nature (ad-hoc versus structural), duration and reasons for establishment. The latter includes the need for a certain expertize, knowledge or capabilities that is not present in-house (e.g. money laundering, document forgery, bomb-making), as well as operational support (e.g. access to smuggling routes and black markets, protection). Examples include: alliances between drug traffickers and terrorist organizations, such as AQIM's delivery of security to criminal networks involved in drug trafficking in the Maghreb and the establishment of a successful heroin smuggling operation during the Kosovo conflict by the Albanian mafia and the Kosovo Liberation Army (KLA); arms trafficking collaborations (sometimes involving arms-for-drugs), such as the relationship between the Italian mafia (including the Comorra and the 'Ndrangheta) and terrorist groups such as ETA and the Irish Republican Army (IRA); tactical alliances between AQ and other terrorist groups and criminal networks (including the Italian mafia) and to provide trafficking networks and safe houses.

Further down Makarenko's continuum we find the appropriation of tactics; i.e. criminal groups developing or acquiring in-house capabilities nor-

11 West Sands Advisory LLP, "Europe's Crime-Terror Nexus," 2012, p. 17.

mally associated with terrorist groups and vice versa. This process of integration increases operational and organizational security and avoids intergroup differences of opinion and distrust compared to the forming of alliances, which might explain its current prevalence as the most common linkage between terrorism and organized crime. Given the post-Cold War loss in financial support from state sponsors, terrorist groups have increasingly engaged in criminal activities to fill their coffers, for instance through active involvement in the illicit drug trade, human smuggling and financial scams. The narcotics trade has been one of the fundamental revenue streams for terrorist organizations over the last two decades. According to the United States (US) Drug Enforcement Administration (DEA), 39 percent of foreign terrorist organizations have connections to the drugs trade as of November 2011. Taliban militants confirm this telling the Telegraph in 2007 that a key source of income was the opium trade,[12] while ETA, the Kurdistan Workers Party (PKK) and Sendero Luminoso are among the many terrorist organizations linked to the drugs trade.[13] It has also been well documented that the perpetrators of the Madrid bombings were previously convicted drug traffickers and the explosives themselves were paid for using hashish.[14]

More recently, hostage taking has become increasingly used as a tactic by terrorist organizations. According to a 2011 Financial Action Task Force (FATF) report,

> Kidnapping for ransom (KFR) as a means of financing terrorism has been identified by law enforcement agencies worldwide as significant source of revenue for terrorist groups often operating in politically unstable countries where central authority is often weak, public and private corruption is endemic, and the social fabric of those nations has unravelled to a considerable degree. Millions of dollars in ransom payments have been collected by terrorist organizations which use networks of facilitators to move the proceeds of KFR through alternative remittance systems, but, more ominously, through legitimate financial institutions such as banks and exchange houses.[15]

---

12 See Ansari, "Taliban use hostage cash to fund UK blitz," 2007, http://www.telegraph.co.uk/news/worldnews/1566163/Taliban-use-hostage-cash-to-fund-UK-blitz.html, accessed 18 October 2013.

13 See Makarenko, "The Crime–Terror Continuum," p. 134.

14 See White, "Madrid train bombings probe finds no al-Qaeda link," 2004, http://usatoday30.usatoday.com/news/world/2006-03-09-madrid_x.htm, accessed 18 October 2013.

15 Financial Action Task Force Report, 2011, http://www.fatf-gafi.org/dataoecd/40/13/48426561.pdf, accessed 10 October 2013.

Take for instance the well documented attack on the In Amenas gas facility in Algeria undertaken by the (al Qaeda affiliated) Katibat al-Mu-lath-ameen ("The Masked Brigade", also known as al-Muwaqqi'ūn bi-d-Dimā', or "Those who Sign with Blood") in January 2013. The demands in this case were not monetary but to seek the cessation of airstrikes over Mali and the release of various prisoners throughout the region and the US held on terrorism charges.[16] Similarly, AQIM are also no strangers from kidnapping for ransom. The FATF reports that AQIM alone has collected at least $65 million (U.S. dollars) in KFR payments from 2005 through 2011, which is a substantial portion of its annual budget that is reported to total approximately $20 million USD per year.[17] The Taliban also admitted it had profited handsomely from a hostage operation in August of that year. Taliban militants claimed that the South Korean government had paid over $10 million USD after 20 South Korean nationals were captured. The militants said the money had contributed greatly to replenishing weapons supplies and for undertaking attacks.[18]

Perhaps the largest increase in recent years has been the involvement of terrorist groups in online crime. According to the United Nations Office on Drugs and Crime (UNODC), terrorists are known to use the internet to finance their efforts through four general methods: direct solicitation and spam, e-commerce, the exploitation of online payment tools (e.g. identity theft, credit card theft, wire fraud, etc.) and through charitable organizations.[19] One of the most famous examples that involves a combination of these methods is the case of Younis Tsouli, a young British man known online as "Irhabi 007". After posting various videos depicting terrorist activity, al Qaeda in Iraq (AQI) established connections with him and started to feed him videos directly. Soon thereafter, Tsouli and his partner Tariq al-Daour began purchasing stolen credit card numbers on the web. By the time they were arrested, they had accumulated 37.000 stolen credit card numbers, which they had used to make more than $3.5 million USD, laun-

---

16 See Jazeera, 2013, http://www.aljazeera.com/news/Africa/2013/01/2013116154848726750.html, accessed 18 October 2013.

17 See The Financial Action Task Force, "Organised Maritime Piracy and Related Kidnapping for Ransom," 2011, p. 31, available at http://www.fatf-gafi.org/media/fatf/documents/reports/organised%20maritime%20piracy%20and%20related%20kidnapping%20for%20ransom.pdf.

18 See Ansari, "Taliban use hostage cash to fund UK blitz".

19 See United Nations Office on Drug and Crime, "The use of the Internet for terrorist purposes," 2012, p. 7.

dered through various online gambling sites.[20] Furthermore, according to Thomas Holt, both terrorists groups and criminal organizations have engaged in hacktivism, using the internet to damage political targets in a variety of ways.[21] Such attacks have included Turkish hackers defacing the website of Jyllands-Posten that published the Muhammad cartoons in 2005, or the Liberation Tigers of Tamil Eelam (LTTE) "suicide email bombing" Sri Lankan embassies in 1998, which involved sending over 800 e-mails per day for an extended period to disrupt communication and voice dissent. More recently, it has been alleged that terrorist groups may have made use of "dark websites" such as Silk Road to launder money or conduct illegal activity. Silk Road, which was recently seized by the FBI, was hidden from the typical internet browser and provided an anonymous marketplace for buyers exclusively using a difficult-to-trace virtual currency called Bitcoin to trade for illicit goods ranging from heroin, explosives, and handguns to hacking tools. The website further advised sellers on shipping methods to avoid detection.[22] As of yet, there has been no naming of specific groups who may have been using it, but concerns have already been raised about the potential for terrorists to finance themselves using Bitcoin.[23]

Although less common, organized criminal groups have also incorporated terrorist modus operandi such as bombings and assassinations as a tactic – not to achieve long-term political aims or to change the status quo but to confront the powers that be and force them to compromize, often following governmental crackdowns on the criminal organization itself. Examples include the Italian mafia's reaction to governmental anti-mafia actions in the 1990s, as well as more recently the reactions to government crackdowns and challenges by rival groups of prison-based gangs in Brazil and Mara Salvatrucha (MS-13) and other criminal cartels in Mexi-

20 See Jacobson, "Terrorist Financing on the Internet," 2009, p.18.

21 See Holt, "Exploring the Intersections of Technology, Crime, and Terror," 2012, pp. 343-345.

22 See Kleiman, "Beyond the Silk Road: Increased Scrutiny of Decentralized Virtual Currencies Used in Illicit Online Activities," 2013, at http://nationalsecuritylawbrief.com/beyond-the-silk-road-increased-scrutiny-of-decentralized-virtual-currencies-used-in-illicit-online-activities/.

23 See Brito and Castillo, "BITCOIN: A Primer for Policymakers," 2013, p.21, http://mercatus.org/sites/default/files/Brito_BitcoinPrimer_embargoed.pdf, accessed 18 October 2013.

co.[24] However, it is important to note that terror is generally not a preferred tactic of organized crime syndicates: they prefer not to openly challenge the regime but deal with political problems through palm-greasing and blackmailing.

The third type of linkage between terrorism and organized crime described in Makarenko's continuum involves a full convergence between the two, either through one group integrating into the other or a merger leading to the formation of a hybrid entity that has both criminal and political motivations. Generally, these hybrids either begin as a terrorist organization that acquires in-house criminal capabilities that are utilized to the extent that the political motivation is pushed to the background or merely functions as a façade, or as organized crime groups that appropriate terrorism tactics that are deployed consistently with a sustained long-term political goal as opposed to short-term operational gains. Examples of the latter are scarce, one case being the Albanian organized crime groups, which Ralf Mutschke referred to as "hybrid organizations, often involved both in criminal activity of an organized nature and in political activities", with strong links to "Pan-Albanian ideals, politics, military activities and terrorism".[25] In addition to opposing the authorities and gaining political leverage, transforming into a crime-terror hybrid is beneficial for criminal organizations since this rallies the public behind their "cause", which in turn provides them with new support networks and access to a new pool of recruits. Examples of hybrids that started as terrorist organizations are more commonplace. FARC being the most obvious example with its intimate involvement in the Colombian drug trade, resembling more a criminal cartel than a revolutionary party. Another example is the Abu Sayyaf Group (ASG), which has proved to be extremely successful at undertaking and profiting from KFR in the Philippines. ASG has alternated between periods of criminal activity and terrorist activity: currently, it seems that criminal activity has completely replaced the initial political goals of seeking to establish an independent Islamic province in Mindanao and the Sulu Archipelago.[26]

---

24 See West Sands Advisory LLP, "Europe's Crime-Terror Nexus," p. 34.

25 Mutschke, "The Threat Posed by the Convergence of Organized Crime, Drugs Trafficking and Terrorism," (Written Testimony to a Hearing of the Committee on the Judiciary Subcommittee on Crime, 13 December 2000).

26 See O'Brien, "Fluctuations between Crime and Terror: The Case of Abu Sayyaf's Kidnapping Activities," 2012, pp. 320-336.

The fourth and last type of linkage at the far end of the continuum is transformation, when both the tactics and the motivations have changed from one type of group into another. Although a theoretical possibility, organizations that demonstrate a complete change of nature without ever reengaging in their "old habits" are extremely rare. FARC and the Provisional Irish Republican Army (PIRA) are two examples that come closest, but their continued involvement in politically motivated rhetoric and actions make it difficult to speak of a full transformation – certainly in the case of FARC, as it is currently engaged in peace talks with the Colombian government.

Having established the various different types of linkages between organized crime and terrorism, this paper will now turn to some of the motivations behind these linkages, as well as discuss several reasons that have inhibited the establishment of relationships between the two.

### *D. Incentives and Disincentives*

As mentioned previously, for terrorist organizations, a primary reason for engaging in crime is to bolster their finances, where smuggling, kidnapping, identity fraud or drug dealing can provide easy access to black market revenue. Additionally, according to James Forest, "in some cases, a terrorist group's involvement in – or protection of – illicit economies like the drug trade can help them attain local legitimacy" and increase their influence.[27]

For criminal organizations reasons for cooperation may be more complex. Again, criminal organizations may focus on the financial benefits, but Louise Shelly also notes that cooperation with terrorist groups may be advantageous by helping to destabilize the political structure and undermining governmental countermeasures.[28]

Overall, ties between terrorist and criminal organizations are often straightforward customer-supplier relationships to facilitate a specific need. A high profile example is the case of the 2011 Iranian plot to assassinate the Saudi Arabian Ambassador in Washington. John Rollins and Liana Sun Wyler detail how several members of the Iran-based Islamic

---

27 See Forest, "Criminals and Terrorists," p. 175.

28 See Shelley, "Identifying, Counting and Categorizing Transnational Organised Crime," 1999, pp. 1-18.

Revolutionary Guards Corps-Quds Force (IRGC-QF) allegedly hired members of the Mexican Drug Cartel, Los Zetas, to conduct the assassination of Ambassador Adel al-Jubeir, for a fee of $1.5 million USD.[29]

However, there are also certain disincentives for cooperation. For terrorists, specifically religious extremists, alliances with criminal organizations or engaging in organized crime themselves may undermine their political ideology, as the conduct of many of the illicit activities concerned often goes directly against the belief system. This, in turn, may diminish their popular support base, which risks decreasing the recruitment pool as well as the logistical support and "cover" that complicit communities often provide terrorist organizations with. Moreover, it will likely attract increased unwanted attention from law enforcement actors they have not dealt with before, and compromize internal security through a higher chance of infiltration. Similarly, it also increases the likelihood of (deadly) competition with other organized crime groups, something that is far less common among terrorist organizations.

On the other side, it is important to note that, although criminals gladly make use of terrorist tactics, these always "form part of a violence-for-profit strategy rather than the other way around" – hence, "criminal motivations may fluctuate according to market opportunities, while terrorist motivations are ultimately removed from profit".[30] Moreover, according to Mark Galeotti,

> on the whole organized crime groups have not shown any particular enthusiasm to work with terrorists, whom they regard as not only unreliable and amateurish but also dangerous, in that any evidence of such a connection is likely to trigger a much more immediate and heavy-handed law enforcement response in the post-11 September era.[31]

Importantly, these motivations and disincentives for cooperation may differ on the individual versus group level and are time and place specific. As in most types of relationships, personal connections and trust are the basis for establishing sustained, mutually beneficial relationships between such differing groups. The following section will briefly explore some of the structural drivers and enablers that create a breeding ground for the crime-terror nexus to grow.

29 See Rollins and Wyler, "Terrorism and Transnational Crime," 2013, p. 9.

30 Mullins, "Parallels between Crime and Terrorism: A Social Psychological Perspective," 2009, p. 815.

31 Galeotti, "Hard Times – Organized Crime and the Financial Crisis," 2009.

*E. Drivers and Enablers*

In addition to considering the types of linkages between organized crime and terrorism and the motivations behind it, it is important to consider where these overlaps occur most frequently and, as such, identify contextual drivers and enablers that facilitate the growth of the crime-terror nexus. Forest argues that "[c]ommon factors that influence a terrorist or criminal organization's activities include access to weapons, illicit economies, and safe haven", which leads him to conclude that "[t]here are specific locations throughout the world within which greater criminality, terrorism, and crime-terror collaboration have been facilitated in the past or are likely in the future."[32]

Firstly, on the international level, globalisation of communication and travel has contributed to the possibility for terrorist and criminal groups to operate beyond borders and collaborate more intensively. During an international meeting on the topic in 2011, Yuri Fedotov, the Executive Director of the UNODC, stated:

> Thanks to advances in technology, communication, finance and transport, loose networks of terrorists and organized criminal groups that operate internationally can easily link with each other. By pooling their resources and expertise, they can significantly increase their capacity to do harm.[33]

Moreover, the loss of state sponsorship following the end of the Cold War, as well as the increase in effective (inter)national counter-terrorism measures following 9/11 has likely led to increased collaboration between terrorists and criminals in order to overcome this restricted operating environment.

In an overview of nations hospitable to organized crime and terrorism, La Verle Berry et al. discern a number of common national and local enabling factors in the case of Africa:

> Weaknesses of state institutions;
> Limited law enforcement capacity;
> Widespread poverty;
> Political and systemic corruption;

32 Forest, "Criminals and Terrorists," p. 176.

33 "UNODC brings victims and criminal connections to the fore of the fight against terrorism," 2011, http://www.unodc.org/unodc/en/press/releases/2011/March/unodc-brings-victims-and-criminal-connections-to-the-fore-of-the-fight-against-terrorism.html, accessed 1 November 2013.

Incomplete or weak anti-terrorism and organized crime legislation and agencies;
Lack of respect for the rule of law in society;
Long porous and unpatrolled borders;
Geographic location along international trafficking routes; and
The existence of transnational ethnic/tribal networks whose members move freely across borders.[34]

These enablers are based on generalized notions of poor governance, rule of law, historical factors, geopolitical issues and socio-economic deficits that hold true beyond the African continent. This concurs with Forest's observation that many analysts and scholars have "drawn links between terrorism, crime, and local conditions like government oppression or corruption, foreign occupation, poverty, discrimination (ethnic, racial, religious), injustice (real or perceived), and a lack of political or socio-economic opportunities", which clearly emphasizes "the importance of a central government's weakness as a potential enabler for criminal and terrorist activity".[35] Moreover, "[w]hen analyzed critically most factors or a combination of factors are present in most developing nations and in some cases developed nations as well."[36] Nevertheless, the crime-terror nexus is likely to be most powerful in (post-) conflict states like Afghanistan, Pakistan, Mali, and Somalia, where government is weak to nonexistent and socio-economic problems are virulent.

The same holds true for specific spaces that lack proper monitoring and control, such as prisons and detention centers, where it is often very difficult to recognize (and where needed, to isolate) terrorists from ordinary and/or organized criminals. These environments offer a perfect place to recruit individuals and acquire new skills and techniques. And this is not only the case in subpar prisons in underdeveloped countries: the Madrid train bombers of 2004 used to be ordinary criminals but were recruited by terrorists in a Spanish jail to carry out this plot.[37]

34 Adapted from Berry et al., "Nations Hospitable to Organized Crime and Terrorism," 2003, pp. 2-4.

35 Forest, "Criminals and Terrorists," p. 176.

36 Hübschle, "From Theory to Practice: Exploring the Organized Crime-Terror Nexus in Sub-Saharan Africa," 2011, p. 87.

37 See Shelley, "Growing Together: Ideological and Operational Linkages between Terrorist and Criminal Networks," 2006, p. 3.

### F. Impact and Policy Implications of the Crime-Terror Nexus

Although criminal activity and terrorism are security threats that cause legitimate concern on their own, "the growing nexus of terrorism and organized crime is creating a dynamic which perpetuates conflict and emboldens and sustains insurgencies".[38] The crime-terror nexus has global, governmental and societal repercussions directly and indirectly affecting governance, security, finances, health and development. It weakens states and sustains failed states. Governments susceptible to corruption are specifically at risk, especially transit countries to the lucrative markets in Europe and the United States. Legal trade is weakened; human security and development decreased; investments, government revenues, and GDP are lost; economic disparity increases; corruption rises; and so the list goes on.

Although the extent and specific details of linkages between terrorist and organized crime groups are not fully known, there is no doubt that the crime-terror nexus has disastrous consequences on effective governance, the economy and human security. In order to address this nexus successfully, a number of actions must be taken.

#### I. Cutting off the Money Supply

Given that the primary purpose for both terrorist and organized crime groups to get involved with one another seems to be financial gain, it is important that key financial institutions are bolstered nationally, regionally and internationally to effectively play their crucial role in combating crime and terrorist financing by identifying and reporting fraud, money laundering and other suspicious transactions. In general, institutions use the same tools to investigate money laundering and financing of organized crime and terrorist groups, so these tools should be refined and made available across borders to ensure swift and effective action.

Furthermore, strengthening the mechanisms to monitor the financing of crime and terrorism is a collaborative effort and public-private partnerships are crucial in this respect. A mechanism such as the Terrorist Finance Tracking Program (TFTP) is an example of successful international cooperation alongside private companies, including national governments,

38 Liang, "Shadow Networks: The Growing Nexus of Terrorism and Organised Crime," 2011, p. 3.

international organizations such as Europol, and private firms. In addition to tracking and intercepting financing to prevent the funding of terrorist activities, the TFTP is also utilized in the immediate aftermath of terrorist incidents such as, for instance, the Breivik attacks. There, TFTP-based information helped Norwegian and other European investigators to identify the channels through which Breivik collected and moved the funds used for the preparation of his attacks, within hours. Moreover, based on the TFTP data collected in the Breivik case, Finnish authorities were able to arrest a person pursuing similar terrorist objectives before he was able to put them into practice.[39] The TFTP is just one example of the effectiveness of such partnerships and cooperation to both prevent crimes and assist in the prosecution of terrorists and criminals.

The listing of terrorist organizations and related sanctions (e.g. asset freezing, travel ban, arms embargo, etc.), for instance on the basis of UN Security Council Resolutions 1267[40] and 1373,[41] can also be effective at helping to deter organizations from collaborating. For instance, a criminal organization may try to steer clear of associating itself with a terrorist group in order to avoid becoming associated with, or potentially even listed as, a designated terrorist organization with all of the sanctions that this entails.

However, the challenge of both the TFTP and various international sanctions is that they can have unintended, indirect consequences. At the minimum level, this can greatly hinder the operating space for civil society organizations[42] that have an important role to play in addressing some of the root causes of conflict and terrorism. At the maximum, these mechanisms can be abused by governments far beyond their intended scope. UN Security Resolutions 1267 and 1373 stand out in comparison to other sanctions in that they seem both temporally and spatially limitless. Furthermore, with the recent disclosures related to US surveillance undertak-

39 See European Commission, 2012, http://europa.eu/rapid/press-release_IP-12-1366_en.htm, accessed 5 November 2013.

40 See UN Security Council Resolution 1267,S/RES/1267, 1999, http://www.un.org/ga/search/view_doc.asp?symbol=S/RES/1267(1999), accessed 8 November 2013.

41 See UN Security Council Resolution 1373, S/RES/1373, 2001, http://www.un.org/News/Press/docs/2001/sc7158.doc.htm, accessed 8 November 2013.

42 For a discussion on this topic see for example, Cortright et al., "Friend not Foe: Opening Spaces for Civil Society Engagement to Prevent Violent Extremism," 2011, http://www.fourthfreedomforum.org/wp-content/uploads/2011/05/Friend-not-Foe_Fnl_May.pdf, accessed 5 November 2013.

en by the National Security Agency (NSA), issues related to data protection have come greatly to the fore. Therefore, it is important to ensure that strict checks and balances are put in place to ascertain that these mechanisms are not used beyond their intended purpose, transfers of financial and private data are protected, functional oversight mechanisms are put in place, and there are ways to appeal against listings and sanctions.

Lastly, with an eye to the recent rise in KFR as a source of income for both organized crime and terrorist organizations, solid cooperation mechanisms should be built between (inter)national intelligence agencies, law enforcement and prosecution services. Adequate tools and resources should be devoted to these actors, and, to bolster the efforts against the use of KFR and deny the benefits of hostage taking, regional and international common approaches need to be established. This is exactly what the Global Counterterrorism Forum's 30 members have attempted with the adoption of the Algiers Memorandum on Good Practices for Preventing and Denying the Benefits of Kidnapping for Ransom by Terrorists.[43] However, the difficulties of establishing a uniform approach soon become clear, with the introduction to the document stating that

> while recognizing that implementation of these practices must be consistent with applicable international law, including human rights law and international humanitarian law, as well as applicable domestic law, reaffirming that ensuring the security of the hostage should be the first priority of any rescue operation and that the state where the hostage is held should take all appropriate measures, in close cooperation with the state of nationality of the hostage where appropriate, to secure the safe release of the hostage, and taking into account the unique contexts surrounding each KFR incident, as well as the varied histories, cultures, and legal systems among states.[44]

### *II. Improving Governance and Reducing Areas of Ungoverned Space*

In order to effectively prevent the growth of the crime-terror nexus, it is important to create and maintain national, regional and international governance regimes that do not allow these groups to operate on their territory

43 See Global Counterterrorism Forum, "Algiers Memorandum on Good Practices for Preventing and Denying the Benefits of Kidnapping for Ransom by Terrorists," 2012, https://www.thegctf.org/documents/10162/159874/Algiers+Memorandum-English.pdf, accessed 8 November 2013.

44 Global Counterterrorism Forum, "Algiers Memorandum," p. 2.

unpunished. States harboring ungoverned areas or with corrupt or failing government institutions and public services must start improving on this – where needed with support from international partners – since terrorist and criminal organizations exploit these structural weaknesses.

It is equally important to foster a strong sense of rule of law and social resilience. For instance, awareness-raising efforts need to focus on the responsibility of individuals and communities to denounce violence (including violence fuelled by a political ideology) and dry up demand by stopping the purchase of illegal products or services since they could potentially fund terrorists and organised crime groups.[45] While this is no mean feat, capacity building efforts to improve judicial, law enforcement and intelligence systems may be necessary to help improve these processes in affected states.

Similar to cooperation on financial monitoring, it is equally important to bolster information sharing on all fronts. Naturally, improved information and intelligence sharing between relevant agencies, both domestically and internationally, is vitally important. There is a dire need for more data gathering, sharing and analysis to identify existing and emerging linkages and continuously monitor developments. Additionally, given the prevalence of illicit (international) trade as a primary income source for both terrorist and organized crime groups, border control and cross-border cooperation need to be improved. A last space that demands increased attention is the internet. It plays a growing role in online radicalization and recruitment as well as in the funding of both terrorist and organized crime groups. Hence, it is of great importance that intelligence, security and law enforcement agencies develop adequate technical capabilities to be able to investigate and monitor illegal activities both on- and offline.

## *G. Concluding Remarks*

As the linkages between organized crime and terrorist groups become more complex, it is vital that national, regional and international responses incorporate the knowledge, experience and lessons learned from both anti-crime policies and counter-terrorism measures, as well as from other countries. This article provides an overview of the crime-terror nexus and uses

---

45 See Global Counterterrorism Forum, "Algiers Memorandum," p. 5.

various examples to demonstrate the complex nature of this fluid relationship. As Kaldor's new wars thesis demonstrates, we are increasingly moving away from traditional forms of conflict. Correlated to this is that there is a much greater blurring of those actors undertaking various forms of contemporary violence. This has distinct policy implications where all forms of violence should then require an integrated policing rather than political or military response, whether it is drugs/gang related violence or terrorism.[46] If this is the case, there clearly need to be greater mechanisms for coordination across the board with experts of each sector – both anti-crime units and counter-terrorism agencies – communicating more efficiently and participating in joint operations. Furthermore, a shared, comprehensive set of tools needs to be developed that can be applied in various contexts. Those responsible for tackling the organised criminals and terrorists alike, must embrace innovative and creative solutions. The leaps that have been made in information and communication technology over the past two decades should help drive simpler and more efficient coordination. Of course strict checks and balances must be built into this system to prevent its abuse, but it is crucial that law enforcement agencies have the resources and talent available to outwit terrorists and criminals on- and offline.

Finally, it is crucial to realize that governments, the military, police, regional and multilateral organizations cannot do this on their own. They will also need to engage civil society actors in order to effectively implement anti-crime and counter-terrorism policies and strategies and address the underlying conditions that give rise to conflict, violent extremism and organised crime.[47] These non-governmental actors are often much better placed than the authorities to address grievances within society that could otherwise potentially develop into participation in violent extremist actions and other types of crime. It is only through sound data analysis and the implementation of a comprehensive approach involving a wide variety of actors, that the complex crime-terror nexus can be addressed effectively.

46 See Kaldor, "In Defence," p. 6.

47 See Ginkel, "Engaging Civil Society in Countering Violent Extremism: Experiences with the UN Global Strategy," 2012, http://www.icct.nl/download/file/ICCT-van-Ginkel-Civil-Society-in-CVE-August-2012.pdf, accessed 8 November 2013.

## Bibliography

Aljazeera, "Algerian army surrounds hostage-takers," 17 January 2013, at http://www.aljazeera.com/news/Africa/2013/01/201311615484872675O.html

Ansari, Massoud, "Taliban use hostage cash to fund UK blitz," *The Telegraph* (14 October 2007), at http://www.telegraph.co.uk/news/worldnews/1566163/Taliban-use-hostage-cash-to-fund-UK-blitz.html

Brito, Jerry, and Andrea Castillo, "BITCOIN: A Primer for Policymakers," *The Mercatus Center, George Mason University publication*, 2013, pp. 1-48, at http://mercatus.org/sites/default/files/Brito_BitcoinPrimer_embargoed.pdf.

Berry, LaVerle, Glenn Curtis, John Gibbs, Rex Hudson, Tara Karacan, Nina Kollars and Ramón Miró, "Nations Hospitable to Organized Crime and Terrorism," A Report Prepared by the Federal Research Division, Library of Congress under an Interagency Agreement with the United States Government, Washington: Library of Congress, 2003, pp. 2-4.

Cortright, David, Alistair Millar, Linda Gerber-Stellingwerf, George A. Lopez, Eliot Fackler and Joshua Weaver, "Friend not Foe: Opening Spaces for Civil Society Engagement to Prevent Violent Extremism," report to Cordaid from the Fourth Freedom Forum and the Kroc Institute for International Peace Studies at the University of Notre Dame, 2nd ed., May 2011.

European Commission, "Terrorist finance tracking: citizen's safeguards are in place," 14 December 2012, at http://europa.eu/rapid/press-release_IP-12-1366_en.htm.

Financial Action Task Force (FATF), "Organized Maritime Piracy and related Kidnapping for Ransom," FATF Report, July 2011, 1-48.

Forest, James F., "Criminals and Terrorists: An Introduction to the Special Issue," *Terrorism and Political Violence* 2 (2012): 171-179.

Galeotti, Mark, "Hard Times – Organized Crime and the Financial Crisis," *Jane's Intelligence Review* (July 2009).

Ginkel, Bibi van, "Engaging Civil Society in Countering Violent Extremism: Experiences with the UN Global Strategy," ICCT Research Paper, The Hague: ICCT, 2012.

Global Counterterrorism Forum, "Algiers Memorandum on Good Practices for Preventing and Denying the Benefits of Kidnapping for Ransom by Terrorists," 2012, at https://www.thegctf.org/documents/10162/159874/Algiers+Memorandum-English.pdf.

Holt, Thomas J., "Exploring the Intersections of Technology, Crime, and Terror," *Terrorism and Political Violence* 2 (2012): 337-354.

Hübschle, Annette, "From Theory to Practice: Exploring the Organized Crime-Terror Nexus in Sub-Saharan Africa," *Perspectives on Terrorism* 3/4 (2011): 81-95.

Jacobson, Michael, "Terrorist Financing on the Internet," *CTC Sentinel* 6 (2009): 17-20.

Kaldor, Mary, "In Defence of New Wars," *Stability: International Journal of Security and Development* 4 (2013): pp. 1-16.

Kleiman, Jared A., "Beyond the Silk Road: Increased Scrutiny of Decentralized Virtual Currencies Used in Illicit Online Activities," 8 October 2013, at http://nationalsecuritylawbrief.com/beyond-the-silk-road-increased-scrutiny-of-decentralized-virtual-currencies-used-in-illicit-online-activities/.

Laqueur, Walter, *The New Terrorism, Fanatism and the Arms of Mass Destruction*, Oxford: Oxford University Press, 1999.

Liang, Christina Schori, "Shadow Networks: The Growing Nexus of Terrorism and Organised Crime," GCSP Policy Paper No 20, September 2011, pp. 1-6.

Makarenko, Tamara, "The Crime–Terror Continuum: Tracing the Interplay between Transnational Organised Crime and Terrorism," *Global Crime* 1 (2004): pp. 129-145.

Makarenko, Tamara, "A Model of Terrorist-Criminal Relations, "*Jane's Intelligence Review* 8 (2003): 6-11.

Makarenko, Tamara, "Terrorist Use of Organized Crime: Operational Tool or Exacerbating the Threat?," in *Defining and Defying Organized Crime: Discourse, Perceptions, and Reality*, ed. Felia Allum, London: Routledge, 2009, pp. 180-193.

Mullins, Sam J., "Parallels between Crime and Terrorism: A Social Psychological Perspective," *Studies in Conflict and Terrorism* 9 (2009): 811-830.

Napoleoni, Loretta, "The New Economy of Terror: How Terrorism is Financed," *Forum on Crime and Society* 1/2 (2004): 31-48.

O'Brien, McKenzie, "Fluctuations between Crime and Terror: The Case of Abu Sayyaf's Kidnapping Activities," *Terrorism and Political Violence* 2 (2012): pp. 320-336.

Rollins, John, and Liana Sun Wyler, "Terrorism and Transnational Crime: Foreign Policy Issues for Congress," Congressional Research Service report, June, 2013, pp. 1-39.

Schmid, Alex P., "The Definition of Terrorism," in *The Routledge Handbook of Terrorism Research*, ed. Alex P. Schmid, London: Routledge, 2011, pp. 39-98.

Schmid, Alex P., "The Links between Transnational Organized Crime and Terrorist Crimes," *Transnational Organized Crime* 4 (2013): 40-82.

Sanderson, Thomas M., "Transnational Terror and Organized Crime: Blurring the Lines," *AIS Review of International Affairs* 1 (2004): pp. 53-56.

Shelley, Louise, "Identifying, Counting and Categorizing Transnational Organised Crime," *Transnational Organised Crime* 1 (1999): pp. 1-18.

Shelley, Louise, "Growing Together: Ideological and Operational Linkages between Terrorist and Criminal Networks," Fund for Peace Threat Convergence Publications, Washington, D.C., 2006, pp 1-5.

United Nations Office on Drugs and Crime, "UNODC brings victims and criminal connections to the fore of the fight against terrorism," 16 March 2011, at http://www.unodc.org/unodc/en/press/releases/2011/March/unodc-brings-victims-and-criminal-connections-to-the-fore-of-the-fight-against-terrorism.html.

United Nations, "Security Council Unanimously Adopts Wide-Ranging Anti-Terrorism Resolution," (UN Security Council Resolution 1373, S/RES/1373), 23 September 2001, at http://www.un.org/News/Press/docs/2001/sc7158.doc.htm.

United Nations Office on Drugs and Crime, "The use of the Internet for terrorist purposes," Vienna, 2012, pp. 1-158.

West Sands Advisory LLP, "Europe's Crime-Terror Nexus: Links between terrorist and organised crime groups in the European Union," Study for the EU Directorate General for Internal Policies, Policy Department C, Citizens' Rights and Constitutional Affairs, Brussels, 2012, pp. 1-65.

White, Paul, "Madrid train bombings probe finds no al-Qaeda link," *USA Today* (3 October 2004), at http://usatoday30.usatoday.com/news/world/2006-03-09-madrid_x.htm.

# *Part II: Essay*

# The Margin of Maneuver: Responding to the Terrorist Threat in Times of the Global War on Terror's Third Phase

*Henning Glaser*

In an essential sense, today's counter-terrorism is a different one than it has been before 9/11, 2001. In form the Global War on Terror (GWOT) counter-terrorism (CT) has in fact become an overarching governance paradigm of unprecedented reach and vigor. Its weight and importance arguably tend to predetermine the margin of maneuver for choosing, calibrating and executing any strategy and measure in responding to the terrorist threat. At the same time, the new paradigm has changed the realities it was supposed to contain in unexpected, unwanted ways. Instead of drying out the designated breeding grounds of terrorism, it has expanded them widely transforming especially the Middle East in a region of disintegrating borders and collapsing normative orders and social structures. These destructive dynamics have over-spilled from the initial target countries of the GWOT to a growing number of other countries reaching from West to Central Africa and Turkey to Central and Southeast Asia. The repercussions of these developments are especially relevant also for Europe which is feeling them in form of waves of refugees, a rising radicalization of both Muslim and non-Muslim populations alike, and an increasing terrorist threat. The latter is caused by the number of returning 'foreign fighters', the general influx of trained and traumatized former fighters from the Middle Eastern civil war theaters, and the mutual radicalization in the European societies.

In this situation, attempts to counter the accelerating processes of radicalization and to foster the de-radicalization and disengagement of violent and potentially violent extremists are evidently worth of being taken up and translated into action.

Somehow in this direction, the 2006 revamped U.S. counterinsurgency (COIN) doctrine that has been developed especially for the Middle Eastern COIN theaters stresses a people- rather than an enemy-centered approach which is, after all, much in line with the classical 'winning the hearts and the minds of the people' rationale.

Against this background an eternal question in combating terrorism and insurgencies comes to the fore, the question how a given CT approach conceives the communicative dimension of CT.

This question is raised here from a European perspective on the GWOT and its repercussions on Europe. Guiding is the assumption that all conceptions and practices of CT are ultimately governed by certain fundamental choices that crystallize in two competing ideal-typically derived CT paradigms. They are defined here by their respective preferences for the dominating core values, the imagery of the terrorist and the way to conceive the communicative dimension of CT.

Starting from these considerations it will be argued that contemporary CT is overly defined by the GWOT paradigm as the manifestation of one of the two competing major CT approaches. It is further assumed that the gravitational force of the GWOT as an encompassing and crucially important governance regime will profoundly imply the consequentional choices that are defining the given margin of maneuver in designing almost every particular CT measure including especially the communication with the adversary. This essay argues that the GWOT is not supporting certain ways of engaging with the adversary and that it is too powerful to be overlooked as a definitional factor in shaping contemporary CT.

## *A. Counter-Terrorism: A Paradigm Shift?*

Starting point of this essay was the assumption of a historic change in the way of responding to terrorism that is exerting significant effect on the space of maneuver in defining and applying single CT measures and strategies. However, closely related to this assumption, present-day terrorism itself is also seen as fundamentally different from the one that has dominated before 9/11. This assumption has largely supported the construction of the new CT paradigm. While the mere fact that the 9/11 event represents a veritable turning point of historical dimension is largely consented, the assumed change of the nature of terrorism is more contested. While the GWOT orthodoxy is inclined to consider the 9/11 attack as the apotheosis of a new form of terrorism that suggests a corresponding change in countering it, others disagree denying substantial changes of the socio-political phenomenon of terrorism itself while acknowledging a fundamental change of CT.

*I. A new Terrorism?*

Having emerged during the 1990s, the concept of a 'new terrorism' claims to describe a significant and substantially different type of terrorism posing the "central threat" for national and international security.[1] Having risen to prominence since 9/11, the 'new terrorism' model is supported by a broad range of policy makers, security officials and academics. They identify the birth of a totally 'new breed' of terrorists which they characterize as more networked, sophisticated, ad hoc, ruthless, dangerous and essentially defined by religious extremism of predominantly jihadist provenance.[2] Often implied is a corresponding concept to counter the threat: the project to annihilate this enemy as the overarching goal and yardstick of CT, often at all costs. With the 'declaration' of the GWOT the 'new terrorism' motif has immediately taken up in practice. Then U.S Atty.-Gen. Ashcroft, for instance, reiterated in his announcement on the American response to the 9/11 attacks the 'new terrorism' motif prominently saying that "*[t]he terrorist enemy that threatens civilization today is unlike any we have ever known.*"[3] In his resulting conception of CT there is thus no space for the terrorist within the confines of the international legal order and no other way for the state than to address him by sheer force. It reads similarly in the words of then US President George W. Bush: "[…] in the face of terror you've got to be strong, not weak. […] the only way to deal with these people is to bring them to justice. *You can't talk to them.* […]"[4] – 'Bringing them to justice', this might be clarified, is not meant as bringing them before the courts of justice rather than to the worldly instruments of a divine justice with the U.S. President as the major instrument of providence.[5]

---

1 See Hoffman, "Terrorism Trends and Prospects," 1999, p. 7.

2 See Hoffman, "Terrorism Trends and Prospects," pp. 7 ff.

3 Ashcroft, December 6, 2001, quoted from Kappeler and Kappeler, "Speaking of Evil and Terrorism: The Political and Ideological Construction of a Moral Panic," 2004, pp. 175, 181. Italics by the author.

4 Bush, "The President's News Conference With President Gloria Macapagal-Arroyo of the Philippines," May 19, 2003, accessed at http://www.presidency.ucsb.edu/ws/?pid=64449. Italics by the author.

5 Even if the analytical concept of how to perceive terrorism and the consequential approach to counter it are not necessarily linked, the affinity between them is striking where it comes to the concept of the 'new terrorism'. Especially the GWOT,

Although the concept of the 'new terrorism' that would require new means of CT had almost become the post 9/11 orthodoxy, both, its empirical base and normative implications remain contested.[6] Its opponents assume instead that contemporary terrorism does not *substantially* differ from previous manifestations – "except for the somewhat increased likelihood that a chemical, biological, nuclear or radiological weapon might be used".[7] Consequentially, in this view, the very nature of the terrorist threat alone is not inclined to indicate the need for a new form of CT. What is nevertheless agreed on by this side is, however, the fact that the GWOT does represent a major change: "Terrorism is today obviously no longer a new phenomenon. *What is new is the central place that it occupies* [...]."[8] The centrality of anti-terrorism as a policy, discourse and regime seems indeed to represent a certain consensus with diverging normative assessments of the question of how desirable this is.

Coming back to the adversary positions claiming the emergence of a 'new terrorism', one might differentiate. Obviously, terrorism is historical-

---

however, is inextricably linked with the concept of the 'new terrorism' which is forming an integral part of its guiding narrative.

6 See Evans, *Liberal Terror*, 2013, p. 11, according to whom terrorism, including its prominent emanations in the 21st century, is not a new phenomenon but a "permanent feature of the modern political vernacular."

7 Tucker, "What's New About the New Terrorism and How Dangerous Is It?," 2001, pp. 1-14; Coady, "How New is the 'New Terror'?," 2006, pp. 49-65; Fukuyama, *America at the Crossroads: Democracy, Power, and the Neo-conservative Legacy*, 2006, pp. 73 f.; Primoratz, *Terrorism: A Philosophical Investigation*, 2013, p. 43. Scholars like Walter Laqueur or Martha Crenshaw employed especially an historical perspective to falsify the 'new terrorism'-concept. Crenshaw, "'New' versus 'Old' Terrorism. Is today's 'new' terrorism qualitatively different from pre-September 11 'old' terrorism?," 2003; Laqueur, "Postmodern Terrorism: New Rules for an Old Game," 1996, pp. 24-36. Laqueur finds that what he calls the "recent upsurge of terrorist activity" during the 1990s "not particularly threatening" claiming that figures of terror victims would be among the "almost meaningless" criteria in assessing the nature of terrorism, "because of both the incidents they disregard and those they count" while Crenshaw reiterates that "the idea of a 'new' terrorism is often based on insufficient knowledge of history, as well as misinterpretations of contemporary terrorism." See also Smith, "The Concept of Security in a Globalizing World," 2006, p. 34: "For the vast majority of the world's population the events of 9/11 represented the 'normalization' of US´s security situation [...]."

8 Benoist, *Carl Schmitt Today: Terrorism, 'Just' War, and the State of Emergency*, 2013, pp. 56 f.

ly a very old phenomenon[9] that is – like other forms of human activity – at the same time nevertheless a contextual and changing one. As much as it is thus true that "[t]he use of terror against innocents [...] has been a reality since men first went to war against other men"[10], it is still justified to ask if the ways in which terrorism unfolds have changed over time. Whereas terrorism and counter-terrorism have always existed especially in the context of empires such as the Roman, British or Soviet Empire, their actual manifestations and the ways they have been perceived have changed significantly. Even over the span of the past few decades, however, both terrorism and CT have been marked by quite diverging contexts and perceptions. Examples are the anti-colonial struggles and the responding anti-revolutionary warfare in Africa and Asia, the multiform European terrorism of the 1970s and 1980s, the arrival of Latin-American narco-terrorism or jihadi terrorism in the 1980s and 1990s. The perception of these forms of terrorism changed as much as their contexts and phenomenologies. Before the 1970s, terrorism was seen primarily as a means and component of anti-colonial insurgencies with the insurgents occasionally termed 'terrorists' for propaganda reasons to delegitimize their cause. Yet, on the national and international security agendas and forums the phenomenon as such was dominantly still addressed as (counter-) insurgency or irregular, 'revolutionary warfare' rather than terrorism. This changed during the 1970s in the West when the term 'terrorists' became connoted with a notion of radicalized individuals who were pathologically alienated from the respective societies and their core values. In this view, terrorists appeared mostly as deviant and dangerous individuals, as unrepresentative, high potential criminals who were somehow organized in small, more or less isolated groups. In reality, most of these groups were nevertheless more or less closely linked to other terrorist movements, foreign govern-

9 European anarchists of the late 19th century for instance instilled the public of the 'civilized world' with fear bombing and shooting indiscriminately and targeting even the elected and crowned heads of state and government. In the 19th century's last two decades Tsar Alexander II of Russia, French President Carnot, Spanish Prime Minister Cánovas, Austrian-Hungarian Princess Elisabeth, Italy's King Umberto I, and US President McKinley were assassinated for instance whereas the assassination of Austria-Hungary's Crown Prince Franz-Ferdinand by a state sponsored Serbian terror movement eventually started the Great War from 1914-1918 in which the adversaries mutually accused each other again of large acts of terrorism.

10 Ball, *The USA Patriot Act: A Reference Handbook*, 2004, p. 3.

ments, intelligence agencies, or the organized crime even if this element was not highlighted in the dominant public perception of the terrorists. Today, terrorism appears again much more interconnected with civil war and insurgency as a network-based expression of a highly contagious form of enmity between major representative groups defined by culture and religion. In a certain sense, the contemporary perception of terrorism seems to take notice of and somehow recapitulate all major forms of terrorist structures. In the focus are the lone wolves and small terrorist cells as much as larger networks and large territorialized organizations competing with the state or even assuming notions of statehood. The corresponding reality of contemporary terrorism covers terrorist acts in Western capitals as well as in insurgency, partisan- and civil war theaters far abroad and yet closely connected due to the fact that the same groups claim responsibility for them. With the advent of globalization very different forms of political violence seem in fact to be highly interconnected and floating into each other. Evidently, terrorism is and has always been a changing phenomenon that can take very different forms. It is therefore suggested to be cautious with essentialistic claims about the uniqueness of one of them. This pertains even to the often claimed unprecedented dangerousness of the 'new terrorism', which might be measured by the quality and quantitity of damage caused or the potential of the available weapons. Whereas the anticolonial terrorism of the 1950s and 60s has coalesced with large-scale insurgencies that produced massive atrocities in the wake of entrenched warfare on both sides, the European forms of a more smallscale terrorism during the 1970s and 80s were marked by large numbers of single attacks. In 1978, Italy alone suffered from more than 2000 attacks in one year for example.[11] Even the claim of the 'new terrorism's' unprecedented weaponry is historically less convincing as it might appear at a first glance. The hijacking of air planes as a terrorist technique to use them Kamikaze-like has been on the focus of security agencies since decades prompting the implementation of response systems that were just not working at 9/11. Given, moreover, that a 20-year-old undergraduate from the Massachusetts Institute of Technology had designed a technical conceivable

11 See Brzezinski, *Strategic Vision: America and the Crisis of Global Power*, 2012, p. 100.

nuclear bomb already in 1975, the scenario of a potential WMD-application is also much older than Al-Qaida.[12]

What is indeed new concerning Islamic terrorism as emerging in the 1990s is the high intra- and interregional connectivity of different forms and distant theaters of political violence which are altogether unfolding a much larger impact on geopolitical agendas and the international order. This change, however, is rather one of the contexts of international governance than the socio-political phenomenon terrorism itself. On the other side, the international dimension and network character of terrorism is not new. Certain notions of 'internationalization' characterize most insurgencies and civil wars in modern times whereas those which were only barely supported from the outside like the Kenyan insurgency often suffered badly from this fact.

Generally, the problem with qualifications like the 'new terrorism' is the degree to which they carry an implied supposedly unquestionable truth deemed to be automatically legitimating not only the cause but also the modes and means of CT. It is thus not the focus on the contextual changes of terrorism but the doctrinal and purposive essentialism which poses a problem concerning the claimed novelty of contemporary terrorism.

How contra-factual the involved assumptions often are is reflected by prominent perceptions of Al-Qaida and the Islamic State (IS). Both are often named as the most visible emanations of the 'new terrorism'. However, while the allegedly outstanding nature of Al-Qaida has often been found in its network-like deterritorialization, the IS is often considered as outstanding just due to its specific territorial character in terms of statehood. Both characteristics can hardly be claimed as significantly expressing a particular novelty of the new terrorism at the same time, both are not totally new in relation to older phenomena of political violence in the Middle East – one might only think of the Mahdist Uprising – and, most important, both represent only a half-truth. Concerning the 'deterritorialization' of Al-Qaida it has to be acknowledged how deep Al-Qaida is actually rooted in traditional, so to say 'telluric'[13] tribal societies whereas the 'state-like' IS is claiming the universalistic, inherently borders- and

12 See Wardlaw, *Political Terrorism: Theory, Tactics and Counter-Measures, 1989,* p. 191.

13 See for the typical 'territorial link' that characterizes the "telluric character" of the partisan, Schmitt, *Theory of the Partisan: Intermediate Commentary on the Concept of the Political*, 2007.

states-transcending *caliphate*. In other words: Catchphrases might be useful to focus the attention but can not replace careful analysis and should not carry far-reaching normative implications if they are not backed by a differentiated doctrine.

### *II. A new Counter-Terrorism?*

This is leading to the question in how far CT has become a different one after 9/11. What has changed least so far is the arsenal of basic strategic and tactical options at hand, an assessment that is reflected by the unabated and even increased interest in the craft's 'classics', the writings of the influential French 'counter-insurgents' of the Algerian War for instance. The operationalization and adjustment of the given conceptional instruments, however, faces new realities and challenges in many respects. That applies already to the number of newly emerging weapons and battlefields of CT. Examples are the revolution in mass surveillance, the ability to launch robot-like long-distance extermination strikes against individuals at any place in the world or new battlefields like the cyber-space. The vast technical innovations that became apparent after the end of the Cold War broadened the scope of analysis and operations largely, created new vulnerabilities and pose a different challenge for the constitutional and legal frame domestically than 'anti-revolutionary warfare' in Malaya, Algeria, Kenya or Vietnam did. Rather a whole set of new legal CT-instruments has been forcefully crafted that is entrenching the reach and the teeth of contemporary CT by legal means on a global scale to an unprecedented degree covering nowadays issues like travelling, finance or trade to name just a few.

Yet, the most significant change in contemporary CT pertains to the overarching function and impact of CT as such. In response to 9/11, CT has actually shifted into the center of gravity of national, regional and global governance as such.[14] The consequentially emerging "culture of counterterrorism"[15] is aligning or at least affecting major segments of both, the domestic and international public order alike. In an official account of the country in which the transformation has started, the United

14 See Smith, "The Concept of Security in a Globalized World," pp. 33, 46.

15 Zulaika, *Terrorism: The Self-Fulfilling Prophecy*, 2009, p. 197.

States of America, CT has indeed "become, *beyond any doubt, the top national security priority*".[16] The corresponding transformative change affects not only the domestic constitutional system but in particular also foreign relations and the global order. In this sense, it has been described as nothing less than forming "*the single hegemonic agenda of U.S. policy*".[17] To put it from another side, a "counterterrorism [of this impact] could not stand alone; it had to defer to the Grand strategy of securing America's status as an unrivalled unipolar power."[18] According to Brzezinski "[…] September 11, 2001, fundamentally altered America's own view of its global purpose." Now, combating terrorism "became synonymous with foreign policy [...]."[19]

On this basis, the unfolding GWOT became not only the hallmark of a new peak of American power, exceptionalism and unilateralism, but also the single agenda that started to define and transform numerous globally relevant legal regimes and practices of global ordering. Among the most obvious and probably most important changes are those directly pertaining to the basic tenets of the international rule of law. These changes fundamentally affect the laws of war, the core primciple of state sovereignty, and vital parts of international humanitarian law and human rights law. Other significant changes pertain to an emerging global law that is far exceeding the classical areas which are typically addressed by CT. Nevertheless, the scope of these normative 'sideshows' of the GWOT profoundly affects global governance as well. Examples are the post-9/11 regimes on export control, anti-money laundering, aviation security and migration law just to name a few of them. Altogether, these 'sideshows' alone enable far-reaching global and domestic control regimes for all kinds of cross-border movements which are essential in a globalized world, namely on the flow of *people*, *money* and *goods*.[20] In this sense, the GWOT has been conse-

16 "Commission on Terrorist Attacks Upon the U.S., The 9/11 Commission Report 361 (2004)," quoted from Londras, "Prevention, Detention, and Extraordina-riness," 2013, p. 117. Italics by the author. See also Kienscherf, *US Domestic and International Regimes of Security: Pacifying the Globe, Securing the Homeland,* 2013, p. 1: "Security has become a veritable obsession in both the United States and Europe."

17 Zulaika, *Terrorism: The Self-Fulfilling Prophecy*, p. 197. Italics by the author.

18 Walker, *National Security and Core Values in American History*, 2009, p. 262.

19 Brzezinski, *Strategic Vision*, p. 122.

20 The next wave of recalibrating the CT-arsenal in the GWOT will probably result in tighter internet control and more limitations on the use of hard cash.

quently described as the manifestation of a project "to establish a new world order implying the global opening of the markets, guaranteed access to energy resources, the suppression of regulations and borders, the control of communications and so on."[21]

The result is a complex and remarkable transformation which represents the real novelty in the wake of 9/11, a novelty that is truly justifying the classification of the 9/11 events as a major turning point. Three aspects of this transformation might be highlighted. First, historically unprecedented, CT became the dominating issue of national, regional and international security. Second, the so initiated trend of an encompassing *securitization* of the public order created a similarly unprecedentedly dense, differentiated, and pervasive security paradigm. Consequently, CT was neither just one security policy among others, nor was national/international security just a policy among other similar important policy issues. In fact, the GWOT became the dominating governance paradigm that not only openly competed with essential principles of domestic and international law but successfully claimed to supersede them while a broad range of policy fields originally unrelated to CT or national security became redefined under the GWOT's precepts. Thirdly, the emerging GWOT paradigm has stunningly been created by the U.S. at a critical juncture after the end of the Cold War that successfully implanted the GWOT which became reinforced by a large number of regimes and institutions on the international level and reproduced by the legal and political agenda of numerous states all over the world. Never before was any government so successful in internationally implanting an agenda of such an impact so quickly and pervasively.

Whether only the massive body of powerful "new rules for an old game"[22] (of CT) is forming the significant novelty since 9/11, or if a whole 'new game' of terrorism actually exists beside it, is therefore not so important to decide. With respect to the claimed 'new terrorism' the actually decisive development since 9/11 is in any case the emergence of a new global governance regime that is facilitated by a transformative nexus of the perception of terrorism and the new approach to counter it.

All in all, it is on this basis that the GWOT develops an unusual gravitational force with respect to all developments and decisions on the CT

---

21 Benoist, *Carl Schmitt Today: Terrorism, 'Just War' and the State of Emergency,* p. 61.

22 Laqueur, "Postmodern Terrorism: New Rules for an Old Game," pp. 4-36.

agenda where it effectively defines the room for maneuver in designing and executing single CT measures and policies on all levels – tactical, operational and strategic to a large degree. Characteristic is the GWOT's transformative ambivalence: On the one hand, it serves the construction of a general governance regime of national and international impact far beyond the immediate threat of terrorism. On the other hand, the sheer weight and importance of this process retroacts onto the margin of maneuver when it comes to the preferences in adopting and executing particular CT measures. While there are still other CT approaches, the GWOT enjoys the status of a highly dominant hegemonic paradigm that is commanding most of the relevant resources and successfully claiming orthodoxy in its view on terrorism and the ways to respond to it. This applies especially to the dimension of communication in CT: As much as communication has been a crucial dimension for the construction of the GWOT as an overarching governance regime (see below) as much is the GWOT paradigm due to exactly this quality assumed to closely determine how communication might be employed as a strategy and means of CT.

## B. *Reconstructing the Choices: Two Model Approaches in Countering Terrorism*

Given the understanding that CT has become an overarching regime and discourse that goes far beyond the classical confines of the business to combat terrorism, the above mentioned thesis of a high degree of determination of any CT measure in the framework of the GWOT deserves some more attention. It shall, in particular, be assumed that the GWOT tightly influences the margin of maneuver for any adjustment of the communication strategies towards actual and potential adversaries. In fact, there are basically two principled angles in form of two overarching CT 'philosophies' or paradigms that might be distinguished to conceive the function and nature any CT measure including the various communication strategies in the frame of CT might actually obtain. The first paradigm manifests in the GWOT, the other in a number of alternative approaches to combat terrorism.

Arguably, any decision to adjust the established CT-related communication to the changing realities in Europe and the Middle East might be considered as being ultimately confined and influenced by the principled choices concerning these basic CT paradigms which shall therefore be reconstructed as ideal-typical models. Before they are unfolded in more detail the two most distinguishing criteria might be highlighted, firstly the question of how communication figures in CT and secondly which constitutional core values are preferred as dominantly guiding CT.

### *I. Communication and Counter-Terrorism*

To understand terrorism as a distinct form of political violence due to its inherent communicative character indicates already a certain centrality of the nature, function and strategy of communication in CT and suggests to conceive the basically available approaches towards CT as a matter of far-reaching consequential choice. CT-related communication is in this sense covering a broad variety of different CT means which are defined by the fact that they all *convey a message* – directly or indirectly, intended and unintended. In this broad sense, every piece of information that potential or actual terrorists or their potential or actual supporters and sympathizers receive being suitable to affect their behavior is considered as 'communication'. Insofar it might be further differentiated. A first layer of CT-related communication covers those measurers which are not primarily intended to convey a message rather than to serve other purposes. Examples are various forms of target hardening (in cities, of plants or airports), embassy fortification and force protection measures in hostile areas or any public surveillance mechanisms.[23] All these measures primarily aim at increasing protection against attacks or preventing them. Often, however, these kinds of measures also carry a calculated or uncalculated element of communication in form of a message of deterrence. Often they have also unintended effects.[24] Embassy fortification, for instance, can produce a powerful symbol of hostile hegemonic intrusion in a sphere of claimed national integrity and purity while massive force protection has been claimed as aggressively distancing military forces from the local population "both phys-

23 See Fussey, "Deterring terrorism? Target hardening, surveillance and the prevention of terrorism," 2011, pp. 164 ff.

24 See Enders and Sandler, "The Effectiveness of Anti-Terrorism Policies: A Vector-Autoregression-Intervention Analysis," 1993, p. 843; see also Fussey, "Deterring terrorism? Target-hardening, surveillance and the prevention of terrorism," p. 174.

ically and philosophically."[25] Similarly, preventive surveillance measures at public spaces might reinforce notions of alienation of potential target populations if they are linked to alleged or real forms of racial or other discriminative forms of profiling. On a second layer, 'communication' might be understood as everything that is *predominantly meant and intended* to convey a message including all forms of indirect and symbolic communication. Examples are CT measures that are intended to convey a message 'without words', be it in the language of 'law and order', crude violence or social support for family members. Here, the adversary can be addressed as both, a rational actor making cost/benefit decisions or an emotional subject exposed to compassion, fear or other strong feelings. The corresponding means are manifold including targeted killings or retaliations by house demolitions and all practices that appeal to actual and potential terrorists to consider the hardships of their choice. These might also be for instance various forms of 'harsh' interrogation methods or hopeless forms of incarceration such as undetermined detention under isolation and sensory deprivation etc. On the other hand, terrorists who are considered as being prone to disengage might receive support and positive incentives in various forms. Similarly, social groups and individuals at risk of radicalization are subject to various 'winning the hearts and minds' approaches. All forms of deterrence by laws, court decisions and administrative practices might also be understood as means of communication in the CT framework. A third layer of communicative relations in CT contains all direct engaging forms of explicit communication like conducting peace talks or programs of disengagement, de-radicalization and counter-radicalization. – All these layers of 'communication' can now be linked to both major 'philosophies' notwithstanding the fact that some approaches might be more typical for one or the other of them while they will often be employed in very different ways within the different paradigms. While typically 'harsh' CT measures like 'enhanced interrogation methods' or targeted killings are inclined to almost exclusively express the approach represented by the GWOT, other forms of CT related communication are equally employed by both approaches like peace talks, disengagement, de-radicalization and counter-radicalization programs, amnesties, financial and other support programs.

25 See Zweibelson, "The US in Afghanistan: Follow Sun Tzu rather than Clausewitz to Victory," 2010, p. 3.

In how far 'communication' figures actually differently in the frame of the two competing CT paradigms will be shown below.

## II. Core Values and Counter-Terrorism

The second major relation that shall serve as a criterion to generate ideal-typical paradigms is the relation between CT and the respectively preferred 'core values'. Basically, two dichotomous classes of core values are inherently competing with each other so far.

On the one hand, there are those values defining *secular humanistic constitutionalism* which might be called the 'constitutional core values'. They are based on the nexus of popular sovereignty, representative democracy, rights and the rule of law as mutually reinforcing elements of a value sated concept of law that claims normative supremacy. They are supposed to constitute the normative core and identity of the body politic. The other class of core values represents the claim that, in the last instance, it is the *reason of state* and the concerns of *national security* that have to be regarded as the supreme norm and overarching rationale guiding the state.[26] Evidently, the conceptual consequences resulting from the preference for one of these sets of core values can affect every aspect of the design and application of CT. The difference is particular relevant for the use of and approach towards the law. An example of conceiving CT has been provided by the German Constitutional Court. In 2006 it decided on the Aviation Security Act that empowered the Minister of Defense to order the shooting down of civilian passenger air planes used as 9/11-like instruments of a terrorist attack. In a widely regarded decision the Court stroke down the act setting a strong sign in preference of the overarching constitutional core values trumping the evident concerns of national security.[27]

Among other issues the Court found that the act violated the protection of human dignity which is acknowledged by the German Constitution as unrestrictable (Art. 1 Basic Law). For the hypothetical case that a passenger plane was shot down in the given scenario despite the lack of a justifying legal basis, the Court notably stated that it had nevertheless not decid-

---

26 See Poole, *Reason of State: Law, Prerogative and Empire*, 2005, p. 246.

27 See the decision 1 BvR 357/05 of the Federal Constitutional Court, on its webpage https://www.bundesverfassungsgericht.de/SharedDocs/Entscheidungen/EN/2006/02/rs20060215_1bvr035705en.html.

ed by its judgment how such an act would have to be judged by any competent court of justice. In other words: While the judges thus accepted the factual possibility of such a shot down without legislative mandate in a state of a supra-legal emergency, it refused to legalize such a legitimizing law as it would violate core constitutional principles. By doing so, the Court reiterated the unquestionable supremacy of the constitution and its core values even in the light of a terrorist attack of catastrophic dimensions and refused to set a symbol for the possibility to supersede them by legislation. Ultimately, this stance expresses the claim that CT has to be organized within the confines of the constitution and affirms a concept of the (rule of) law that perceives the legal order as inherently charged with supreme values enjoying a principled validity.

The opposing concept of law is effectively based on a preference for the demands of national security and framed by the reason of state as the ultimate value and normative benchmark of CT. It is characterized by more latitude towards the rule of law and constitutional rights and liberties where it comes to combating terrorism and the willingness to supersede such core values for the sake of CT. Adherents of this perspective are inclined to see the law as an instrument rather than a limiting frame of CT and the legal order as an arsenal of "lawfare". Initially, the concept of 'lawfare' has been used defensively to refuse arguments of the adversaries of the reason of state-based approach towards the law as an instrument of CT. 'Lawfare' has been used in this context to discredit those seeking redress to the rule of law in order to confine CT to the constitutional and legal boundaries. In reverse, however, 'lawfare' has effecttively become an integrated part of CT and COIN as the "continuation of warfare by political or legal means".[28] It is supposed in this sense to make use of law as "a weapon of war, an affirmative tool for advancing strategic and tactical interests during conflict."[29]

28 Carter, "Legal Combat: Are enemies waging war in our courts?," 2005, at http://www.slate.com/articles/news_and_politics/jurisprudence/2005/04/legal_combat.html. See from a critical perspective Luban, "Carl Schmitt and the Critique of the Lawfare," 2010, pp. 458 f.

29 Sitaraman, *The Counterinsurgent's Constitution: Law in the Age of Small Wars*, 2013, p. 109.

Accordingly, within the post 9/11 security paradigm the "existing institutions including courts become conceived merely as 'instruments for use in the service of national security […]'."[30]

Moreover, the legal and extra-legal exemption of extended spheres of CT-operations from the constraints of constitutional and international law and a 'thick' notion of the rule of law as being based on the constitutional core values has become another manifestation of the reason of state based approach towards CT. Here it is the strategic neutralization of those legal regimes dominated by constitutional core values that forms a typical strategy. Such "legal black holes"[31] can be created in both ways, legally by statutes or secretly by practice. A striking example for a bold statutorily ordered exemption from one of the core regimes of international humanitarian law is contained in the 2006 Military Commissions Act (MCA). Strikingly, (10 U.S.C.) § 948b(g) (2012) orders for example that:

> [n]o alien unlawful enemy combatant subject to trial by military commission under this chapter may invoke the Geneva Conventions as a source of rights.

Moreover, according to 28 U.S.C. § 2241 (2011), the MCA also provides that

> [n]o person may invoke the Geneva Conventions or any protocols thereto in any habeas corpus or other civil action or proceeding to which the United States, or a current or former officer, employee, member of the Armed Forces, or other agent of the United States is a party as a source of rights in any court of the United States or its States or territories.

These provisions eventually enacted in pursuit of the GWOT exemplify the relation between CT, rights and the rule of law in the second major CT paradigm *pars pro toto* for a large arsenal of similar legal and informal measures that are attempting to secure CT from being constrained by those core values that characterize Western constitutional and international law. They are considered as opposing the supremacy of the preferred core values represented by the reason-of-state and national security.

---

30 Poole, *Reason of State: Law, Prerogative and Empire*, p. 260, referring to Butler, *Precarious Life: The Power of Mourning and Violence*, 2006, p. 95.

31 The term has been used to describe the detention center at Guantanamo Bay as well as the network of black sites operated by the CIA especially in the context of the extraordinary rendition program. See Steyn, "Guantanamo Bay: The Legal Black Hole," 2004, pp. 1-15.

Although these fundamental and fundamentally competing notions of which ultimate normative order is supposed to guide CT express two inherently different classes of core values, they are yet not representing an either/or relation rather than a dynamic form of coexistence in the frame of the res publica's normative fabric. In fact, adherents of both basic approaches pertaining to the guiding core values of CT will be inclined to acknowledge the basic importance of the values preferred by the respective other side. The decisive question distinguishing them is yet the question which class of core values would deserve priority in the case of colliding interests. This problem of a latently irreducible tension in handling the coexistence of two essentially different layers of normative ordering that are each claiming superior validity, appreciation and effect is not confined to CT but becomes particularly acute here and strongly influences the categorical approaches to conduct the business of CT. With the GWOT, this tension between two normative orders constituting the Western society has reached a veritable peak. Pertaining to the understanding and operation of CT, the decision in favor of one of these two sets of core values shapes the overall character and deep structure of CT as much as it affects almost every single measure taken by the CT community in practice.

### *III. Deriving a Dichotomous Model View on Counter-Terrorism*

Starting from these considerations, two ideal-typical models of CT shall be suggested that are basically distinguished by both, different conceptions of communication with the adversary and different notions pertaining to the ultimately preferred 'core values'. Beyond these principled relations, both models are developed as open phenomenologies characterized by a range of additional affinities and preferences. Before they are unfolded, it is useful to ask for other attempts to classify the basic approaches towards CT as addressed in the CT discourse. Generally, the range of issues to cover by any encompassing CT model is as broad as diverse including the rationales, strategies and tactics of CT to be applied to a wide spectrum of preventive and repressive, deterrent and defensive measures. These are for instance investigative and intelligence activities, retaliation-, kill- and capture missions, diplomatic approaches and multilateral cooperations on the legislative level and in terms of police and intelligence cooperation, the conduct of military and intelleginence operations as well as domestic social programs and all efforts intended to foster de-radicalization, disengagement and counter-radicalization. Most of the various approaches to classify and describe this complex business of CT have as a common denominator the fact that they are developed along opposing view points and dichotomous pattern. This is the angle from which some given approaches shall be accessed before a different yet also dichotomous model approach shall be presented.

An older, quite simplistic differentiation between 'soft' and 'hard' CT measures has, however, been largely replaced by the search for 'smart' approaches (see Gunaratna in this book).[32] The heuristic value of focusing on smart solutions lies mostly in the possibility to avoid the contra-factual notion of an either/or relation between 'soft' and 'hard' approaches in CT. That opens space for reflection which, yet, has still to be filled conceptually. Instead of providing a substantial concept, the focus on 'smart' CT therefore poses basically the question which combination of CT measures running across the hard-soft distinction might actually be 'smart' enough to promise success.

With the GWOT the discussion on conceptually more coherent approaches to envision the encompassing project of CT has, indeed, significantly gained in weight and size, with respect to both operations and theoretical reflection alike. As CT became so unprecedentedly important, complex and entrenched, encompassing models to combat terrorism became more intensively discussed as well to assess potential chances and challenges and to design, adjust and execute contemporary CT in the frame of a holistically integrated, systemic and flexible approach.

This interest is fully justified. Given the expansion and impact of CT, overarching model views can help acknowledge and avoid unanticipated effects of particular CT measures which might eventually develop not only in a complete "diffusion of benefit"[33] but even be "far more costly than the intended consequences".[34] Among the most harmful unintended consequences outweighing the actual benefits and achievements of CT are triggering critical levels of international resistance or significant processes of

32 Evans, *Liberal Terror*, p. 47, according to whom the "claim that soft and hard approaches are incompatible or ideologically opposed is misguided."

33 Clarke, *Situational Crime Prevention: Successful Case Studies*, 1997, p. 175.

34 Enders and Sandler, "The Effectiveness of Anti-terrorism Policies: A Vector-Autoregression-Intervention Analysis," p. 843; see also Fussey, "Deterring terrorism? Target-hardening, surveillance and the prevention of terrorism," p. 174.

radicalization and surging support for hostile developments which strengthen the terrorist's cause. This is for example deliberated – essentially as a question of communication – with respect to the effects of targeted killings. Generally, the employment of brute force beyond the constitutional constraints of regular law enforcement is discussed as further radicalizing and thus eventually increasing terrorism. Ultimately, the negative effect might turn out not only against the respective CT campaign but profoundly the domestic state of affairs of the state employing it. The edge is the point where a corrupted legitimacy of the state's fight against terrorism raises the likelihood that terrorism will prevail durable and significant encouraging the state to only further engage in the chosen direction. Then dysfunctional CT policies might become domestically detrimental and even start to transform constitutional core values not only as constraining CT but as a matter of the own identity of the CT-conducting society posing greater risks to it than single terrorist cells can do:

> The most serious danger currently posed by terrorists is probably their capacity to provoke ill judged, extravagant, and counter-productive state responses, rather than their own direct actions themselves (which statistically continue to representative comparatively limited danger).[35]

If success in neutralizing terrorists is paid by tarnishing the normative identity of state and society that are fighting terrorism, the disadvantages might, indeed, outnumber the advantages of certain CT measures by both the damage done to the own society and the surge of hostile forces in favor of the enemy's cause.

From this perspective, it is exactly the impact and complexity of contemporary CT that indicates the need to observe and analyze different CT measures, dimensions and layers with respect of an overarching conceptual context. As striking this is as much is a fully convincing proposal lacking by which, in the ideal case, consequentional choices, crucial points and critical junctures of encompassing CT campaigns could be analytically addressed and adjusted. Before the marginal spaces for such assessments from a meta-sphere can be discussed below, some thought-provoking conceptions to envision CT shall be visited briefly. Given that the

35 See English, *Terrorism: How to Respond*, 2010, p. 119 and also p. 124; for the compromising effects of the War on Terror on the identity of the liberal-democratic U.S. society in the immediate aftermath of the attacks see Kellner, *From 9/11 to Terror War: The Dangers of the Bush Legacy*, 2003, pp. 68 ff.

GWOT framework inherently integrates classical counterinsurgency (COIN) and even conventional warfare, it makes some sense to start with an originally military distinction that has frequently been operated in COIN and CT contexts as well.

In fact, the developing modern military strategy of the 19th century displays an interesting prefiguration of one of the recurring dichotomous notions of current CT philosophies. It is reflected by the opposing views on the ultimate rationale of military operations by two leading military strategists of their time. One is Antoine-Henri Jomini, a former member of Marshall Ney's staff who became influential with his "Summary of the Art of War" (first published in 1837), the other is Carl v. Clausewitz. In this relation, Jomini represents a military doctrine which primarily aims at the enemy's annihilation. It is driven by the assumption that the total destruction of the enemy forces is the sole factor deciding the outcome of the war.[36] Clausewitz on the other hand, who was opposed to Jomini's ideas on strategy, famously introduced the influential dictum of the supremacy of politics over military rationales.[37] This approach became the doctrinal precondition for the classical French and British concept of anti-revolutionary warfare during the anti-colonial insurgencies after WW II. One of its key elements is the "winning the hearts and minds" approach which still figures as the probably most discussed single element of any modern COIN-doctrine.[38] Only gradually different from some of its older versions, it is today mostly embedded in an explicit nation-building context of COIN-strategy.[39] Yet, it should be clarified that this approach has historically always been combined with elements of annihilation and other 'harsh' methods of the CT arsenal. Central for it is just the acknowledgement of a political dimension of the political violence that is to be addressed and the consequential need to include the population in the strategic calculus. This activates an inherent communicative aspect of COIN which is essential for the 'winning hearts and minds' strategy pursued by a classical carrot-and-

36 See Nagl, *Learning to Eat Soup With a Knife: Counterinsurgency Lessons From Malaya and Vietnam, 2005,* pp. 17 f.

37 See Nagl, *Learning to Eat a Soup With a Knife*, pp. 17 f.

38 See Galula, *Counterinsurgency Warfare: Theory and Practice*, 2006, p. 1, who starts his classical book with a paraphrase of Clausewitz' famous dictum on warfare as the continuation of politics with other means.

39 See Sitaraman, *The Counterinsurgent's Constitution*, pp. 147 ff.

stick approach. – Compliance with COIN forces will be rewarded, non-compliance punished.

Based on these basic approaches, Kilcullen distinguishes two contrasting schools of thought pertaining to classical COIN campaigns: an 'enemy-centric' and a 'population-centric' model.[40]

The first one understands COIN as a variant of conventional warfare primarily aiming at the enemy's defeat. This *enemy-centric approach* includes a combination of 'hard' and 'soft' measures including decapitation and marginalization strategies. Yet, ultimately decisive for it is the focus on the enemy and the priority to destroy this prime target as a sufficient condition for success in combating terrorism.

The *population-centric approach* on the other hand, focuses on a governance challenge that crystallizes in form of the insurgency. It addresses primarily not the fighter but the relevant population as the essential target while it includes both 'hard' and 'soft' methods as well. Frequently studied and influential in the American discourse as one of the classical COIN-scholars in favor of this approach is David Galula, a military intelligence veteran of the French Algerian war. His thoughts on COIN are basically a reprise to Mao's legendary concept of revolutionary warfare that Galula had experienced himself in China and according to which the people are the sea in which the revolutionary swims like the fish in the water.[41] Galula's approach to dry out this 'sea' as a strategic priority of COIN warfare is reflected to a certain degree by the 2006 U.S. FM 3-24.

Kilcullen himself proposes another more elaborated distinction by which he confronts what he labels the "terrorism" and the "counter-insurgency paradigm" respectively.[42] His ideal-typical model differentiation represents a more analytical and encompassing CT concept that is practically important due to his consultancy activities to General David Petraeus who initiated an adjustment of the military strategy for the COIN theaters in Iraq and Afghanistan that was continued by General Stanley McCrystall

40 See Kilcullen, *Counterinsurgency*, 2010, p. 94; see also Kilcullen, "Two Schools of Classical Counterinsurgency," 2007, accessible at http://smallwarsjournal.com/blog/two-schools-of-classical-counterinsurgency.

41 See Galula, *Counterinsurgency Warfare*, pp. 3 ff. For a critique of *Galula* see Mathias, *Galula in Algeria: Counterinsurgency Practice versus Theory*, 2011, pointing at the discrepancy between the French counterinsurgency practice in Algeria and Galula's counterinsurgency theory.

42 See Kilcullen, "Two Schools of Classical Counterinsurgency," pp. 186 ff.

and somehow manifested in the mentioned U.S. FM 3-24.[43] According to Kilcullen's distinction, the 'terrorism paradigm', envisions the enemy, the terrorist, as an unrepresentative aberration of the normal population, someone who is psychologically and morally flawed, characterized by his unacceptable methods and objectives and thus being no subject for any negotiations. Methodological, CT is considered by this view as a law enforcement problem that adopts a case-based approach focused on arresting the suspects.[44]

The 'COIN paradigm' on the other hand, envisions the enemy – thus the insurgent – as being representative of actual societal root causes for unrest, as someone who uses unacceptable means while potentially having acceptable objectives. Kilcullen's 'insurgent' uses violence instrumentally "within an integrated politico-military strategy" that requires a corresponding 'winning hearts and minds approach' in response.[45] COIN is thus considered as a "whole-of-government problem" with a strategy that is focusing on defeating the insurgent's *strategy* whereas the objective of arresting or killing the enemy ranks secondary.[46]

Appreciating the perspective offered by this differentiated approach, a partly different one is suggested here. Whereas the presently suggested one shares with Kilcullen the centrality of the taken *perspective on the adversary*, it differs in other respects. This is largely the result of the basically different underlying interests and heuristic contexts. Whereas Kilcullen prescribes an effective versus ineffective approach, the perspective taken here is confined to suggest an empirical assessment of how CT is actually conducted. While Kilcullen puts emphasis on the primary question of the best *'counter-method'* against the terrorist threat to define the *paradigmatic difference* between the basic approaches, this distinction plays no *defini-*

43 See Gurman, "Introduction," 2013, p. 2; Sitaraman, *The Counterinsurgent's Constitution: Law in the Age of Small Wars*, pp. 32 ff.

44 See Kilcullen, "Two Schools of Classical Counterinsurgery," pp. 186 ff., especially p. 188.

45 Correspondingly opposing to a strategy of predominant militarily annihilation, Gen. David Petraeus stressed that the ultimate CT/COIN goal for Iraq was "a negotiated settlement – in fact, a series of them". Insofar, the American troops were supposed to offer the hostile parts of Iraq's Sunni population "a new option instead of treating them as the enemy". See Robinson, *Tell Me How This Ends: General David Petraeus and the Search for a Way out of Iraq*, 2008, pp. 177 and 252.

46 See Kilcullen, "Two Schools of Classical Counterinsurgency," pp. 186 ff., especially p. 188.

*tional* role for the model distinction suggested here. Consequently and different from Kilcullen, a case-focused criminal law approach or a socio-politically defined governance approach are necessarily representing two paradigmatically divided approaches from the perspective taken here. While Kilcullen focuses moreover much on the population of potential or actual insurgency theaters, the perspective provided here includes also the 'lone wolves' and the radicalizing youth from urban European contexts. Most important, however, is another difference, namely the inclusion of the category of core values. Whereas it is the merit of Galula and Kilcullen to have emphatically included the communicative dimension in the calculus of operations, they do, however, not prominently address the guiding core values.

Differently, the relation between communication and core values is considered here as the Archimedean point in deriving ideal-typical models of actual CT. From here, a third central criterion ensues as a sort of missing link between the former two. That is the perception of the adversary's *gestalt*, the dominant imagery of the adversary as being shaped by the dominant core values and further influencing the way how appropriate communication with the adversary is perceived. These three criteria form the characteristic constellation that distinguishes the two ideal-types of CT from a fundamental perspective. From these interconnected basic points of reference, a number of additional dichotomous characteristics will be suggested as being inclined to be displayed in the frame of the two paradigms. These additional characteristic dichotomies follow partly almost compellingly from the outlined basic configuration, partly they represent attributions that are circumscribing typical yet not necessary predispositions in the frame of the basic models. Additional elements of the paradigmatic configurations pertain for instance to the interventionist rationale of CT, the dimensions and modes of action and the respectively leading actors but also the respectively preferred foreign relations rationale.

The resulting ideal-typical and ideal-typically opposing paradigms are addressed here as the *subject-related communication* (SRC) model and the *danger-directed measures* (DDM) model of which the GWOT is the contemporary by far most prominent expression.

The DDM model is focused on the *elimination of the danger* that the terrorist represents and aims first and foremost at effectively 'taking the threat out'. The SRC model maintains that CT is *dealing with subjects in a legal and moral sense* while aiming at countering the terrorist threat due to the rule of law to be upheld, irrespectively of the wickedness and danger to be addressed or the actual operational oportunities.

This basic distinction indicates already the preferences for the dominating normative order, the guiding core values, and, more concretely, the interventionist rationale of CT. While the SRC approach acknowledges the predominance of secular humanist constitutional core values, the DDM approach is predominantly oriented at consequent reason-of-state thought. As pointed out above, the former reference manifests especially in Western constitutionalism that is embodied by the mutually reinforcing nexus of human rights, democracy and a 'thick' version of the rule of law. Whereas the DDM model is well at ease with exceptions from the regular constitutional and legal order to achieve its end, if it is not even favoring a permanent state of emergency, the SRC model is oriented at maintaining the regular constitutional and legal order as much and far as possible. Whereas the SRC model prefers as the dominating interventionist rationale that of orthodox criminal justice, strict observance of constitutional restrictions for interventions and deliberate dialogue, the DDM approach aims at the effective deterrence of potential enemies and tight control of broadly defined risks where it is not simply advancing a 'capture or kill' rationale. Different from the SRC model, it takes a skeptical stance towards all possible restrictions based on constitutional rights and considerations of democratic accountability. Different from the SRC approach, the DDM perspective will favor less the open dialogue rather than forms of influencing and manipulation in terms of communication with the adversaries.

While regular law enforcement by civilian agencies dominates the SRC understanding, the broad understanding of warfare and covert action is inclined to represent the preference according to the DDM model. This may lead to a preference of conducting CT militarily or by militarizing the police and giving the intelligence apparatus broader space and leeway. While the SRC approach is inclined to integrate different CT actors under overt civilian control down to the operational level where it prefers prosecutors and police as the lead/main agency, the DDM concept is inclined to prefer an intelligence and military thinking and lead with more covert forms of civilian involvement.

Another typical preference pertains to the predominant stance towards foreign relations and international law. While the DDM perspective is easier inclined to manifest in 'exceptionalism', unilateralism and '*strategic* multilateralism', the SRC-based approach is inclined to suggest the strict adherence to the international rule of law and correspondingly justified and mandated international interventions. Whereas a SRC-based strategy would favor inclusive nation-building based on constitutional core values, the DDM approach would currently prefer the maintenance of relative control over strategic areas based on a superior military/intelligence infrastructure – forward operating bases, the deployment of drones and reconnaissance electronics for instance – and an essentially opportunistic and often shifting system of alliances with local clients whose value is defined strategically or tactically irrespective of their assessment in legal or moral terms. This stance has been described as a preference for a 'martial plan' rather than a Marshall Plan[47] and reinforced by the experience of large scale nation building failure in the GWOT context.

Pertaining to the dominant imagery of the terrorist, the DDM approach will be shaped by a Manichaean view based on the perception of an absolute good/evil divide with the terrorist as the incarnation of the very evil that CT is called to eliminate. This, and this alone, is the moral mission of the counter-terrorist and the state's overarching interest following a Hobbesean imperative to maintain the own population's safety as the state's foundational purpose.

In this perspective, the imagery of the terrorist as the embodiment of evil as such had an outright foundational function especially for the implementation of the GWOT. In President George W. Bush's words:

> [T]hey're flat evil. That's all they can think about, is evil. And as a nation of good folks, we're going to hunt them down, and we're going to find them, and we will bring them to justice.[48]

In this context, 'justice' evidently refers to punishment by an eye-for-an-eye approach of the Old Testamentarian provenance rather than due legal process. Importantly, 'justice' as retaliation follows here from the consequent dehumanization of the enemy and the danger he outrageously represents. In President Bush's words again: "My hope is that all nations will heed our call and *eliminate the terrorist parasites* [...]"[49] who are "spread

47 Krugman, "The Martial Plan," *New York Times* (Feburay 2003), quoted from Koh, "America's Jekyll-and-Hyde Exceptionalism", 2005, p. 121.

48 Bush, September 25, 2001 quoted from Kappeler and Kappeler, "Speaking of Evil and Terrorism: The Political and Ideological Construction of a Moral Panic," pp. 175, 184.

49 Bush, State of the Union Address, January 29, 2002, at http://edition.cnn.com/2002/ALLPOLITICS/01/29/bush.speech.txt/. Italics by the author.

throughout the world like ticking bombs", tens of thousands in number and threatening not only entire nations but even "civilization as such".[50] Waging war on terrorism is thus, in this perspective nothing less than to "save civilization itself".[51] For, as an often reiterated theme of the imagery of the 'new' terrorism, the latter belongs to those few crimes "so terrible [that] *they offend humanity itself*. Therefore, the aggressions and ambitions of the wicked must be opposed early, decisively and collectively before they threaten us all."[52]

The SRC approach on the other side will be inclined to acknowledge with Kilcullen the political if not moral cause of the terrorist while condemning the means he employs. They are not regarded as an isloted expression of absolute wickedness rather than as an unacceptable tactic employed in an ugly game that all too often actually two are playing to a certain extent. Adherents of the SRC model would thus easier contemplate the possibility of a certain exchangeability pertaining to the driving forces on both sides of the terrorism-counterterrorism relation. While the SRC advocates uphold the distinguishing line between them and the terrorists by linking the means they employ to their core values, the adherents of the DDM defend their core values occasionally in ways that might reflect an exchangeability of the means on both sides which is yet comfortable for them due to their perception of an almost ontological difference between them and their enemies. Those applying the SRC perspective on the other hand perceive the 'other' still as subjects in the moral and legal sense while they would avoid *essentialist* or even *ontological* claims in terms of good and evil when defining them operationally. Consequently, the SRC approach considers CT as a matter of law and due process while the DDM perspective is inclined to accept that the end justifies the means. With respect to the own core values, there is, from the SRC perspective furthermore always the possibility that 'what we do to the enemy we might even-

50 Bush, January 29, 2002, quoted from Kappeler and Kappeler, "Speaking of Evil and Terrorism: The Political and Ideological Construction of a Moral Panic," p. 179. See also Colin Powell's, "assault […] against civilization", 2002, quoted from Kappeler and Kappeler, "Speaking of Evil and Terrorism: The Political and Ideological Construction of a Moral Panic," p. 182.

51 Bush, November 8, 2001, quoted from Kappeler Kappeler, "Speaking of Evil and Terrorism: The Political and Ideological Construction of a Moral Panic," p. 181.

52 Bush, November 10, 2001, quoted from Kappeler and Kappeler, "Speaking of Evil and Terrorism: The Political and Ideological Construction of a Moral Panic," p. 176.

tually also do to us' which, on the other hand, would be inclined to be alien to a DDM approach.

Coming back to the imagery of the terrorist once more, the idea of a 'new terrorism' with normative implications like the absolute necessity of rooting this danger by all means would very much express a DDM perspective while it would be refused from a SRC perspective. Pertaining to the terrorism-counterterrorism nexus there are thus two typical disconnections with respect to the imagery of terrorism dominating the opposing models. Whereas there is no 'new terrorism' in the sense that it would necessarily imply a 'new CT' strategy from the point of view of a SRC-based perspective, it is not relevant for the DDM model to ask for exchangeability of the means of terrorism and counterterrorism. From the DDM perspective, wrong and evil are therefore always on the side of the hostile other, right and good on the own. For the DDM model, the heuristically most decisive distinction is thus the one which absolutely separates the own and the other along the lines of 'good' and 'evil'. It is reinforced by a consequent reason-of-state rationale whereas almost all other significant distinctions are inclined to be blurred against the clarity and supremacy of this first and truly foundational one. This is affecting important distinctions between regular rule and rule of emergency, criminal law on the one hand and prevention and warfare on the other, overt and covert action, between being 'within' and 'beyond' the legally defined institutional competences and between the qualification as 'terrorists', supporter or sympathizer or those being just suspected or found guilty, and so on.

From the perspective of the SRC approach, on the other hand, the major heuristical distinction is made from the constitutional and moral point of view that acknowledges the enemy's quality as a human subject with all inherent legal restrictions in engaging with him or her. This focus on the moral and legal subject-quality of the adversary entails the notion to take both sides of the terrorism-counterterrorism nexus in consideration while preserving the enemy's subject quality, the integrity of the rule of law and constitutional core values and eventually maintaining the normative identity of the own state and society in combating the terrorist. Pertaining to the above mentioned distinctions, it implies the inclination to strictly observe their boundaries which are inclined to be blurred by the DDM approach.

Accordingly, the basic approaches towards the communicative dimension of CT are shaped. From an SRC perspective, the counter-terrorist is more likely able and willing to put himself in the shoes of the adversary as one of the basic conditions of any authentic open communication. He adopts this attitude, however, notwithstanding the *continuing and principled demand* of those constitutional core values that are prescribing the state's *duty to prosecute and punish* crimes. Thus, all crimes committed in the context of the terror-CT nexus, those committed by the enemy as well as those committed on the state's side in the wake of CT operations, are to be strictly subjected to criminal investigations and legal punishment.

From a DDM based perspective, open dialogical communication is not impossible as well but will be inclined to be governed by its typical reason of state rationale. Communication is thus neither desirable nor manageable in the frame and the guidance of constitutional core values. A preferred mode of communication will be the covert contact to the enemy, be it for purposes of negotiation, infiltration or manipulation. DDM-based communication will thus preferably involve all forms of disinformation, propaganda, and manipulative persuasion. Legally induced investigations and punishments on the other side are often inclined to be easier superseded by opportunistic interests when it comes to infiltrate or manipulate the enemy's networks from a DDM perspective.

All in all, the distinction between the DDM and the SRC paradigm transcends those between 'soft' and 'hard' CT approaches. Both might well be employed in the frame of both models whereas the concrete character, the *gestalt* they actually adopt may differ drastically. 'Winning the hearts and minds of the people' campaigns for instance fit well in the SRC model, but have originally been developed as a major strategy tool of colonial anti-revolutionary warfare against insurgents/terrorists where they were based on a pure reason-of-state rationale. After all, this core strategy has regularly and without conceptual inconsistency been complemented by repressive means to enforce compliance. Typically winning the hearts and minds campaigns were supplemented for instance by extended practices of forced resettlements, torture, rape and summarily executions. Again: the communicative setting remained fully instrumental to the overarching national security and reason of state rationale rather than reflecting and being integrated by constitutional core values. A manifestation of the instrumental rather than principle sated nature of communication in the DDM framework which is leading to a kind of opportunistic fragmentation of the overarching communication strategy are amnesties. Amnesties of hardened terrorists who are convicted for severest crimes are for instance evidently more likely to be regarded as a valuable instrument to gain information from a DDM perspective than from a SRC-based perspective that is confined to invariably maintain the rule of law and substantial justice. Similarly different is the basic attitude towards the de-radicalization and dis-engagement of adversaries which is especially relevant in terms of prevention.

Generally, both CT models, the SRC and the DDM model, face their typical challenges whereas both will only be successful as long as they are applied consistently, determinedly and consequently. Both are derived from a clearly defined basic configuration, namely the respective choices in terms of 'core values', 'enemy perception' and 'communication' while they are representing open and party non-exclusive models. Some of their characteristics follow almost compellingly from the respective basic configuration while others represent typical preferences and tendencies. In reality these models may not necessarily appear in their 'pure form' but often in form of a paradoxical coincidence and with occasionally blurring boundaries on all levels: in the frame of national policies, the policies of single CT agencies and even on the level of individual actors. The respective choices might be conscious as well as unreflective. In this regard, it is helpful to remember that a melange of different, often opposing conceptions is nothing unusual in the field of governance and public policy. Grand national security strategies are in fact often shaped – or confused – by coexisting influences of inherently opposing and competing paradigmatic approaches.[53] Such a paradoxical complexity might be as beneficial as detrimental to the underlying purposes and can gradually be addressed if a meta-perspective is possible. Pertaining to contemporary CT, the concurrence of the DDM and the SRC approach runs across all the different levels involved from grand strategy and single national security policies to those of operational tactics involving all CT agencies and stakeholders and covering national, regional and international discourses and theaters. Against this context it is assumed that the actual figuration or *gestalt* of both paradigms is somehow reflected on all levels, in all dimensions and by every aspect of a broadly understood CT in form of permanent processes of reproduction and interaction with a shifting relative weight that each of them enjoys in general and in a given context.

It is important to note, however, that choices between the two paradigms are not choices between even alternatives. The GWOT that is largely expressing the DDM paradigm has quickly become an encompass-

53 See Biddle, "Strategy in War," 2008, p. 5.

ing and far reaching governance paradigm that has shifted into the very center of gravity of domestic and international politics. It goes much beyond the classical confines of CT and enjoys a much greater weight than CT policies ever did in other contexts. This distinguishes it significantly from the alternative approach, the SRC model, which seems to be in retreat.[54] Different from the GWOT paradigm, it is most notably not inhabited by an expansive, transformative rationale on its own. Is the GWOT always working in favor of entrenching a particular trend of *securitization*, the SRC approach seeks to ensure compliance with the core values that are subject to a general trend of *constitutionalization*. Most notably, the GWOT is representing a hegemonic discourse that is not only claiming orthodoxy but also continuously reinforced by the accumulating power resources of the very regime it creates. Yet, despite the impressive impact and shape of the GWOT, contemporary CT remains an inherently contested and somehow contradictory subject. This is leading to the initially posed question: How much space of maneuver actually exists for choosing, calibrating and executing strategies and measures in responding to the terrorist threat in terms of communication? What are, in particular, the prospects for counter-radicalization, de-radicalization and disengagement in the given context? To approach not an answer to these questions but the context in which such answers might be discussed, it is necessary to further understand, qualify and quantify the weight, compactness and reach of the GWOT paradigm.

## C. *The Global War on Terror and its Gravitational Force*

To determine the given scope of the margin of maneuver to choose, adjust and employ dialogical forms of CT communication it has to be acknowledged that the GWOT paradigm is barely inclined to foster such approaches with any priority. It is, for example, a typical expression of the DDM based GWOT paradigm to question "[h]ow helpful it really [is] to search for causes and try to 'understand' terrorists as victims of despair and the

54 In some jurisdictions like the German the GWOT or DDM approach meets a much stronger resistance by the SRC approach than in othe countries like England for instance. Moreover, the actual appearance of any given country's CT paradigm is always distinguishable from those of other countries with different manifestations and different forms of coexistence of the ideal-typical basic models.

voices of the repressed?"[55] The instead recommended basic attitude is rather enshrined in the following words:

> We must take precisely the opposite approach to terrorism. We *must commit ourselves never to try to understand or eliminate its alleged root causes*, but rather to place it beyond the pale of dialogue and negotiation.[56]

Notably, the 'pale of dialogue' in CT especially addresses not so much the terrorists themselves as main target but their support environment and those who shall be prevented from engaging in violence. In the pure version of DDM/GWOT approach their perception is tertiary, the annihilation of the enemy the primary goal. Consequently, the preferred forms of communication are often those by retaliation – notwithstanding the potential costs concerning the effect on third parties and the given constitutional constraints:

> If the way liberal democracies behave *sends the message* that they are hesitant to pay a price in order to win the war – be it in casualties or in showing readiness to reexamine their commitment to the idea of sovereignty, in order to cope with the threats emanating from ungoverned areas – there is no chance that they will convince terror groups that they should worry about the reaction to their activities. In other words, by inconsistent words and actions, liberal democracies undermine their own credibility and, at the same time, their own ability to deter armed groups.[57]

This notion of an almost unlimited form of preventive warfare is, indeed, very much in line with a consequent DDM approach and has been advocated most famously in the early days of the GWOT when it has been advocated with a very specific understanding of preemption that goes far beyond everything what has formerly understood by the term. In this sense, John Yoo has advised President Bush that he could attack any government or private organization, anytime, anywhere in the world on the basis of no more than mere suspicion.[58] Accordingly, with breathtaking frankness, the global hegemon officially declared its will to pursue warfare against its enemies in the face of international law and the international community according to its reason of state alone: As "a nation at war", the National

---

55 See Sznaider, "Terrorism and the social contract," 2006, pp. 8 f.

56 See Dershowitz, *Why Terrorism Works: Understanding the Threat, Responding to the Challenge*, 2002, pp. 24 f. Italics by the author.

57 See Kupferwasser, "Is It Possible to Deter Armed Groups?," 2008, p. 132.

58 See Pyle, *Getting Away With Torture: Secret Government, War Crimes, and the Rule of Law*, 2009, p. 10.

Defense Strategy of the United States of America 2005 announced for instance, that

> [a]t the direction of the President, we will defeat adversaries at the time, place and in the manner of our choosing – setting the conditions for future security.[59]

Even if the rhetoric of the GWOT has been occasionally less bold, the direction of the path taken remained and remains unchanged. The more the contemporary GWOT enters the dangerous terrain of conventional proxy warfare with strong state adversaries as it is looming at the horizon of possibilities with respect to the Syrian civil war, the more the lines between 'good' and 'bad' allies are blurring and the less probable is an adjustment of the basic notion of 'talking to the enemy' in principle.

This status suggests to explore the actual weight and reach of the GWOT in more detail in order to assess its gravitational force where spaces might open up to raise the cause of counter-radicalization, de-radicalization and disengagement in line of the SRC understanding.

Turning point in the understanding and formation of CT were, as mentioned, the 9/11 attacks. Through them, CT emerged as a central policy paradigm of unprecedented reach and impact. As a uniquely intense act of terrorism they were followed by a corresponding sea change in the CT discourse and practice that profoundly affects domestic constitutionalism, global governance and international relations under the label of GWOT. To understand this transformation and its full impact it is, however, necessary to take a historical perspective back to the previous decade that was inaugurated by the end of the Soviet empire. In many respects, the years following the fall of the Berlin Wall should turn out as the breeding ground of the global order that would eventually be shaped under the precepts of 9/11 CT. Three subsequently emerging historical constellations need to be differentiated to comprehend the grand transformation induced by the attacks on American soil. These are the initial moment of confusion after the unanticipated end of the Cold War, the soon emerging visions of global governance that were competing during the decade prior to 9/11, and, finally, the forceful translation of the 'transformative moment' of 9/11 into a dominating global regime. Against this background the following aspects shall be oberserved more closely: After a look at the compet-

59 National Defense Strategy of the United States of America 2005, p. 1, accessible at: http://www.au.af.mil/au/awc/awcgate/nds/nds2005.pdf.

ing normative orders and governance visions during the 1990s (I.), the paradigm shift by which CT was positioned at the center of gravity of domestic and international ordering shall briefly be reconstructed (II.). This will then be complemented by some remarks on the construction and endurance of the new security order (III.) eventually leading to a final assessment of the outlooks of the GWOT and the margin of maneuver for SRC based communication strategies (D.).

### *I. Filling the Gap: The Global War on Terror and the Cold War*

In brief, the development between the end of the Cold War and the establishment of the GWOT can be described as follows. Soon, the initial confusion over the sudden end of the Cold War gave room to a period of orientation and preparation in the search for a 'new world order' that was supposed to replace the vanished Cold War order of 'mutually assured destruction' and the corresponding realities of the international rule of law.[60] Under these precepts, for almost a decade the 1990s witnessed several tentative attempts to craft a global order out of quite different normative thrusts. Throughout this period, different visions of global governance competed against a still open horizon of possible developments. That ended with the post 9/11 implementation of a hegemonic "Empire of Security"[61] leaving not only those disillusioned who had hoped for the final dominance of a universal human rights regime or even 'world democracy' but also those who had more conservatively believed in a strict adherence to a unilaterally conceived international rule of law.[62] This transformative process deserves some closer attention. It is marked by three passages: a certain continuity of forerunning thrusts, a sharp catalyzing break with the

60 See for the American 'confusion' after the end of the Cold War and the New World Order, Dallek, *Hail to the Chief: The Making and Unmaking of American Presidents*, 1996, p. 119.

61 Bain, "Introduction," 2006, pp. 5 f.

62 The extent to which adherents of human rights, world democracy or a fairer international order engaged in optimism pertaining to the realities of global order prior to 9/11 was quite different. In America, the New Haven School for instance, placed the concern for human dignity at heart of the future international legal-political system, a hope which, however, has aptly been described as "more fiction than reality". See Andreas Paulus, "The Influence of the United States on the Concept of the 'International Community'," 2003, p. 72.

old and breakthrough of a new order, and an evolutionary entrenchment of the new order that turned out to be as sustainable as it was pervasive from the onset.

Against this background, the 1990s might be seen as an era that begun with the question for a new vision for global governance and in which the cornerstones for several competing global regimes were already put in place. Starting point was the sudden discovery of the chances and challenges of a 'new world order' that were still surrounded by a mist of very different sentiments ranging from diffuse fears to sublime feelings of hope based on notions of an almost mystical provenance. While "it seemed for a while after 1991 that America's triumph might last for a long time, with no rival in sight, imitation worldwide, and history seemingly halted"[63], it would soon became clear that a more coherent form of global governance was needed than those implied by the momentous status of a de facto U.S. dominance in absence of any serious rival. The crafting of such a 'new world order' loomed already in 1989 as the historical mission of the 'last man standing' in a turn of eras after the decadelong U.S.-Soviet struggle for global dominance had ended.[64] Yet, the opportunity came unexpected[65] and even those who started to realize its implications seemed initially not to be fully aware of how to live up to its demands and potentials. While President George H. W. Bush prominently reintroduced and relentlessly repeated the reference to the 'new world order' imagined as a "commonwealth of freedom"[66] the vision had still to be complemented by a supporting grand strategy. In the same time, the mission met a moderately resisting, subjectively very complex and in many respects contradictory reality. The thaw of the frozen world order released not only space for quickly spreading conflict spots across the globe but also some confusion within the prevailing NATO camp. In fact, the vacuum left by the crumbling Soviet Empire and disintegrating or shifting security interests in Europe caused some initial confusion over the future roles of major actors and institutions. Some German and French security experts and politicians considered even to end the NATO, as for example then German Minister

---

63 Brzezinski, *Strategic Vision*, p. 44.

64 Francis Fukuyama famously took the success of this mission almost for granted. See Fukuyama, "End of History?," 1989.

65 See Zulaika, *Terrorism: The Self-Fulfilling Prophecy*, p. 146: "[A]s the Soviet Union was imploding, the CIA reported that its economy was growing."

66 See Kissinger, *World Order*, 2014, p. 315.

of Defense Rudolph Scharping, or at least their country's engagement within the NATO as proposed by some French politicians. Moreover, the German unification that quickly followed the turn of tides troubled other European powers like France fearing of her national security with surprising intensity. With not only Russia but also Germany figuring prominently in France's heated security debates of the early 1990s, the "fairly aggressive nuclear arms tests of the early 1990s" indicated the whole volatility of the European situation.[67] – Generally however, the initial uncertainty about the world's new status quo was filled with great hopes and great fears alike while reality still seemed to leave much space for the striving pioneers on the search of a new world order.

The effective shaping of the international security order that still waited to be transformed into a hegemonic vision of global governance under U.S. leadership started early with *Operation Desert Shield/Storm* in 1990/91 which exemplified the overwhelming military might of the U.S. Moreover, with the surging human rights revolution and the strongly advanced neoliberal project, two additional, inherently expansive conceptions of governance could claim to have the potential to substantially contribute to the global order to come. All these visions were ideologically boosted by the Western victory of the Cold War and competed in various modes of conflict and cooperation during the 1990s, more or less entangled, and on more or less on equal footing with each other. Altogether they met an undecided reality, similarly inviting for optimism and pessimism as well. Both, hopes and fears, seemed to be equally justified. Before the end of the Soviet empire, the compelling rationales of the Cold War that were evolving from the threat of nuclear annihilation, had also rammed some normative pillars of almost biblical dimension into the globe's geopolitical ground. At least, they had provided the world with seemingly predictable steering impulses that were defining global and domestic governance in the frame of the world's frozen instability. When this stable-instable global order suddenly ceased to exist, it left numerous spaces in which power vacuums or violent internal conflict emerged or continued on a new level, – meanwhile unleashed from the rigid constraints of a bipolar 'nuclear world'. With some reason, the new global scenario seemed to pave the way for an era of confusing deterioration of regional and global ordering

67 See, also for the quotation, Hagmann, *(In)Security and the Production of International Relations: The Politics of Securitization in Europe,* 2015, p. 153.

with spreading civil wars, insurgencies and domestic terrorism. Yet, all these theaters seemed to pose a threat predominantly not to the prevailing 'West' but the margins of the old world and, due to scale of atrocities, to human dignity as such. Most of the mushrooming conflicts were charged by the colonial and the Cold War heritage, fueled by claims of self-determination of ethnical and religious minorities and often interwoven with desires to exploit the fatal gift of natural resources. Old and new actors grasped the changing opportunities to violently engage with new vigor in the shadows of global change that also sponsored them with a dramatic increase of proliferating weapons. Many of the crises that blossomed throughout the new vacuums of order were driven by forces that had been supported by the Cold War adversaries. From these roots, a range of violent scenarios grew during the 1990s which should later become the main theaters of the GWOT. However, before the current landscape of *jihadi* re- and insurrection took shape, the accumulated potentials of violence that were now deprived of their disciplining Cold War-frame spread diffusely throughout culturally and religiously defined large-spaces. While the Middle East still seemed to charge its potential for more violent conflict, former Yugoslavia and several places in Africa emerged as global stages for a newly visible horror of what men could do to men. The unleashed dynamics of large-scale brutality that started with the Yugoslavian and the Algerian civil wars which were beginning in 1991 peaked with the 1994 genocide in Ruanda and the subsequent Congo wars. Together they demonstrated a new threat to one universal good before all: human rights. Notably, all the atrocities that became visible were still inherently 'glocal' in a significant sense: Situated at the margins of the old world, in the classical European and African 'hearts of darkness', they seemed to prove precisely the same locally confined otherness that had figured greatly as the opposite to the claimed Western superiority for a long time.[68] Arguably, it was exactly this clear-cut localization of the orderliness and chaos the world witnessed that allowed the new global rights discourse to take off as a global norm that claimed practical enforcement, a claim that seemed to be able to be fulfilled without hurting anyone relevant. The underlying notion of political chaos and the danger of new atrocities which were lurking throughout the alleged uncivilized parts of the world were widely perceived as some

68 See for instance Holt, *The Problem of Freedom: Race, Labor and Politics in Jamaica and Britain 1832-1838*, 1992.

of the most pressuring challenges demanding a global order that would have to be defined by the originally Western rights discourse. In other words: the gross and systemic human right violations that challenged the vision of a more humane future at the margins of the new world in principle were the 'present danger' of the day. Especially the failure to prevent the genocide in Rwanda demonstrated and confirmed the need for an international order and an international security architecture that could prevent large scale human right violations. At the same time, the apparent victory of the free market economy over the Soviet style planning economy and the keen interest of numerous old and new states to profoundly reform their economies under the signs of an advancing neo-liberal global economy contributed to another global project of ordering that was reflected by a strongly advancing free trade, a revolution of the global financial markets and an enhanced global role for the Bretton Woods institutions.

In the mid of the 1990s, these three grand visions of global governance – human rights and democracy, security and safety, and neo-liberally conceived free trade and market economy – still appeared to be much more compatible with each other than they should be some years later. While free trade and market economy enjoyed an almost immaculate authority as the immediate gains of the historic turn among the larger population, human rights and democracy appeared as the more distant but shining fix stars of a dignified future of humanity. While security governance was not any more the sole global issue it still figured prominently as the necessary precondition to secure the integrity of rights and the free market. Despite the impressive and unrivalled American military might the dominating vision in the U.S. was yet vague and modest. High-profile analysts like Joseph Nye, a former assistant secretary of defense, concluded that, "[a]lthough the United States still has leverage over particular countries it has far less leverage over the system as a whole".[69] His advice was therefore to rely on "soft power" to shape global foreign policy rather than on military force. This line was taken up especially by Georg H. W. Bush's successor in office, President Bill Clinton (1993-2001). Convinced of the need to pursue the new global order under U.S. leadership like most American politicians, he preferred to pursue this aim however, along the avenues of free trade. Generally, integrated by a new wave of constitutionalism across the globe, free trade and human rights became further en-

69 Nye, "Soft Power," 1990, p. 156.

trenched as major visions of global ordering despite or even because of the mentioned setbacks in Africa and the Balkans. Optimists could even claim during the 1990s that "the idea of democratization of the entire world has turned into a mighty social, political force" reinforcing the inherently linked idea of human rights.[70] Having been a powerful rhetoric (and arguably less powerfully enforced norm) in U.S. foreign policy since long, especially the rights discourse enjoyed a veritable renaissance that somehow resembled the much shorter, similar hopeful historical moment at the end of World War II. In the wake of the post Cold War confusion, especially the rights-currency's value seemed to enjoy an unexpected increase almost 'overnight' that manifested institutionally in a number of major innovations like the implementation of the United Nations High Commissioner for Human Rights in 1993, the establishment of international criminal tribunals for the former Yugoslavia (1993) and Rwanda (1994), the emerging doctrinal foundation of the later acknowledged Responsibility to Protect and the Rome Statute (1998) paving the way for the International Criminal Court (ICC) in The Hague. Whereas only few believed that a real world democracy could soon emerge, a palpable will to end mass atrocities by means of internationally sanctioned military intervention or criminal prosecution contributed to a widespread believe in the prospects of the new global order of rights. Especially the ICC was expected to augur a "new world order based on the international rule of law" which itself was supposed to be reigned by human rights.[71] This was very much an understanding of international law that duplicated the substance of Western constitutionalism on the domestic level reinforcing a unitary vision of a morally charged international law that just needed to be developed into a matrix of effective global governance.

Similarly successful was the neoliberal agenda's global spread which was driven by the reformed Bretton-Woods institutions and a number of Western governments with the U.S. and the UK in the lead. Under the sign of the Washington Consensus and with the 1995-commenced World Trade

70 Walker, *National Security and Core Values in American History*, pp. 196 f., quoting Shultz, *Turmoil and Triumph: My years as Secretary of State*, 1993, p. 1106.

71 Koskenniemi, *The Politics of International Law*, 2011, p. 113.

Organization (WTO) neoliberal global governance took impressive shape across the globe.[72]

Against this background, the project of a new international security order was pursued from the hegemonic position the only country called to do so, the United States of America. Supposed to respond to the felt need for global ordering and to preserve the fruits of its righteous victory over the Soviets, the process was also reinforced by the particular interest of partisan players that realized a window of opportunity. These were in particular the neoconservative circles and think tanks in the U.S. and more generally what might be called the military(-intelligence)-industrial complex of which President Eisenhower had warned so staunchly in his farewell address to the American people.[73] In fact, when the Cold War was won serious steep cuts loomed on the side of the victors due to the dramatically decreased threat perception. In the light of shrinking budgets the end of the Soviet 'empire of evil' pointed therefore at a frightening peace for the former warriors and institutional spearheads of the Cold War. Not only could they claim little to have made it happen or at least foreseen, but rather it took away the foundational foe of the whole national security state which was feeding them. Victory, thus, threatened to turn into a

---

72 See Glaser, "Visions of the Good Society: Good Governance, Corruption and Public Law – Reflections on Selected Thai, German and Global Discourses," 2015, pp. 389 ff.

73 It is worth to comprehend the warning of the politician turned general who pointed to a development that has, arguably, seen a major boost by 9/11, a boost that no other single event beside the attack on Pearl Harbor ever had on the structure of the American state and society: "This conjunction of an immense military establishment and a large arms industry is new in the American experience. The total influence – economic, political, even spiritual – is felt in every city, every statehouse, every office of the federal government. We recognize the imperative need for this development. Yet we must not fail to comprehend its grave implications. Our toil, resources and livelihood are all involved; so is the very structure of our society. In the councils of government, we must guard against the acquisition of unwarranted influence, whether sought or unsought, by the military-industrial complex. The potential for the disastrous rise of misplaced power exists, and will persist. We must never let the weight of this combination endanger our liberties or democratic processes. We should take nothing for granted. Only an alert and knowledgeable citizenry can compel the proper meshing of the huge industrial and military machinery of defense with our peaceful methods and goals so that security and liberty may prosper together." (Eisenhower, "Farewell Radio and Television Address to the American People," 17 January, 1961, *Public Papers of the Presidents*, at http://www.presidency.ucsb.edu/ws/index.php?pid=12086).

"death knell for the CIA's war against godless Communism" which had become the company's very raison d'être.[74] These vested interests of particular actors notwithstanding, it can hardly surprise, however, that the sole remaining superpower aimed to enhance its global military standing in a strategic situation like those in which the US found itself in the early 1990s. Consequently, the project to deal with the new hegemony started as a diverse and open discourse in which the voices of the existing national-security-apparatus and their policy backers had a strong impetus that yet needed some time to bear fruits. Before a differentiated grand strategy emerged history offered the opportunity to take a first step in direction to affirm and consolidate the new U.S. hegemony in form of the Gulf War against Saddam's Iraq. In its wake and due to further military engagements during the subsequent years, the U.S. gained access to regions that were formerly closed or at least much less accessible to them whereas a workable grand strategy for the new "empire of security" has not yet been built. For some neoconservatives like Donald Rumsfeld America had thus not done enough during the 1990s to engage its historic mission of shaping the world; rather "America […] had taken a 'holiday from history' […]"[75]. Indeed, compared to the GWOT, the then dominating security vision might have appeared benign. President Bush's call for a new world order, most visibly stated in his January 29, 1991, State of the Union message, was initially still perceived as being much dependent on good relations to Russia and an indispensible role of the UN in facilitating it as a sort of Wilsonian Pax Americana.[76] Nevertheless, "Bush and Baker were not supporters, however, of the political parity that multilateralism implies, although the deference to that concept proved highly useful in forging a coalition against Saddam Hussein."[77] In other words, despite a lacking preference for multilateralism and principled parity among the nations, the thread of 'hegemonic multilateralism' was yet too young and thin to be solely spun from a unilateralist national-security fabric. Still, the U.S.

74 See Zulaika, *Terrorism: The Self-Fulfilling Prophecy*, p. 145.

75 Rumsfeld, "Terrorism is a Threat to National Security," 2007, p. 23. From this perspective there was thus a "period of strategic pause" in terms of military strategy which eventually ended with the Joint Vision 2020 preparing for asymmetric challenges to the "sole superpower" based on 'full spectrum dominance' making the U.S. forces ready for a 'global strike'. See Applegate, "Preparing for Asymmetry: As Seen Through The Lens of Joint Vision 2020," 2001, p. 10.

76 See Walker, *National Security and Core Values in American History*, p. 208.

77 Walker, *National Security and Core Values in American History*, p. 208.

needed to be compliant with the rules of an international order they had claimed to defend for decades while "Baker did not contemplate a return to Roosevelt's humanistic globalism"[78] at all. Furthermore, from the perspective of the more prudent promoters working for U.S. security dominance it was still more conceivable to firstly create, enhance or upgrade all the necessary pre- and marginal conditions for a more unilateral and aggressive shaping of global hegemony. This applies especially to the systematic opening of new dimensions of spatial control that could be established largely undisputed, particularly in Europe and the Middle East during these years. Yet, not-withstanding the discrete force of the inherent laws of timing, some groundbreaking normative claims were already made. During the 1990s, Secretary of State Madeleine Albright for instance ceaselessly reiterated that the United States were "the world's indispensable nation", a claim that was quickly taken up by American officials and commentators to describe the overarching role of the United States as the sole and uncontested superpower in the post-Cold War world.[79] Unequivocally, the claim was made with reference to the possibilities of a unilateral military based order:

> If we have to use force it is because we are America. We are the indispensable nation. We stand tall. We see further into the future.[80]

New in this statement was less the lofty tone of imperial self-confidence but the fact that it was raised among friends and in the absence of the Cold War restraints preventing its transformation into action. From this point of view, the future fullblown "degradation of international law" in the wake of 9/11 might be seen as the continuation and culmination of a process that was going back to the "degradation that can be just readily discerned in the earlier bombings of Libya in 1986 and Belgrade in 1999."[81] Military action, however, was still stronger connected to rights and democracy is-

---

78 Walker, *National Secutity and Core Values in American History*, p. 209.

79 Ruggie, "American Exceptionalism, Exemptionalism and Global Governance," 2005, p. 335. Clinton, in his second inaugural address 1997, reiterated the claim as well: "At the dawn of the 21st century […] America stands alone as the world's indispensable nation." Short before 9/11, Georg W. Bush went even a step further: "Our nation is chosen by God and commissioned by history to be a model for the world." See for these quotes Brzezinski, *Strategic Vision*, p. 44.

80 Blackburn, *The Imperial Presidency, the War on Terrorism, and the Revolutions of Modernity*, 2002, p. 9.

81 Ward, *Law, Text, Terror*, 2009, p. 13.

sues during the 1990s than it would be in the GWOT. Yet, in the early 1990s some neoconservative planers had already started to craft a 'purer' and more consequent agenda to achieve 'full spectrum' global security dominance. One of the first manifest indications of the project to develop a new military doctrine suiting the construction of a global order under the precepts of a hegemonic security paradigm is what has been called "Dick Cheney's masterwork", the *Defense Planning Guidance Draft* of 1992.[82] Very explicitly it introduces the idea of a possible necessity of unilateral military action, the preemptive use of military force, and the possession of a U.S. nuclear arsenal strong enough to deter the development of nuclear programs elsewhere including the option to use the bomb.[83] Around a decade later "Cheney's masterwork" should become the first draft of the Bush doctrine of 2002.[84]

Occasionally, however, even some more visible agents of the official doctrine made clear how serious they were about the new security order that had already started to take shape. Telling is an episode that reveals a stunning willingness to apply the merciless logic of warfare on Iraq's peacetime order for pure reason-of-state considerations at the expense of huge humanitarian costs: In a public debate in 1996, then Secretary of State Madeleine Albright responded to the question whether the death of 500.000 Iraqi children would be worth as a price of upholding the wartime blockade of Iraq after such a long time that the U.S. had won the war: "I think that this is a very hard choice, but we think the price is worth it."[85] This bold statement is a remarkable affirmation of the U.S.' determination to lead globally while resting lastly on a consequent reason-of-state based security paradigm at all costs.[86] Notably, in 1996 the realities of global or-

82 Hoffmann, "American Exceptionalism: The New Version," 2009, p. 228.

83 See Hoffmann, "American Exceptionalism: The New Version," p. 228.

84 See Hoffmann, "American Exceptionalism: The New Version," p. 228.

85 Albright, Madeleine, "CBS, 60 Minutes," 12 May 1996, quoted from Benoist, *Carl Schmitt Today: Terrorism, 'Just' War', and the State of Emergency*, p. 31. Legal basis of the blockade were the UNSCR 661 and 687.

86 See on the other side Dennis Halliday, the then responsible UN coordinator occupying a position on the Assistant Secretary-General level of the UN, who resigned in 1998 over the Iraq sanctions which he qualified as "genocidal". Later he explained his decision by the following statement: "I often have to explain why I resigned from the United Nations after a 30 year career […]. In reality there was no choice, and there remains no choice. You all would have done the same had you been occupying my seat as head of the UN Humanitarian program in Iraq. I was

dering where still a long way away from the grand transformation that should be levered by the GWOT. The emergence of a much tighter, dynamic and pervasive security paradigm under the precepts of CT was not even yet in sight. This raises the question how terrorism and CT actually figured during the 1990s on the national security agenda. In fact, before the end of the Cold War they had already formed essential parts of the U.S. national security and foreign policy agenda of the Reagan administration when terrorism was targeted as being linked to communist insurrection and 'narco'-politics. Despite being already "central to the selfimage of the American nation allowing it to define itself against its enemies"[87] under Reagan, CT did, however, not immediately start to transcend the confines of its established function when the Cold War ended. Although Islamic terrorism was a widely recognized security issue during the late 1980s and early 1990s it was far from becoming a central target of American national security planning. On the contrary, while the risk of a backlash of the US-sponsored *jihadi* buildup in Afghanistan quickly manifested after the Soviets withdrew in 1989, terrorism was still perceived mainly as a threat in form of Latin American 'narco-terrorism', famously personified by Pablo Escobar. On the other side, when the Cold War ended, some of the conflicts that had been particularly shaped by terrorism in other parts of the world had already ended or were running towards an end. In other words, CT was not new as an important element of the national security agenda but lacked a clearly defined and prominent place at the end of the millennium.

When George W. Bush entered office, all essential threads to spin the new national security were nevertheless at place while they still had to be picked up to weave the totally new fabric of what would become the

driven to resignation because I refused to continue to take Security Council orders, [...] that had imposed and sustained genocidal sanctions on the innocent of Iraq. I did not want to be complicit. I wanted to be free to speak out publicly about this crime. And above all, my innate sense of justice was and still is outraged by the violence that UN sanctions have brought upon, and continues to bring upon, the lives of children, families [...]. There is no justification for killing the young people of Iraq, not the aged, not the sick, [...]. [...] and international law has no provision for the disproportionate and murderous consequences of the ongoing UN embargo – for well over 12 long years." Halliday, "2003 Gandhi International Peace Award Acceptance Speech", accessible at https://gandhifoundation.org/2003/01/30/2003-peace-award-denis-halliday-2/.

87 See Aksan and Bailes, "Introduction," 2012, p. 3.

GWOT. Yet, both of its central components, a U.S. 'empire of security' at the top of the global order and CT as its core, had neither been readily developed nor were they inherently interconnected. Nevertheless, the paths taken on the terrain of national security almost from the onset of the post-Cold War decade would prove to be of crucial importance for the later implementation of the hegemonic global security order.[88] To this avail, the Bush administration could assemble several of the set pieces of the security legacy of the 1980s and 1990s, put them together on the basis of an already impressively entrenched and consolidated geopolitical U.S. position and finally manage the construction of a global empire of security with the U.S. as its hegemon. When Bush entered office, he started to realize what conservative think tanks openly expected from his foreign policy – irrespective of any international law constraints:

> An unprecedentedly dominant United States [...] is in the unique position of being able to fashion its own foreign policy. After a decade of Prometheus playing pygmy, the first task of the new [George W. Bush] Administration is precisely to assert American freedom of action.[89]

Indeed, President George W. Bush went on to endorse the policy of unilateral action, preemption and regime change long before the attacks of 9/11.[90] Prior to 9/11, his government seemed only to lack the necessary political leverage to realize its plans.[91]. In this sense, the newly implemented security order is not at all the sole result of the 9/11 incident rather than the final breakthrough of a longer emerging 'imperial grand strategy'.[92] This breakthrough was initiated by a deep re-formation of older normative and strategic visions, enabled by a geopolitically entrenched position and catalyzed by the 9/11 events. Now, a newly crafted security paradigm was able to be driven at the heart of both, the constitutional order of the U.S. and the global governance agenda – with CT as the new security pivot. Crucial for this development was the increasing terrorist

88 See for theses continuities Patman, "Globalization, the End of the Cold War and the Doctrine of National Security," 2006, p. 16.

89 Charles Krauthammer, quoted in Daalder and Lindsay, *America Unbound: The Bush Revolution in Foreign Policy*, 2003, p. 12.

90 See Wrage, "The Department of Defense and the Department of State: Out of Balance and into Trouble," 2008, p. 21.

91 See Wirls, "Hidden in Plain Sight: The Bush Military Buildup," 2008, pp. 99 ff.

92 See Patnam, "Globalization, the End of the Cold War and the Doctrine of National Security," p. 16.

threat in form of *jihadi* Islam that had started to take shape on a serious level at the end of the 1990s, for example with the World Islamic Front's 1998 announcement "Jihad Against Jews and Crusaders", and the attacks on the Kenyan embassy and the USS Cole.[93] From a constructivist point of view this offered the chance for national security planers to eventually fully replace the communist threat of the Cold War time with a new functional threat. – Now, "[t]he fear of the terrorist serve[d] as a displacement for the nuclear threat and [a justification for the] double standard of the existing system".[94] After 9/11, the fight against the 'new terrorism' would eventually not only justify the own nuclear arsenal but also re-regulate post-Cold War proliferation according to the rationale that no other power than those accepted by the U.S. should possess nuclear weapons. Here, the manifold connections between the Cold War and the GWOT become especially evident. The unwillingly produced terror threat from the former Cold War battlefields in the Middle Eastern and the well-established CT stance that had been developed against Latin-American 'narco-terrorism' were the nods that had just to be connected. It needed, however, some time until CT could eventually mutate into something much bigger than before, namely the GWOT:

> If, with Clinton, terrorism turned into an autonomous prime mover of enormous consequences, affecting national policy and legislation, with President George W Bush, the War on Terror has *become the sole mission of American politics*. If with Reagan and Clinton terrorism has been 'naturalized' into a constant risk that is omnipresent, a sort of chaotic principle always ready to strike and create havoc, with Bush, it became the prime raison d'état, the one enemy against which society must now marshal all its resources in an unending struggle.[95]

It needs to be reiterated in this context that even if terrorism had prominently figured on the national security agenda during the 1980s and 1990s, the gap to the post 9/11-attention represents a whole gulf.[96]

Significant is also the change pertaining to the normative fabric of the whole web of global governance which was essentially consisting of 'security', 'rights' and 'free trade' threads and the established international

---

93 See Mastors, *Breaking Al-Qaeda: Psychological and Operational Techniques*, 2014, pp. 511 ff.

94 Zulaika, *Terrorism: The Self-Fulfilling Prophecy*, p. 170.

95 Zulaika, *Terrorism: The Self-Fulfilling Prophecy*, pp. 5 f. Italics by the author.

96 See Hastedt, "Washington Politics, Homeland Security, and the Struggle Against Global Terrorism," 2014, p. 397.

rule of law. Now, the former steady state between the three competing orders changed substantially with the rights-thread becoming much 'thinner' in relation to the others. 'Rights' should be understood in this context as representing the whole range of constitutional values of secular humanistic governance that form the identity of Western constitutionalism and figured strongly in international law as well. Here it is the nexus of rights, the rule of law and democracy that has been mostly affected by the profound transformations catalyzed by 9/11 compared to the prior status and standing. While the national security and the neo-liberal governance regime entered into a perfect marriage in the wake of 9/11, the fate of the 'rights revolution' was less fortunate. Soon after the GWOT was launched much hope for the further enhancement and even the preservation of the status quo in terms of rights governance yielded to the new realities ascending. With them, the former utopian faith and "triumphalist confidence"[97] in a global rights regime to come was almost gone.[98] Largely the discursive space that has formerly been occupied by a staunch rights-optimism became intruded by a wave of patriotic self-assurance in domestic debates, accompanied by almost ubiquitous expressions of compassion and loyalty on the side of allies and the marvel of few over the decisiveness with which the new empire of security became constructed. This construction was very much staged as a zero-sum game, not only with respect to the demand of unconditioned loyalty but also the affected normative orders and principles, namely democracy, rights and the rule of law which were supposed to be superseded in the interests of security. In consequence, the attacks had "crushed all the optimism which a newly envisaged age of human rights had brought a decade earlier."[99]

The way in which the response to 9/11 and its repercussions on the international legal-political system had changed the world will be assessed in more detail below. At this point it needs to be acknowledged how decisive the consequential transformation has been staged to conceive the force with which the change came:

97 Tamanaha, *On the Rule of Law: History, Politics, Theory*, 2004, p. 1.

98 See for such optimistic visions during the 1990s Pogge, *Realizing Rawls*, 1989, pp. 242 ff; Téson, "The Kantian Theory of International Law," 1992, pp. 84 and 97.

99 Ward, *Law Text, Terror*, p. 11, referring to Steyn, "Guantanamo Bay: The Legal Black Hole," p. 6.

> Those of us who have lived through these challenging times have been changed by them. We've come to know truths that we will never question: Evil is real, and it must be opposed. [...] In a single instant, we realized that this will be a decisive decade in the history of liberty – that we have been called to a unique role in human events. Rarely has the world faced a choice more clear or consequential.[100]

In fact, according to this new orthodoxy the carefully and deliberately crafted paradigm shift follows almost naturally from an inevitable, powerfully invoked turn of eras. In fact, the actual dimensions of the 'empire of security' that was rising from the ashes of the Twin Towers fully justifies the assessment that

> [t]he crisis unleashed by the events of 11th September is one that is global and all encompassing. [...] More than any other international crisis yet seen, it affects the multiplicity of life's levels, political, economic, cultural and psychological.[101]

Indeed, President Bush's claim that "rarely has the world faced a choice more clear or consequential" than in the wake of 9/11 was echoed also by those who analysed the developments more critically, nevertheless agreeing that "9/11 has had a series of major effects on world politics"[102] – even to the extent that "September 11 has given us a planet we barely recognize"[103]. Reflecting this change from the perspective of constitutional core values a leading American international lawyer concludes:

> Since September 11, we have almost literally left the light and entered the shadows of a new age of global pessimism, in which we have realized with alarm that all of the interdependent dimensions of the age of globalization could be equally turned against us.[104]

Remarkably, major political actors appreciated specifically the *constructive potential* of this watershed in global ordering. While Donald Rumsfeld stated that 9/11 had created "the kind of opportunities that World War

---

100 Bush, State of the Union Address, January 29, 2002, accessible at http://edition.cnn.com/2002/ALLPOLITICS/01/29/bush.speech.txt/.

101 See Halliday, *Two Hours that Shook the World: September 11, 2001: Causes and Consequences*, 2013, p. 31, quoted from English*, Terrorism: How to Respond,* p. 94.

102 Smith, "The Concept of Security in a Globalizing World," p. 46.

103 See Amis, *The Second Plane, September 11: 2001-2007*, p. 21, quoted from English, *Terrorism: How to Respond*, p. 94.

104 See Koh, "On American Exceptionalism," 2003, p. 1496.

II offered to refashion the world"[105], Condoleezza Rice reportedly told senior members of the National Security Council to

> think about 'how do you capitalize on these opportunities' to fundamentally change American doctrine, and the shape of the world, in the wake of September 11.[106].

The National Security Strategy 2002 repeats accordingly that: "The events of September 11, 2001, […] *opened vast, new opportunities*."[107] In another public address, Condoleezza Rice elaborated on the impact of the transformative moment that 9/11 offered more differentiated, claiming that

> there is one […] important truth […]: an earthquake of the magnitude of 9/11 can shift the tectonic plates of international politics. The international system has been in flux since the collapse of Soviet power. Now it is possible – indeed, probable – that that transition is coming to an end. If that is right, if the collapse of the Soviet Union and 9/11 bookend a major shift in international politics, then this is a period not just of grave danger, but of enormous opportunity. Before the clay is dry again, America and our friends […] must move decisively to take advantage of these new opportunities. This is, then, a period akin to 1945 to 1947, […] to create a new balance of power that favored freedom.[108]

Consequently, 9/11 actually emerged into a major turning point of world politics and global ordering due to the fact that it had provided a stunningly successfully exploited

> unique opportunity […] to reshape the rules and norms of the international order, with or without the support of long-standing allies.[109]

Technically, that has to be reiterated, this whole process was wrapped in and enabled by a DDM model based CT paradigm labeled as the GWOT.

---

105 Donald Rumsfeld, "Secretary Rumsfeld Interview with the New York Times," *New York Times*, October 12, 2001.

106 Condoleezza Rice, quoted in Lemann, "The Next World Order: The Bush Administration May Have a Brand-New Doctrine of Power," *New Yorker*, April 1, 2002, accessible http://www.newyorker.com/fact/content/articles/020401fa_FACT1).

107 The White House,"The National Security Strategy of the United States of America 2002," 2002, p. 28. Italics by the author.

108 Condoleezza Rice, "Remarks by National Security Advisor Condoleezza Rice on Terrorism and Foreign Policy," April 29, 2002, accessible at https://georgewbush-whitehouse.archives.gov/news/releases/2002/04/20020429-9.html.

109 Lee, *US Hegemony and International Legitimacy: Norms, Power and Followership in the Wars on Iraq*, 2010, p. 2.

Its actual impact on the global order shall be analyzed in more detail below.

## *II. Paradigm Shift*

Even if it might be evident that the historic opportunity of the 9/11 incident has actually led to a change of "not interstitial but architectural"[110] nature, it is useful for the purpose of this essay to qualify and quantify the nature and weight of the change pertaining to some selected aspects.

A first issue is the changing balance between the above-described competing normative regimes and visions of global ordering. Deep transformative change in form of a veritable paradigm shift manifests here in the American domestic constitutional order on the one hand and the country's commitment to the international order on the other. Quickly this process triggered similar changes in international law and the constitutional order of numerous other states across the globe.[111] Given the importance of the US as the global hegemon and the leading force of the GWOT focus is however put on the transformations taking place here. In this context, it is important to acknowledge the inherent ambiguity of global legal regimes from an American perspective that is directed at preserving global hegemony. From this point of view global legal regimes are perceived and treated as both constraining and enabling alike. In terms of hegemony it is notably not only military or economic power or global presence that makes the American might but very much also its 'normative capital', the fact that the US are in the lead in defining almost any form of global legal orders. It might be argued with respect to the global balances of power that arguably all new legal regimes with global reach tend to contribute in the last instance relatively more to US interests than to those of other powers. After all, as Isaiah Wilson III stated, "[a]s a hegemon of the prevailing international system, the United states is not merely a player on the stage of international affairs: it also shapes and defines the system."[112] And it

---

110 Koh, "America's Jekyll-and-Hyde Exceptionalism," p. 125.

111 See for selected European countries Oehmichen, *Terrorism, and Anti-Terror Legislation: The Terrorized Legislator? A Comparison of Counter-Terror Legislation and Its Implication for Human Rights in the Legal Systems of the United Kingdom, Spain, Germany and France*, 2009, pp. 384 ff.

112 Wilson III, "Military Intervention and International Law," 2008, p. 69.

might be added that the law is indeed one of the distinct substances by which this happens. In this context it is important to perceive that it is particularly the 'West' which, more than any other regional or global power in the history of mankind, made use of the law as a matrix to extend and entrench hegemonic power. Consequently, modern law is almost purely rooted in the West which still enjoys the interpretational supremacy and dominates its reproduction. It is this combination of military and economic power on the one hand and a particular norm-based power on the other that ensures the ability of the U.S. Empire to define the rules of the game to a large extent. Exactly this so crafted position creates the important margin between the U.S. and other aspirants for hegemony where it comes to the capitalization of global legal regimes. This is also true for human right regimes where the ambiguity in terms of hegemonic interest is most intense. On the one hand, human rights contribute well to the U.S. hegemonic interests as more recently demonstrated by the 2011 U.S. dominated multilateral intervention in Libya (see UNSCR 1973). On the other hand, the implementation of the GWOT was marked by a significant and partly sustaining shift to diminish the global rights regime. In fact, different from the neoliberal discourse and regime[113], the domestic and interna-

113 Significant are the close entanglements in the post 9/11 evolution of the neoliberal order and the GWOT that are manifest in a boost of privatization of security services. During the 1990s, a large number of private security firms had already started to engage in major security tasks including counterterrorism, ranging from hostage negotiations, target hardening and -protection, private investigations to identify terrorists and their locations up to paramilitary operations to release kidnap victims and even ferreting out terrorists in pre-emptive missions. See Wardlaw, *Political Terrorism: Theory, Tactics and Counter-Measures*, p. 196. In the wake of an advancing neoliberal agenda in the 1990s, this privatization became constantly propelled to new dimensions when the process became strongly accelerated and entrenched after 9/11. Now, security and profit rationales amalgamized on a totally new level. Significant is the change in comparison to the 1970s and 1980s, where the employment of private CT forces, especially in Latin America, was largely a reaction to what has been perceived as a failure of state organized CT. Today, privately organized and exercised CT is officially complementing the state's CT mission. Main contract partners of the state are not anymore private individuals frustrated by the state's inefficiency to accommodate their individual interests but governments and government contracted companies hiring privates to support or even execute the public mission of maintaining security as formerly entrusted to the state. These contractors are one of the major problems in the context of SRC based communication related CT which is evident concerning the handling of detainees and the interrogation of suspects by

tional rights order proved in large parts – albeit not in total – detrimental to the objectives and strategies of the GWOT whose rhetoric did partly reject and partly refer to rights and democracy.[114] Especially the implementation of the GWOT has been managed by largely delineating the grand national security strategy and its definition of the national interest from human rights. When the U.S. took the historic opportunity to "reshape world order" in 2001, this process was indeed consequently accompanied by a determined move to supersede or suspend central areas of the established right discourses and regimes. This process already started short before 9/11 when the Bush administration took over. Almost immediately after taking office, President George W. Bush started to redraw the lines of the American participation in international human right regimes or those other international legal regimes that serve a humanist or peace cause respectively. One of the most remarkable expressions of this trend became the hitherto unprecedented practice of 'un-signing' international treaties like the Kyoto Protocol and the ICC statute. Auspiciously, already in April 2001, the U.S. also withdrew from the United Nations Commission on Human Rights and confirmed its refusal to ratify the International Convention on the Prohibition of the Development, Production and Stockpiling of Bacteriological and Toxin Weapons and on their Destruction in November 2001 which had already been ratified by 144 countries.[115] Only

---

such contractors. Significant for the success of the amalgamization of neoliberal and security notions of international regime building is the different reaction of international law towards terrorism on the one side and mercenaries on the other. Since 9/11 terrorism has shifted obviously into the very center of international law with the terrorists as the 'new pirates', thus enemies of mankind par excellence. They are standing outside the law in a very distinct way allowing for their capture or killing by bounty hunters and extra-legal elimination but state-run robot programs. The epidemic increase in the proliferation of mercenaries in exactly the same scenarios however remained on the other side almost completely beyond the focus of international law despite its vast destructive potentials with respect to peace and the rights of the peoples affected by their uncontrolled action as witnessed by the Blackwater scandals.

114 See for this multilayered and largely ideological character of the legitimizing discourses of the GWOT Koskenniemi, "The Subjective Dangers of Projects of World Community," 2012, p. 9. According to him the GWOT "may have been designated to counter a global threat – but despite the universal values it invokes, it is hard not to conceive the way it has shifted institutional priorities in favor of the developed world."

115 See Benoist, *Carl Schmitt Today: Terrorism, 'Just' War, and the State of Emergency*, p. 39.

some days later, the U.S. unilaterally revoked the Antiballistic Missile Treaty of 1972 limiting the deployment of anti-missile defenses.[116] Since 9/11, U.S. international law-exceptionalism grew then not only in significance[117] but became an integral part of the construction of the new empire of security while "the debate on the globalization of rights seemed to give way to the practice of globalization of violations".[118]

Among the various measures taken in this direction, some are outstanding. The most aggressive delineation from a robust international human rights regime became manifest in the U.S.' "extraordinary vendetta"[119] against the International Criminal Court[120] that culminated in an unprecedented degradation of international human rights law in form of the so called 'Hague Invasion Act'. This *American Service-Members' Protection Act* of 2002 particularly authorizes the U.S. President to use "all means necessary and appropriate to bring about the release of any U.S. or allied personnel being detained or imprisoned by, on behalf of, or at the request of the ICC." It allows, in other words, a military rescue mission of American soldiers having been indicted by and committed to the ICC due to suspected gross human rights violations.

A second outstanding expression of the trend to set an end even to a sham compliance with international human rights protection is the suspension of central parts of the Geneva Convention. An indication of how deep all these changes affected the domestic human right culture in America as a true turn of eras is the fact that some leading American scholars of hu-

116 See Benoist, *Carl Schmitt Today: Terrorism, 'Just' War, and the State of Emergency*, p. 39.

117 In this context it might be remembered that the U.S. had, for example, already reserved the right to be the sole judge of what constituted a war of aggression and of the rules of recognition of other states on occasion of the signing of the 1928 Kellogg-Briand-Pact, after which it also had refused to join the League of Nations.

118 Palma, "The Possible Contributions of International Civil Society to the Protection of Human Rights," 2012, p. 78.

119 See Hoffmann, "American Exceptionalism: The New Version," p. 229.

120 Notably, the hostilities towards the ICC had been initiated even before Bush took office when the Congress was already in Republican hands and increasingly moved by the reemerged neoconservative faction among them. Here it is of great irony that the ICC ratification was dead on arrival basically because of a feared giving away of American's constitutional due process guarantees.

man rights and international law saw the human rights era ending – without expressing too much regret.[121]

At this point of the argumentation, the decisive withdrawal from central rights-related international law regimes that accompanied the unleashing of the GWOT is considered to sufficiently demonstrate the deliberate preparation and eventual creation of a major shift in the global order. It is, thus, not deemed necessary to go into all the violations of domestic constitutional and international law by different practices that have surfaced as integral elements in the GWOT. One of its architects, John Yoo, himself infamous for his contribution to the 'torture memos', referred tellingly to the basic attitude underlying these practices in the title of his memoirs as "*War By Other Means: An Insider's Account of the War on Terror*" (2006) resounding both Clausewitz as well as the old maxim of *inter arma enim silent leges*. Even if these practices might amount to rendering international legality to become nothing less than a "gigantic irrelevance" as a British newspaper concluded[122], the above-described delineation from international regimes directly or indirectly protecting rights shows already how decisive the project to reshape the global order has been initiated as early as 2001.

However, the expansion of the new security order did not stop with neutralizing central human right regimes – let alone the widespread employment of practices in direct violation of them – but also superseded other core principles of the international legal order. Remarkable is how directly, undisguisedly and assertively the principle of state sovereignty became targeted and brushed aside by means of a totally redefined principle of preventive war against all "entities [...] hostile to freedom, democracy, and other U.S. interests". In the words of the U.S. National Security Strategy 2005:

> Allowing opponents to strike first [...] is unacceptable. Therefore, the United States must defeat the most dangerous challenges early and at a safe distance, before they are allowed to mature.

This new form of preemption allowed precautionary attacks for which it would no longer be required to wait for the threat to materialize. This doctrinal change was the key to pull out all the legal stops for unleashing the

121 See Koh, "On American Exceptionalism," pp. 129 f.

122 *Sunday Telegraph*, February 29, 2004, quoted from Ward, *Law, Text, Terror*, p. 11.

GWOT against any adversary. The man who had suggested the blueprint for the corresponding grand military strategy almost ten years ago, Dick Cheney, concretized the preemption-rule in November 2001 in an extreme way with his infamous 1%-rule. According to it, military attacks would be appropriate, if there would exist only a one-percent chance of a prevention of a nuclear terrorist attack on the U.S.[123] Yet, even without this extreme reading, the new doctrine of preemption was radical. The manifesting national security strategy built on it represented an unleashing of all those forces neoconservative advocates wanted to see. With preemption defined by terms like 'early', 'at a safe distance' and 'before they are allowed to mature', and the highly questionable procedures how such a threat probability has actually been assessed in the context of the 2003 war against Iraq[124], it becomes obvious how much the new doctrine challenges the common understanding of Art. 51 of the UN Charter.[125] Effectively, the established international rule of law pertaining to collective security and the question of starting a war against another sovereign state was single-handedly replaced by a hyper sensitive risk assessment on U.S. terms. Manifesting in the invasion of Iraq, the new doctrine materialized as another "transitional moment".[126] While the world could not do much more than taking notice of the change, many American observers reacted with an attitude of outright triumphalism claiming that in a one-superpower world American exceptionalism and double standards would be a good

123 See Bzostek, *Why Not Preempt?: Security, Law, Norms and Military Activities*, 2016, p. 205.

124 In the days following September 11, the US government announced a White Paper by September 18 that was supposed to outline the evidence which it claimed to have against Al Qaeda proofing that the latter had committed the attacks. While Britain did release such a paper-based on infamous distortions of the facts, the U.S. eventually refrained and never distributed the announced evidence. – Finally, the administration had started the GWOT without even fulfilling the self-defined and self-composed yardstick of its legitimacy to do so, and this, most notably, without any consequence. See Kellner, *From 9/11 to Terror War: The Dangers of the Bush Legacy*, p. 59.

125 See also Chesterman, "The Spy who Came in From the Cold War: Intelligence and International Law," 2006, p. 1105; Fukuyama, *America at the Crossroads*, p. 83. See for the general problems with the whole spectrum of variations pertaining to preventive wars Buchanan, *Human Rights, Legitimacy and the Use of Force*, 2010, pp. 280 ff.

126 Stromseth, "Law and Force After Iraq: A Transitional Moment," 2003, pp. 628-642.

thing, something to which the rest of the world ought better get used to.[127] Robert Kaplan suggested in this sense, that America should use its power unilaterally to "manage an unruly world" leaving behind "the so-called international community," especially the United Nations, with its "antiquated power arrangement."[128]

However, the crafting of a new order through the GWOT is not sufficiently sketched by focusing only on the impressive acts of diminishing of competing normative orders by unilateral acts. Remarkable are also the 'constructive' innovations with respect to international organizations like the NATO, OAS, and UN. In response to the 9/11 attack, *for the first time* in their history both NATO and the OAS invoked the respective mutual defense clauses declaring the 9/11 terroristic attacks as military attacks against all NATO/OAS member states.[129] This move was not only unprecedented like so many others in the context of the 9/11 transformation but also exemplifies the paradigm shift at a critical juncture: the connection of CT with warfare. By applying the mutual defense clause the NATO and the OAS sanctioned and reinforced the central conception of CT as the conduct of warfare including all its problematic vagueness with respect to the adversary as well as the legitimate target against which it was supposed to be waged. In consequence, without any international resistance, the U.S. had succeeded in taking the first major step in establishing a new global order under the signs of a 'war against terrorism'. The U.S. has, indeed, been remarkably successful in both, defining conceptionally and leading practically the international efforts to combat terrorism in terms of military engagement. Unprecedented is also the further reaction of the United Nations. Initiated by the U.S. they quickly created an "international web of mechanisms for battling terrorism" in form of a considerably diversified arsenal of terror-directed law, which, "unlike international human rights law, has teeth".[130] Moreover and most notably, already on 28 September 2001 and

---

127 See Koh, "*On American Exceptionalism*," pp. 129 f.

128 Kaplan, "Supremacy by Stealth: Ten Rules for Managing the World," 2003, pp. 66-83.

129 Gray, *International Law and the Use of Force*, 2008, p. 193; Mendelsohn, *Combating Jihadism: American Hegemony and Interstate Cooperation in the War on Terrorism,* 2009, p. 94.

130 See Schepelle, "The Migration of Anti-Constitutional Ideas: The Post-9/11 Globalization of Public Law and the International State of Emergency," 2009, p. 350.

> with hardly any recorded debate, the Security Council passed Resolution 1373, a far-reaching and essentially legislative resolution that, *for the first time* in the Security Council's history, used a binding authority under Chapter VII of the UN charter to require all member states to change their domestic laws in very specific ways.[131]

With this resolution, imposing "unprecedentedly detailed and intrusive demands on states for cooperation and assistance"[132] the UNSC departed "radically […] from its previous practice and language"[133].

These changes on the level of the international order – including the subsequent introduction of legal regimes putting the global streams of people, money and goods under close scrutiny – were accompanied by domestic changes all around the world. Almost everywhere the 9/11 momentum led to an expansion of the realm of security at the expense of rights.[134] In the U.S., however, these changes were more swift and encompassing than in most other Western countries.

Altogether, the fast, vast and forceful shifts that created the GWOT regime reflect a stunning determination and impact with which CT was made the very pivot of the national security agenda for the purpose of expanding and valorizing this same agenda as the vehicle of a new 'reason of empire'.

On the domestic level of the U.S., this trend is exemplified by concerted efforts to strengthen the federal executive to a formerly unknown degree, including a huge buildup of the national security apparatus. A few examples shall be mentioned among all the sweeping changes that were implemented for the purpose of adjusting the established CT-infrastructure but affected the entire national security community in depth, indirectly affecting also the balances of power in general.

---

131 See Schepelle, "The Migration of Anti-Constitutional Ideas: The Post-9/11 Globalization of Public Law and the International State of Emergency," p. 350.

132 See Roberts, "Intervention: Beyond 'Dictatorial Interference'," 2006, p. 176.

133 See Cohen, *Globalization and Sovereignty: Rethinking Legality, Legitimacy, and Constitutionalism*, 2012, p. 272.

134 See Oehmichen, *Terrorism, and Anti-Terror Legislation: The Terrorized Legislator?*, p. 384, who identifies for selected European countries an "apparent fragility of basic human right principles" in the wake of 9/11, a shift marked by the "tendency […] to ignore human rights […]" and introduce new "drastic measures" and issues of debate "that have long been considered as obsolete". See also the country-specific contributions in Ramraj, Hor, and Roach (eds.), *Global Anti-Terror Law and Policy*, 2012, pp. 273-634.

As a direct response to the 9/11 attacks in general and to their qualification as an intelligence failure in particular, the Intelligence Reform and Terrorism Prevention Act of 2004 charted a major reorganization of the *intelligence community* at large. Accompanied by a huge increase of the intelligence budget of at least[135] almost a half over the next years[136] it represents its most far-reaching structural reorganization since the establishment of institutionalized national intelligence in the U.S. by the National Security Act 1947 after WW II.[137] Among other changes, the 2004 Act created the Office of the Director of National Intelligence (DNI) charged with the oversight of all (originally 16, now) 17 intelligence agencies. As the country's new prime intelligence official the DNI replaces the Director of Central Intelligence[138] in this function having the National Counterterrorism Center (NCTC) at his direct disposal.[139] More interesting than the question to which extent the reform has actually created any real integration and efficient centralization of power at top of the intelligence community[140] are the *claims* made by it. In this sense, the reform exemplifies most notably an encompassing redefinition of national intelligence *in the frame of CT*. Secondly, the reform was explicitly formulated in this regard as a *global vision* pertaining to which the new DNI stated that his office would be a "*globally networked and integrated intelligence enterprise*".[141]

135 The budget is classified but can be roughly estimated.

136 See Betts, *Enemies of Intelligence: Knowledge and Power in American National Security*, 2007, p. 126.

137 See Betts, *Enemies of Intelligence: Knowledge and Power in American National Security*, p. 126.

138 See for the reform in more detail Betts, *Enemies of Intelligence: Knowledge and Power in American National Security,* pp. 150 ff. Until 2005, the Director of the CIA concomitantly served as the head of the intelligence community (DCI). With the new office of the DNI, the Director of the CIA (D/CIA) became subordinated to this new office.

139 See Betts, *Enemies of Intelligence: Knowledge and Power in American National Security*, pp. 126 f. and 146 f.; Ransom, *Intelligence and National Security: A Reference Handbook*, 2007, p. 21.

140 See Betts, *Enemies of Intelligence: Knowledge and Power in American National Security*, pp. 150 ff.

141 While much earlier formulated, the vision *of a globally networked and integrated intelligence enterprise* was more recently reiterated as the title of the Office of the Director of National Intelligence's Vision 2015, see Office of the Director of National Intelligence Vision 2015, http://www.au.af.mil/au/awc/awcgate/dni/vision_2015_july08.pdf. Instead of the old restriction to the clandestine business of intelligence, the new intelligence apparatus embraces its global mission like an

Yet, beyond the introduction of new offices and interesting rhetoric claims there were also considerable changes in terms of the intelligence community's 'real' power: Almost all of America's intelligence units grew significantly in size while being legislatively supported by the USA Patriot Act and the Intelligence Reform Bill which both enhanced their scope of competencies.[142] An especially visible structural change is, furthermore, reflected by the establishment of the Department of Homeland Security not even one year after the attack. With it, the Congress mandated the largest reorganization in the history of the U.S. administration since the Defense Department was created in 1947.[143] It brought together twenty-two agencies in a single administrative structure with some 170.000 employers.[144] Another cornerstone of the intelligence community, the NSA, was structurally largely enhanced as well. While the NSA's budget has been "dramatically increased every year since 9/11", its manpower has also been "shooting upward".[145] In this context, the huge clandestine domestic and international eavesdropping activities in the aftermath of 9/11 might be mentioned.[146] Significant change was also experienced by the CIA as the classical centerpiece of the American intelligence community: With 9/11 its institutional profile was substantially reformed to create an organization focused on waging counter-terrorist operations while its manpower and budget were largely increased. In the words of former CIA deputy director Morell:

> Never before had CIA refocused so abruptly and dramatically as we did after 9/11. The number of officers working on terrorism – including contractors – more than tripled, and the dollars flowing to the terrorism problem jumped even more.[147]

---

economic enterprise resounding notions of a perfect cooperation of the security apparatus and the neoliberal forces of privatization that emerged after 9/11 to an unprecedented degree.

142 See Davis, "Intelligence Analysts and Policymakers: Benefits and Dangers of Tensions in the Relationship," 2006, pp. 106 f.

143 See Ransom, *Intelligence and National Security: A Reference Handbook*, p. 21.

144 See Ransom, *Intelligence and National Security: A Reference Handbook*, p. 21.

145 See Aid, "Prometheus Embattled: A Post 9/11 Report Card on the National Security Agency," 2014, p. 424.

146 See Aid, "Prometheus Embattled: A Post 9/11 Report Card on the National Security Agency," pp. 431 ff.

147 See Morrell, *The Great War of our Time: The CIA's Fight Against Terrorism, From Al Qa'ida to ISIS*, 2015, p. 73.

At the same time, the post 9/11 revamp of national security profoundly affected the military, too. One commentator put the change in a nutshell answering the question "what did 9/11 change": "[W]hile very little changed in actual military policy and planning, politically everything changed."[148] Political change, however, was accompanied by significant structural change. Most obvious are the changes in terms of defense spending of that nation in the world that already spends by far the biggest part of its budget and by far the biggest budget in absolute terms on the military. From 2000 to 2008 military expenditures increased by 66% while the president's request for 2009 raised them up to 77%.[149] This alone meant a military spending that was above the average of the Cold War years and soon crossing the mark of 50% of the world's overall military expenditures[150], let alone the subsequent increases. In fact:

> Within a few years, the Bush administration's total military spending reached and then exceeded the peak spending (adjusted for inflation) of the Cold War era, including the Korean War, the Vietnam War, and the Reagan buildup.[151]

Moreover, despite the abovementioned claim that policy and planning were less affected by the changes, the grand transformation is in fact also reflected in terms of strategy and the corresponding institutional setup. Embedded in a new national security strategy that had been initiated in parts before the 9/11 incident, significant institutional changes took place. They have to be seen against the background of a new focus of perceiving and addressing the contemporary global security context with respect to the challenges by asymmetric warfare and irregular conflicts.[152] The corresponding CT-oriented National Security Strategy marks indeed a profound and highly dynamic realignment of military strategy. With the vision of a WMD-prone, deterritorialized 'new' terrorism figuring as a major national security threat that is perceived as permanently acute, potentially devastating and as invisible as omnipresent on the one hand and an engagement strategy based on precautious preemption on the other, it establishes a highly 'trigger-friendly' doctrinal combination at the heart of

148 Wirls, "Hidden in Plain Sight: The Bush Military Buildup," p. 101.
149 See Wirls, "Hidden in Plain Sight: The Bush Military Buildup," p. 99.
150 Wirls, "Hidden in Plain Sight: The Bush Military Buildup," p. 99.
151 Wirls, "Hidden in Plain Sight: The Bush Military Buildup," p. 103.
152 See Shultz, Godson, Hanlon, Ravich, "The Sources of Instability in the Twenty-First Century: Weak States, Armed Groups, and Irregular Conflict," 2011, p. 74.

national security politics.[153] A major institutional expression of these transformations is the upgrading of the Special Operations Command (SOCOM), especially its subunit, the Joint Special Operation Command (JSOC) in the GWOT framework. While SOCOM comprises overt and covert operations, JSOC is responsible particularly for the latter which largely grew in size and importance in the GWOT framework, especially where it comes to the training of indigenous special operation forces and kill and capture missions.[154] John Nagl, advisor to General Petraeus, described the JSOC-wing of SOCOM as an extraordinary military lever for the sake of DDM-based CT, "an almost industrial-scale counter-terrorism killing machine".[155]

Even if SOCOM and especially JSOC had already been structurally enhanced in line with the changing military strategy of the post-Cold War period, they reached a completely new level of institutional, infrastructural and functional empowerment in the wake of 9/11.[156] Most importantly, it was not anymore the CIA but the SOCOM that became the designated

153 See Fukuyama, *America at the Crossroads*, p. 82.

154 SOCOM's outlook is thus characterized by a twofold structure. On the one hand there are the units commissioned with 'white', overt operations – Army Special Forces, the 'Green Berets'; most Ranger units; most Navy SEAL units and numerous support units. On the other hand, there are the units under the JSOC that are basically commissioned with 'black', covert operations – the Special Forces Operational Detachment-Delta, the 'Delta Force'; the Naval Special Warfare Development Group, 'DEVGRU' or 'SEAL-Team 6'; the Air Force's 24th Special Tactics Squadron; the Army's 160th Special Operation Aviation Regiment, 'Airborne' or 'Night Stalkers'; and the Army's 75th Ranger Regiment, 'Rangers'. See for SOCOM's double structure Kibbe, "Covert Action and the Pentagon," 2014, pp. 218.

155 Turse, "A secret war in 120 countries," *The Nation*, August 5, 2011, accessible at http://nation.com.pk/international/05-Aug-2011/A-secret-war-in-120-countries.

156 Going even further back in the development of U.S. Special Forces it is interesting to compare the size of OSS-directed units during World War II with present day SOCOM capabilities. It would be also interesting to compare the huge institutional uplifting of SOCOM as the designated lead agency of covert operations with Pres. Kennedy's efforts to strengthen the role of the Special Forces during the Vietnam War. Convinced that a stronger COIN stance was badly needed within the grand strategy of the Vietnam War, he took great personal interest in the development and supply especially of the Green Berets. Although he had doubled the number of the Special Forces and increased the size and standing of their headquarter in Fort Bragg, Kennedy, who was somehow obsessed with the Special Forces, eventually did not succeed in giving the Vietnam War a new nature and major strategic design like it has been done so consequently after 9/11. See

lead agency to wage the GWOT abroad.[157] As such SOCOM is closely connected and independently managing its contacts to a range of other government agencies, and foreign militaries and intelligence services reinforced by its presence in countries around the globe.[158]

This unprecedented shift was the result of fierce bureaucratic battles that had created some "friction within the national security apparatus".[159] In fact, SOCOM represents the nucleus of a security apparatus within the national security apparatus. A former SOCOM chief, Admiral Eric T. Olson, revealed the newly adopted nature of SOCOM as a "microcosm of the Department of Defense, with ground, air, and maritime components, a global presence, and authorities and responsibilities that mirror the Military Departments, Military Services, and Defense Agencies".[160]

Probably more than any other institutional change, the vast upgrading of SOCOM represents the fact that the GWOT is not a mere metaphor but a precisely labeled project to merge CT and warfare under the precepts of the latter and for the sake of maintaining a global empire of security. The consequences mirror some of the major characteristics of the GWOT in general. In particular, by putting SOCOM in the lead of CT, the lines between military and intelligence operators were blurred with far-reaching constitutional implications pertaining to the accountability of the new lead agency's operations. This is due to the fact, that SOCOM reports directly to the Defense Secretary and is thus not part of the revamped intelligence community overseen by the newly created DNI.[161] When then Secretary of Defense Donald Rumsfeld installed SOCOM as the "lead combatant commander for planning, synchronizing, and, as directed, executing global operations", SOCOM also received its own intelligence budget. Simultaneously, it operated increasingly in fields formerly dominated or even exclusively handled by the CIA, – largely by JSOC as its subunit for most covert operations.[162] Legal basis of JSOC activities in global CT, includ-

---

McClintock, *Instruments of Statecraft: U.S. Guerrilla Warfare, Counterinsurgency, and Counter-Terrorism, 1940-1990*, 1992, p. 180.

157 See Kibbe, "Covert Action and the Pentagon", p. 219.

158 Turse, "A secret war in 120 countries," *The Nation*, August 5, 2011, accessible at http://nation.com.pk/international/05-Aug-2011/A-secret-war-in-120-countries.

159 See Kibbe, "Covert Action and the Pentagon", p. 219.

160 Turse, "A secret war in 120 countries," *The Nation*, August 5, 2011, accessible at http://nation.com.pk/international/05-Aug-2011/A-secret-war-in-120-countries.

161 See Ransom, *Intelligence and National Security*, p. 22.

162 See Kibbe, "Covert Action and the Pentagon", p. 219.

ing operations in countries not at war with the U.S., became a classified 2004 order by Donald Rumsfeld known as the "AQN ExOrd" or Al Qaeda Network Execute Order that was intended "to cut through bureaucratic and legal processes, allowing US Special Forces to move into 'denied' areas or countries beyond the official battle zones of Iraq and Afghanistan".[163] The fact that JSOC increasingly engages in the type of covert action that had formerly been the domain of the CIA affects congressional oversight substantially while the under-regulated covert operations of JSOC arguably create a new realm of secrecy: Whereas the CIA is required to obtain a specific Presidential mandate, a so called 'finding', and notification of Congress, there are no similar requirements for military covert operations.[164]

Moreover, the above indicated major military build-up in the context of the GWOT has to be regarded more differentiatedly. Besides the spending necessary to conduct military CT operations the GWOT has in fact also justified an impressive military buildup in general. In other words, under the cover of the GWOT a buildup entirely separated from the GWOT and the funding necessary for it had been justified.[165] From this perspective, fighting the GWOT was, at least not solely, the end but also the means to achieve a greater project, the building up of an encompassing global security regime based on unprecedented military superiority.[166] To name only one among many examples in this context: at 75.7 billion USD, the military budget for 'research and development' alone figured more than double than the entire budget for the Department of Homeland Security.[167] Moreover, through the backdoor of 'emergency supplemental funding' the military budget has been massively increased in a completely unorthodox way. Before 9/11, emergency supplemental budget composed, "at most, a

163 Scahill, "Obama's Expanding Covert Wars," *The Nation*, 2013, accessible at: https://www.thenation.com/article/obamas-expanding-covert-wars/. See also Shah, "A Move Within the Shadows – Will JSOC's Control of Drones Improve Policy?," 2014, p. 162; Schmitt and Mazzetti, "Secret Order Lets U.S. Raid Al Qaeda," *The New York Times*, November 9, 2008, accessible at: http://www.nytimes.com/2008/11/10/washington/10military.html?_r=0.

164 See Ransom, *Intelligence and National Security*, p. 22; Kibbe, "Covert Action and the Pentagon," pp. 222 ff.; Shah, "A Move Within the Shadows – Will JSOC's Control of Drones Improve Policy?," pp. 163 f.

165 See Wirls, "Hidden in Plain Sight: The Bush Military Buildup," p. 99.

166 See also Wirls, "Hidden in Plain Sight: The Bush Military Buildup," p. 111.

167 See Wirls, "Hidden in Plain Sight: The Bush Military Buildup," p. 99.

few percentage points of total defense spending. In 2007, already not less than about 23% of total military spending was in the form of supplemental funding."[168] In other words, military budget increased in the wake of the GWOT completely independent from the purpose of CT and, that is "the extraordinary thing",[169] extensively also in form of supplemental funding that is effectively functioning as an actual backdoor buildup. However, "[i]n the wake of 9/11, no politician could afford even the perception that he or she did not support the troops while the nation was at war, even if much of the money had nothing to do with the war on terror."[170] This aspect of the post 9/11 transformation, the unassailability of the claimed validity of everything brought forward under the label of the GWOT, points once more to the pervasive gravitational force of this deeply entrenched paradigm and its orthodoxy. – Altogether, these examples highlight how the outlines of a deep and concerted transformation of global and domestic governance took manifold shape in form the GWOT.

In order to assess the actual impact of the GWOT more palpable as a paradigm shift of great magnitude, it is instructive to further ponder the question in how far it is distinguished from other major national security projects reflecting a similar willingness to enforce the reason-of-state against contravening normative interests in form of humanitarian issues and the international rule of law. From such a comparative perspective it would hardly surprise that the war against Iraq lacked the claimed factual basis or that the U.S. exhibit a strong pattern of exceptionalism or non-compliance with established human right norms "more persistently" than other Western nations.[171] Moreover, looking back at the 1990s, reason of state politics have shockingly clashed with a humanitarian vision of the international order several times. Examples are the upholding of the past-war blockade of Iraq that implied the sacrifice of half a million children or the abandoning of former Shiite allies in Iraq by the U.S. that invited for their slaughter by Saddam or the French *Opération Turquoise*, the French intervention in the Rwandan massacre. Disguised as a humanitarian mission, it has been accused to have purely served the French national interest expressed by an engagement "which may have contributed more to protecting the Rwandan genocidaires than it did to establishing peace" and, to

168 Wirls, "Hidden in Plain Sight: The Bush Military Buildup," p. 106.
169 Wirls, "Hidden in Plain Sight: The Bush Military Buildup," p. 107.
170 Wirls, "Hidden in Plain Sight: The Bush Military Buildup," p. 110.
171 See Ratner, "Comments on Chapter 1 and 2," 2003, p. 107.

put it more concretely, to protect innocents from being murdered in masses.[172] In fact, trade-offs between reason of state rationales and rights are the regular shadow of warfare, but often even ordinary foreign policy as such. During the last decades the reason of state often trumped however grossly over international law and humanitarian concerns with much higher casualties than those caused by the GWOT. Yet, while the GWOT is thus not outstanding in terms of non-compliance with international law; with the damages or sacrifices caused by it or the attention it receives as an historical event[173], the GWOT *is* outstanding as a paradigm shift in global ordering creating a distinct, differentiated and extended normative order that is succesfully fostering U.S. global hegemony.[174]

### *III. Constructing the New Order: The Foundational Moment and its Continuation*

This claim is better understood with a look at the deliberate 'construction' of the GWOT itself, precisely the foundational moment, its 'translation' into the crafting of a new order and the continuation of the latter. The argument suggested here is that the all-pervasive 'constitutional moment' at the edge of the new order should be understood as a concerted construction with which a new regime is forcefully implemented as a matter of strategic choice. To understand the GWOT as a socio-political construct is nothing extraordinary: "Security policies are 'constructed', – that is, produced by rhetorical strategies that define some problem as being of type A rather than of type B", given especially that "every problem definition car-

172 Paulus, "The Influence of the United States on the Concept of 'International Community'," p. 80.

173 It should nevertheless not be overlooked that the Afghanistan War is the longest ever in U.S. history, longer than the Vietnam War, the two World Wars or the Independence War and that the Iraq War turned out to be third longest War – if the present U.S. involvement in the fight against the IS is not counted as a continuation of the original Iraq War given the fact that there the US military engagement continued after the official withdrawal in various forms of disguise the whole time.

174 In fact, incidents like the Rwandan civil war and the failure to prevent it were not only not linked with the goal to establish a global regime but provoked on the contrary eventually stronger demands in direction of a global order to be based more effectively on the respect and protection of human rights and dignity.

ries with it a prescription for one solution rather than another".[175] The GWOT, however, is not just 'a security policy' but has to be conceived as the foundational act merging and setting in force a powerful regime strongly reinforcing the U.S. hegemonic position in the global order. Specifically, it is the autonomy of such a construction and its endurance after having successfully been established that explains a lot of the GWOT's nature and dynamics. Social constructions might generally be conceived with respect to the assumption that social 'truth' is fabricated as Giambattista Vico said (*verum ipsum facit*) and that social 'facts' are largely a matter of perception as Bishop Berkeley famously stated (*esse est percipi*).

With respect to global ordering it has been claimed in this sense that a new policy paradigm is ready to be implemented when the presently dominating policies create expectations about world order that "are no longer borne out by events in the international system – when it no longer 'fits' with what observers see happening around them".[176] When constructing a new order, it is therefore essential to frame the epistemic pattern along which the relevant realities are to be perceived to define a 'truth' on the actual state of affairs and the appropriate order it requires. This can be done by the authoritative 'eventization' of catastrophic incidents that are carrying a catalyzing potential and their narrative framing with definitional scripts. If successful, such a construction enshrines sufficient epistemic impact to henceforth manage the related discourses by limiting acceptable arguments and effective access to the definitional mechanisms and the corresponding reflection and discursive reproduction. In this sense, the implementation of the GWOT as being rooted in a transformative 'super-constitutional' moment shall be understood here as the deliberate construction of a new normative reality. It is then decisive to analyze as how sustainable the foundational moment turned out with the respect to the evolution of the regime emanating from it.

---

175 Burgos, "Problem Definition in Foreign and Security Policy," 2008, p. 77.

176 Burgos, "Problem Definition in Foreign and Security Policy," p. 78, who refers to Jeffrey Legro, *Rethinking the World: Great Power Strategies and International Order*, 2005.

### 1. Foundation

The *zeitgeist* that manifested in the post 9/11 order has lucidly been exemplified by an influential neoconservative intellectual, Charles Krauthammer, about six months before the attacks:

> In the liberal internationalist view of the world, the U.S. is merely one among many – a stronger country, yes, but one that has to adapt itself to the will and the needs of 'the international community.' […] This is folly. *America is no mere international citizen. It is the dominant power in the world*, more dominant than any since Rome. Accordingly, America is *in a position to reshape norms, alter expectations and create new realities*. How? *By an unapologetic and implacable demonstration of will.*[177]

Once the project to decisively implement a new order as an "implacable demonstration of will" had commenced, it had to follow the procedural autonomy of such a building of a new socio-political reality. In this sense, it had not only to be rooted in a sufficient narrative basis but also to construct a foundational act that would stand out in its symbolic singularity. Staging the attacks as one, if not *the* ineffable national catastrophe in the country's history was the first step on this way. This included the designation of the ruins of the World Trade Centre as a 'ground zero' and justified the special character of everything that followed. However, the new security order was not to be created in a normatively empty space but at the expense of contravening orders, especially central parts of international and domestic constitutional law. This implied two notions of the 'constitutive/constitutional moment': The need of an effective supersession of those legal regimes standing in the way of the foundational project and the sharp symbolic disentanglement of the new order from competing normative orders that could diminish the foundational force necessary. In order to achieve these purposes, the immediate response of the U.S. administration to the attacks was almost immaculate. It appeared less as a "postmodern onslaught on international law as a means to contain conflict and implement shared values"[178] rather than an expression of foundational vigor against any order blocking the transformative moment from unfolding. Vi-

177 Krauthammer, "The Bush doctrine: In American Foreign Policy, a new motto: Don't ask. Tell," 2001, accessible at http://edition.cnn.com/ALLPOLITICS/time/2001/03/05/doctrine.html. Italics by the author.

178 Paulus, "The Influence of the United States on the Concept of 'International Community'," p. 77.

olence is in the foundational discourse predominantly not any more a means to achieve a higher good called 'rights' and 'democracy' but the essence of a new mission called the GWOT. In a certain way, this foundation mirrored the initial spark that had set it in motion sacrificing some of the cornerstones of the formerly established order by a sort of controlled demolition of high symbolic value that transcended the established practices of American exceptionalism by far. The corresponding message of the grand project that took off from 'ground zero' amounted indeed to an "implacable demonstration of will" that was accompanied by a bold 'whoever is not with me is against me'. Consequently, the inauguration of the new regime saw an unprecedented delineation from and expressive devaluation of key elements of the old domestic and international order affecting rights regimes, democratic accountability, the separation of powers and the adherence to the rule of law. For the moment, the new normative order in foundation was to be punched out as clear as possible, with as much visible determination as possible. With ostensibly little interest in the existing legal restraints, its constructors were not willing to grant any space in between acceptance and non-acceptance of the fait accompli, no degree of deference or resistance along the lines of "either you are with us, or you are with the terrorists".[179]

From a constructivist perspective, however, it was the sometimes stunningly reckless verve with which some of those who crafted the new architecture tended to openly ignore all existing barriers and contravening core values by which they drew the clear-cut delineations that demonstratively separated the new from the old. The decisive ignorance of these transgressions exemplified and reinforced the will and potential to craft a new order that was surpsingly accepted without considerable resistance, a veritable regime change on own terms

Notably, however, the subsequent evolution of the emerging empire of security is then marked by the gradual, yet not complete re-acknowledgement of the continuing existence and principled relevance of the competing legal regimes which nevertheless remained in a much weaker position compared to the status before 9/11.

Especially the initial phase of this project was all communication: the decisive communication of a paradigm shift whose visible occurrence alone proved the new order's claimed superior validity, appreciation and

179 See Benoist, *Carl Schmitt Today*, p. 41.

effect. Decisive for this construction of a new normative order was an epistemic turn whose narratives were supposed to create a new orthodoxy. President Bush put it in a nutshell when he claimed that in the face of the 'new terrorism' the U.S. and its allies would have to *deconstruct and reinvent "our thoughts, language, and imaginary"* which *"dictate the question we ask and the methods we use* […]".[180] A typical feature of any foundational act of normative ordering is also the claim of an awakening expressed by the evocation of a new clarity and corresponding decisiveness. Interestingly, such a notion dominates not only frequent public speeches and announcement of various representatives of the Bush administration but found its way also into the National Defense Strategy of the United States of America 2005. Claiming that "America is a nation at war" it also underlines that "[t]he attacks of 9/11 *gave us greater clarity* on the challenges that confront us".[181]

The clarity of a foundational awakening that is defining the project of the GWOT is expressed in an outright religious language in one of the big liberal American newspapers lucidly celebrating the decision to wage war against Iraq as nothing less than *"a vision of great sweep and imagination: comprehensive, prophetic, evangelical – […] wholly foreign to the modesty of containment [of the Cold War order]"*, a vision that signals the iron determination "to remake the world" by dealing with the "evil of terror".[182] This text is a perfect example of how consequently and intensely the novelty of the new order was marked out in the aftermath of 9/11 for a long foundational moment. One expression of the grand foundational gesture reflected in this text is the momentary dropping even of the masks of compliance with the rule of law that was accompanied by the almost total suspension of the tempering democratic practices of listening to opposing ideas in the public discourse.

The most concise sketch of this foundational *zeitgeist* is the public clarification of a presidential aide when responding to a critic who dared to

---

180 Bush quoted from Kappeler and Kappeler, "Speaking of Evil and Terrorism," p. 183. Italics by the author.

181 U.S Department of Defense, "The National Defense Strategy of the United States of America 2005," 2005, p. 1, accessible at http://www.au.af.mil/au/awc/awcgate/nds/nds2005.pdf. Italics by the author.

182 See Danner, "The Struggles of Democracy and Empire," 2002, *The New York Times*, 2009, accessible at http://www.nytimes.com/2002/10/09/opinion/the-struggles-of-democracy-and-empire.html. Italics by the author.

refer to the 'old' order – the law, the constitution, international conventions: "We're an empire now, and when we act, we create our own reality."[183]

From this perspective, the torture practices that were part and parcel of the GWOT's toolkit[184] could claim to have at least an indirect discursive purpose for the foundational drama, despite widespread doubts whether torture would be effective at all.[185] After all, serious claims have been brought forward that torture would not only not produce any actionable intelligence but also alienate other countries and peoples all over the world from the U.S.' cause. Yet, there is at least one functional argument that could be held against such criticism. Arguably, the value of torture for the foundation of a hegemonic empire of security lies in the systematic transgression of a taboo that conveys an important message. By breaking the taboo the perpetrator can demonstrate the fact of a sovereign foundation of a new order or, in other words, "to demonstrate America's unrestrained sovereignty by disregarding international laws and conventions."[186] This process was remarkably successful in the initial phase of the GWOT. Those who did not join the large and heterogeneous chorus of the new security regime's supporters but tried to complain – many even from within the security apparatus, the FBI, CIA or the various intelligence units of the armed forces – were quickly silenced. Others, especially most of the leading voices in the public debate, remained deaf and dumb in the face of the overwhelming transformation. All this reflects the sweeping success of the grand transformation including especially its discursive dimension. An evident manifestation is the widespread "assimilation of the culture of counterterrorism, even by the liberal media."[187] Likewise, the normally expectable resistance of NGO's like Human Rights Watch largely failed to materialize when the new order took shape at the obvious expense of hu-

183 See Rich, *The Greatest Story Ever Sold: The Decline and Fall of Truth From 9/11 to Katrina*, 2006, p. 4.

184 See the finding of the 2012 US Senate Select Committee on Intelligence, "Committee Study of the Central Intelligence Agency's Detention and Interrogation Program," 2012/2014, accessible at https://www.amnestyusa.org/pdfs/sscistudy1.pdf.

185 See the Senate Select Committee on Intelligence opening its report with the finding: "The CIA's use of its enhanced interrogation techniques was not an effective means of acquiring intelligence or gaining cooperation from detainees."

186 See Zulaika, *Terrorism: The Self-Fulfilling Prophecy,* p. 214.

187 See Zulaika, *Terrorism: The Self-Fulfilling Prophecy,* p. 197.

man rights.[188] Similarly, the international community responded either with passionate support or pale acceptance. If "[a]ttempting to alter the way friends and foes perceived reality and deny others the right to interpret their own history had long complemented US grand strategy"[189], this craft reached its peak in the wake of 9/11 when definitional sovereignty towered remarkably high above contravening norms and realities. Altogether, the Bush administration's decisive narrative framing and discursive design of the 9/11 events and the forceful erection of the GWOT as a new order eventually ensured that "an immediate war and the longer-term equivalent of the Cold War were launched"[190] for the sake of establishing an empire of security. This is the first phase of the GWOT.

### 2. *Continuation*

Given that the crafting of a new order as an "unapologetic and implacable demonstration of will" was surprisingly successful the crucial question was then how sustainable and resilient the new order would prove to be after the smoke over its foundation would have settled. Two markers for this second phase of implementing a new global order and its successful accomplishment might be discussed. A first and immensely important hurdle was cleared when the GWOT passed the 'succession test' and continued unimpaired under a new presidency since 2009, namely the Obama administration. The second accomplishment in terms of sustaining continuity could be noted with the elimination of Osama bin Laden by the same *Obama* administration on May 1, 2011.

Especially the 'succession test' was an evident indicator of sustainability as it was a shift of power from a hawkish, evangelical 'neocon'-administration to a mildly 'leftist' Democrat as U.S. President who had criticized central aspects of the GWOT prior to his presidency. This discrepancy irrespective, the GWOT-paradigm remained substantially unaffected and continued uninterruptedly under the new administration.

Evidently, when Barack Obama took over, the new order was firmly implemented. It had survived numerous scandals and already entered a

---

188 See Osiel, *The End of Reciprocity: Terror, Torture, and the Law of War*, 2009, p. 55.

189 Walker, *National Security and Core Values in American History*, p. 273.

190 Wirls, "Hidden in Plain Sight: The Bush Military Buildup," p. 109.

more moderate phase of its reproduction. Obviously, despite having held some alternative views on the GWOT, Obama seems to have been well aware of the nature of the overall normative order he was supposed to defend as U.S. President. Before his election, he had hinted to a foreign policy stance that would not be too far away from a moderate conservative stance. Six months before he became President, Obama told the New York Times for example that "I have enormous sympathy for the foreign policy of George H. W. Bush"[191] – a clever assurance of his determination to not sheer off the basic direction while maintaining the necessary distance to his rival, the President. When he eventually took office, the tone of the official GWOT-discourse moderately changed while the melody continued loud and clear. This matched the realities as the already achieved autonomy of the reproductive processes underlying the GWOT regime did, at this point, not any more require the same strident tone that had dominated the initial period. The milder tones that became gradually interspersed in the GWOT discourse now were in fact not induced by Obama alone. Some normalization had already been fostered by the fact that Congress and the judicial branch had corrected some expressions of Bush's most extravagant interpretations of the dominating CT score.[192] Moreover, by the time the Obama administration took office there was more consensus than discord within the political establishment's notion towards the GWOT[193] which, as a regime, had successfully passed its foundational period and could be reproduced with a less aggressive tone now.[194] Arguably it even *required* a more 'settled' operationalization at this more mature stage of its enforcement, – something which Obama did well provide. The aggressive way by which Bush had established the new regime had mobilized some resistance which was well responded now by Obama's modest moderation of the GWOT tone which effectively stabilized the basic direction taken. To show some notions of compliance and rhetorical appeasement towards human rights and democratic oversight could only serve the well established 'empire of security'. Metaphorically speaking, it might be said that, the stronger the security regime's roots had become, the more the new plant invested its energy in its green cover, – and for that Obama proved to

191 Obama, *New York Times*, May 16, 2008.

192 Katyal, "Stochastic Restraint," 2013, p. 992.

193 Katyal, "Stochastic Restraint," p. 992.

194 See Taylor and Wittes, "Looking Forward, Not Backward: Refining U.S. Interrogation Law," 2010, pp. 289 f.

be compatible, domestically and internationally. However, some modest initiatives of self-criticism and careful reacknowledgment of the relevance of rights and the rule of law *in principle* have commenced already under the late Bush administration, especially when such moves seemed to be unavoidable to deal with growing criticism triggered by leaking scandals. Yet, at heart, under the late Bush as well as under the whole Obama administration, changes in publicly presenting and overtly regulating the GWOT seem to have been more reflecting a natural departure from the initial rugged rhetoric that had accompanied the aggressive foundation of the new order rather than fostering substantial reform. Basically, most of the changes represent only modest readjustments without correcting the direction. All in all, they remained, in the words of Koh, rather interstitial in nature than that they became architectural. From an overarching long-term perspective on the underlying processes of regime building it might even be justified to conclude that these modifications were introduced without moving the GWOT paradigm an inch out of the national policy pivot or giving in substantially when it came to its adamant enforcement. Whereas the GWOT's rendition, detention and interrogation programs became strongly criticized and – even if limitedly and temporarily – scrutinized at an official stage, they continued at least partly, just more carefully embedded in the shape of sham compliance with the countervailing constitutional core values and the mollifications of toothless oversight. Notwithstanding some single serious interventions and mitigations, the essential objectives and practices of 'warfare' against global terrorism, the whole ideological, normative and practical substance of the established CT-paradigm and the deadly machine executing it remained largely untouched.

While President Obama, officially and repeatedly banned domestic torture declaring an end to "the CIA's detention and interrogation program"[195], he did not fully rescind maltreatment and rendition practices but partly reaffirmed them even on the official track with a more discretely formulated executive order.[196] Noteworthy, he also used preferably these tentative legislative instruments, executive orders, to execute his mitigat-

195 See Taylor and Wittes, "Looking Forward, Not Backward: Refining U.S. Interrogation Law," p. 291.

196 Ahmed, "The United States Is Committing Brutal Acts of Torture Right Now," 2014, accessible at http://www.truth-out.org/news/item/28177-america-is-committing-brutal-acts-of-torture-right-now.

ing policies and retained the freedom to make secret exceptions if deemed necessary.[197] Moreover, instead of putting continued focus on the kidnapping of terrorism suspects or buying them from warlords and bounty hunters as it was more widespread under Bush, his administration shifted its focus to just killing them on the spot. Targeted killings, executed by commandos and drones, form a key element of the present GWOT shaped by the Obama administration. Being operated without any regard of due judicial process and, if necessary, by superseding the national sovereignty of affected states, these (capture or) kill operations mark the same determination to reproduce the GWOT as a hegemonic governance paradigm as President Bush had expressed it.[198] While the GWOT became partially embedded in more sophisticated discourses, it arguably remained essentially the same.[199]

An interesting example for this trend of filling old wine in new skins is the 2006 version of the Army Field Manual for Human Intelligence Collector Operations. On the one hand, it indeed employs a more careful lan-

---

197 See Taylor and Wittes, "Looking Forward, Not Backward: Refining U.S. Interrogation Law," p. 291.

198 Attorney General Eric Holder defended the legality of the lethal targeting program in a speech delivered March 5, 2012, at Northwestern University School of Law. According to him, the U.S. Constitution "empowers the President to protect the nation from any imminent threat of violent attack" noting that "international law recognizes the inherent right of national self-defense." Moreover, Holder made explicitly clear again that such authority would not be limited to Afghanistan, citing the AUMF and domestic court decisions, while he also stated that international legal principles would constrain such operations abroad. However, lethal operations would be legal in other countries, he maintained, if the host nation provided its consent or a (unilateral) determination had been made that the respective nation "is unable or unwilling to deal effectively with a threat to the United States." See Attorney General Holder, "Speech at Northwestern University School of Law," March 5, 2012, prepared text available at http://www.lawfareblog.com/2012/03/text-of-the-attorney-generals-national-security-speech/#more-6236.

199 It is remarkable, for instance, how the American stance for unilateralism has further developed in the frame of the GWOT since 2001. After the US had initially pursued the construction of the new security order by an unprecedented advancement of NATO and UN, it largely abandoned both forums when it engaged in concrete militarily CT-operations abroad later.

guage and more limited scope of officially sanctioned methods[200] which, on the other hand, still cover interrogation techniques that go "far beyond the original Geneva-inspired restrictions of the original version of the manual."[201] At large, it displays thus the continuation of the established 9/11-CT/COIN regime in a softer tone.[202] Interestingly in this context, President Obama's Director of National Intelligence, retired Admiral Dennis Blair, told the Senate Intelligence Committee in 2009 that the Army Field Manual would be amended to allow even new forms of enhanced interrogation but these changes *would remain classified*:

> We have large amounts of unclassified doctrine for our troops to use, but we don't put anything in there that our enemies can use against us. And we'll figure it out for this manual [...] there will be some sort of document that's widely available in an unclassified form, but the specific techniques that can provide training value to adversaries, we will handle much more carefully.[203]

Realistically seen, the reformed manual meant basically a back-to-normal, a normal which entails the two usual layers of any manifest security regime: an overt, practically often less significant regime consisting of reason of state affirmations softened by more or less rhetorical right appeasements, and the often really significant, largely covert practices on the ground. Both layers are well connected with the overt layer often providing valuable disguise for covert politics:

> Obama recalibrated the covert torture apparatus, and is attempting to leverage the [Senate's] torture report's damning findings to claim moral high ground his administration doesn't have. The torture regime is alive and well, but it

200 The manual explicitly prohibits some of the most notorious abusive techniques used on security detainees in the War on Terror including waterboarding, the use of sexual humiliation and military dogs.

201 In the 2006 version of the Field Manual the former explicit prohibition of the – regularly employed – use of stress positions and sleep manipulation has been removed. Furthermore, the Field Manual's Chapter 8 still allows the 'fear-up' of detainees, a technique that is normally used in conjunction with 'separation' to create strong feelings of fear and hopelessness in the detainee: "In the fear-up approach, the HUMINT collector identifies a pre-existing fear or creates a fear within the source." Fear-up is also used together with 'emotional love or hate approaches' where feelings of love of detainees, especially to their family, are exploited to break them down. FM 2-22.3, Ch.8, p.11.

202 Ahmed, "The United States Is Committing Brutal Acts of Torture Right Now".

203 Ahmed, "The United States Is Committing Brutal Acts of Torture Right Now".

> has been put back in the box of classified secrecy to continue without public scrutiny.[204]

In this context, it should be remembered that the Bush government saw itself forced to modify its concept of enhanced interrogation only after great scandals. The latter came as a "public outcry after the leak of the 'torture memos'", especially the leaked photographs of "grotesque abuse of prisoners" in Iraq and additionally the President's nomination of a lawyer to head the nation's Justice Department who was directly connected to the 'torture memos'.[205] Eventually, these scandals forced the government to modify its concept of interrogation "with something more closely resembling the prevailing domestic and international standard".[206] Even if Obama much more deliberately gave in to softening the tone of the GWOT-discourse and the mitigation of official practices, the patterns remained the same. This becomes also clear with respect to the rendition and targeted killing practices under his administration. Allegedly, extraordinary renditions did not only continue but were taken on with even renewed significance as an officially endorsed counter-terrorism tool of the US government since he assumed office.[207] Similar, targeted killings became nothing less than the very hallmark of his COIN/CT strategy as the Commander-in-Chief in the GWOT's second round.[208]

Another example for the continuation of the GWOT with only some new accentuations pertains to the commissioning of JSOC as the GWOT's operative lead agency. Under the Obama administration JSOC's function as the CT-spearhead was not only confirmed but even further enhanced. A former top JSOC commander stated, for instance, that "Obama gave JSOC *unprecedented authority to track and kill terrorists*, to 'mow the lawn'."[209] Responding to the question of a journalist if he would think that JSOC

---

204 Ahmed, "The United States Is Committing Brutal Acts of Torture Right Now".

205 See Minow, "What is the Greatest Evil," 2005, p. 2166.

206 Minow, "What is the Greatest Evil," p. 2166.

207 Whitlock, "Renditions continue under Obama, despite due-process concerns," 2013, accessible at https://www.washingtonpost.com/world/national-security/renditions-continue-under-obama-despite-due-process-concerns/2013/01/01/4e593aa0-5102-11e2-984e-f1de82a7c98a_story.html.

208 See Roach, *The 9/11 Effect: Comparative Counter-Terrorism*, 2011, pp. 226 f. and 229 ff.; Anderson, "Targeted Killing in U.S. Counterterrorism Strategy and Law," 2009, pp. 347 ff.; see for Pakistan Siddique, "The Other Pakistan: Special Laws, Diminished Citizenship and the Gathering Storm," 2015, pp. 250 f.

209 See Kibbe, "Covert action and the Pentagon," pp. 219 f.

would hit harder under Obama than it did under Bush, a former JSOC operative answers: "harder, faster, quicker, – with the full support of the White House". Indeed, based on the Bush doctrine, the Obama administration expanded JSOC's covert actions in number and scope, designating the whole world as the GWOT's battlefield. While under the Bush administration US Special Forces were operating in 60 countries, they quickly reached 75 under President Obama.[210] According to the quoted veteran, "JSOC has been more empowered under this administration than under any other in recent history. No question. [...]. The *Obama* administration took the [Bush] order and went above and beyond."[211] This assessment corresponds with the fact that core practices of the GWOT like targeted killings in sovereign countries were not only taken up but also lifted to a new level by the Obama administration.

This is leading to the second indicator for the continuation of the GWOT-paradigm under President Obama, the elimination of Osama bin Laden. On a symbolic or communicative level it might be seen as a telling contra-part to the GWOT's initial foundation that is somehow completing a central thread of its foundational narrative. This becomes evident in the tone of President Obama's speech after the lethal mission had been accomplished:

> Let us think back to the sense of unity that prevailed on 9/11. I know that it has, at times, frayed. Yet today's achievement is a testament to the greatness of our country and the determination of the American people.

Moreover, "[t]o those families who have lost loved ones to al-Qaeda's terror," he claimed that, "justice has been done" echoing President Bush's statement following the 9/11 attacks that "justice will be done".[212] This achievement notwithstanding, the show had to go on, the GWOT had to be transferred into a subsequent version. The one who communicated that the GWOT's next chapter had to be opened along the established lines of a solemn foundation was then Secretary of State Hillary Rodham Clinton who declared that the

---

210 See "Jeremy Scahill Testifies Before Congress on America's Secret Wars," 2010, accessible at: www.thenation.com/article/jeremy-scahill-testifies-congress-americas-secret-wars/.

211 "Jeremy Scahill Testifies Before Congress on America's Secret Wars".

212 Obama quoted from Mandel, *Coercing Compliance: State Initiated Brute Force in Today's World*, 2015, p. 61.

> fight against terrorism continues, and we will never waver. I know there are some who doubted this day would ever come, who questioned our resolve and our reach. But let us remind ourselves, this is America. We rise to the challenge, we persevere, and we get the job done.[213]

Getting "the job done" was thus obviously not confined to the killing of Osama but just finishing one chapter of the GWOT to open the next one that would unlikely be the last one too. Like the foundation of the GWOT, the accomplishment of its first partial victory was successfully staged as a monumental act of perseverance beyond any constraints of the 'old order'. In the official testimony the elimination of Osama bin Laden (and of four other people including one of his sons) by a JSOC-operated DEVGRU commando delivered a testament to the greatness of the American nation in memory of 9/11. Taking visibly revenge by literally executing the Bush/ Obama doctrine against Osama as the GWOT's arch enemy closed a circle. While it completed the foundational narrative of the GWOT during its second phase under President Obama it symbolically initiated its third phase, its detachment from its foundational foe and its continuation in other theaters.

Noteworthy, Osama's carefully staged execution presented the world public the reality of an extra-judicial killing of an unarmed man with an assertiveness that resembled the demonstrative determination of the Bush administration when the GWOT had been constructed as a narrative in the wake of 9/11.

## D. *Conclusion and Outlook: Counterterrorism and Communication in Times of the GWOT*

Starting point of this essay was the assumption that the current threat assessment for the European CT-theater would suggest to ponder the prospects of an adjustment of the predominant communication strategies with respect to actual and potential CT adversaries. This would largely be dependent on choices with respect to the discussed ideal-typical CT approaches. Purpose of the ensuing argumentation was it then to provide an explanatory matrix for the gravitational forces of the GWOT as a manifes-

---

213 Clinton, "Remarks on the killing of Usama bin Laden", May 2, 2011, US State Department, accessible at http://www.realclearpolitics.com/articles/2011/05/02/secretary_clintons_remarks_on_the_killing_of_osama_bin_laden_109721.html.

tation of one of these approaches which are arguably largely determining the state of affairs in contemporary CT. As a vastly entrenched framework it is assumed that the GWOT influences the trends and defines the margin of maneuver in designing and directing almost all strategies, tactics and operations of CT post 9/11. In the wake of this turning point, CT became immensely valorized as a powerful discourse and regime in the U.S. that shifted into the center of national security from where it emerged into the single dominating national and international policy objective to become closely entangled with a broad range of central policy fields originally not linked to national security. While this trend of an encompassing securitization was globally reproduced on national agendas, the domestic national security structures were tighter linked with the U.S.' security matrix. Meanwhile, the U.S.-defined anti-terrorism policy became the overarching discourse in international law and policy making. Largely on U.S. initiative, this led to the gradual establishment of an unprecedented intense, differentiated and entrenched international security regime. By it, the U.S. GWOT was reinforced with huge leverage for the declared project to reshape world order at a critical juncture after the Cold War had been won and before rival powers could challenge the realities of the unipolar world. Expression of the gravitational force inherent in the emerging regime, that was, after all, deliberately crafted for no lesser purpose than to "shift the tectonic plates of international politics" after the "international system [had] been in flux since the collapse of Soviet power"[214], is its above demonstrated actual reach and weight. In fact, the "enormous opportunity"[215] offered by the 9/11 events has been impressively seized by the Bush administration transforming it into a major turning point of global ordering. Since then the hegemonic position of the U.S. has been significantly backed and entrenched by the newly crafted international security order. The ongoing unfolding and further entrenchment of this international regime is mirrored by the synchronized securitization of domestic orders around the globe. The transformative impetus of this process not only on the national security structure but the constitutional core values as well has been shown in a nutshell for the U.S. Here, a massive institutional revamp

---

214 See Rice, "Remarks by National Security Advisor Condoleezza Rice on Terrorism and Foreign Policy," April 29, 2002, accessible at https://georgewbush-whitehouse.archives.gov/news/releases/2002/04/20020429-9.html.

215 Rice, "Remarks by National Security Advisor Condoleezza Rice on Terrorism and Foreign Policy".

was accompanied by crucial challenges to the constitutional core values: rights and liberties, the balances of power and democratic oversight. Against the historical depth of its mission, its actual pervasiveness and transformative impact, the GWOT's gravitational force has indeed to be acknowledged as completely unprecedented by any other CT approach in history. Where policy makers and academics, professionals and experts would therefore come to the conclusion that the initially described dynamics of the European security environment would demand an adjustment especially of the basic communicative CT approach in direction of the SRC model, the GWOT represents the most significant confining constant for the discussion, reflection and implementation of such a restatement.

At this point it serves to remind that the preferred communication strategy in CT is one of the distinguishing criteria between the two essentially different ideal-typical CT approaches, the DDM and the SRC framework, both being defined by their configuration of the respectively dominant core values, preferred modes of communication with, and imagery of the adversary. As ideal-types, the actual manifestations of both models are considered as basically coexisting. Yet, since 9/11 the GWOT as a current expression of the DDM model has evidently become the by far dominant discourse and regime which is enjoying a sheer weight and reach as no other CT discourse did before. While the GWOT strongly dominates the European CT-discourses, policies and strategies, a certain interest in structurally more dialogical communication measurers like SRC-based de- and counter-radicalization and disengagement programs is also discussable. Western CT experts have for instance increasingly studied the design and execution of such programs in predominantly Muslim countries to learn from them[216] to improve the own programs in place with respect to political Islam. The widespread implementation of de- and counter-radicalization and disengagement programs across the whole Muslim world – in Africa, the Middle East, Central Asia, South-, Southeast and even East Asia – does, however, not imply at all that the SRC approach is advancing even if these programs might include stronger or weaker notions of the SRC model. In many of these programs, compared to Western pendants, Muslim addressees are treated with greater ease and natural respect that grows out of the shared cultural and religious identity but also the more vital risk to alienate more members of the own Muslim population from

216 Hamed El-Said, "Conclusion," 2013, pp. 262 ff.

the state. Communication is here much easier than the required cross-cultural communication in Western programs and might thus indeed resemble a more subject-related basic figuration resembling the SRC model. However, most of these programs are yet inclined to be different with respect to the influence of constitutional core values that are, after all, definitional elements of the SRC approach. In a certain way, the turn towards radicalized or radicalizing citizens in these programs often resembles what has been said above about the winning-the-hearts-and-minds approach in COIN strategies. It might thus be assumed that the ideal-typical distinction between the DDM and the SRC paradigm carries much more weight in Western countries that are defining themselves by the constitutional core values in question under a DDM model regime. Nevertheless, the increasing interest in Western countries in de- and counter-radicalization and disengagement is not automatically implying a turn towards a stronger recognition of the SRC approach at all. Given their low impact on the overall CT-approach, the detrimental development of the general political and societal conditions to engage in an authentic dialogue and the ongoing alienation of increasing parts of the European Muslim communities, their prospects to shape the fundamental philosophy in dealing with violent Muslim radicalization seem to be rather bleak. Even if Western de- and counter-radicalization and disengagement programs might therefore structurally display a stronger affinity with a SRC approach, such programs can hardly be developed, organized and implemented isolated from the fundamentally underlying trend in CT. That trend, however, is the GWOT. It is therefore inclined to informe those who generally grant funds, hire people and assess programs and has thus to be expected to have more or less subtle influences on the successful calibration and execution of most de- and counter-radicalization and disengagement programs. This trend presently seems to be stable and leaving much space to significantly valorize or enlarge SRC-related elements of CT. European responses to the terrorist attacks in Paris in November 2015 were notably fully in line with the established GWOT approach. This already applies to their semantics that were almost identical to those of the formative discourses in the wake of 9/11. Addressing the 2015 incident as an "attack on all of humanity", the French and other European governments significantly repeated the narrative framing of 9/11 quickly resounded by President Obama.[217] Notably, the narrative did not lose its power. Almost immediately after issuing this definitional response to the attacks France engaged in militarily retaliation strikes against Syria. Given that the repercussions of the GWOT are increasingly hitting Europe, which already responded by echoing the GWOT's grand narratives with more verve, impulses of change are unlikely in the foreseeable future. Nevertheless, appreciating the fact that GWOT is still a changing, contextual and contingent phenomenon, it might be asked if its exceptional gravitational force will indeed unfold with basically the same impact and in the same direction in the near future almost 15 years after it has been launched.

Two perspectives shall be taken into consideration. One is directed at the deep structure of the present global order which has been shaped by the West. Focus is put here on the Western inclination to approach global order with a particular preference for legal constructions and the consequences for a more fundamental assessment of the GWOT. The other perspective is directed at the coalface of current CT, especially with respect to the Middle Eastern dynamics that is increasingly affecting the European situation.

Taking the latter perspective first, the general situation on the Middle Eastern battle-fields and their repercussions on Europe unequivocally worsened indicating an intensification of the GWOT rather than a substantial change of the underlying CT paradigm. Since 2001, civil war has wildly spread to and in countries like Syria, Iraq, Yemen, Libya, Somalia, or Mali, interlocking terrorism and conventional warfare. From this perspective it can be hardly avoided to say that the GWOT failed not only to root out terrorism but also tumbled almost all of its designated theaters and bordering countries into large scale destruction and further radicalization. In geopolitical perspectives the GWOT led to an unhealthy mutation of the strategic landscape from the very perspective of those who had unleashed it. As a direct consequence of the GWOT Shiite regimes in Iran, Iraq, and Syria could form a Shiite axis that extend to the Lebanese Hezbollah and the Yemenite Huthi. Strategic pivot of this axis is the battle for Syria with the Assad government's survival being of significant strate-

217 Obama, "Statement by the President on the Situation in Paris," November 13, 2015, accessible at: https://www.whitehouse.gov/the-press-office/2015/11/13/statement-president-situation-paris.

gic interest to Russia which is conducting air strikes from Iranian soil.[218] Another supporter of the Assad regime that is also advancing Iran is China. On the other side, Israel, Saudi Arabia, several Gulf States and Turkey support Sunni groups, partly even those with (former) affiliations to Al Qaida and the IS while some of the Syrian Sunni rebel groups receive support also from the U.S., France and other NATO members. Against this background, the GWOT emerged in a potentially perpetual battleground that is shaped by various interconnected layers of conflict which in turn will almost inevitably fan the flames of terror in the times to come. With the Western involvement on the one side and the Russian and Chinese on the other, the conflict has got a global dimension that is reinforced by the involvement of the four most powerful regional rival powers that are concomitantly linked to these global powers: – Saudi Arabia, Israel and Turkey on the anti-Assad side and Iran on the other. With this constellation a massive military potential is involved that has already led to an entangled and intensifying proxy war. On the ground, a tribal and an outright criminal element are additionally interwoven in the conflict as are almost all of the region's various ethnic and religious minorities. Altogether this has turned the battle for Syria into a maelstrom of destruction and radicalization which might well be expected to continue to affect Europe for some time to come, not to speak of the more or less connected, yet independent conflict scenarios like those in Turkey, Yemen or Libya. From this perspective, starting with the invasion of Iraq, the whole Middle East has transformed into an entrenching zone of overlapping conflicts with religious warfare between Sunnis and Shiites, civil warfare between shifting alliances of numerous players and proxy warfare by regional rivals and along the Cold War divide including massive conventional warfare, vested criminal interests and designated terrorist groups like the IS or the al-Nusra Front attracting large numbers of foreign fighters, many of them from Europe. All this is eventually prone to reinforcing the GWOT paradigm that has changed its outlook since 9/11. Given this status and the prospects of the Middle Eastern theaters it is justified to ask if the GWOT itself might even radicalize in the future despite its obvious failure. In this re-

218 Syria's importance for Russia follows from its strategic value with the only Russian Mediterranean naval base that is connecting the 5th Mediterranean warship squadron to the Russian Navy's Black Sea bases and as it connects the Russian access to the Mediterranean Sea through the Shiite belt with Russia again, offering an opportunity to transport Russian and Iranian gas from Russia to Europe.

gard, it has to be differentiated: On the one hand, the increasing threat of a further escalation and greater mutual destruction of the region with threatening spillover effects in all directions and high costs for most involved powers might eventually lead to a strengthening of mitigating tendencies in the short to medium term. Whereas on the other hand the game of proxies and allies blurs the propagandist lines that are dividing radical and bloodthirsty terrorists from non-terrorist freedom fighters, serious concern remains that the European scenario will become increasingly shaped by divisional rhetoric, policies and practices as a direct outcome of the conflict. The shock waves that are evolving from the Middle Eastern disaster can not only be expected to arrive in even greater density but also to continue to erupt long after the arms of conventional forces will have become silent. The then possibly ongoing implosion of ordering structures at large would result in a longterm destabilization producing further breeding ground for massive radicalization for a long time. As a probable side effect, the European societies would further radicalize in all directions and further contribute to the terrorist's cause at home and abroad. This whole process, despite being a testament of great failure of the GWOT, would likely to be inclined to paradoxically reinforce the reproduction of the very same GWOT. In other words, a turn away from the established approach towards CT-related communication strategies and practices is rather improbable.

This grim outlook might, however, be at least partly differentiated from the second perspective on the deep structure of the present global order. First, as a military strategy, the GWOT, as important it is and probably remains, is no exclusive approach. As there are other CT approaches despite the GWOT paradigm's overwhelming might there are also other military strategy approaches than COIN warfare in the frame of the GWOT. Given this fact of a strategic pluralism, a grand military strategy favoring conventional rather than COIN warfare could divert some attention from the GWOT/COIN paradigm. Such a rebalancing could receive increasing support due to current trends on the global 'chess board' like the growing tensions with Russia following the eastward enlargement of NATO and the endangerment of Syria or the conflict with China over the South-China Sea. In these and other scenarios like a potential war with Iran or North-Korea a COIN strategy would indeed prove totally useless. The limited value of a COIN strategy as the center of the grand military strategy of the U.S. is evident and could lead to a rebalancing of the overall strategy to the disadvantage of COIN and CT.[219] From this perspective, it is probable that the strong focus on COIN as it had been reinforced by and in the frame of the GWOT will be increasingly adjusted again, towards more support for conventional warfare. Especially where such an adjustment with all involved budgetary, institutional and personal interest will cause frictions however, it might well be that the GWOT itself is increasingly defined as a hybrid of CT/COIN and conventional firepower. Possible is also that the form of the GWOT remains with a much more diversified content yet without effectively increasing the ensuing spaces of maneuver to define CT. In other words, even if CT will figure less prominent it will probably remain part of a militarily defined approach. After all, strategic pluralism allows and even encourages the coexistence of diverging strategic preferences[220], so that a shift back to conventional warfare would not necessarily affect the conventional GWOT paradigm too much.

Second, taking a more fundamental perspective on the GWOT as a lever to achieve and preserve hegemony in terms of global order, there are on the other hand no signs of a further *shrinking* of the current, comparatively small margin of maneuver in favor of alternative CT approaches based on the SRC model. In a certain sense, the deep structure of hegemonic global ordering by a Western power like the U.S. seems even to imply a guarantee that some notions of the SRC model with its accent on constitutional core values will always be retained as an option. Point of this argument is that the GWOT serves a strategic purpose that would be greatly endangered if the same constitutional core values that it is pushing back so significantly would completely be neutralized in the context of CT. What has to be acknowledged is the fact that the GWOT, although it greatly helped to foster U.S. hegemony, did not cement it and did not render the values and structures of the pre 9/11 global normative order obsolete. Today the U.S. is even more contested in its hegemonic position than it has been around 9/11. It is at the same time still a "liberal hegemon"[221], proven by the thousands of pages of revealing official documents made available on central issues pertaining to the GWOT by due legal process. In fact, the same constitutional core values that have been superseded so forcefully by the GWOT are still forming a large part of the normative identity of the Western state and the international rule of law. While the

219 See Reveron and Stiehm, "Introduction," 2008, p. XV.
220 See Biddle, "Strategy in War," p. 5.
221 Ratner, "Comments on Chapter 1 and 2," p. 111.

protection of this normative identity is a central argument of the SRC approach it is so evident and fundamental that it can hardly be denied in principle also from the angle of the DDM, even if as a much more distant and secondary benchmark where it comes to security related decision making. After all, at least in principle the constitutional core values and norms of the Western liberal-democratic state still represent the beating heart of the Western project of civilization or, as Henry Kissinger put it:

> When the United States began to take up the torch of international leadership, it added a new dimension to the quest for world order. A nation founded explicitly on an idea of free and representative governance, it identified its own rise with the spread of liberty and democracy and credited these forces with the ability to achieve the just and lasting peace that had thus far eluded the world.[222]

Consequently, constitutional core values have still to be considered as at least somehow indispensable even for the most hawkish promoters of the GWOT – as long as they preserve themselves a sense of reality. Notably, this applies in a specific way directly to the interests of national security in the preservation of a strategic position in terms of global hegemony. In other words, constitutional core values are, to a certain degree, subject of the reason of state of Western nations. Historically, Western constitutional core values have always been of great strategic importance for the preservation of relative global hegemony and the legitimacy of Western global security policy. Amidst growing counter-vailing powers in form of the BRICS, most notably China, American hegemony is increasingly challenged which, in turn, is rendering Western constitutional core values strategically more important than ever. It might be argued that universalistic norms like those manifested in the concept of secular humanism – human rights, democracy and the rule of law – are more important in shaping government and governance for the Western tradition than they are in other cultural spaces which have they alternate normative orders fullfiling similar functions. The neutralization of these core values and their support structure by any empire emerging out of the Western civilization that is claiming any meaningful continuing contact to its cultural substance and identity would thus amount to wield the axe against one's very own roots of life. The civilizational fabric that is 'producing' a strong notion of

222 Kissinger, *World Order*, p. 361.

rights is the very same matrix that is nurturing potentially all significant emanations of the Western culture – including those supporting the national security state. To completely marginalize the claim of human rights universalism as a constitutional core value is thus not conceivable for any Western empire that does not want to suddenly embody the very negation of its own cultural deep structure, normative identity, and productive potentials. That is why these norms and values representing the "liberal model of the international community, stabilize – voluntarily or involuntarily – American hegemony".[223] After all, it is still the West that comfortably commands the interpretational sovereignty over most parts of the global and international law's content, if not global legal regime building in general. In fact, legal norms have been an essential and significant substance of Western entrenchments of power since the Dark Ages. This centuries-old and particular Western preference to advance political influence via legal norms and claimed universal values is currently emphasized by the essentially different ways in which the U.S. and China compete in enhancing their global economic power in the post-WTO world. While the U.S. approach in form of 'free trade agreements' like TPP, TISA or TTIP is inherently developed on the basis of *legal platforms* the Chinese response in form of the 'One Belt, One Road'-project is primary constructed by means of diplomatic relations, investment and infrastructure. Whereas legal norms are a key in the U.S. approach that is repeating long established pattern of European empire building, the law is actually not the clay out of which Chinese entrenchment is essentially made. From this angle, legal norms as such but also the constitutional core values defining Western identity in particular are somehow indispensible for any Western advancement to create or preserve an Empire. Even if the most ardent supporters of a unilateral, purely reason of state-based 'empire of security' would be called to freely decide they would thus be well advised to not completely dismiss these norms and values in principle. Especially vis-à-vis a rising rival like China that is growing to global dominance from a culture which is much less shaped by the matrix of law it would be a prudent choice to not give up the vast edge the West has in ruling by the rule of law. In this light there is a paradox and distant affinity between the 'empire of security' and human rights regimes even if hardly in the way that human right

223 See Paulus, "The Influence of the United States on the Concept of International Community'," p. 75.

interests would largely supersede security objectives. Arguably, the revival of the rights based invocation of the Responsibility to Protect to end the Ghaddafi regime in Libya might be seen as such an expression of a strategically enforced reentanglement of the competing normative orders.[224] A good example for such entanglements of human right and security issues are No-flight-Zones (NFZs). Having been established in Iraq, Bosnia and Herzegovina, and Libya to enable humanitarian corridors they are also suitable to destabilize an enemy regime or to maintain zones of relative domination in destabilized regions with multiple warring parties. NFZs offer great opportunities to provide allied local forces with shelter and air-ground support against their adversaries.[225] The more the initially ambitious nation building projects of the GWOT's early days have failed leaving large spaces for spreading terrorist organizations, the more NFZs seem to offer a promising military strategy to regain space control by proxies on the ground. In conclusion, it might be expected also from this perspective that constitutional core values will continue to play a strategic role which might have some effects on the margin for the SRC approach as well. However, an expansion of this margin can hardly be expected as much as this status cannot satisfy those promoting the SRC approach at all.

A last issue to ponder is the question if the GWOT paradigm has not already been modified to a certain extent with respect to constitutional core values and strategic communication. In fact, since its implementation

---

224 See Obama, "Presidential Study Directive on Mass Atrocities," The White House, August 04, 2011, https://www.whitehouse.gov/the-press-office/2011/08/04/presidential-study-directive-mass-atrocities: "Our security is affected when masses of civilians are slaughtered, refugees flow across borders, and murderers wreak havoc on regional stability and livelihoods. America's reputation suffers, and our ability to bring about change is constrained, when we are perceived as idle in the face of mass atrocities and genocide." For the R2P with respect to Libya see Bellamy and Williams, "The new politics of protection? Côte d'Ivoire, Libya and the responsibility to protect," 2011, pp. 825-850. See for a more critical stance Chesterman, "Leading from Behind: The Responsibility to Protect, the Obama Doctrine, and Humanitarian Intervention After Libya," 2011, and Hehir, "The Permanence of Inconsistency: Libya, the Security Council, and the Responsibility to Protect," 2013, pp. 137-159. The latter warns of practices to operationalize the R2P "compelled by the occasional coincidence of interests and humanitarian need, rather than an adherence to either law or norms".

225 Other expressions of the re-entanglement of human rights and security orders is the current trend of an increasing securitization of humanitarian aid or the extension of material support offenses on humanitarian aid on the other.

the GWOT paradigm has undergone some adjustments. Interesting among them is especially the indicated shift from an enemy-centered to a population-centered COIN approach.[226] It might be asked in how far the new doctrine is indeed representing a certain convergence of the the SRC and the DDM model approach. Despite all optimistic praise,[227] it is assumed here that the new COIN doctrine rather adjusted and improved the established doctrines of counter-revolutionary warfare (especially the French doctrine de guerre révolutionnaire or DGR) than that it actually transcends the confines of the DDM model. Despite some wise modifications and good intentions, the basic tenets of the DDM model remained effectively untouched – at least by the corresponding practice. Like traditional winning the hearts and minds approaches, the new doctrine had no expressive effect on the guiding core values. Population centric warfare based on the DDM model has for instance often included resettlements and the destruction of villages with severe violations of constitutional core values involved as exemplified by anti-revolutionary warfare in Malaya, Vietnam, Algeria and Kenya.

In Afghanistan for instance, besides the resettlement of thousands of families and the systematic destruction of entire villages by explosives in 2010, the introduction of the new COIN strategy was accompanied by an increase of enemy-centric operations in terms of drone attacks, air strikes and lethal night raids by special operation forces with a reportedly high the rate of uninvolved civilians killed.[228] Given the employment of harsh population-centered measures like resettlements and due to the bifurcation of 'normal' military missions and special operations, the new COIN approach did indeed fully remain within the confines of the established DDM approach. Moreover, it also failed to achieve its objectives.[229] Even Afghan President Hamid Karzai badly complained to his allies from the NATO-led International Security Assistance Force (ISAF) after another strike on the 'harsh track' that was killing eleven children in May 2011: "If they continue their attacks on our houses, then their presence will

---

226 See Sitaraman, *The Counterinsurgent's Constitution: Law in the Age of Small Wars*, 2013, pp. 27 ff.

227 See Sitaraman, *The Counterinsurgent's Constitution: Law in the Age of Small Wars*, passim.

228 See Gurman, "Introduction," pp. 3 ff.

229 See Eikenberry, "The Limits of Counterinsurgency Doctrine in Afghanistan: The Other Side of the COIN," *2013, pp.* 59-74.

change from a force that is fighting terrorism to a force that is fighting against the people of Afghanistan."[230] – After the celebrated shift towards a population-centered COIN strategy this criticism could hardly be more scathing from an ally who was militarily and politically dependent on the ISAF. Soon the new COIN doctrine lost further in relevance when NATO started to partly withdraw from Afghanistan. The value of the remaining NATO support in form of advice and ongoing CT operations, most notably by special operation forces, left not much room to define operational success primary by village building, the rule of law dialogue and the cross-cultural competence of NATO soldiers. Success is rather measured by keeping the domestic government's enemy at bay, be it by kill and capture activities or cooptation. It might still be advisable to establish good relations to the population from this perspective wherever possible but it will not define failure or success of the current security support mission. What remains is basically to directly or indirectly increase the government's potential of lethal force and independent kill and capture missions of domestic special operation forces against the background of a disillusioning rearguard action. The large majority of the ground force which is made up by governmental forces, domestic forces allied with them and the stunning number of private military contractors who are operating within another form of legal 'black hole', might altogether not be expected to do better with a population-centered approach than the NATO forces did. Additionally, the full criminal immunity of US soldiers from the Afghan justice system as being granted by the Bilateral Security Agreement for the remaining troops will hardly contribute to an environment conducive to a working people-centered COIN approach in Afghanistan. Similarly sobering are the developments in Iraq, let alone Syria or Yemen where conventional warfare shapes the picture and local militia rather than the population at large are the main subject of communicative efforts in the ongoing operations in complex and shifting scenarios.

Taking the people-centered COIN strategy as one piece in the puzzle of the grand project of global ordering under the precepts of the GWOT, the nature and failure of this doctrinal innovation is instructive for the prospects of CT in the overarching GWOT paradigm in general. Especially its contemporary entanglement with more conventional forms of warfare and the fact that the overall political trend is increasingly influenced

---

230 Hamid Karzai quoted from Gurman, "Introduction," p. 5.

by a populism that has to respond to the radicalization of the European societies the gravitational force of the current DDM approach towards CT will remain unbroken. Consequently, the situation in Europe seems to point to a continuing paradox of societies that badly need a new approach to respond to a trend of frightening radicalization while the signs of the time point to forces that will not allow a significant change of the course taken. The margin of maneuver through the stormy waters of radicalization ahead is and will remain marginal where it comes to alternative approaches.

## Bibliography

Ahmed, Nafeez, "The United States Is Committing Brutal Acts of Torture Right Now," *AlterNet, News Analysis*, December 23, 2014, at http://www.truth-out.org/news/item/28177-america-is-committing-brutal-acts-of-torture-right-now

Aid, Matthew M., "Prometheus Embattled: A Post 9/11 Report Card on the National Security Agency," *Essentials of Strategic Intelligence,* ed. Loch K. Johnson, Santa Barbara: ABC-CLIO, 2014, pp. 417-446.

Aksan, Cihan, and Jon Bailes, "Introduction," in *Weapon of the Strong: Conversations on US State Terrorism*, ed. Cihan Aksan and Jon Bailes, Chicago: University of Chicago Press 2012, pp. 1-31.

Anderson, Kenneth, "Targeted Killing in U.S. Counterterrorism Strategy and Law," in *Legislating the War on Terror. An Agenda for Reform*, ed. Benjamin Wittes, Washington: Brookings Institution Press, 2009, pp. 346-400.

Applegate, Melissa, *Preparing for Asymmetry: As Seen Through The Lens of Joint Vision 2020*, Collingdale: DIANE Publishing, 2001.

Bain, William, "Introduction," in *The Empire of Security and the Safety of the People*, ed. William Bain, New York: Routledge, 2006, pp. 1-14.

Ball, Howard, *The USA Patriot Act: A Reference Handbook*, Santa Barbara: ABC-CLIO, 2004.

Bellamy, Alex, and Paul D. Williams, "The new politics of protection? Côte d'Ivoire, Libya and the responsibility to protect," *International Affairs* 87, 4 (2011): 825-850.

Benoist, Alain *de, Carl Schmitt Today: Terrorism, 'Just' War, and the State of Emergency*, London: Arktos, 2013.

Betts, Richard K., *Enemies of Intelligence: Knowledge and Power in American National Security*, Columbia University Press: New York, 2007.

Biddle, Stephen, "Strategy in War," in *Inside Defense: Understanding the U.S. Military in the 21st Century*, ed. Derek S. Revenon and Judith Hicks Stiehm, New York: Palgrave Macmillan, 2008, pp. 3-13.

Blackburn, Robin, *The Imperial Presidency, the War on Terrorism, and the Revolutions of Modernity*, New York: Constellations, 2002.

Bzostek, Rachel, *Why Not Preempt?: Security, Law, Norms and Military Activities*, London and New York: Routledge, 2016.

Brzezinski, Zbigniew, *Strategic Vision: America and the Crisis of Global Power*, New York: Basic Books, 2012.

Buchanan, Allen, *Human Rights, Legitimacy and the Use of Force*, Oxford: Oxford University Press 2010.

Burgos, Russell A., "Problem Definition in Foreign and Security Policy," in *Inside Defense: Understanding the U.S. Military in the 21st Century*, ed. Derek S. Reveron and Judith Hicks Stiehm, New York: Palgrave Macmillan, 2008, pp. 75-86.

Bush, George W., "The President's News Conference With President Gloria Macapagal-Arroyo of the Philippines," May 19, 2003, at http://www.presidency. ucsb.edu/ws/?pid=64449.

Butler, Judith, *Precarious Life: The Power of Mourning and Violence*, London: Verso, 2006.

Carter, Philip, "Legal Combat: Are enemies waging war in our courts?," *Slate* (April 2005), at http://www.slate.com/articles/news_and_politics/jurisprudence/2005/04/legal_combat.html.

Chesterman, Simon, "The Spy who came in From the Cold War: Intelligence and International Law," *Michigan Journal of International Law* 27 (2006): 1071-1130.

Chesterman, Simon, "Leading from Behind: The Responsibility to Protect, the Obama Doctrine, and Humanitarian Intervention After Libya," *New York University Public Law and Legal Theory Working Papers* 282 (2011), at http://lsr.nellco.org/nyu_plltwp/282/.

Clarke, Ronald, *Situational Crime Prevention: Successful Case Studies*, New York: Harrow and Heston, 1997.

Coady, Cecil A. J., "How New is the 'New Terror'?," *The Jeruslam Philosphical Quarterly* 55 (2006): 49-65.

Cohen, Jean, *Globalization and Sovereignty: Rethinking Legality, Legitimacy, and Constitutionalism*, Cambridge: Cambridge University Press, 2012.

Crenshaw, Martha, "'New' versus 'Old' Terrorism: Is today's 'new' terrorism qualitatively different from pre-September 11 'old' terrorism?," *Palestine-Israel Journal of Politics, Economics and Culture* 10, 1 (2003), at http://www.pij.org/details.php?id=80.

Daalder, Ivo H. and James M. Lindsay, *America Unbound: The Bush Revolution in Foreign Policy*, Washington, D.C.: Brookings Institution Press 2003.

Dallek, Robert, *Hail to the Chie: The Making and Unmaking of American Presidents*, Oxford: Oxford University Press, 1996.

Danner, Mark, "The Struggles of Democracy and Empire," 2002, *The New York Times*, October 2, 2009, accessible at http://www.nytimes.com/2002/10/09/opinion/the-struggles-of-democracy-and-empire.html.

Davis, Jack, "Intelligence Analysts and Policymakers: Benefits and Dangers of Tensions in the Relationship," Intelligence and National Security 21, 6 (2006): 999-1021.

Dershowitz, Allan, *Why Terrorism Works: Understanding the Threat, Responding to the Challenge*, New Haven: Yale University Press, 2002.

Eikenberry, Karl W., "The Limits of Counterinsurgency Doctrine in Afghanistan: The Other Side of the COIN," *Foreign Affairs* 92, 5 (September/October 2013): 59–74.

Eisenhower, Dwight D., "Radio and Television Farewell Address to the American People," 17 January, 1961, *Public Papers of the Presidents*, at http://www.presidency.u csb.edu/ws/index.php?pid=12086.

El-Said, Hamed, "Conclusion," in *De-radicalizing Violent Extremists: Counter-radicalization and De-radicalization Programmes and Their Impact in Muslim Majority States*, ed. Hamed El-Said and Jane Harrigan, London/New York: Routledge, 2013.

Enders, Walter and Todd Sandler, "The Effectiveness of Anti-Terrorism Policies: A Vector-Autoregression-Intervention Analysis," *American Political Science Review* 87, 4 (1993): 829-844.

English, Richard, *Terrorism: How to Respond*, Oxford: Oxford University Press, 2010.

Evans, Brad, *Liberal Terror*, Cambridge: Polity Press, 2013, p. 11.

Fukuyama, Francis, "The End of History?," *The National Interest* (Summer 1989): 3-18.

Fukuyama, Francis, *America at the Crossroads: Democracy, Power, and the Neoconservative Legacy*, New Haven and London: Yale University Press, 2006.

Fussey, Peter, "Deterring terrorism? Target-hardening, surveillance and the prevention of terrorism," in *The Psychology of Counter-Terrorism,* ed. Andrew Silke, Oxford: Routledge, 2011, pp. 164-185.

Galula, David, *Counterinsurgency Warfare: Theory and Practice*, London: Praeger, 1964, 2006.

Glaser, Henning, "Visions of the Good Society: Good Governance, Corruption and Public Law – Reflections on Selected Thai, German and Global Discourses, *Thammasat University Law Journal* 44, 2 (2015): 384-414.

Gray, Christine, *International Law and the Use of Force* Oxford: Oxford University Press, 2008.

Gurman, Hannah, "Introduction" in *Hearts and Minds: A People's History of Counterinsurgency*, ed. Hannah Gurman, New York and London: The New Press, 2013, pp. 1-16.

Hagmann, Jonas, *(In)Security and the Production of International Relations: The Politics of Securitization in Europe*, New York: Routledge, 2015.

Halliday, Dennis, "2003 Gandhi International Peace Award Acceptance Speech," at https://gandhifoundati on.org/2003/01/30/2003-peace-award-denis-halliday-2/.

Hastedt, Glenn, "Washington Politics, Homeland Security, and the Struggle Against Global Terrorism," in *Essentials of Strategic Intelligence,* ed. Loch K. Johnson, Santa Barbara: ABC-CLIO, 2014, pp. 387-416.

Hehir, Aidan, "The Permanence of Inconsistency: Libya, the Security Council, and the Responsibility to Protect," *International Security* 38, 1 (2013): 137-159.

Hoffman, Bruce, "Terrorism Trends and Prospects," in *Countering the New Terrorism*, ed. Ian O. Lesser, Santa Monica: RAND, 1999.

Hoffmann, Stanley, "American Exceptionalism: The New Version", in *American Exceptionalism and Human Rights,* Michael Ignatieff, Princeton: Princeton University Press, 2009, pp. 225-240.

Holder, Eric, "Speech at Northwestern University School of Law," March 5, 2012, at http://www.lawfareblog.com/2012/03/text-of-the-attorney-generals-national-security-speech/#more-6236.

Holt, Thomas, *The Problem of Freedom: Race, Labor and Politics in Jamaica and Britain 1832-1838*, Baltimore: Johns Hopkins University Press, 1992.

Kaplan, Robert D., "Supremacy by Stealth," *Atlantic Monthly* 292, 1 (2003): 66-83.

Kappeler, Victor E., and Kappeler, Aaron E., "Speaking of Evil and Terrorism: The Political and Ideological Construction of a Moral Panic", in *Terrorism and Counter-Terrorism: Criminological Perspectives,* ed. Mathieu Deflem, Oxford: Elsevier, 2004, pp. 175-197.

Katyal, Neal Kumar, "Stochastic Restraint," *Harvard Law Review* 126 (2013): 990-1010.

Kellner, Douglas, *From 9/11 to Terror War: The Dangers of the Bush Legacy,* Blue Ridge Summit: Roman & Littlefield, 2003.

Kibbe, Jennifer D., "Covert Action and the Pentagon," in *Essentials of Strategic Intelligence*, ed. Loch K. Johnson, Connecticut/London: Praegerl, 2014, pp. 217–236.

Kienscherf, Markus, *US Domestic and International Regimes of Security: Pacifying the Globe, Securing the Homeland*, New York: Routledge, 2013.

Kilcullen, David J., "Two Schools of Classical Counterinsurgency," *Small Wars Journal* (January 2007), at http://smallwarsjournal.com/blog/two-schools-of-classical-counterinsurgency.

Kilcullen, David J., *Counterinsurgency*, Oxford: Oxford University Press, 2010.

Kissinger, Henry, *World Order*, New York: Penguin Books, 2014.

Koh, Harold Hongju, "On American Exceptionalism," *Stanford Law Review* 55 (2003): 1480-1527.

Koh, Harold Hongju, "America's Jekyll-and-Hyde Exceptionalism," in *American Exceptionalism and Human Rights*, ed. Michael Ignatieff, Princeton: Princeton University Press, 2005, pp. 111-144.

Koskenniemi, Martti, *The Politics of International Law*, London: Bloomsbury Publishing, 2011.

Koskenniemi, Martti, "The Subjective Dangers of Projects of World Community," in *Realizing Utopia: The Future of International Law*, ed. Antonio Cassese, Oxford: Oxford University Press, 2012, pp. 3-13.

Krauthammer, Charles, "The Bush doctrine: In American Foreign Policy, a new motto: Don't ask. Tell," *Inside Politics*, February 26, 2001, at http://edition.cnn.com /ALLPOLITICS/time/2001/03/05/doctrine.html.

Kupferwasser, Yosef, "Is It Possible to Deter Armed Groups?," in *Armed Groups: Studies in National Security, Counterterrorism and Counterinsurgency*, ed. Jeffrey H. Norwitz, Newport: U.S. Naval War College, 2008, pp. 127-133.

Laqueur, Walter, "Postmodern Terrorism: New Rules for an Old Game," *Foreign Affairs* 75, 5 (1996): 24-36.

Lee, Lavina Rajendram, *US Hegemony and International Legitimacy: Norms, Power and Followership in the Wars on Iraq*, New York: Routledge, 2010.

Legro, Jeffrey, *Rethinking the World: Great Power Strategies and International Order*, Ithaca, NY: Cornell University Press, 2005.

Lemann, Nicholas, "The Next World Order: The Bush Administration May Have a Brand-New Doctrine of Power," *New Yorker*, April 1, 2002, at http://www. newyorker.com/fact/content/articles/020401fa_FACT1.

Londras, Fiona de, "Prevention, Detention, and Extraordinariness," in *Guantanamo and Beyond: Exceptional Courts and Military Commissions in Comparative Perspective*, ed. Fionnuala Ni Aolain and Oren Gross, Cambridge: Cambridge University Press, 2013, pp. 117-136.

Luban, David, "Carl Schmitt and the Critique of the Lawfare," *Western Reserve Journal of International Law* 43, 1, 2 (2010): 457-471.

Mandel, Robert, *Coercing Compliance: State Initiated Brute Force in Today's World*, Stanford: Stanford University Press, 2015.

Mastors, Elena, *Breaking Al-Qaeda: Psychological and Operational Techniques*, New York: CRC press, 2nd ed., 2014.

Mathias, Grégor, *Galula in Algeria: Counterinsurgency Practice versus Theory*, Santa Barbara: Praeger, 2011.

McClintock, Michael, *Instruments of Statecraft: U.S. Guerrilla Warfare, Counter-insurgency, and Counter-Terrorism, 1940-1990*, New York: Pantheon Books 1992.

Mendelsohn, Barak, *Combating Jihadism: American Hegemony and Interstate Co-operation in the War on Terrorism*, Chicago: The University of Chicago Press, 2009.

Minow, Martha, "What is the Greatest Evil," *Harard Law Review* 118 (2005): 2134-2169.

Morrel, Michael, *The Great War of our Time: The CIA's Fight Against Terrorism, From Al Qa'ida to ISIS*, New York: Grand Central Publishing, 2015.

Nagl, John A., *Learning to Eat Soup With a Knife: Counterinsurgency Lessons From Malaya and Vietnam*, Chicago: The University of Chicago Press, 2005.

Nye, Joseph, "Soft Power," *Foreign Policy* 80 (1990): 153-171.

Obama, Barack, *New York Times*, May 16, 2008.

Obama, Barack, "Presidential Study Directive on Mass Atrocities," The White House, August 04, 2011, at https://www.whitehouse.gov/the-press-office/2011/08/04/presidential-study-directive-mass-atrocities.

Obama, Barack, "Statement by the President on the Situation in Paris," November 13, 2015, at https://www.whitehouse.gov/the-press-office/2015/11/13/statement-presi dent-situation-paris.

Obama, Barack, "Presidential Study Directive on Mass Atrocities," The White House, August 04, 2011, at https://www.whitehouse.gov/the-press-office/2011/08/04/presidential-study-directive-mass-atrocities.

Oehmichen, Anna, *Terrorism, and Anti-Terror Legislation: The Terrorized Legislator? A Comparison of Counter-Terror Legislation and Its Implication for Human Rights in the Legal Systems of the United Kingdom, Spain, Germany and France*, Antwerpen: Intersentia, 2009.

Office of the Director of National Intelligence, "Vision 2015: A Globally Networked and Integrated Intelligence Enterprise," at http://www.au.af.mil/au/awc/awcgate/dni/vision_2015_july08.pdf.

Office of the Press Secretary, "Remarks by National Security Advisor Condoleezza Rice on Terrorism and Foreign Policy," April 29, 2002, at https://georgewbush-whitehouse.archives.gov/news/releases/002/04/20020429-9.html.

Osiel, Mark, *The End of Reciprocity: Terror, Torture and the Law of War*, Cambridge: Cambridge University Press, 2009.

Palma, Mauro, "The Possible Contributions of International Civil Society to the Protection of Human Rights," in *Realizing Utopia: The Future of International Law*, ed. Antonio Cassese, Oxford: Oxford University Press, 2012, pp 76-88.

Patman, Robert G.,"Globalization, the End of the Cold War and the Doctrine of National Security," in *Globalization and Conflict, National Security in a 'New' Strategic Era*, ed. Robert G. Patman, New York: Routledge, 2006, pp. 3-29.

Paulus, Andreas, "The Influence of the United States on the Concept of 'International Community'," in *United States Hegemony and the Foundations of International Law,* ed. Michael Byers and Georg Nolte, Cambridge: Cambridge University Press, 2003, pp. 57-91.

Pogge, Thomas W., *Realizing Rawls*, Ithaca, London: Cornell University Press, 1989.

Poole, Thomas, *Reason of State: Law, Prerogative and Empire*, Cambridge: Cambridge University Press, 2005.

Primoratz, Igor, *Terrorism: A Philosophical Investigation*, New Jersey: John Wiley & Sons, 2013.

Pyle, Christopher H., *Getting Away With Torture: Secret Government, War Crimes, and the Rule of Law*, Washington, D.C: Potomac Books, 2009.

Ramraj, Victor V., Michael Hor and Kent Roach (eds.), *Global Anti-Terrorism Law and Policy*, Cambridge: Cambridge University Press, 2012, pp. 273-634.

Ransom, Clark, J., *Intelligence and National Security: A Reference Handbook*, Westport, Connecticut/ London: Praeger, 2007.

Ratner, Steven, "Comments on Chapter 1 and 2," in *United States Hegemony and the Foundations of International Law,* ed. Michael Byers and Georg Nolte, Cambridge: Cambridge University Press, 2003, pp. 101-108.

Reveron, Derek S., and Judith Hicks Stiehm, "Introduction," in *Inside Defense: Understanding the U.S. Military in the 21st Century*, ed. Derek S. Reveron and Judith Hicks Stiehm, New York: Palgrave Macmillan, 2008, pp. XIII-XXII.

Rich, Frank Kelly, *The Greatest Story Ever Sold: The Decline and Fall of Truth From 9/11 to Katrina*, New York: The Penguin Press, 2006.

Roach, Kent, *The 9/11 Effect: Comparative Counter-Terrorism*, Cambridge: Cambridge University Press, 2011.

Roberts, Adam, "Intervention: Beyond 'Dictatorial Interference", in *The Empire of Security and the Safety of the People*, ed. William Bain, New York: Routledge, 2006, pp. 158-187.

Robinson, Linda, *Tell Me How This Ends: General David Petraeus and the Search for a Way out of Iraq*, New York: Public Affairs, 2008.

Ruggie, John Gerard, "American Exceptionalism, Exemptionalism, and Global Governance," in *American Exceptionalism and Human Rights,* ed. Michael Ignatieff, Princeton: Princeton University Press, 2005, pp. 304-338.

Rumsfeld, Donald, "Secretary Rumsfeld Interview with the New York Times," *New York Times*, October 12, 2001.

Rumsfeld, Donald H., "Terrorism is a Threat to National Security," in *National Security*, ed. David Haugen, Michigan: Greenhaven Press, 2007, pp. 21-29.

Scahill, Jeremy, "Obama's Expanding Covert Wars," *The Nation*, 2013, at https://www.thenation.com/article/obamas-expanding-covert-wars/.

Schepelle, Kim Lane, "The Migration of Anti-Constitutional Ideas: The Post-9/11 Globalization of Public Law and the International State of Emergency," in *The Migration of Constitutional Ideas,* ed. Sujit Choudhry, Cambridge: Cambridge University Press, 2009, pp. 347-373.

Schmitt, Carl, *Theory of the Partisan: Intermediate Commentary on the Concept of the Political*, trans. G. L. Ulmen, New York: Telos Press Publishing, 2007.

Schmitt, Eric, and Mark Mazzetti, "Secret Order Lets U.S. Raid Al Qaeda," *The New York Times*, Nov. 9, 2008, at: http://www.nytimes.com/2008/11/10/washington/10military.html?_r=0.

Shah, Naureen, "A Move Within the Shadows – Will JSOC's Control of Drones Improve Policy?," in *Drone Wars: Transforming Conflict, Law, and Policy*, ed. Peter L. Gergen and Daniel Rothenberg, Cambridge: Cambridge University Press, 2014, pp. 160-184.

Shultz, George P., *Turmoil and Triumph: My years as Secretary of State*, New York: Charles Scribner's Sons, 1993.

Shultz, Richard, Roy Godson, Querine Hanlon, and Samantha Ravich, "The Sources of Instability in the Twenty-First Century: Weak States, Armed Groups, and Irregular Conflict," *Strategic Studies Quarterly* 5 (2011): 73-94.

Siddique, Osama, "The Other Pakistan: Special laws, Diminished Citizenship and the Gathering Storm," in *Norms, Interests, and Values – Conflict and Consent in the Constitutional Basic Order*, ed. Henning Glaser, Baden-Baden: Nomos, 2015, pp. 249-290.

Sitaraman, Ganesh, *The Counterinsurgent's Constitution: Law in the Age of Small Wars*, Oxford: Oxford University Press, 2013.

Smith, Steve, "The Concept of Security in a Globalizing World," in *Globalization and Conflict: National Security in a 'New' Strategic Era*, ed. Robert G.Patman, New York: Routledge, 2006, pp. 33-55.

Steyn, Johan, "Guantanamo Bay: The Legal Black Hole," *The International and Comparative Law Quarterly* 53, 1 (2004): 1-15.

Stromseth, Jane, "Law and Force After Iraq: A Transitional Moment," *American Journal of International Law* 97 (2003): 628-642.

Sznaider, Natan, "Terrorism and the Social Contract," *Irish Journal of Sociology* 15, 1 (2006): 7-23.

Tamanaha, Brian Z., *On the Rule of Law: History, Politics, Theory*, Cambridge: Cambridge University Press, 2004.

Taylor, Stuart, and Benjamin Wittes, "Looking Forward, Not Backward: Refining U.S. Interrogation Law," in *Legislating the War on Terror: An Agenda for Reform*, ed. Benjamin Wittes, Washington: Brookings Institution Press, 2010, pp. 289-345.

Téson, Fernando R., "The Kantian Theory of International Law," *Columbia Law Review* 92, 53 (1992): 53-102.

The White House, "The National Security Strategy of the United States of America 2002," 2002, at http://www.state.gov/documents/organization/63562.pdf.

Tucker, David, "What's New About the New Terrorism and How Dangerous Is It?," *Terrorism and Political Violence* 13 (2001): 1-14.

Turse, Nick, "A secret war in 120 countries," *The Nation*, August 5, 2011, at http://nation.com.pk/international/05-Aug-2011/A-secret-war-in-120-countries.

US Department of Defense, "National Defense Strategy of the United States of America 2005," March 2005, at http://www.au.af.mil/au/awc/awcgate/nds/nds2005.pdf.

US Senate Select Committee on Intelligence, "Committee Study of the Central Intelligence Agency's Detention and Interrogation Program," 2012, 2014, accessible at https://www.amnestyusa.org/pdfs/sscistudy1.pdf.

Walker III, William O, *National Security and Core Values in American History*, Cambridge: Cambridge University Press, 2009.

Ward, Ian, *Law, Text, Terror*, Cambridge: Cambridge University Press, 2009.

Wardlaw, Grant, *Political Terrorism: Theory, Tactics and Counter-Measures*, Cambridge: Cambridge University Press, 1989.

Wilson III, Isaiah, "Military Intervention and International Law," in *Inside Defense: Understanding the U.S. Military in the 21st Century*, ed. Derek S. Reveron and Judith Hicks Stiehm, New York: Palgrave Macmillan, 2008, 67-74.

Wirls, Daniel, "Hidden in Plain Sight: The Bush Military Buildup," in *Inside Defense: Understanding the U.S. Military in the 21st Century*, ed. Derek S. Reveron and Judith Hicks Stiehm, New York: Palgrave Macmillan, 2008, pp. 99-114.

Whitlock, Craig, "Renditions continue under Obama, despite due-process concerns," The Washington Post, January 1, 2013, at https://www.washingtonpost.com/world/national-security/renditions-continue-under-obama-despite-due-process-concerns/2013/01/01/4e593aa0-5102-11e2-984e-f1de82a7c98a_story.html.

Wrage, Steven D., "The Department of Defense and the Department of State: Out of Balance and into Trouble," in *Inside Defense: Understanding the U.S. Military in the 21st Century*, ed. Derek S. Revenon and Judith Hicks Stiehm, New York: Palgrave Macmillan, 2008, pp. 15-29.

Zulaika, Joseba, *Terrorism: The Self-Fulfilling Prophecy*, Chicago: University of Chicago Press, 2009.

Zweibelson, Ben, "The US in Afghanistan: Follow Sun Tzu rather than Clausewitz to Victory," *Small Wars Journal* (December 2010): 1-6.

# *Part III: Additional Material*

# Interview with Major General Ashok Hukku (ret.) on the Islamic State

The jihadist group Islamic State has been capturing the attention of the world since it burst on the international scene with its claim to establish a caliphate and with seizures of territories in Iraq and Syria in 2014. It has become infamous for mass killings, abductions and beheadings. In the interview below, conducted at the sidelines of the international conference "Peace and Stability in Asia" of the German-Southeast Asian Center of Excellence for Public Policy and Good Governance (CPG), Faculty of Law, Thammasat University, and the Taiwan ASEAN Studies Center from 17-18 December 2015 in Bangkok, Major General Ashok Hukku (ret.), Y.S.M., expert on strategic development and international relations in South and East Asia and former chief intelligence advisor to the Indian government, shares his insights on the Islamic State and its geopolitical impacts on international peace and security.

Q: Gen. Ashok, the Islamic State (IS) stands as one of the most threatening jihadist groups next to Al-Qaeda. What is the background of the emergence of the IS? Where is it coming from?

The Islamic State movement basically started in Iraq. Initially Al-Qaeda in Iraq was operating against the United States forces in Iraq. The Islamic State grew out of Al-Qaeda in Iraq and – after the withdrawal of the US forces in 2011 – became the main group fighting government forces in Iraq and Syria under the leadership of al-Baghdadi who himself was a prisoner of Camp Bucca, a US military maintained detention facility in Iraq. The Shia government which came into power after the withdrawal of the US continued to promote the Shia agenda backed by Iran. And, therefore, the Sunni insurgent movement was very displeased and angry and they started reacting. So basically, the IS is a Sunni jihadist organization expanding from Iraq to Syria and further.

Q: So, the root cause for the emergence of the IS is the failure to build a stable state?

Exactly. I would go to the extent of saying that when Saddam Hussein was alive, the region was stable despite the conflict with Iran and in spite of the internal problems in Iraq. At least, the Islamic State and al-Qaida were not as active as they are today. Moreover, when the US withdrew from Iraq in 2011, they left a very big power vacuum which was eventually occupied by the Islamic State. It was basically a failure on part of the political leadership of Iraq which failed to govern the country properly. Saddam Hussein's army and its leadership were completely destroyed. It was replaced by a new leadership which was inexperienced and pro Shia and pro Iran. This was a hotbed for internal turbulences out of which the Islamic State could grow.

Q: How is the IS structured with regards to its organization, process of decision-making and financing?

The Islamic State is essentially a one man organization. And that man is al-Baghdadi. He is a very strong leader, highly respected within the Islamic State, and the real source of authority in the Islamic State: What he says happens. And there is no dissent against him. I'm sure that if there is any dissent that person will be eliminated. But that does not mean that the organization will collapse when Baghdadi is killed. There is the Shura Council, a committee on which some important leaders sit. They are the people controlling the operations on the ground and ready to take over the leadership in case al-Baghdadi would be killed.

One person is called Abu Ala al-Afri. There is slight doubt whether he is alive or not. There are conflicting reports that he is alive or dead. But he is a very strong leader in running day to day operations. And if he is alive, he is likely one of the runners.

Another person is called Abdullah al-An. He is another leader, about 51 years old and an ex al-Qaida man, who joined al-Qaida 10 or 11 years ago. He has transferred himself from al-Qaida to the Islamic State. He is an influential leader and claims divine lineage which, according to the Islamic State leaders, is necessary to become the leader of the Islamic State.

Then there is Unus al Bash Adan. He's not very old. He is 55 years old and holds a PhD degree in Islamic studies from Iraq University. Again he was an al-Qaida man, is very forceful and well-known as religious scholar.

He also claims divine leadership. So again a front-runner if something happens to the present leader.

Another interesting person is Muhamad al-Adnan. He is a very young man. He is 38 years old and of Syrian origin. In Syria, he is the most powerful leader of the Islamic State. He was the official spokesman of Syrian leadership for quite some time. He has been articulating that there should be lone wolf attacks. That means that a believer in the Islamic State, e.g. in the United States or in Europe does not wait for a link-up with the Islamic State, does not wait for help, but acts on his own will, on his own resources and does damage, e.g. by killing people or destroying something.

So, even though I say that al-Baghdadi is the undisputed leader of the Islamic State today, killing him alone will not destroy the Islamic State. And as of now, there are now rivalries – at least not visible – within the leadership of the IS. But I would not rule that out for the future. Because this happens in all organizations and also within al-Qaida it happened. In all major organizations I have seen eventually rifts develop, either based on philosophy or simply on power. So I would not rule that out for the future.

With regards to the financial resources of the IS: One big reason for its success is the kind of money the IS has access to. Their major part of their finances is coming from the oil fields they have captured in Iraq and Syria. And these are supposed to provide them with about 2 million USD per day, i.e. 50-60 million USD per month. Besides that, the second largest source of finances is extortion and taxes. In the areas they have occupied they are taxing especially the non-Sunni people and other minorities very heavily, also the business people. They allow them to do business, but of course they have to pay taxes. In fact, from taxation they are earning around 3 to 5 million USD per month which is also a very large amount. And then, of course, there are the ransom payments as another source of funding. Overall, the income is around 60 to 70 million dollars per month.

Q: The IS has been claiming to establish a caliphate. How do you assess IS' political and military strategies in this light?

The aim of the Islamic State is basically to establish a caliphate in the region of Levant which is where they are and extending slightly to Georgia, Israel, Palestine, Syria and Iraq. No, I am quite certain that this is not the end of the story. Even if they gain control over this area, they will want to extend beyond that. They want to renew the old empire which existed once upon a time and that is what their goal is as far as their political strategy is concerned.

Their military strategy is good in the sense that it is how this sort of insurgency has to be done. There are good fighters, very well armed and equipped. But there is one problem. As long as insurgency under pressure can disappear and mix with the civilians it will survive. But if you can delineate the extent of insurgency, then there is a problem. By that I mean. If they want to establish an Islamic State they need three things: First they need to hold ground, they have to say that the Islamic State extents from point A to point B and these points have to be clarified ideally. If these points are identified, the extent of the Islamic State is defined by ISIS, they have to ensure that the borders are guarded. And then you have a very much defined enemy position for somebody to attack. But as long as it is a nebulous organization operating here and if too much pressure comes in they hide and mix with we civilians and we do not know who is member of the Islamic State, it is very difficult to defeat this kind of insurgency.

But as soon as they establish a so-called state, they have to establish and guard borders and to hold those borders. This will become vulnerability in the future. So, the Islamic State will never be established as a state, as a nation.

Now, they are playing by the rules of insurgency. They are very cruel, they withdraw under heavy pressure when they know they cannot fight. They withdrew when they were north of Raqqah and very heavy pressure came on them even though that was their capital. And they knew that against strong military forces in an area they cannot put up a fight. But guerilla warfare, insurgency warfare, that is endless. And you only need one insurgent who can take care of thousands of troops. All that he needs to do is to hide.

Q: How do the terrorist attacks fit in this strategy?

Terrorist attacks are basically part of their propaganda strategy. It is just mental propaganda. The Islamic State does not plan or even hope to extent to France or the UK, but a terrorist attack shows their strength and it is a great attraction for people to see that the Islamic State is strong, that they can launch an attack in the United States, launch an attack in France, so it is a great moral boosting factor for the fighters of the Islamic State as well as for recruits and to tell the world: "Look, we mean business and we are capable. So even though you have launched 5,500 flight attacks against me, I still get the opportunity to attack you in France today and I will now attack in another country." It is a great propaganda feature for them and great recruitment policy to launch attacks in distant countries.

Q: The IS poses a tremendous challenge to the international community. How do you see the positions and geo-political moves of major powers involved such as Turkey, the USA and Russia?

Turkey sits on top of Syria. Turkey has played a very intriguing role in this whole drama. Turkey is a member of the NATO, not a member of the European Union – what they are very unhappy about. However, up to now, until one month ago, President Erdogan had, in a sense, been supporting the Islamic State. And when I say supporting, I mean two things. First, no insurgency can survive without logistics. They must get reinforcements, weapons, ammunition; they must get finances and medical treatment. The logistic support was going through Turkey. Through the border of Turkey and Syria the logistic support was going in and Erdogan was aware of it but did not stop it. Second, he did not allow the US to operate against the Islamic State from the Incirlik Air Base in Turkey. The US wanted to send fighters from Incirlik Air Base, but they were refused. In fact, there was a lot of tension about this issue. Basically, Erdogan was more interested in Syrian politics. He wanted Assad out and therefore he was supporting the rebel groups in Syria. However, when IS attacks happened on Turkish soil such as the Suruc bombing in July, he has got extremely worried. Turkish intelligence has warned Erdogan that there already are some Islamic sleeper cells existing in Turkey, but he was ignoring this. But now, after the incidents, things have changed. Now, he does allow the airbase to be used by the US coalition. And he has also helped close down the supply routes. But some are still open, not all of them are closed. Basically, he is operating against the Kurdish rebels. That is his focus of attention and not so much the Islamic State. But since some recent incidents have happened, perhaps he will be more cooperative.

The United States of America leads a coalition against the Islamic State. The US are in a very awkward dilemma. President Obama, who happens to be a "lame-duck" president now because his term of office will terminate, had a very clear policy. He was out to destroy al-Qaida in Afghanistan. 150.000 troops operated in Afghanistan. Then they were stopped. He promised his countrymen that he would take the American troops out of Afghanistan. And there was a tremendous public opinion against the loss of US human life in Afghanistan, and not only loss of life, also expenditure incurred, billions of dollars every month, people injured, families destroyed. So, there was a strong public opinion in the United States against operating in Afghanistan. When he gave a public commitment to remove the troops, the Islamic State came up. He is politically, psychologically and in every sense of the word not in a position to put troops on the ground again against the Islamic State. Even in Europe no one is willing to put troops on the ground because they have seen what happened in Iraq and in Afghanistan with so many lives lost, thousands of families destroyed, billions of dollars gone, and the problem still not solved, neither in Iraq nor in Afghanistan. So, no one wants Syria and Iraq on his shoulders now. Considering that, the only option left to the US was airstrikes. And, therefore, they have carried on with intensified airstrikes. This year and last year they have launched more than 5,500 airstrikes in the coalition together in Iraq and Syria. It is interesting to note, that France initially was of the opinion that we need to negotiate with the Islamic State and refused military reaction. But after the attacks in France, they absolutely changed their outlook. They increased the intensity of airstrikes in Syria in Iraq. Now, the trouble is, that an insurgency of this kind cannot be eliminated by airstrikes. Air strikes can kill a lot of jihadists; they can destroy their strongholds, their weapons and their buildings. But they cannot destroy the organization or the idea of the Islamic State. And it is that that needs to be addressed but is not being addressed with full force.

Russia supports the Assad regime. They are not for a replacement of Assad. The airstrikes which are being carried out by Russia in Syria were actually not targeting the Islamic State but the rebel forces against Assad. If Islamic State members were killed in the process, that was an additional bonus. But now, it seems that Russia is changing its opinion slightly – not against Assad but towards the Islamic State to a certain extent.

Q: How do you assess the recent steps taken by the international community against the IS?

The UN Security Council has passed Resolution 2253 on 17 December saying that the financial resources of the Islamic State have to be choked, which means oil. Oil will not be bought from the Islamic State. Buyers of their oil are Turkey, the Kurds and the Syrians. So let us see how this happens. It was a US proposed resolution and Russia signed it. So to that extent I think there is some cooperation from Russia but it remains to be seen if they will operate against the Islamic State more effectively.

A day after the attacks in Paris the US, Russia, Britain, France, Iran and Saudi Arabia signed a statement in Vienna which supports 1 January 2016 as deadline for the start of talks between the Syrian government and opposition, with the aim of agreeing on a ceasefire by 14 May. Saudi Arabia in this case of course wants to oust Assad and has been supporting Islamic forces operating against Assad other than the Islamic State. Saudi Arabia is very worried about the Islamic State because the Islamic State will also not tolerate a monarchy in Saudi Arabia – but of course that is not very easy to do.

So the Vienna meeting of 14 November shows some promise as does the UN resolution.

Q: What are the prospects for the fight against the Islamic State in the near future?

There is no mandate for troops on the ground. And I also do not see that coming in the near future. If we try to project in this light what kind of environment is likely to prevail in the foreseeable future 2016-2017, I see the present struggle going on, air strikes going on, one leader killed here, another there, a new leadership emerging, the Islamic State losing certain territory here, gaining some territory there. These kinds of things are going to happen unless there is a categorical change in the offensive policy of the coalition – and especially depending on what Russia is going to do. Until that happens, the Islamic State will not be knocked out. Today the Islamic State is the world's richest extremist organization. They have the weapons, the money, the logistic lines running even now. They have a very strong presence on the Internet, on Twitter, on the electronic media which seems to attract a lot of people from all over the world. So the idea of the Islamic State is very much in existence and the more you suppress them, the more they reach out to the world and look for people who are against Muslim people. So, the status quo will remain for an unforeseeable future.

*Thank you very much Gen. Ashok for this interview.*

The interview was conducted by Dr. Duc Quang Ly,
CPG Project Manager.

# Report: Strategic Engagement of Ideologically Driven Individuals: Towards Achieving Sustainable Peace and Development

*A. S. A. Safras*

It is important to understand that, in any society, there are individuals with different ideologies. When it comes to its implementation either they can be directly involved in execution of antisocial attack or as financial supporters or as planners. In any scenario it is vital to identify the root causes of their behaviour as "What changed them?" or causes of radicalization.

Radicalization is a process by which an individual or group comes to adopt increasingly extreme political, social, or religious ideals and aspirations that reject or undermine the status quo or reject and/or under-mine contemporary ideas and expressions of freedom of choice. For example, radicalism can originate from a broad social consensus against progressive changes in society. Radicalization can be both violent and nonviolent, although most academic literature focuses on radicalization into violent extremism (RVE). There are multiple pathways that constitute the process of radicalization, which can be independent but are usually mutually reinforcing. Radicalization serves as a kind of sociological trap that gives individuals no other place to go to satisfy their material and spiritual needs.

## *A. Sri Lankan Context*

Sri Lanka faced a number of civil conflicts during the past four decades, two in the Sinhala-dominated south in 1971 and 1989 and the protracted conflict which later grew into a full scale war between the government military forces and the Liberation Tigers of Tamil Eelam (LTTE) in the Northern and Eastern Provinces of the country, which eventually disturbed the entire social fabric of the island. This conflict brought tragedy and pain to communities in all the regions of the country especially the Northern and Eastern Provinces. Thousands of young people lost their lives. With the military defeat of terrorism in May 2009, a door opened for a new era of peace and development.

It is well known that youth are more vulnerable when it comes to conflicts and they tend to get radicalized more often than the others. Therefore, it is important that we identify the vulnerable youth including adults, and empower them of tolerance, moderation and importance of coexistence in a multi-ethnic and multi-religious community, make them aware of the need of unity in diversity and the importance of diversity in coexistence.

### *B. Rehabilitation of Ex-LTTE Combatants*

Sri Lanka's multifaceted and multiagency rehabilitation program to reintegrate approximately 12,000 ex-combatants was set up by the Bureau of the Commissioner General of Rehabilitation (BCGR) under the guidance of the Ministry of Defence and in collaboration with the Ministry of Rehabilitation and Prison Reforms. The government of Sri Lanka adopted an approach to rebuild the lives of the ex-combatants through rehabilitation programs carried out at Protective Accommodation and Rehabilitation Centers (PARCs) in the Northern and Eastern provinces of Sri Lanka.

The Bureau of the Commissioner General of Rehabilitation (BCGR) came into being for the purpose of rehabilitating and re-integrating LTTE Ex Combatants who either surrendered or were forced to surrender during the final stages of the 30 years-long conflict.

The programs were geared towards engaging the hearts and minds of the ex combatants (beneficiaries of rehabilitation) through several modes of rehabilitation programs. The 4R model of rehabilitation (Rehabilitation, Reinsertion, Reintegration and Reconciliation) was specially developed and designed to suit the culture, religion, ethics, norms and values of Sri Lankans especially to suit the Tamil speaking people of the North and East. The rehabilitees/beneficiaries were able to get in touch with their inner self and develop an appreciation for peaceful co-existence. Through the several rehabilitation programs and interactions with the service personnel (who conduct the rehabilitation program), beneficiaries have come to value the need for a society free of violence and hatred. Most have transformed and rejected violence and expressed remorse. Many are working to build a new Sri Lanka where moderation, toleration and co-existence have become the guiding principles. A few of the beneficiaries have emerged as champions of peace where they are actively working to rebuild bridges between the different communities, with the end of terrorism in Sri Lanka.

It was found necessary to rectify the existing imbalances of conceptual, physical and moral facets of rehabilitees prior to the implementation of the 4R (Rehabilitation, Reinsertion, Reintegration and Reconciliation) process to achieve the desired results. It is no secret that by making the best use of issues listed below terrorist leadership took advantage to remold susceptible individuals, especially the youth, to their liking to meet their vested ends. These perceived anomalies need to be rectified in an overall perspective whilst moral and physical aspects of individuals are taken care of through a well articulated, deliberately designed and individually targeted rehabilitation process in a secured but collective environment. This process is currently being implemented with great success.

a) Distorted morals and social values.
b) Indifferent perceptions of different communities.
c) Disintegrated social fabric.
d) Unresolved issues related to fundamental rights and implied deprivation.
e) Falsified/misleading connotation of facts.

The Action Plan for rehabilitation is primarily based on the Sri Lankan context drawing on lessons learnt from International Best Practices and International Legal Principles and Precedents, and in accordance with the mandate vested upon the Commissioner General of Rehabilitation (CGR) and the Bureau of Commissioner General Rehabilitation (BCGR) on the continuation and expansion of a range of initiatives being undertaken to rehabilitate, reinsert, reintegrate and reconcile rehabilitees into civilian life in Sri Lanka. Rehabilitation and reinsertion both will be centre-based and community-based, whereas the social reintegration and economic reintegration will take place at the community level.

All reintegration processes worldwide are largely shaped by their contexts, including the nature of the conflict and conflict settlement, the socio-political environment, economical integration, public sentiment and natural, human, technical and financial resources at hand. The terrorist nature of the conflict makes it imperative for reintegration programs to pay substantial attention in providing psychosocial care and civic education to rehabilitees. Careful programming to prepare the host communities and the public as a whole in accepting and reintegrating rehabilitees back into the society is also a primary issue.

The goals of the 4R (Rehabilitation, Reinsertion, Reintegration and Reconciliation) Action Plan is threefold:

a) To safeguard the human rights of rehabilitees, victims and host communities, including the responsibility to protect and assist them in accordance with the Constitution of the Democratic Socialist Republic of Sri Lanka and the State's international obligations;
b) To contribute towards sustainable peace, reconciliation and social cohesion;
c) To increase the employability of rehabilitees, minimize their risk of socio-economic marginalization and utilize their underutilized knowledge and skills to create opportunities for economic revitalization in post-conflict development efforts.

## *C. Engagement of Individuals with Extremist Ideology*

I prefer to use the term "engagement", because the word "rehabilitation" is sensitive for many. As in medicine individuals who are rehabilitated are with some sort of a disability. When it comes to counter extremist ideology, the engagement has to be at different levels and context specific. As in Figure 1 below, when pyramid ascend number of individuals are less but the effort required for engagement is more or else it is more difficult to engage in negotiation.

*Figure 1: Different levels of ideologically driven individuals.*

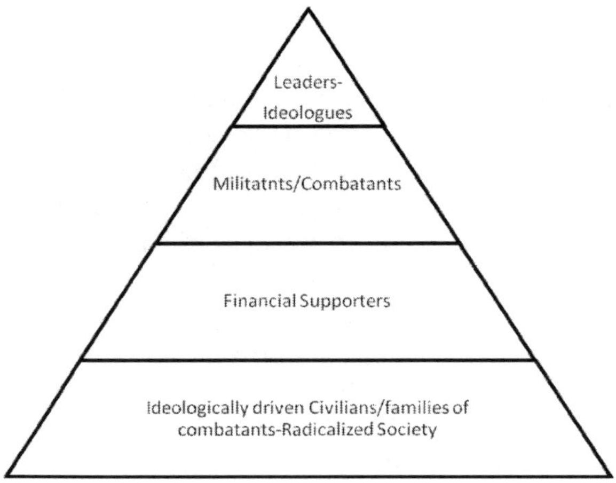

Communities might look at an individual with radical/extremist behaviour or ideology in a very emotional and impulsive way. Therefore, we look at what we see, not what is beyond. It is essential to understand the root causes of a certain ideology or a certain behaviour of an individual or a group. A very simple example is given in the below figure 2. It is an ice-berg. At an instant when we see someone with antisocial behaviour what we see is their physical attribute, behaviour, skin colour etc. What is important to identify is what lies underneath the water, like social status, beliefs, values etc.

*Figure 2: Iceberg model*

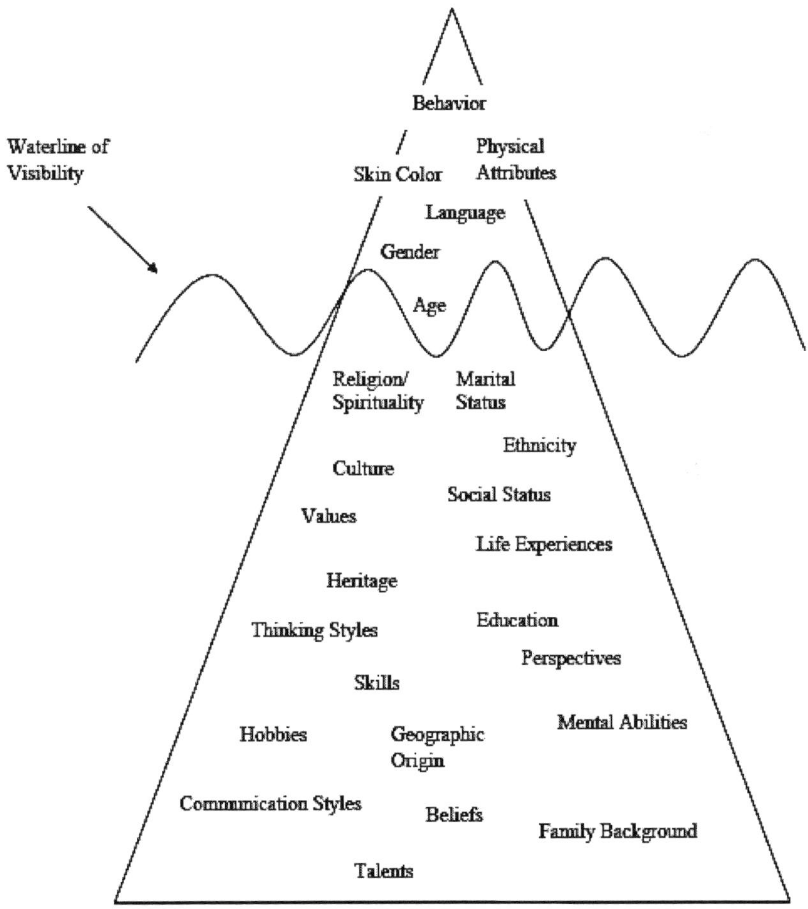

## D. Conclusion

In conclusion, the human brain is very well malleable when right conditions and situations are met. It can be radicalized, deradicalized and also re-radicalized. It is always important to identify root causes of conflict of interest or the extremist behaviour to find solution. Engagement with extremist individuals at different levels as described above has to be context-specific and tailor-made, not a free size which fits for all.

# List of Contributors

**Arabinda Acharya, Ph.D,**
is Associate Professor at the National Defense University Washington D.C. and Adjunct Fellow at the International Centre for Political Violence and Terrorism Research at S. Rajaratnam School of International Studies, Nanyang Technological University, Singapore. His research interests include security policy, regionalism, conflict studies and terrorism.

**Rommel C. Banlaoi**
is Chairman of the Board of the Philippine Institute for Peace, Violence and Terrorism Research (PIPVTR) and Director of its Center for Intelligence and National Security Studies (CINSS). His work reflects various issues of regional security, foreign and defense policy, local governance, civil-military relations and international terrorism.

**Michael Fischer**
is research assistant and lecturer at the Research Institute of Security and Crime Prevention Hamburg (ISIP). His focus of work lies in sociology of morals and cleavages, critical criminology as well as violence and terrorism studies.

**Oliver Gerson, Ph.D,**
is research associate at the Chair of German, European and International Criminal Law, Criminal Procedure Law and White-Collar-Crime of Prof. Dr. Robert Esser, Faculty of Law, University of Passau.

**Henning Glaser**
is Director and Member of the Supervisory Board of the German-Southeast Asian Center of Excellence for Public Policy and Good Governance (CPG), Faculty of Law, Thammasat University, and lecturer at the Faculty of Law, Thammasat University. His research areas cover comparative constitutional law and constitutional theory, international human rights protection, as well as national and regional security law and policy.

**Rohan Gunaratna, Ph.D,**
is Head of the International Centre for Political Violence and Terrorism Research (ICPVTR) and Professor of Security Studies at S. Rajaratnam School of International Studies, Nanyang Technological University, Singapore. His areas of expertise include Islamic State and Al-Qaeda, counter terrorism, financing of terrorism and rehabilitation.

**Orla Hennessy**
is expert for conflict and fragility, security and terrorism at Clingendael, Netherlands Institute of International Relations.

**Major General Ashok Hukku (ret.), Y.S.M.,**
is former Chief Military Intelligence Advisor in the Cabinet Secretariat at New Delhi.

**Eelco Kessels**
is Director of the London office of and Senior Analyst at the Global Center on Cooperative Security (UK). He manages research and programming activities related to managing and reintegrating violent extremist offenders, identifying and addressing violent extremist radicalization in prisons, countering violent extremism, and rule of law-based approaches to counterterrorism.

**Eva-Maria Reh**
is student assistant at the Research Institute of Security and Crime Prevention Hamburg (ISIP).

**Thomas Koruth Samuel**
is Director of the Research and Publications Division of the Southeast Asia Regional Centre for Counter-Terrorism (SEARCCT), Kuala Lumpur. His main research areas cover the dynamics of terrorism and counter-terrorism, including narratives and counter-narratives.

**A.S.A. Safras, Ph.D.,**
is psychosocial advisor of the National Reconciliation Unit Sri Lanka.

# Index